*The Earnest Men*

# The Earnest Men

★ ★ ★

REPUBLICANS OF THE CIVIL WAR SENATE

## Allan G. Bogue

CORNELL UNIVERSITY PRESS

*Ithaca and London*

International Standard Book Number 0-8014-1357-5
Library of Congress Catalog Card Number 81-67176
Printed in the United States of America
*Librarians: Library of Congress cataloging information appears*
*on the last page of the book.*

*For Margaret,*
*who has always understood*
*that history is important*

# Contents

PREFACE                                            9

ACKNOWLEDGMENTS                                   15


PART I    *Men, Context, and Patterns*

1    THE SENATORS                                 25

2    COMMITTEES, RULES, AND LEADERS               61

3    RADICALS AND MODERATES                       88

4    CONNECTIONS                                 125


PART II    *The Substance of Disagreement*

5    SLAVES, SOLDIERS, AND TAXES                 151

6    EMANCIPATION AND "HUMAN" RIGHTS             182

7    PUNISHMENT AND REHABILITATION               219

8    COURTS, BORDER STATES, AND SELF-CONTROL     261

9    DESIGNS AND PERSPECTIVES                    296

10   AFTERWORD                                   330

# 8    Contents

*Appendix A*  Roll-Call Analysis Procedures                               343

*Appendix B*  The Screening Procedure for the Selection of
              "Divisive" Votes                                           353

*Appendix C*  Roll Calls Used Initially in Scaling Analysis              357

*Appendix D*  Divisive Roll Calls—Radical-Moderate Division              358


INDEX                                                                    361

# Preface

This book is an inquiry into the nature of radicalism in the Civil War Senate. Although the degree of emphasis which historians have placed upon radical and conservative elements within the Republican party has varied through time, the distinction has been a basic theme in much writing about the Civil War. Yet it is a theme frustratingly difficult to understand on the basis of much of the secondary literature. Writers using the word "radical" often employed it without explanation, or when radicals were specifically identified they proved to be a heterogeneous crew of cabinet members, party functionaries, senators, and representatives, whose reactions to the same events could not be realistically compared. Sometimes, indeed, leopards seemed to change their spots, and the switch was not always noted as unusual nor did the phenomenon seem to discourage some authors from giving the impression that radicals were radicals, conservatives were conservatives, and that was that. At the same time a good many actors lurked in the background, unidentified as either.

Other historians of the Civil War have used the word "radical," and various synonyms and antonyms, with little qualification, but their work suggests that such practice sometimes leads to confusion when particular lawmakers are followed through debates and voting on a number of major issues. Some have tried to solve this problem of identification by arguing that they use the word "radical" or "conservative" as explanatory terms merely indicating how legislators confronted specific issues, irrespective of subsequent behavior.[1] This is an attractive strategy, but it clearly was not the contemporary practice of the Civil War generation.

1. Herman Belz, *Reconstructing the Union: Theory and Policy during the Civil War* (Ithaca: Cornell University Press, 1969), p. 129.

To call a lawmaker a radical in the Civil War clearly meant more than simply that this man had taken an extreme position on a specific piece of legislation. And it is this broader meaning of radicalism that concerns us to a large extent in what follows.

(For the sake of clarity I have in one respect altered contemporary word use. The generation of the 1860s typically used the terms "radical" and "conservative" in writing or speaking of the opposing positions on Civil War issues among the Republicans, although "Jacobin" and "ultra" and "moderate" also appear. But the word "conservative" was frequently used to describe the position of Democrats as well, and I have therefore in general used "moderate" to refer to those Republicans who most disagreed with the radicals of their party. Of these men probably only Browning and Cowan, and perhaps Ten Eyck, in general took positions that were truly conservative if the Democracy is taken into consideration.)

This book is not meant to be an all-embracing study of radicalism in the Civil War Senate; it is primarily an analysis of that phenomenon as it was revealed in the Senate's voting patterns. The legislative roll call demands an expression of position from all members of the chamber upon a question, a question that is put to every lawmaker in exactly the same way. Although some legislators may absent themselves or make pairing agreements, such deviations from the mainstream are not unduly hampering when any appreciable number of roll calls are examined. The votes in the United States Senate during the Civil War, therefore, provide a great body of systematically recorded observations of the behavior of the senators, an extremely important segment of the Republican party elite. We can also find, particularly in the pages of the *Congressional Globe,* a considerable amount of explanation for their individual votes. If any data will allow us systematically to note differences of attitude and behavior among the senators, surely the roll calls offer the most promising beginning. We cannot, of course, assume that the distinctions we document among the senators were necessarily also found among members of the party outside that forum, but certainly knowledge of these differences will allow us to bring additional perspective to our study of such individuals.

In recent years, some historians have come increasingly to set their research within a social-science framework of hypothesis or model testing. Although I find this approach attractive under certain conditions and have myself practiced it elsewhere, I have not pursued it in this book. Rather I have tried to confront a number of questions that are still of great importance to those who study one of the most dramatic and interesting eras of our national history: Is it indeed possible to distinguish objectively between radicals and other varieties of Republicans in such a body as the Civil War Senate? Is it appropriate to view these distinctions as permanent divisions that set various senators apart from one another within the Republican party during the course of the war? If so, did the distance between radical and moderate increase or diminish through time? What were the substantive issues that elicited radical or nonradical behavior? Did these change over time? Did personal attributes of the senators seem to be associated with moderation or radicalism? Were these modes of behavior associated with other, more general attitudes toward aspects of American institutions and society? Was the institutional structure of the Senate during the Civil War such as to encourage or discourage factional behavior? We look back to the 1850s as one of the great periods of electoral realignment in our history; what can we say of the congresses of the Civil War, particularly the Thirty-seventh, in that context? (Of course, whatever we suggest about behavior in post-realignment congresses must be speculative, because we have as yet no comparable studies of the other congresses that immediately followed realignment.)

Why study the senators rather than the representatives? The latter were popularly elected for two-year terms, and should better reflect public opinion than did the members of the smaller chamber, who were elected by their state legislatures, usually for six-year terms. This objection is well put in a sense, but I was interested in discovering whether federal lawmakers adapted in some degree to the changing pattern of issues throughout the great conflict. Any such adjustment is difficult to discover in dealing with the House, since one of the greatest turnovers in congressional history occurred in that chamber between the Thirty-seventh Congress and the Thirty-eighth. Fifty-eight percent of the members of the House during the Thirty-eighth Congress were serving their first term, and the proportion of new members rises to 67 percent if we also count those with previous congressional experience who did not serve during the Thirty-seventh Congress.[2] There was turnover within the Senate but it was much less marked than in the popularly elected body.

It should also be pointed out that I am not attempting to rewrite T. Harry Williams' great monograph, *Lincoln and the Radicals*. That work is primarily an analysis of the uses of congressional investigatory power and the mobilization of pressures upon the executive branch. I do not touch upon such matters in this book, important though they were. Undoubtedly Abraham Lincoln and members of the cabinet influenced the position of senators on occasion. A thorough reconsideration of such relationships is in order but I have not attempted it here; basically I am

2. Morris P. Fiorina, David W. Rhode, and Peter Wissel, "Historical Change in House Turnover," in Norman J. Ornstein, ed., *Congress in Change: Evolution and Reform* (New York: Praeger, 1975), pp. 29–31.

trying to establish where the senators stood and *their* explanations for those positions.

Nor is this a general legislative history of the Senate during the Civil War. The measures I discuss are those that in some respect caused disagreement between the radicals and moderates within the party, and I have been much more interested in why the issues provoked disagreement than in the final content of the legislation, unless that was significantly shaped by factional disagreement. Indeed, some of the proposals examined in this book never became law; but in discussing them and voting upon them the senators revealed differences in attitudes or objectives that allow us better to understand the form and substance of radicalism and its antithesis.

When I began this work, I planned to devote a considerable section of it to a description of the ways in which other historians have dealt with the issue of radicalism. As that section of the book became increasingly substantial I decided that it must be reserved for separate publication; I have tried to keep dialogue with other historians to a minimum in the text. I should, however, note that several authors completed works of related interest during the years while my research was under way. Of most direct interest in various respects were: Glenn M. Linden, "Congressmen, 'Radicalism' and Economic Issues, 1861 to 1873" (Ph.D. dissertation: University of Washington, 1963); John L. McCarthy, "Reconstruction Legislation and Voting Alignments in the House of Representatives, 1863–1869" (Ph.D. dissertation: Yale University, 1970); Michael Les Benedict, *A Compromise of Principle: Congressional Republicans and Reconstruction, 1863–1869* (New York: Norton, 1974); Leonard P. Curry, *Blueprint for Modern America: Nonmilitary Legislation of the First Civil War Congress* (Nashville: Vanderbilt University Press, 1968); Hans L. Trefousse, *The Radical Republicans: Lincoln's Vanguard for Racial Justice* (New York: Knopf, 1968); Herman Belz, *Reconstructing the Union: Theory and Policy during the Civil War* (Ithaca: Cornell University Press, 1969); and Harold M. Hyman, *A More Perfect Union: The Impact of the Civil War and Reconstruction on the Constitution* (New York: Knopf, 1973).

The first three of these authors used quantitative analysis, but only Linden ranged across all of the wartime legislative sessions. His selection of roll calls, however, was a very small one, and both his selection procedures and averaging method of analysis left important questions unanswered. Although McCarthy used sophisticated scaling methods and other types of agreement analysis, he began his study in the Thirty-eighth Congress and concentrated upon the House of Representatives. Benedict used the second war congress as his starting point also, concentrated primarily on reconstruction policy, and used procedures that excluded many legislators from his analysis. Curry's study of the Thirty-seventh Congress was primarily a reconstruction of the bill histories of major war legislation in both houses; it did not focus on differences between radicals or moderates or on roll-call behavior, and discussed only one of the two wartime congresses. Trefousse, on the other hand, produced a wide-ranging study concerned primarily with the tension between the radicals and Lincoln, and did not examine legislative behavior in detail. The brilliant studies by Belz and Hyman in legal-constitutional history provide a strong contrast: the former is concerned with one category of legislation during the war, and the latter surveys the changing constitutional ethos of the era. These works, as well as many others, have been helpful. None of the authors attempted to do what I have done, nor in areas of mutual concern are my conclusions identical with theirs.

All historians face the danger of finding only what they set out to find. When one is using such an amorphous source as the *Congressional Globe,* that danger is very great indeed. One historian has accused such sinners among us of engaging in "proof by selective omission." I cannot claim to have produced *the* truly objective book, but I have used methods of selecting materials for analysis that are objective, subject to the basic assumptions involved in them, and I have tried to let the senators speak for themselves to a large degree in explaining their actions.

During the last generation there has been much examination of minds, cultures, and ideologies. Undoubtedly we, as members of the historical profession, are much·more sophisticated as a result of these endeavors than we once were. In such research, however, there is the ever-present danger of creating a reified set of labels which, to borrow a caustic metaphor, "magically resolves the problem by failing to confront it."[3] Those who have used the term "radicalism" in connection with the Civil War have sometimes fallen into this trap, I suspect. Perhaps I have not fought completely free of such entanglements, but my strategy has been to identify radicals and moderates in terms of the positions in which their votes place them upon voting scales constructed in an objective fashion, and then look to the explanations that the lawmakers gave for their votes for the ideas and some suggestion of the attitudes that characterized those whose voting fell into particular patterns. Thus it is possible to develop a set of ideas and policies which radicals held in common and which may be collectively called radicalism. But it is also true that the ideas that identified a radical in this fashion had no life or

3. Ronald P. Formisano, "Toward a Reorientation of Jacksonian Politics," *Journal of American History,* 63 (June 1976), 65.

vital power other than what men gave them—then as now, lawmakers looked to ideas as referents, but they also used them in self-justification, amended them, rejected them, and sought more satisfactory constructs.

An incident at the annual meeting of the Mississippi Valley Historial Association in 1964 solidified my determination to inquire more deeply into the nature of Civil War radicalism. As program chairman, I was obligated to write a summary of the proceedings but patently unable to attend all of the panels. When I asked how the discussion had developed in a session dealing with the politics of the Civil War, I was told, "Oh, it degenerated into the usual argument over 'who was a radical.'" I hope that my research in the years since has made possible a better answer to that question than was then available.

ALLAN G. BOGUE

*Madison, Wisconsin*

# Acknowledgments

Many individuals and institutions have helped me during the preparation of this book. I am much indebted for fellowship aid to the Social Science Research Council, to the John Simon Guggenheim Memorial Foundation, and to the Sherman Fairchild Distinguished Scholars Program of the California Institute of Technology, as well as for research assistance provided by the Mathematical Social Science Board and, particularly, by the Research Committee of the Graduate School of the University of Wisconsin–Madison.

William O. Aydelotte, Robert W. Fogel, and Joel H. Silbey have been continuing sources of friendship and inspiration. It was a privilege to work with Lee Benson on a variety of plans and projects during the 1960s and 1970s, and the sessions of "the floating seminar" during the preparation of *American Political Behavior: Historical Essays and Readings* (New York: Harper & Row, 1974) particularly stimulated my thinking about American political history. I have gained much knowledge and insight on this subject also from collaborations with Jerome M. Clubb and William H. Flanigan. Lance E. Davis, J. Morgan Kousser, and their colleagues of the Division of Humanities and Social Sciences at California Institute of Technology were ideal hosts, and stimulating to boot, during a semester while I was completing a draft of this book.

My former colleague Aage R. Clausen was a never-failing source of information and encouragement in the quantitative phases of my work. Richard H. Sewell generously shared his knowledge of the Civil War period with me on various occasions, and William L. Sachse kindly identified the source of Charles Sumner's allusion to "a lion in the lobby." At the Social Sciences Data and Computation Center of the University of Wisconsin, Edward Glaaser, Max E. Ellis, Jerome L. Kreuser, and, later, Alice R. Robbin assisted me greatly. On several occasions, Richard A.

Baker, Historian of the United States Senate, and his staff responded to inquiries with overwhelming generosity.

I owe a great debt to a number of talented young historians who assisted me during my years at the University of Wisconsin: James R. Turner, Ballard C. Campbell, Dennis East, David A. Walker, Mark P. Marlaire, Julienne L. Wood, Kenneth J. Winkle, George C. Brown, and Charles H. Schoenleber. All were meticulous researchers and several had unique skills of varying sorts; equally important, they volunteered some interpretations of the data which were extremely helpful. In the final stages of its preparation, George C. Brown read the manuscript and provided useful comments. So, under somewhat different circumstances, did Brooks Simpson, and it is thanks to him that I have clarified some important details about the voting on the Wade-Davis bill. The manuscript was typed and retyped by two cheerfully efficient and patient secretaries, Roberta R. Schambow and Carol Birkholz.

I believe that quantitative research can be most effective when combined with research in so-called literary sources and, as a result, I owe much to librarians and archivists in many institutions across the country. Providing continuous assistance were staff members of the Wisconsin State Historical Society. The helpfulness of Peter Draz, Ellen Burke, Josephine L. Harper, William F. Thompson, John A. Peters, Gerald Eggleston, and others of the Society staff made my research much easier. I am grateful also to staff members of the Manuscript Division of the Library of Congress, the Iowa Historical Society, the Minnesota Historical Society, the Lawson Library of the University of Kansas, the Illinois State Historical Library, the Indiana Historical Society, the Indiana State Archives, the Western Reserve Historical Society, Rochester University Library, the Vermont Historical Society, the Maine Historical Society, the New Hampshire Historical Society, the Massachusetts Historical Society, the Connecticut Historical Society, the Pennsylvania Historical Society, the Maryland Historical Society, the Oregon Historical Society, The Library of the University of Maine at Orono, the Houghton and Widener libraries at Harvard University, the Special Collections Division of the Cornell University Libraries, and the Henry E. Huntington Library and Art Museum, San Marino, California. I must particularly acknowledge the kindness of Mary Louise Rice Mallam of the University Library staff at St. Lawrence University, Canton, New York. Although I had coded the roll calls of the Civil War senates before the Historical Archive of the Inter-University Consortium for Political and Social Research in Ann Arbor was able to offer the same material to researchers in machine-readable form, that organization provided me with important data in the later stages of my research. In trying to find biographical information about some of the more obscure members of the Civil War senates, I wrote for information to many other libraries and local historical societies. These inquiries were received with unfailing courtesy and helpfulness, and I am most grateful.

During the course of this research I have published a number of progress reports as articles or contributions to collections of essays. I am indebted for permission to reprint excerpts or otherwise draw upon these publications as follows: part of Chapter 2 is taken in somewhat revised form from my analysis of power relations among the Republican senators which was originally published in William O. Aydelotte, Allan G. Bogue, and Robert W. Fogel, eds., *The Dimensions of Quantitative Research in History* (Princeton: Princeton University Press, 1972), copyright © 1972 by Center for Advanced Study in the Behavioral Sciences, pp. 285–95. Republication rights have been granted by my coeditors, Princeton University Press, and the Center for Advanced Study in the Behavioral Sciences, Stanford, California. In preparing Chapter 3, I drew upon some materials originally published in David M. Ellis et al., eds., *The Frontier in American Development: Essays in Honor of Paul Wallace Gates* (Ithaca: Cornell University Press, 1969), pp. 20–30, and upon the article "Bloc and Party in the United States Senate: 1861–1863," *Civil War History*, 13 (September 1967), 221–41. Republication rights were kindly granted by Cornell University Press, *Civil War History*, and Kent State University Press. In this chapter I also used some material from my article "The Radical Voting Dimension in the U.S. Senate during the Civil War," reprinted from *The Journal of Interdisciplinary History*, 3 (1973), 449–74, by permission of *The Journal of Interdisciplinary History* and M.I.T. Press, Cambridge, Mass. I presented a preliminary version of some of the material in the later chapters in a paper at the annual meeting of the Organization of American Historians in 1972. Most of the book, however, represents research and findings that have been hitherto unpublished.

I must also thank the directors and staffs of the following manuscript repositories for permission to quote from their collections as follows: from the Fessenden Family Papers, the Bowdoin College Library, Brunswick, Maine; from the Orville Hickman Browning Papers, the Illinois State Historical Library, Springfield; from the John Parker Hale Papers, the New Hampshire Historical Society, Concord; from Mss 577, James Willis Nesmith Papers, the Oregon Historical Society, Portland; from the James Rood Doolittle Papers and from the Timothy Otis Howe Papers, the State Historical Society of Wisconsin, Madison. In the absence of information about the copyright holders of unpublished letters in the Zachariah Chandler Papers, deposited in the Manuscript Division,

Library of Congress, I have quoted briefly from one letter, as noted in my text, in the belief that the quotation illustrates the "fair use" of research materials as set forth in the Copyright Act of 1976.

A.G.B.

# Part I

MEN, CONTEXT, AND PATTERNS

★　★　★

The junior senator from Wisconsin in 1861 was Timothy Howe, a man of some detachment and, as time would prove, considerable perception and staying power. Early in the long session of the Thirty-seventh Congress he wrote to a member of his family: "Every thing about us portends the coming of a rupture in the ranks of the war party and if so[,] a fierce struggle between the two factions. The organization of a party designing either to rule the administration or to supplant it has *I* think already commenced. Emancipation—the utter extinction of slavery will be the watchword & the effort of one faction. Where the other faction will plant itself is not so certain."[1] And, the following spring, in debates on the confiscation bills, one finds the senators describing, explicitly or implicitly, the differences among Republicans. Some opponents of a harsh confiscation bill invoked the Constitution against those who were maintaining that Congress should exercise war powers and urging "legislative encroachment upon the prerogatives of the other departments."[2] But men who complained in this fashion, retorted Senator Wade, were advocating the "irresponsible power of the Chief Magistrate in time of war," a doctrine which he characterized as "most slavish and un-American."[3] Senator Dixon, who feared that the powers of the states might be diminished, maintained that the rebel states were still within the Union, and their residents, therefore, were entitled to the guarantees of the Constitution if they were to be punished. He also implied that the chairman of the Judiciary Committee was an "opponent of this Administration."[4] To this the chairman, Lyman

1. Timothy O. Howe to Grace Howe, Dec. 13, 1861, Timothy O. Howe Papers, Wisconsin State Historical Society.
2. *Congressional Globe* (hereafter *CG*), 37 Cong., 2 sess., 2919.
3. Ibid., 2930.
4. Ibid., 2924–2928, 2973.

Trumbull, responded by suggesting that Dixon was a "courtier" and a "sycophant" who did "not mean to be in opposition to the Administration let what will happen."[5]

Senator Cowan referred to "the ultra school of the Republican party," whose members had decided that the rebellion of "some of the slave States" would be "put down by main force, and by an utter disregard of the will of the whole people of the slave States," and were insisting on measures "utterly obnoxious and distasteful" to every senator from the slave states.[6] More personally still, Wade described himself and his friends as "the earnest, up and down, through thick and thin Republicans of this body," leaving the character of recusant Republicans to the imagination.[7] But on one occasion, Senator Fessenden, in exasperation with Wade and his friends, spoke of "certain gentlemen on this floor," who "seem to think that they are the representatives of all righteousness . . . and that if anybody differs from them he is either a fool or a knave."[8]

Expression of such differences appeared in the senators' correspondence. Writing to Zachariah Chandler after the close of the second session and as the election of 1862 neared, Morton Wilkinson worried only about the success of root-and-branch men like himself.[9] As he reviewed the Illinois election for Chandler's benefit a few weeks later, Lyman Trumbull remarked sarcastically: "Do you think it will be any loss to exchange Browning for a responsible Democrat?"[10] To Browning, after the Thirty-seventh Congress had ended, Ira Harris lamented that the President had "been drawn into the views" unfortunately "of a miserable lot of politicians"; a "lot" of which the New Yorker obviously did not consider himself a member.[11]

Actors in the drama of the Civil War frequently used the terms "radical" and "conservative" to describe distinctions of the sort indicated here, and historians have accepted such precedent with varying degrees of interest, imagination, and amplification. Yet despite the emphasis that some historians have placed upon the political role of the radicals, we have only recently begun to demand a precise definition of radicalism and to explore with real intensity the ways in which the phenomenon was related to the development of legislative policy. It is, of course, no simple

5. Ibid., 2973.

6. Ibid., 2993.

7. Ibid., 3002.

8. Ibid., 2203.

9. Morton Wilkinson to Zachariah Chandler, Oct. 20, 1862, Zachariah Chandler Papers, Library of Congress.

10. Lyman Trumbull to Zachariah Chander, Nov. 9, 1862, ibid.

11. Ira Harris to Orville H. Browning, May 30, 1863, Orville H. Browning Papers, Illinois State Historical Library.

matter to disentangle one strand from the intricate pattern of legislative life in Washington and, indeed, any single element can have full meaning only within the perspective of the whole. This is worth remembering as we probe the meaning of radicalism or its antonym, moderation, in the Civil War Senate.

Chapter 1 of Part I introduces the members of the Senate and examines some of their characteristics, both individual and collective. The next chapter investigates the institutional structure within which the senators served and devotes some attention to the character of leadership exercised in the chamber. In Chapter 3 we analyze the roll calls to establish whether the voting patterns of the senators justify the description of individuals as radicals or moderates. Having established in qualified fashion that such distinctions did exist, we turn in Chapter 4 to a brief examination of the ways in which they related to the personal characteristics of the senators and the institutional arrangements within the Senate.

# 1

# The Senators

The congresses of the Civil War were unusual assemblages, deliberating under conditions unparalleled in the lifetime of their members and, indeed, in later years as well. For the first time in its short history the Republican party was in control of the executive branch and of both houses of Congress. In the Senate the Republicans had no effective opposition; the consolidating influence that powerful opponents provide was absent. The Thirty-seventh Congress was therefore the scene of competition among the abler or more ambitious Republican lawmakers for control of the legislative process, a situation that subjected the committee structure to stresses and strains at the very time that the chairmen were struggling to perfect unprecedented amounts of wartime legislation.

Republicans had various party antecedents—they had been Whig, Know-Nothing, or Democrat, not to mention various shadings within those political persuasions. Former Whigs were a majority among the Republican legislators, and in that party they had cherished the theory of legislative supremacy over the executive. Efforts of the President to exercise strong leadership over congressional activity might therefore have been expected to meet opposition. The Republican party had accepted much of the economic orientation of the Whigs, a circumstance that may have left former Free-Soil Democrats within the Republican ranks extremely uncomfortable when economic matters were under discussion. The Republicans were most strongly united in their opposition to slavery, but, even in that respect, there were great differences of opinion among them as to the most appropriate policies to follow. The national government was directing a great war against most of the men and women who maintained the peculiar institution, and it was to be expected that the disasters and triumphs of the conflict would affect the thinking of different men in different ways. In fact, the war created an atmosphere of recurrent crisis in which extreme proposals might attract, for a time at least, even congenitally moderate men. It would have been surprising indeed had not differences of opinion developed, as to both the objectives of the war, and the degree to which the Republicans should build a record in other legislative areas.

No one has ever considered the conditions under which members of the Congress worked during the first seventy years of the Republic to be ideal. When dry, the streets of Washington puffed dust at the pressure of the lightest foot or slowest turning wheel; when wet, they were quagmires. And when sessions lingered into late spring or summer, the marshes and minor water courses all stank; household "slops" putrefied in yard and street; privies became malodorous; and generations that knew no air conditioning steamed in high temperatures, oppressive humidity, and their own sweat. The wartime influx of humanity exacerbated conditions immeasurably as the problems of human waste and garbage disposal reached crisis proportions, and army slaughterhouses and makeshift hospitals added their unwholesome increment to the atmosphere.

From the capital's earliest days congressmen generally lived in boardinghouses or hotels, sharing accomodations and meals with a small group of more or less congenial colleagues. Frequently wives shared a rented room or two with their husbands. However charming the chatelaine of the boardinghouse, or excellent her cooking, boardinghouse life was restrictive and uncomfortable and afforded little privacy or opportunity for contemplation. After 1840 increasing numbers of congressmen resided individually or with family members at hotels, boarded separately in the home of some respectable, if not genteel, family, or acquired private dwellings. But when not in committee room or on the floor, most congressmen of the Civil War still moved to the rhythm of the boardinghouse or hotel life. And although Doolittle of Wisconsin could write to his wife of pleasant evenings in Mrs. Carter's parlor when a younger Doolittle and a Cowan scion tuned up their fiddles, it was not a life that protected a man's free hours or encouraged contemplation of public issues.[1]

Whatever his dwelling place, the individual senator or representative quite literally lived in the midst of war. As various observers noted, Washington in 1861 had become an armed camp. Regiments were encamped or billeted in and around the city and for a time the senators

---

1. An introduction to the Washington milieu and its bibliography is provided by Constance M. Green, *Washington: Village and Capital, 1800–1878* (Princeton: Princeton University Press, 1962), pp. 200–312, 415–27.

hacked and coughed as the smoke from an army bakery in the lower regions of the Capitol filtered into their chamber. Marching men, army trains, or cavalry troops churning up dust from the wretched streets, lounging soldiers on pass, epaulettes and braid in the lobbies of the Willard, the National, and other hotels—these were the surface manifestations of the war in Washington. To federal lawmakers, these also symbolized the fact that their own lives had become vastly more complicated as a result of the conflict. To the inconveniences of boardinghouse or hotel life and the unpleasantness of the Washington climate, there was now added the pressure of greatly increased work. The committee room and late sessions held the senators in thrall until it was pure ecstasy to ride a horse or drive a buggy out to visit one of the state regimental encampments in company with friends or army officers. Less happy but even more essential were the visits to army hospitals, which became routine once the grim game was begun in earnest across the rolling Virginia countryside. The number of errands run to the various government departments on behalf of constituents before the "morning hour" or on Saturdays increased sharply. The senators were entreated to arrange compassionate leaves and speed the bandages and apple sauce contributed by volunteer groups at home to the proper hospitals or camps. Some of them rose at 5 A.M. to attack the piles of correspondence that mounted remorselessly on their writing tables.

While they tried to perform their legislative and related duties, the senators were besieged by constituents, job seekers, aggrieved officers, and lobbyists. The importunities of such visitors emphasized the fact that the war effort was also making huge amounts of patronage at least potentially available to legislators, tempting them to try to use it for partisan or personal ends or, at the very least, complicating the relations of the lawmakers with both their constituencies and the executive branch of government. If, in theory, more patronage was available than ever before in the nation's history, legislators were more fearful perhaps than ever before that political rivals might use it to their own ends. Victory in the field must be left to the generals but, for the individual senator, political survival might rest on the choice of the next postmaster in Hartford, Connecticut, or the question of whether he was receiving his fair share of his state's federal list.

Even had they wished to, the senators could not put the war from their minds for any length of time. At night the rumbling of army freight trains, the clatter of artillery caissons, the tramp of marching columns, and the serenades of military bands disturbed their rest. Some agonized over the knowledge that their decisions and the legislation they passed might send thousands of men to their deaths. And when the strong young voices of a passing regiment rose in song, others might have wondered how many more such songs those lusty throats would sing. And how much more poignant such thoughts must have been to senators such as Fessenden and Doolittle, whose sons were marching or riding in the armies of the Union.

But even though the senators of the Civil War years were certainly men burdened with unprecedented responsibilities and confronted with new and perplexing challenges, theirs was by no means a *tabula rasa*. James Harlan was doubtless naive when he explained to Iowans how he would conduct himself if elected to the Senate of the United States in 1854 ("in all *Constitutional* questions . . . I would expect to be guided in my action by the decisions of the Supreme Court and the well settled principles of Constitutional Law—in all questions of *Legislative Expediency,* by the views and wishes of the Legislature and people of Iowa— and in all questions of *Conscience* by the Bible."[2] But all these men brought to their work their own conceptions of the nature of life, the Union, and the Constitution. In addition, they were linked by membership, tradition, and institutional arrangements to preceding congresses. The patterns of sectional opposition and the institutional frictions of the past could be expected to continue at least to some extent within this Congress, despite the extraordinary conditions under which its members met.

This book is a study of the similarities and differences in the acts and words of the United States senators; but at this point we must introduce the cast of characters whom visitors in the Senate galleries saw settling into the work of the session during the closing weeks of 1861. Most of the same men had met in the special summer emergency session, but the brevity of that assembly, and the general solidarity exhibited on most issues by the Republicans at that time, suggest that our consideration should begin with the regular session.

The Thirty-seven Senate was the second to meet in the "new" Senate Chamber, where the skylighted ceiling suspended thirty-six feet above them, lateral dimensions of slightly more than one hundred and thirteen by eighty feet, and encircling galleries filled with rustling and occasionally applauding or hissing spectators, challenged the senators to make themselves heard. Sometimes the thrumming of rain on the roof provided an additional muffling layer of sound to frustrate those of weak voice. By no means everything worked to stifle the orator, however. Since the chamber rested within a cocoon of corridors, lobbies, cloak-rooms, and functionary and administrative offices, there were no win-

2. Johnson Brigham, *James Harlan* (Iowa City: State Historical Society of Iowa, 1913), p. 87.

dows to admit the distracting sounds of passerby and military band or the pungent odors of an unsanitary city. In this respect the senators were, as Senator Borah later suggested acerbicly, out of "touch with the outside world."[3]

The senators also labored under the debilitation of a ventilating system that fell far short of its planners' objectives. Designed to blow in cool basement air, on occasion it wafted in smoke from the Army bake ovens, installed in the basement while soldiers were occupying the Capitol during the first excited efforts to organize the defense of Washington. Speaking to his motion for an investigation of improved methods of ventilation, or of moving the chamber to the external wall of the Capitol's north wing, in early June, 1862, Hale likened the conditions under which he and his colleagues labored to having "something like a hothouse, as if it were for rearing exotic plants, over our heads, by which the rays of the sun are concentrated on us," while "the air we breathe is pumped up from a damp and unwholesome place below the surface of the ground."[4]

The senators meeting in their second (or first regular) legislative session of the war convened in the early days of December, 1861, beneath galleries packed with relatives, Washington residents, lobbyists, soldiers, and curious visitors from afar. From these watchers rose a steady murmuring as the initiated identified veteran legislators for their companions, or speculated on the identity of unknown individuals moving amid the three-tiered concentric rows of senatorial desks, shining in polished mahogany splendor in contrast to the brassier glitter of senatorial cuspidors, strategically arranged on the new matting with which the chamber had been provided after its soldier occupants departed. Since relatively unknown senators sometimes played leading roles, albeit briefly, during the Civil War and, since sectional loyalties were of major importance in the congressional events of the 1850s, it is useful to examine the backgrounds of the senators and to consider them within a regional setting.

The legislatures of New England had by this time sent to the Senate a solid phalanx of Republicans, who, because of both years of service and ability, were to provide a disproportionate amount of the chamber's leadership during the war. The "best general debater and practical legis-

3. George H. Haynes, *The Senate of the United States: Its History and Practice* (Boston: Houghton Mifflin, 1938), 2:920. For the physical setting see: Glenn Brown, *History of the United States Capitol* (56 Cong. 1 sess., Senate Doc. 60. Washington: Government Printing Office, 1902), Vol. 2; *Keim's Illustrated Hand Book: Washington and its Environs . . .* (Washington: B. F. Owen, 1884, and other editions); Ihna Thayer Frary, *They Built the Capitol* (Freeport, N.Y.: Books for Libraries Press, 1940).

4. *CG*, 37 Cong., 2 sess., 2569.

The Thirty-sixth Senate, the first to sit in the new chamber, in session. The engraving appeared in *Harper's Weekly*, December 31, 1859.

lator" there, according to "Mack," the political correspondent of the Cincinnati *Commercial,* was William Pitt Fessenden of Maine, a veteran senator of Whig antecedents who presided on occasion within the Republican caucus, and who chaired the Finance Committee. His level gaze, high-bridged nose, and firm lips and chin identified a man who would be intimidated by none; although known as a genial friend and a speaker who on occasion enlivened the chamber with humorous sallies, he was also capable of devastating sarcasm and a remorseless recall and logic that left colleagues rash enough to question either his motives or his acts, licking their wounds in frustrated fury. Since the presidential election had moved Maine's other senator of 1860, Hannibal Hamlin, to the Vice President's rostrum, the state legislature chose Lot M. Morrill, governor of the state during the late 1850s and, like Hamlin, a former Democrat, to work in harness with Fessenden. Bald with a white fringe, slight of figure and birdlike, even somewhat effeminate in manner, Morrill was a man of real ability, and, although less well known to historians than Justin S. Morrill of Vermont, he was to remain active in national politics until the late 1870s.[5]

From Vermont came two older senators who wielded considerable influence among their colleagues, but enjoyed little of the public acclaim afforded to more colorful associates. A "rather heavy set man of medium height," and with long service on the bench, Jacob Collamer was, in Mack's view, the best lawyer in the Senate, given particular attention by his colleagues when, infrequently, he addressed them. His low tones seldom carried into the reaches of the galleries, however, and viewers there were left to read his words in the *Congressional Globe* or merely wonder why Sumner, in some seriousness, called him the "Green-Mountain Socrates." His colleague, Solomon Foot, was president *pro tempore* recurrently during the Thirty-seventh Congress; white haired, massive of head, his "smile full of sweetness," the "most senatorial of senators," he presided with serene and severe fairness, and apparently retained the respect of all in a party and a chamber that had their full complements of difficult individuals.[6]

5. Mack's evaluation was reprinted in the Chicago *Tribune,* March 4, 1864. The standard biographies of Fessenden are: Francis Fessenden, *Life and Public Services of William Pitt Fessenden: United States Senator from Maine 1854–1864, Secretary of the Treasury 1864–1865, United States Senator from Maine 1865–1869,* 2 vols. (Boston: Houghton Mifflin, 1907), and Charles A. Jellison, *Fessenden of Maine: Civil War Senator* (Syracuse: Syracuse University Press, 1962). On Morrill, see George F. Talbot, "Lot M. Morrill: Sketch of his Life and Public Services," in Maine Historical Society *Collections and Proceedings* 2d series, 5 (1894), 225–75; Augusta *Kennebec Journal,* January 17, 1883.

6. Concerning Collamer see: Chicago *Tribune,* March 4, 1864; Philadelphia *Press,* April 28, 1862; Allen F. Davis notes other sources of information in "Why Jacob Collamer?" *Vermont History,* 27 (January 1959), 41–53. Springfield (Mass.) *Weekly Republican,* March 7, 1863; *Dictionary of American Biography* (New York: Scribner, 1931), 6:498–99. His colleague

Like those of the Maine contingent, the political origins of the New Hampshire senators, John Parker Hale and Daniel Clark, served testimony to the realignment which had produced the Republican party. Initially a Democrat, Hale represented the antislavery cause in Congress as early as 1847. Imposing of presence, he caught the attention of the Philadelphia *Press* reporter during the special session, "How jolly he looks! Dark masses of hair; keen roguish eye; broad, bold front, he stands like a great pump, pouring out a constant stream of good-nature. A little gall, however, will drop into the pure torrent." Clark, on the other hand, emerged from the Whiggery of the Granite State. Now well into his first term, he was "tall, easy, elegant in his bearing, with a strong face, deeply lined, . . . [a] man of the deepest conviction" and "the most uncompromising principles." A younger "Black Dan," Clark was a working senator, whose history of solid legislative accomplishments during the war contrasted sharply with the record of his squabbling and quixotic colleague.[7]

In Charles Sumner and Henry Wilson, Massachusetts had two of the senior Republican senators. Both headed important committees, Sumner Foreign Affairs, and Wilson Military Affairs and Militia, and both were to be involved in many of the most tumultous debates of the war years. Sumner was no doubt more frequently described by members of the press and Washington visitors than any other senator. He was surpassed in length of service only by Foot and Wade among the Republicans—and that by less than two months—and marked both in mien and in body by the struggle for freedom; his formidable stature and handsome features, as well as the scholarly adornment in his major speeches, caught the attention of all. Mack called him the Senate's best scholar, but some among his colleagues believed that scholarship was not necessarily the greatest of senatorial virtues. Wilson no doubt suffered, both in his own mind and in those of many observers, from comparison with his colleague. He was "strong and earnest" of face, but his scrambling rise to the Senate owed much to the putrescent forces of Know-Nothingism in Massachusetts. Whereas Sumner's frame could have born

---

is described in *Proceedings on the Death of Hon. Solomon Foot Including the Addresses Delivered in the Senate and House of Representatives on Thursday, April 12, 1866* (Washington: Government Printing Office, 1866); George F. Edmunds, "The Life, Character and Services of Solomon Foot," *Addresses Delivered before the Vermont Historical Society . . . October 16, 1866* (Montpelier, Vt.: Walton's Steam Printing Establishment, 1866).

7. Philadelphia *Press*, July 12, 1861; Richard H. Sewell, *John P. Hale and the Politics of Abolition* (Cambridge: Harvard University Press, 1965). Springfield *Weekly Republican*, March 7, 1863; Isaac W. Smith, "Hon. Daniel Clark," *The Granite Monthly*, 10 (July 1887), 223–29; Charles H. Bell, *The Bench and Bar of New Hampshire* (Boston: Houghton Mifflin, 1894), pp. 269–72. Webster's nickname was used in a description of Clark in the latter's obituary, Manchester *Mirror and American*, January 21, 1891.

a toga with dignity and grace, Wilson's dumpy build would have made such a garment slightly ridiculous, and any attempt on the part of this "Natick cobbler" to garnish his speeches with the classical allusions and scholarly citations offered by his colleague would have been equally laughable. But Wilson was an indefatigable worker, the armies of the Union would owe him much, and along the way he struck more than one notable legislative blow at slavery as well.[8]

The Republican senators from the lower New England states were to leave less imprint upon the form of the Senate's war than the northern delegations. James F. Simmons, a manufacturer from Rhode Island, resigned under a cloud during the summer of 1862 after admitting that he had agreed to obtain contracts for constituents for a percentage of their value. During the third session of the Thirty-seventh Congress, the lawyer-historian, Samuel Greene Arnold, replaced Simmons and in turn gave way to William Sprague. One of the heirs to a Rhode Island man-ufacturing fortune, Sprague had made a name for himself in mobilizing Rhode Island for war and had actually served as an aide to Burnside on the disastrous field at First Manassas. Only thirty-two years of age when he reached the Senate in March, 1863, this somewhat indolent but very rich young man gave Washington its most glittering social event of the Civil War when he married Kate Chase, the talented and charming daughter of the Secretary of the Treasury. It was perhaps his greatest contribution to the war effort subsequent to his election. The senator who held the other Rhode Island seat was of different stripe. Henry B. Anthony, it was said, made the Providence *Journal* into the "Rhode Island Bible," at least to the Republicans of the state, and presided for years over the "*Journal* Sunday School," where each Sunday morning leading citizens met at the "Round Table," in the *Journal* offices to chart the political future of the state. A man of "personal charm and dignity," and not one to make extended speeches or to insult his colleagues he was destined to serve longer than all but a handful of his colleagues of the Thirty-seventh.[9]

8. Chicago *Tribune*, March 4, 1864. David Donald's magisterial two-volume biography provides the best introduction to the extensive Sumner bibliography. The Civil War years are covered in *Charles Sumner and the Rights of Man* (New York: Knopf, 1970). The senators from Massachusetts are contrasted in the Springfield *Weekly Republican*, March 7, 1863. Biographies of Wilson are Ernest McKay, *Henry Wilson: Practical Radical, A Portrait of a Politician* (Port Washington, N.Y.: Kennikat Press, 1971), and Richard H. Abbott, *Cobbler in Congress, The Life of Henry Wilson, 1812–1875* (Lexington: University Press of Kentucky, 1972).

9. Boston *Morning Journal*, July 8, 1862; *Biographical Cyclopedia of Representative Men of Rhode Island* (Providence: National Biographical Publishing, 1881), pp. 248–49. H. W. Shoemaker, *The Last of the War Governors . . .* (Altoona: Altoona Tribune Publishing, 1916); Thomas G. and Marva R. Belden, *So Fell the Angels* (Boston: Little, Brown, 1956). Charles

If Rhode Island provided the Senate with its only historian member during the war, Connecticut provided the only poet, James Dixon. His sonnets, wrote an authority, were characterized by "chasteness of thought and style." Initially a Whig, he had flirted with the Americans during the mid-1850s to his considerable advantage, a fairly common gambit. He was unusual, however, in that his colleagues believed that he had sat adjacent to the congressman from Illinois, Abraham Lincoln, as a member of the House of Representatives during the 1840s, a position that now gave him, some suspected, an unfair advantage in the struggle for political patronage. Dixon's colleague was Lafayette S. Foster, also Whig in background. Although he was historically one of the less prominent Republican senators he enjoyed sufficient esteem among his colleagues to be chosen president *pro tempore* during the Thirty-ninth Congress.[10]

Republican dominance was less firm in the senatorial delegations from the Middle Atlantic states than among the New England senators. Of the states of New York, Pennsylvania, and New Jersey, only the Empire State was continuously represented by two Republican senators during the war. The gallery occupant of early December, 1861, would have seen the massive Preston King, "waddle" in, "fat as a hogshead, with great hanging chops," in Walt Whitman's words. A veteran of New York's Barnburner Democracy, King had impeccable antislavery credentials, and the manuscript collections left by his contemporaries contain numerous examples of his round childish script, expressing faith in both the Almighty and the Union cause. "His vote," wrote a biographer, "often stood with that of the vicious Ben Wade, but never his heart." Though neither his energy nor his good intentions could be questioned, King failed to navigate the shoals and cross-currents of Republican politics in New York; the wealthy merchant and first war governor, Edwin D. Morgan replaced him in March, 1863. Ira Harris replaced William Seward in the other New York seat after Seward's elevation to the cabinet. Veteran of twelve years on the state supreme court and

---

Carroll, *Rhode Island: Three Centuries of Democracy* (New York: Lewis Historical Company, 1932) 2:1092–93; *Dictionary of American Biography*, 1(1928), 316–17; *Chicago Tribune*, January 20, 1863; *Memorial Addresses on the Life and Character of Henry Bowen Anthony (A Senator from Rhode Island), delivered in the Senate and House of Representatives ... January 19 and 21, 1885* ... (Washington: Government Printing Office, 1885).

10. Charles W. Everest, ed., *Poets of Connecticut* (Hartford: Case, Tiffany, & Burnham, 1844), p. 435; William Faxon to Mark Howard, Hartford, Conn., December 15, 1863 (Mark Howard Mss., Connecticut Historical Society, Hartford); *Commemorative Biographical Record of Hartford County, Connecticut* ... (Chicago: J. H. Baers, 1901), 1:1–2. *Dictionary of American Biography*, 6(1931), 553; Jarlath R. Lane, *A Political History of Connecticut during the Civil War* (Washington: Catholic University of America Press, 1941), passim.

lecturer in the Albany Law School, Harris was a man of "splendid personal appearance" and "dignified manner" and, on occasion, a source of great irritation to "hell-for-leather" colleagues.[11]

Perhaps deservedly, John Conover Ten Eyck, the Republican senator from New Jersey, has received little attention from historians. Described by one New Jersey historian as "a lawyer who had not been politically prominent," Ten Eyck apparently did not attract the interest of those who drew pen portraits of the senators, and was dismissed by the Chicago *Tribune* merely as a "conservative" who represented "the most conservative State in the North." Yet on some matters he would speak out and with some force. Nor did his Democratic colleague play a major role in the ranks of the opposition during the second session of the Thirty-seventh Congress. A prominent New Jersey businessman, John R. Thomson had been governor of his state and had served in the Senate since 1853, but, through most of 1862 he struggled to recover from the effects of a stroke and took no real part in the Senate's business.[12] He died and New Jersey's legislators caught the attention of the Union by sending James Walter Wall to replace the governor's appointee, Richard S. Field, and complete the unexpired term. Lawyer and journalist, a former supporter of John C. Breckinridge, Wall was involved in the editorial direction of the New York *Daily News,* a peace organ that the government suppressed in August, 1861. Subsequently Wall was arrested and he languished in Fort Lafayette for a couple of weeks until he was released after swearing allegiance to the Union. New Jersey's Democratic legislators sent this martyr to the Senate as living evidence of the encroachments of the Lincoln administration on the individual American's freedom of speech. Reconsidering, they replaced him at the end of the third session with William Wright, an elderly manufacturer whose establishment in times of peace had supplied the southern chivalry and plain folk with much of their saddlery and harness, and who had served one earlier term during the mid-1850s.[13]

Pennsylvania's Unionists displayed their ambivalence on war issues in 1861 by passing over David Wilmot, the celebrated Free-Soiler, to send Edgar Cowan to the United States Senate. Their choice was a lawyer

11. Ernest Paul Muller, "Preston King: A Political Biography" (Ph.D. diss., Columbia University, 1957), pp. 697, 683. *National Cyclopedia of American Biography* . . . (New York: James T. White, 1921), 2:96; *Dictionary of American Biography,* 8(1932), 310; Chicago *Tribune,* January 22, 1862.

12. Charles Merriam Knapp, *New Jersey Politics during the Period of the Civil War and Reconstruction* (Geneva, N.Y.: W. F. Humphrey, 1924), p. 16; Chicago *Tribune,* January 22, 1862. *Cyclopedia of New Jersey Biography* (New York: American Historical Society, 1923), 1:165–66.

13. Knapp, *New Jersey Politics,* pp. 53–81, passim; Irving S. Kull, *New Jersey: A History* (New York: American Historical Society, 1930), 3:775–86, 830–36; *National Cyclopedia of American Biography,* 10:123–24. *Dictionary of American Biography,* 20 (1936), 570–71.

from western Pennsylvania whose only previous elective office of any moment had been that of presidential elector in the 1860 election. Reared in penury by a widowed mother, Cowan had been a raftsman, boat builder, schoolteacher, and medical student before becoming a lawyer, and he was as formidable in intellect as his height of six-foot-four made him in stature. In the full flight of oratory, he reminded one observer of Carlyle's portrayal of Mirabeau speaking in the Convention of 1789[sic]. As a youngster, Cowan had collected toll on behalf of his mother on the Robbstown Pike. Reportedly, when a mounted traveler threw a dollar on the ground and demanded change, the lad fetched coins from his mother's house nearby and flung them at the feet of the bully's horse. Showing little of the reticence and modesty deemed appropriate in a freshman senator, he displayed similar independence in arguing against the constitutional positions of colleagues such as Sumner, Howard, and Wade, and earned their bitter enmity as a result.[14]

Although passed over once for Cowan, Wilmot was not long denied a senate seat thereafter. He was awarded the remaining two years of Simon Cameron's term when the latter took over the War Department, and was sworn in only ten days after Cowan in March, 1861. Almost a legend by then, Wilmot had been a man of gargantuan appetitie in his younger days and, according to the Pennsylvania congressman Galusha Grow, one of the great barroom speakers of his time. Now in failing health, he did not take a prominent role in the proceedings of the Thirty-seventh Congress. At the conclusion of the third session, he left the chamber amid the angry recriminations of his supporters, who charged that the failure of the Cameron wing of the Pennsylvania Republicans to close ranks behind him had handed the election to Charles R. Buckalew. Republican papers described the Democrat Buckalew as "wireworking, cool, sardonic," and moreover, "a true slave-loving demagogue," who won the prize while an armed and noisy mob demonstrated during the balloting. The "brave and true" Wilmot lost out when Simon "Cameron's dollars" confronted Buckalew's "dirks."[15]

In the Middle West, the Republicans in general held the senatorial seats, but there were exceptions, as well as occasional deep concern about

14. George D. Albert, ed., *History of the County of Westmoreland, Pennsylvania, with Biographical Sketches of Many of Its Pioneers and Prominent Men* (Philadelphia: L. H. Everts, 1882), pp. 334-41; B. F. Pershing, "Senator Edgar A. Cowan, 1861-1867," *Western Pennsylvania Historical Magazine,* 4 (October 1921), 224-33; John Newton Boucher, "Edgar Cowan, United States Senator from Pennsylvania during the Civil War," *Americana,* 26 (April 1932), 247-60.

15. Charles B. Going, *David Wilmot, Free-Soiler* (New York: Appleton, 1924); James H. Duff, "David Wilmot, the Statesman and Political Leader," *Pennsylvania History,* 12 (October 1946), 283-89. Chicago *Tribune,* January 17, 20, 21, 1863; *Ohio State Journal,* January 19, 1863; *Dictionary of American Biography,* 3 (1929), 225-26.

the reelection of some Republican worthies. From Ohio came the redoubtable veteran of the antislavery wars, Benjamin F. Wade, who shared with Foot the honor of having the longest continuous service among the Republicans in the Senate, and who was credited with having stopped the rout of Union soldiers fleeing from First Manassas. Wade was no orator, and his contributions to debate were usually short and, on occasion, intemperate: he once called Cowan a dog and attacked the President in open debate on more than one occasion. A correspondent once described him as stumping into the chamber "grim as a bear in ill health" and left the reader to guess the implications of this condition. His younger colleague John Sherman succeeded Salmon P. Chase in 1861, giving Ohio two senators of Whig origin. Having proven his mettle in the House, Sherman was immediately marked for an important role on the Finance Committee. A "tall, scholarly looking gentleman," characterized by the "quiet elegance of his manners," the youthful Sherman stood out amid the gray heads around him. He was to confide to his brother, the general, that he entered the Senate expecting that at last he would have the leisure to study and analyze legislation in a reflective way—expectations that he admitted were completely unrealized.[16]

Perhaps no other pair of western senators had quite the impact upon legislative events of the Ohio senators, if one considers Wade's contribution to the investigatory activities of the Joint Committee on the Conduct of the War. Nonetheless, other western senators left a strong impress upon senatorial activities. Michigan's Zachariah Chandler was abolitionist in sympathy, a speaker who rolled his eyes and contorted his features, and was generally without the "graces or conventions of eloquence and oratory." The Cincinnati *Commercial*'s correspondent emphasized two of his weaknesses by referring to "the excitable and 'spiritual senator' from Michigan"; paradoxically, a memorialist dubbed him "the Doric Pillar of Michigan." A merchant, adrift with few like companions in a sea of lawyers, he resembled Wade in sentiment and

16. Cincinnati *Daily Commercial*, December 5, 1862. Hans L. Trefousse, *Benjamin Franklin Wade: Radical Republican from Ohio* (New York: Twayne, 1963), is the most recent full-scale treatment but see also Mary Land, "Ben Wade," in Kenneth W. Wheeler, ed., *For the Union: Ohio Leaders in the Civil War* (Columbus: Ohio State University Press, 1968), pp. 157–233, and Albert G. Riddle, *The Life of Benjamin F. Wade* (Cleveland: William W. Williams, 1886). Springfield *Weekly Republican*, March 7, 1863; John Sherman to William Tecumseh Sherman, March 20, 1863, in Rachel S. Thorndike, ed., *The Sherman Letters: Correspondence between General and Senator Sherman from 1837 to 1891* (New York: Scribner, 1894), p. 194; Jeannette P. Nichols, "John Sherman" in Wheeler, *For the Union*, pp. 377–438; Theodore E. Burton, *John Sherman* (Boston: Houghton Mifflin, 1906); Winfield Scott Kerr, *John Sherman: His Life and Public Services*, 2 vols. (Boston: Sherman, French, 1908); John Sherman, *John Sherman's Recollections of Forty Years in the House, Senate and Cabinet; An Autobiography*, 2 vols. (Chicago: Werner, 1895).

approach. He was less effective in the Senate chamber than the Ohioan but a good deal more successful in controlling the Republican machinery of his state.[17]

Chandler moved to Republicanism from an antislavery Whig position; his colleague from Michigan during the special session of July, 1861, was the former governor of Michigan, Kinsley Bingham, a veteran of the Free-Soil Democracy. But Bingham died in the interim between the first and second sessions of the Thirty-seventh Congress, and in mid-January of 1862 his replacement, Jacob M. Howard, took the oath. A Whig lawyer who wrote the platform of the Jackson convention, and reputedly the man who chose the name "Republican" to designate the movement mobilized there, Howard served as attorney general of the state from 1855 to 1861. Known in Michigan as "Honest Jake," he was somewhat portly with iron-gray hair, hazel eyes, and high coloring, used cologne "profusely," and continuously chewed a private blend of fine-cut unsweetened tobacco. His colleagues considered him one of the better constitutional lawyers in the chamber, and he did not demur at that judgment.[18]

Wisconsin also was represented by two Republican senators, James Rood Doolittle and Timothy O. Howe, the latter having taken the oath of office in March, 1861, and the former in 1857. In this delegation too a veteran of the Free-Soil Democracy, Doolittle, served beside a man who had been a Conscience Whig. Though both had served on the Wisconsin bench and neither would run with the ultras of the party, in terms of personality there was a world of difference between them. Doolittle was a stocky man "with locks and beard shaggy as his own northwestern pines," and a rich sonorous voice effective at a "range of forty rods," who brought as much emotional fervor to his defense of the Constitution as Sumner dedicated to excoriating the barbarisms of slavery. Howe, an accomplished speaker who was capable of achieving a wry detachment forever denied to his colleague, impressed the correspondent of the Springfield *Republican* as "very sober" and "somewhat old grannyish," and as the "slow, sedate gentleman from Wisconsin." Never accused of

17. Wilmer C. Harris, *Public Life of Zachariah Chandler, 1851-1875* (Lansing: Michigan Historical Commission, 1917). O. E. McCutcheon, "Recollections of Zachariah Chandler," *Michigan History Magazine,* 5 (January–April 1921), 140-49, see p. 142 for quoted passage; Cincinnati *Daily Commercial,* June 17, 1862; *Zachariah Chandler: An Outline Sketch of His Life and Public Services* (Detroit: *Detroit Post and Tribune,* 1880) App. xviii; Mary Karl George, *Zachariah Chandler: A Political Biography* (Lansing: Michigan State University Press, 1969).

18. Elsa Holderried, "Public Life of Jacob Merritt Howard" (M.A. thesis, Wayne State University, 1950), p. 4; *Dictionary of American Biography,* 9 (1932), 278-79; Hamilton Gay Howard, *Civil War Echoes: Character Sketches and State Secrets* (Washington: Howard Publishing, 1907), has been criticized as unreliable but includes useful information about the author's father.

laziness, however, he apparently thrived under the demanding tutelage of Fessenden on the Finance Committee.[19]

The Republicans were less firmly entrenched in Indiana and Illinois. The son of a man who was an Indian fighter and a genuine Kentucky colonel, Henry S. Lane himself won the rank of colonel in the Mexican War after service in Congress during the early 1840s as a Whig. Prominent in the Indiana canvass for Frémont, he stumped from caucus to caucus at the Republican convention of 1860 in Lincoln's behalf, begging for "success rather than Seward." He stood for governor of Indiana and served for but two days in that capacity before the Indiana legislature elected him to the United States Senate. Although capable of impassioned oratory upon the hustings, he originated few measures and seldom spoke in the Senate. Somewhat Lincolnesque in build, he loved to tell how that other Kentucky-born Whig had once referred to him on circuit as "an uglier man than I." Initially Lane's colleague was Jesse Bright, that ruggedly stout and arrogant doughface Democrat—one reporter preferred "stolid and bull-faced"—whose expulsion was effected before packed galleries during the winter of 1862.[20] In an effort to foster a strong Union movement in the state, Governor Oliver P. Morton chose Joseph Wright to succeed Bright. A former Democratic congressman, who had also been governor of Indiana from 1849 to 1857, and thereafter minister to Prussia, in the latter year, Wright proclaimed in 1862 that there "should be no Republican party, no Democratic party now." The Springfield *Republican* reported that "everybody likes Wright," and called him "frank, pure and honest." But when the Indiana

19. Springfield *Weekly Republican*, March 7, 1863; James L. Sellers, "James R. Doolittle," *Wisconsin Magazine of History*, 17 (1933-34), 168-78, 277-306, 393-401; 18 (1934-35), 20-41, 178-87, 293; Duane Mowry, "An Appreciation of James Rood Doolittle," *Wisconsin Historical Society Proceedings*, 57 (1910), 281-96; Mowry, "James Rood Doolittle of Wisconsin: Gleanings from the Private Letters and Documents of a Senator of the Civil War Period," *Journal of the Illinois State Historical Society*, 4 (July 1911), 165-71; Mowry, "A Northern Statesman's Solution of Some of the Civil War Problems," *Americana*, 9 (February 1914), 94-104. Springfield *Weekly Republican*, April 30, 1864; Albert Erlebacher, "Senator Timothy Otis Howe and His Influence on Reconstruction, 1861-1877" (M.A. thesis, Marquette University, 1956); William H. Russell, "Timothy O. Howe, Stalwart Republican," *Wisconsin Magazine of History*, 35 (Winter 1951), 90-99; Duane Mowry, "Timothy Otis Howe," *Green Bag*, 15 (November 1903), 509-14.

20. Kenneth M. Stampp, *Indiana Politics during the Civil War* (Indianapolis: Indiana Historical Bureau. 1949), p. 39; *Dictionary of American Biography*, 10 (1933), 574-75; Walter Rice Sharp, "Henry S. Lane and the Formation of the Republican Party in Indiana," *Mississippi Valley Historical Review*, 7 (September 1920), 93-112; James A. Woodburn, "Henry Smith Lane," *Indiana Magazine of History*, 27 (December 1931), 279-87; David Turpie, *Sketches of My Own Time* (Indianapolis: Bobbs-Merrill, 1903), 202-3. "Sigma" in the Cincinnati *Daily Commercial*, January 25, 1862; Charles B. Murphy, "The Political Career of Jesse D. Bright," Indiana Historical Society *Publications*, 10 (Indianapolis: Indianapolis Historical Society, 1931), 101-45; "Some Letters of Jesse D. Bright to William H. English, 1842-1863," *Indiana Magazine of History*, 30 (December 1934), 370-92.

legislators replaced him for the short session of 1862–63 with bright young David Turpie, the Democratic representatives from Indiana insisted, contrary to the usual practice, that the new senator's credentials be presented by Senator Powell of Kentucky rather than by Wright. No whit abashed, Wright invited his successor to dinner in his pleasant rooms and helped the young man to rent them following his departure, a considerable favor in crowded Washington.[21]

Ostensibly, the Republican party's situation in Illinois was more satisfactory at the beginning of the second session of the Thirty-seventh Congress than was the case in Indiana. The senior senator from the Prairie State was Lyman Trumbull, who moved in 1855 from the State Supreme Court to the United States Senate while a Free-Soil Democrat, as one of the early beneficiaries of the Anti-Kansas–Nebraska movement. "A rather tall and spare gentleman with a sandy complexion and gold spectacles," Trumbull evidenced his nervous energy in his habit of tearing up little scraps of paper while he smilingly pondered the weaknesses of the arguments developed by colleagues. The "'keenest' debator" in the chamber in Mack's opinion, he held the chairmanship of the Judiciary Committee, the most important committee role played by a westerner, aside perhaps from the dual responsibility of Wade to Territories and the Joint Committee on the Conduct of the War.[22]

Following the death of Stephen A. Douglas, Governor Richard Yates appointed Orville H. Browning to fill the other Illinois seat. Browning who possessed "the suave and formal manners of a Kentucky gentleman," and invariably wore a ruffled shirt, was a friend of Lincoln, and according to one reporter, he suffered fits "of the constitutional ague," such that Trumbull speculated whether it would be "any loss to exchange Browning for a responsible Democrat." Trumbull could hardly, however, have appreciated the act of the Illinois legislature in moving Colonel William A. ("Old Dick") Richardson from the House, as Browning's replacement, early in the third session of the Thirty-seventh Congress. Kentucky-born, this hulking veteran of a state Democratic party in which southern stock voters were very important was accused of sometimes wearing shirts "absolutely black," except where stained from the tobacco juice that ran from each corner of his mouth in a "steady drizzle," and was derided by the Chicago *Tribune* in 1864 as one of the two "habitual drunkards of the Senate." The moratorium on party politics

21. *CG*, 37 Cong., 2 sess., 3345; Springfield *Weekly Republican*, July 19, 1862; *Dictionary of American Biography*, 20 (1933), 559–60. Turpie, *Sketches*, 200–201.

22. "The United States Senate," Portland *Transcript*, January 23, 1864; Chicago *Tribune*, March 4, 1864; Mark M. Krug, *Lyman Trumbull: Conservative Radical* (New York: A. S. Barnes, 1965); Horace White, *The Life of Lyman Trumbull* (Boston: Houghton Mifflin, 1913).

declared by Joe Wright was not for Richardson; his course in the Thirty-seventh and Thirty-eighth Senates was that of a partisan Democrat.[23]

Two trans-Mississippi states sent Republican teams to the Senate. From Iowa came the conscientious former Whigs, James Harlan and James W. Grimes. Harlan—stout, compact, blue-eyed with full light whiskers and clean-shaven upper lip—was one of the handful of western-born Republicans. A lawyer, he had been state superintendent of education as well as president of Iowa Wesleyan College and its professor of intellectual philosophy and moral science. Although he spoke infrequently, he was, claimed the Boston *Journal*, "emphatically a 'working member' of the Senate." So too was his colleague James Grimes, a lawyer from Burlington in the Black Hawk Purchase, the major architect of the Republican party in Iowa and the party's first governor there. Authoritative, full-chested, high-browed, with graying hair and, in curious complement to Harlan, having a full moustache and side whiskers cut to reveal a firm jaw and full underlip, Grimes would become, as the Boston *Journal* put it, locked in "an irrepressible conflict" with his chairman on the Naval Affairs Committee. Finally, as we shall see, he carried the day after a protracted engagement.[24]

Two heroes of the Kansas Crusade represented the young state on the Kaw—James H. Lane and Samuel C. Pomeroy. In general, historians of the twentieth century have given these men low grades; indeed, perhaps no other pair of Republican senators of the war era have fared so poorly. But in the early war years their contemporaries would not have returned that verdict. Former Democrat, Mexican War colonel, commander of the Frontier Guard, Jim Lane was a volatile man, and capable of violence in both word and deed. The Springfield *Republican* described him as being "long" and "eely-shaped," with a "careless, loose-hung look," and "not an especially open countenance." Although he subjected his wardrobe to occasional and spasmodic reformation, Lane's sartorial slovenliness was surpassed only by that of the Democracy's Dick Richardson. Enjoying the fact that he sat at the desk formerly occupied by Jefferson Davis, Lane, "uncaged, fierce, angered, and raging," called for draconian war, but was capable of surprising flashes of sentiment and was extolled by

---

23. *Dictionary of American Biography*, 3 (1929), 175–76; Cincinnati *Daily Commercial*, July 11, 1862; Trumbull to Zachariah Chandler, November 9, 1862, Chandler Mss., Library of Congress. Maurice G. Baxter, *Orville H. Browning: Lincoln's Friend and Critic* (Bloomington: Indiana University Press, 1957). Chicago *Tribune*, January 31, February 3, 1864; *United States Biographical Dictionary and Portrait Gallery, Illinois* (Chicago: American Biographical Publishing Co., 1876), pp. 602–3.

24. Boston *Daily Journal*, December 26, 1863; Brigham, *James Harlan*. Boston *Morning Journal*, February 8, 1864; William Salter, *The Life of James W. Grimes* (New York: Appleton, 1876). *Dictionary of American Biography*, 7 (1931) 631–32.

many as a real "live" one. His colleague's portrait shows a substantial man, with mutton chops, double chin, self-satisfied expression. Reputedly used by Mark Twain as the model of the venal senator in *The Gilded Age*, Pomeroy still wore the aura of mobilized abolitionism in these years, and few read the lesson of his committee assignments—public lands, pensions, and claims, all involving the direct distribution of government largesse.[25]

In contrast to those of Iowa and Kansas, Minnesota's senatorial representation at the beginning of the war was split between the Democrats and Republicans. Henry Mower Rice, the Democrat, a former sutler, fur trader, and Indian treaty commissioner, had been Minnesota's territorial delegate and one of the state's first senators. Slender in build, gentle of voice, respected by the Indians of the Northwest who knew him as "White Rice," he supported Breckinridge for President in 1860, but his Republican colleagues found him dedicated to the preservation of the Union. The cooperation that he gave them on key issues was not sufficient, however, for him to be returned for another term at the conclusion of the Thirty-seventh Congress. He was replaced by the state's first war governor, Alexander Ramsey, a Republican, and "the finest specimen of a physical man in the Northwest." Rice's Republican colleague, Morton S. Wilkinson, entered the Senate in 1859 after brief service in the territorial legislature, several years as a register of deeds, and membership on a commission revising the Minnesota code—one of the less impressive training regimes of the Republican senators. Only thirty-nine when elected, Wilkinson was a tall, handsome man, his wide mouth, beak nose, and high forehead somewhat similar to those of the later William Jennings Bryan. Although one authority congratulated Minnesota on having sent to Washington men far excelling the "shirtsleeve senators and sodcorn representatives usually chosen in the beginning by western constituencies," another primly regretted that Wilkinson's "speeches were always better than his practices." Never backward nor intimidated, Wilkinson could also play the hectoring bully in debate.[26]

25. Springfield *Weekly Republican,* March 7, 1863; Wendell H. Stephenson, *The Political Career of General James H. Lane,* Kansas State Historical Society, *Publications,* 3 (1930) 156–60; Chicago *Tribune,* January 9, 1862. Martha B. Caldwell, "Pomeroy's 'Ross Letter': Genuine or Forgery?" *Kansas Historical Quarterly,* 13 (August 1945), 463–72; *Dictionary of American Biography,* 15 (1935), 54–55; *United States Biographical Dictionary, Kansas* (Chicago: S. Lewis, 1879), 742–44.

26. Committee of the St. Paul Chamber of Commerce, "Henry M. Rice," Ms. Biography in Henry M. Rice Mss., Minnesota Historical Society; *Encyclopedia of Biography of Minnesota* (Chicago: Century Publishing and Engraving, 1900), pp. 364–67; *Dictionary of American Biography,* 15 (1935), 540–51; William R. Marshall, "Henry Mower Rice," Minnesota Historical Society, *Collections,* 9 (1901), 654–58; Erling Jorstad, "Personal Politics in the Origin of Minnesota's Democratic Party," *Minnesota History,* 36 (September 1959), 259–71. *Dictionary of American Biography,* 15 (1935), 341–42 attributes the flattering description of Ram-

From the outposts of Empire on the West Coast, the Oregonians despatched one Republican and one Democratic senator to Washington in 1861: Edward D. Baker and James W. Nesmith. The English-born Baker was a former Whig congressman from Illinois and a friend of Lincoln—according to James G. Blaine, an "irresistibly charming" man, who had been a colonel in the Mexican War and later a gold rush lawyer in California. He had conducted a short but victorious campaign for one of Oregon's Senate seats to the great discomfiture of incumbent Joseph Lane. But the "Gray Eagle" accepted a colonel's commission in the Pennsylvania Volunteers and fell at Ball's Bluff in October, 1861. The Douglas Democratic and Republican legislators who selected Baker balanced that choice by turning to Colonel James W. Nesmith, the former superintendent of Indian Affairs in Oregon. A handsome, rugged, fun-loving and witty Douglas Democrat, he had come as a mere boy to the Pacific Northwest with the Applegate party of 1843. Farmer and lawyer, he was a key member of the "Salem clique," which played an important part in shaping the early history of the Democratic party in Oregon. Following Baker's death, Oregon's governor, a Breckinridge Democrat, appointed still another colonel, Benjamin Stark, to serve in the Senate until the legislature should next meet. Stark too had been an unabashed supporter of Breckinridge, and his loyalty became a major issue in the second session of the Thirty-seventh Congress. When the Oregon legislators met, they replaced Stark with another member of the Salem clique, the Willamette farmer Benjamin F. Harding, who took his seat in the third session of the Thirty-seventh.[27]

Throughout this Congress, California's Senate seats were both filled by Democrats. Conservative young Milton S. Latham, who had briefly

sey to a contemporary. "Memorial Addresses in Honor of Governor Alexander Ramsey," Minnesota Historical Society, Collections, 10, Pt. 2 (1905), 721–66; William J. Ryland, Alexander Ramsey: A Study of a Frontier Politician and the Transition of Minnesota from a Territory to a State (Philadelphia: Harris & Partridge, 1941). Henry A. Castle, "Memorial Addresses in Honor of Harlan Page Hall . . . ," Minnesota Historical Society, Collections, 12 (1908), 733; James H. Baker, "Alexander Ramsey: A Memorial Eulogy, Delivered Before the Minnesota Historical Society . . . ," Minnesota Historical Society, Collections, 10, Pt. 2 (1905), 737; The United States Biographical Dictionary and Portrait Gallery of Eminent and Self Made Men (Chicago: American Biographical Publishing, 1879), 598–99; Mankato: Its First Fifty Years, . . . 1852–1902 (Mankato, Minn.: Free Press Printing, 1903), 156–57.

27. Gayle Anderson Braden, "The Public Career of Edward Dickinson Baker" (Ph.D. diss., Vanderbilt University, 1960), p. 45 repeats James G. Blaine's evaluation. Harry C. Blair and Rebecca Tarshis, The Life of Colonel Edward D. Baker, Lincoln's Constant Ally . . . (Portland: Oregon Historical Society, 1960); William D. Fenton, "Edward Dickinson Baker," Quarterly of the Oregon Historical Society, 9 (March 1908), 1–23; Milton H. Shutes, "Colonel E. D. Baker," California Historical Society Quarterly, 17 (December 1938), 303–24. Homer L. Owen, Nesmith: Pioneer Judge, Legislator, Farmer, Soldier, Senator and Congressman, Reed College Bulletin, 28 (June 1950); Harriet K. McArthur, "Biographical Sketch of Hon. J. W. Nesmith," Transactions of the Fourteenth Annual Reunion of the Oregon Pioneer Association

been governor of California, completed the term of David C. Broderick who perished in a duel with the chief justice of the state in 1859. However, the War Democrat, John Conness, who replaced Latham in March, 1863, would elect to sit with the Republican caucus. Earlier, in March, 1861, Latham was joined by Baker's former law partner, James A. McDougall. Brilliant, eccentric in dress and behavior—he reportedly once rode a horse at breakneck clip down a Washington thoroughfare attired in vaquero dress—and regrettably alcoholic, McDougall was a committed Union man who became increasingly irresponsible in Republican eyes during the course of the war.[28]

The border states from Delaware to Missouri presented the Republicans with unique problems. Here the odious domestic institution of slavery survived, but in the early stages of the war, at least, it was essential that loyal governments be maintained there if the armies of the Union were to be effective and the national capital remain in Washington. The political origins of the senatorial delegations from the region were wonderfully mixed. Democrats of various hues, Old Whigs, Know-Nothing survivors and Constitutional Unionists were all present in the group.

The Delaware senators were both Democrats: James A. Bayard and Willard Saulsbury. Bayard, the second of four generations of the family to serve in the United States Senate, entered that body in 1851, and was an unabashed Peace Democrat who set himself to guard the constitutional freedoms of both individuals and states from the encroachments of Republicans, whom he likened to "the ferocious men" of "the reign of terror" during the French Revolution. His gray hair was thin, his face deeply lined, and he delivered his able constitutional expositions in a rather whining voice. His world, his correspondence shows, lay shattered about him; he struggled against the "madmen" who supported a "horrid pointless war," but with little confidence that he could influence events. Representing the rival Democratic dynasty of Delaware, Willard

for 1886, pp. 28–36; *Dictionary of American Biography*, 13 (1934), 430–31. G. Thomas Edwards, "Benjamin Stark, the U.S. Senate, and 1862 Membership Issues," *Oregon Historical Quarterly*, 72–73 (December 1971–March 1972), 315–38, 31–59. William D. Fenton, "Political History of Oregon from 1865 to 1876," *Quarterly of the Oregon Historical Society*, 2 (December 1901), 339–40; *National Cyclopedia of American Biography*, 12:394; Howard McKinley Corning, *Dictionary of Oregon History* ... (Portland: Binfords & Mort, 1956), p. 106.

28. William Fletcher Thompson, "The Political Career of Milton Slocum Latham of California" (M.A. thesis, Stanford University, 1952); Edgar Eugene Robinson, ed., "The Day Journal of Milton S. Latham," *California Historical Society Quarterly*, 11 (March 1932), Editor's Introduction, 3–28. *National Cyclopedia of American Biography*, 11:369; Boston *Daily Journal*, February 9, 1864. Oscar T. Shuck, ed., *History of the Bench and Bar of California* ... (Los Angeles: Commercial Printing House, 1901), pp. 468–72; Russell Buchanan, "James A. McDougall: A Forgotten Senator," *California Historical Society Quarterly*, 15 (September 1936), 199–212; William Lawrence Shaw, "McDougall of California," *California Historical Society Quarterly*, 43 (June 1964), 119–34.

Saulsbury was but forty years of age, twenty years younger than his colleague, and a solidly built man of middle height with black hair and eyes, clean shaven, well dressed and, when sober, an excellent speaker. In his cups, he was a most irritating man.[29] Like his colleague he staunchly defended the status quo in all respects.

Maryland's senior senator at the beginning of the Thirty-seventh Congress was James A. Pearce, who had represented his state in the Senate since 1843, first as a Whig and later as a Democrat. A "typical Maryland gentleman of the old school," he was a champion of federal educational enterprises such as the Smithsonian Institution, the botanical gardens, and the coastal survey. He had spoken out forthrightly against secession. Although they deplored his acceptance of slavery, many of the Republican senators respected him and even considered him a friend. In ill health during much of the Thirty-seventh Congress, he died in December, 1862, and was replaced by the Unionist governor and former Democrat, Whig, and American, Thomas H. Hicks. Ill health was to plague Hicks as well; as the result of an accident he was forced to have one leg amputated at the knee, and he died of a stroke during the second session of the Thirty-eighth Congress. Pearce's original colleague was Anthony Kennedy, the son of a Baltimore merchant family with planting interests and brother of the better-known John Pendleton Kennedy, the author of Swallow Barn. Whig and thereafter American and Democrat in political affiliation, Anthony was described by his brother's biographer as "an amiable, shallow man devoid alike of talent and experience," at the time of his election in 1856. He seldom took the floor in the wartime Senate. His successor was very different; a seasoned politician, a brilliant lawyer, and formerly Attorney General of the United States, Reverdy Johnson replaced Kennedy on March 4, 1863 and was one of the most effective critics of the constitutional positions of Republicans during the Thirty-eighth Senate.[30]

29. James A. Bayard to Samuel L. M. Barlow, October 28, 1862, September 30, 1862, January 13, 1862, July 20, 1862, S. L. M. Barlow Mss., Henry E. Huntington Library, San Marino, Cal.; Cleveland Plain Dealer, December 26, 1863; Dictionary of American Biography, 2 (1929), 66–67; Biographical and Geneological History of the State of Delaware . . . (Chambersburg, Pa.: J. M. Runk, 1899), 1:227; National Cyclopedia of American Biography, 13:206–7; Harold Bell Hancock, Delaware during the Civil War: A Political History (Wilmington: Historical Society of Delaware, 1961), passim. Dictionary of American Biography, 16 (1935), 379–80; Cleveland Plain Dealer, December 26, 1863; Springfield Weekly Republican, February 21, 1863. James A. Bayard to Thomas F. Bayard, January 26, 28, February 1, 1861. Bayard Mss., Library of Congress.

30. Springfield Weekly Republican, January 17, 1863; Boston Daily Journal, December 26, 1862; Bernard C. Steiner, "James Alfred Pearce," Maryland Historical Magazine, 16 (1921), 319–39; 17 (1922), 33–47, 117–90, 269–83, 348–63; 18 (1923), 38–52, 134–50, 257–73, 341–57; 19 (1924), 13–29, 162–79; Henry Fletcher Powell, Tercentenary History of Maryland, . . . (Chicago: S. J. Clarke, 1926), pp. 870–73. George L. P. Radcliffe, Governor Thomas H. Hicks of Maryland and the Civil War, Johns Hopkins University Studies in Historical and

During July, 1861, Republican leaders recognized Unionist Virginia by seating Waitman T. Willey and John S. Carlile. Both were former Whigs, but Willey had more recently associated with the Constitutional Unionists, while Carlile had used the Know-Nothing movement for political advancement. Termed the ablest lawyer of northwestern Virginia by the Philadelphia *Inquirer,* Willey was a "tall, fine, spectacled specimen of the old Virginia gentleman." Carlile, "very sallow and angular in his face, flat on his head, compact and well-knit in framework," was "somewhat singular looking," but an able speaker, unintimidated by the Republicans and, according to Mack, the Senate's "most eloquent Copperhead." With the creation of West Virginia, Willey would be elected to the chamber from that constituency, but Carlile continued to represent a rather shadowy Old Dominion during the Thirty-eighth Congress.[31]

During the special session of July, 1861, Democrat Lazarus Powell served as Kentucky's senior senator by grace of election in 1859, whereas the former Vice President of the United States, John Breckinridge, had only returned to the Senate on March 4, 1861. Although he served in the July session, Breckinridge had cast his lot with Jefferson Davis by December, and his former colleagues summarily expelled him on December 4. The Kentucky legislators thereupon elected Garrett Davis as his successor. Both Powell and Davis sorely tried the patience of their Republican colleagues. Mack's choice for the "most violent Copperhead" of the Thirty-eighth Senate, Powell was a "large, bluff, sandy-haired, sanguine-faced man," who in repose chewed tobacco, spat on the floor, or munched apples, and in the full flight of oratory waved his arms in violent denunciation of the government's war policies. Garrett Davis was an intriguing character. A spry, peppery, gray-haired little man of about sixty, Davis had been a Clay Whig and a Constitutional Unionist and, in Kentucky's crisis, both a resolute and an inspiring Unionist. But he was

---

*Political Sciences* (Baltimore, 1901), series 19, nos. 11-12: *Dictionary of American Biography,* 9 (1932), 8-9. *National Cyclopedia of American Biography,* 12:481; Powell, *Tercentennary History of Maryland . . . ,* p. 14; Charles H. Bohmer, *John Pendleton Kennedy: Gentleman from Baltimore* (Baltimore: Johns Hopkins University Press, 1961), p. 171. Bernard C. Steiner, *Life of Reverdy Johnson* (Baltimore: Norman, Remington, 1914); *Dictionary of American Biography,* 10 (1933), 112-14.

31. Philadelphia *Inquirer,* July 16, 1861; Springfield *Weekly Republican,* March 7, 1863; Charles H. Ambler, *Waitman Thomas Willey, Orator, Churchman, Humanitarian* (Huntington, W. Va.: Standard, 1954). Richard O. Curry, *A House Divided: A Study of Statehood Politics and the Copperhead Movement in West Virginia* (Pittsburgh: University of Pittsburgh Press, 1964), p. 160, quoting the Wheeling *Intelligencer,* February 21, 1861 concerning Carlile; Chicago *Tribune,* March 4, 1864; *Dictionary of American Biography,* 3 (1929), 493-94; William P. Willey, *An Inside View of the Formation of the State of West Virginia, with Character Sketches of the Pioneers in that Movement* (Wheeling: News Publishing Co., 1901), pp. 207-10; Charles H. Ambler and Festus P. Summers, *West Virginia: The Mountain State* (Englewood Cliffs: Prentice Hall, 1958), passim.

also dedicated to the defense of Kentucky's institutions as they were, rather than as many Republicans wished them to be, and he was prepared to make his points, a book at a time, in a thin, piercing voice. A correspondent of the Chicago *Tribune* called him a "political saurian . . . covered with the imbricated scales of 'the Institution,'" while the Boston *Journal* conceded him a "Union man in his way, only it is a very poor way," and the Springfield *Republican* called him a "little wasp." The reporter of the *Globe* paid his oratory the ultimate compliment early in 1862 when the Kentuckian avowed his willingness to take abolitionist extremists and the "secesh" leaders, and "hang them in pairs." Following this proposition in the *Globe,* its reporter added the interjection "[Sensation.]."[32]

When the senators assembled for the second session of the Thirty-seventh Congress, there was still uncertainty as to whether Waldo P. Johnson and Trusten Polk, the Missouri senators of record, had joined the legions of the Confederacy. Motions for expulsion were approved in early January, and Missouri's governor, Hamilton R. Gamble, appointed replacements pending action of the legislature. Both the new senators, John Brooks Henderson and Robert Wilson, were of Democratic antecedents, although the former's commitment was to the Douglas Democracy and General "Bob" Wilson, a veteran of Missouri's Mormon campaign had supported the Constitutional Unionists in 1860. Bright, eloquent, and still in his mid-thirties, Henderson won respect among Republicans as one of the most realistic of the senators from the border states, and succeeded in winning reelection although his supporters agreed to support the radical candidate, B. Gratz Brown, for the other position.[33]

32. Chicago *Tribune,* March 4, 1864; Springfield *Weekly Republican,* March 7, 1863; *Dictionary of American Biography,* 15 (1935), 148–49; *Biographical Sketch of the Hon. Lazarus W. Powell . . .* (Frankfort: Kentucky General Assembly, 1868); Garrett G. Clift, *Governors of Kentucky, 1792–1942* (Cynthiana, Ky.: Hobson Press, 1942), pp. 64–66. Chicago *Tribune,* December 9, 1863; Boston *Daily Journal,* January 13, 1865; Springfield *Weekly Republican,* February 27, 1864; *CG,* 37 Cong., 2 sess., 453. *Dictionary of American Biography,* 5 (1930), 113–14: *Memorial Addresses on the Life and Character of Garrett Davis, (A Senator from Kentucky), delivered in the Senate and House of Representatives . . . December 18, 1872* (Washington: Government Printing Office, 1873).

33. Certainly one of the most perceptive of the border-state senators, Henderson would reward more study than he has received. See, however, *Dictionary of American Biography,* 8 (1932), 527–29; Dorothy McClure Merideth, "John Brooks Henderson as a Representative of Border-State Public Opinion" (M.A. thesis, University of Missouri, 1939); F. A. Sampson, "Hon. John Brooks Henderson," *Missouri Historical Review,* 7 (July 1913), 237–41; Floyd C. Shoemaker, *Missouri's Hall of Fame: Lives of Eminent Missourians* (Columbia: Missouri Book Company, 1918) pp. 213–17. For Wilson see W. V. N. Bay, *Reminiscences of the Bench and Bar of Missouri . . .* (St. Louis: F. H. Thomas, 1878), pp. 561–63, and Howard L. Conard, ed., *Encyclopedia of the History of Missouri* (St. Louis: Southern Historical Society, 1901), 6:484. Wilson's successor is treated in Norma L. Peterson, *Freedom and Franchise: The Political Career of B. Gratz Brown* (Columbia: University of Missouri Press, 1965).

With the addition of Andrew Johnson of Tennessee, whose major war service would lie elsewhere, these were the senators who served at one time or another during the second and third sessions of the Thirty-seventh Senate. For some, service in that body was their last; others sat in the Thirty-eighth Senate and were joined by others as noted, as well as by Thomas A. Hendricks (Indiana), James W. Nye and William M. Stewart of Nevada—men of some substance—and a few shadowy figures such as Nathan A. Farwell of Maine, George R. Riddle of Delaware, and Lemuel J. Bowden of Virginia. A recital of this sort inevitably under-emphasizes the amount of prior acquaintance and personal relationship that was actually present in the congresses of the mid-nineteenth century. As we have seen, very few of the Republicans from west of the Appalachians had actually been born in the region. Their family ties and educational, and even occupational beginnings, were in the New England or Middle Atlantic states and sometimes these links were the basis of political rapproachments that no written record reveals. Few representatives from new western states received all their political train-ing in those commonwealths; Baker, the hero of Ball's Bluff, for in-stance, successfully campaigned in three states. And, with some excep-tions, the senators were men of considerable prior political experience, which stretched over decades of service at the state level and in the House of Representatives, as well as within the party conventions and canvasses that were so much a part of the frenetic political activity of the American middle period.

The *Tribune Almanac and Political Register for 1860* identified the party affiliations of the sixty-six senators of the first session of the Thirty-sixth Congress, meeting in December, 1859, as being Democratic in 38 cases; there were twenty-five Republicans, two Americans, and one vacant seat in that body. When the second session of the Thirty-seventh Senate assembled in early December, 1861, thirty-one Republicans would sit with seventeen Democrats and Border Unionists, of whom one had been elected as an American. In 1859 the Republicans constituted 38 percent of the senators; two years later they represented 65 percent of the strength of the chamber. What was the political and human meaning of this "realignment?"

There have been few sudden or startling changes in the demographic composition of the United States Congress. From the very beginning of the nation, the representatives and senators constituted an elite group, and elites do not change rapidly in composition unless the political sys-tem of which they are a part suffers a massive shock or dislocation. Even then, the members of an elite who hold formal positions of power in a system may simply be replaced by others of similar social and economic

TABLE 1–1.
Occupation of senators' fathers (in percent)*

|  | Civil War senators | Senators, 1869–1900† |
|---|---|---|
| Farmer | 48 | 50 |
| Businessman | 13 | 17 |
| Professional | 26 | 27 |
| Craftsman | 3 | |
| Laborer | 3 | 3 |
| Other | | 3 |
| Unknown | 7 | |

*See note 34 for a brief description of the sources of this table and those following in this chapter unless otherwise stated.
†David J. Rothman, *Politics and Power: The United States Senate, 1869–1901,* p. 113.

background. But the Civil War dealt a solid blow to the constitutional machinery devised by the Founding Fathers. And in certain trite and obvious ways the composition of the United States Senate during the Civil War reflected systemic malaise. A group of members who shared a very important characteristic—a common regional affiliation—had almost disappeared. The members of a new regional party controlled the United States government, opposed in the Senate chamber by a remnant of the national party that had dominated the federal government for a generation, and by a few others whose own regional or ideological commitments prevented them from making common cause with the newly dominant party. All this is plain enough, and suggests that, under some conditions, the single most important characteristic of the individual legislator may simply be the fact that he represents a particular constituency, located in a particular region.

Once we shift our focus beyond the empty desks, the unique characteristics of the war senators from northern and border states become more difficult to identify. The occupations of their fathers differed surprisingly little, on the whole, from those of the fathers of the senators who served during the latter part of the century (Table 1-1).[34] Farmers sired slightly less than half of the war senators; professionals, mostly lawyers, fathered somewhat more than a quarter of them, and 13 per-

34. The data in Table 1-1 and the following tables are taken from the individual biographical sources listed above, newspaper obituaries and accounts of funerals, the *Biographical Directory of the American Congress* (various editions) and the manuscript records of federal censuses 1800–1840. The two most difficult categories of information to find in all cases were the occupation of the father and the religion of the senator. In a number of cases the denomination of the pastor performing the burial service was used as an indication of religious preference.

cent of the group were the children of businessmen. The fathers of only 6 percent were craftsmen or laborers.

Subdivision of the group does reveal some differences within Republican ranks (Table 1-2). If we use the eastern boundary of Ohio as an arbitrary division, the western Republican was somewhat more likely to come from the farm than was his eastern colleague. And eastern Republicans numbered five manufacturers or merchants among their fathers as well as a craftsman and a laborer. Of their western colleagues, only Orville Browning had a businessman father and the elder Browning had farming interests as well; no westerner was the son of a laborer or craftsman.

When we move from consideration of occupation to a crude measure of class origins (Table 1-3), we again find that the group of war senators was quite similar in composition to that of the senators of 1869–1900 studied recently by David Rothman.[35] The Democrats displayed a somewhat greater tendency to have emerged either from a substantial or from an elite background, but this characteristic is attributable largely to the contingent of that party from the border states. Among senators from both parties from northern constituencies, westerners were more likely to have subsistence-level origins than were eastern senators, but among the Republicans the difference was only 11 percentage points in a population of forty-three men, hardly an impressive distinction.

Quite clearly it would be interesting to compare the social origins of the Civil War senators with those of their predecessors. But as yet researchers have not compiled enough detailed information about the family background of the members of earlier congresses to allow us to make such comparisons. Those data series depicting the social and economic attributes of congressmen that have been extended across the nineteenth century, however, show either little change or gradual change over extended periods of time. If one suspects that the Republicans—the new party—did share unique attributes, the opposition senators provide a useful basis of comparison. And as we have seen the differences in background between Republicans and their opponents were not striking.

The information in *The Biographical Directory of the American Congress* shows that some 58 percent of the senators of the years 1789–1800 had some college education and that the proportion was about the same

35. David J. Rothman, *Politics and Power: The United States Senate, 1861–1901* (Cambridge: Harvard University Press, 1966), pp. 271–72, describes the criteria for inclusion in the various categories. Briefly summarized—the elite father enjoyed sufficient status to suggest that the son would hold positions of leadership and power; the family heads of the middle category could provide some advantages for their offspring, as in the cases of local professionals or prosperous farmers; fathers of the subsistence category apparently did not have the means to give assistance to sons in establishing themselves.

TABLE 1-2.

Occupations of senators' fathers by party group (in percent)

| | Farmer | Lawyer | Other profession | Business | Craftsman | Laborer | Unknown |
|---|---|---|---|---|---|---|---|
| Eastern Republicans (22) | 36 | 18 | 4 | 23 | 4 | 4 | 9 |
| Western Republicans (21) | 62 | 19 | 10 | 5 | | | 5 |
| Northern Democrats (14) | 50 | 14 | 22 | 7 | | | 7 |
| Border Democrats (11) | 55 | 36 | | | | 9 | |
| Unionists (9*) | 33 | | | 33 | 11 | | 22 |
| Republicans (43) | 49 | 19 | 7 | 14 | 2 | 2 | 7 |
| Non-Republicans (34) | 47 | 18 | 9 | 12 | 3 | 3 | 9 |

*Joseph Wright included.

TABLE 1-3.

Social origins of the Civil War senators (in percent)*

|                           | Subsistence | Substantial | Elite | Unknown |
|---------------------------|-------------|-------------|-------|---------|
| Eastern Republicans (22)  | 37          | 50          | 13    |         |
| Western Republicans (21)  | 48          | 38          | 9     | 5       |
| Northern Democrats (14)   | 43          | 50          | 7     |         |
| Border Democrats (11)     | 18          | 55          | 27    |         |
| Border Unionists (8)      | 50          | 37.5        | 12.5  |         |
| Northern Unionists (1)    | 100         |             |       |         |
| Republicans (43)          | 42          | 44          | 12    | 2       |
| Democrats (25)            | 32          | 52          | 16    |         |
| Grand total (77†)         | 40          | 46          | 13    | 1       |

*The relatively weak contrast between the Republicans and the Democrats revealed in Table 1-3 is similar to the party differences appearing in some of the tables that follow. Since we are dealing with a total population rather than samples, significance tests can serve only as analogy and the small values in some cells render the device inappropriate even in that sense. With these reservations, one can report that the $X^2$ values based on the national Republican and Democratic values in this table is 3.159 with two degrees of freedom, reflecting differences that are significant at approximately the .20 level.

†Serving subsequent to the special session of 1861.

during the 1860s.[36] Thereafter, the secular trend has been upward until some 90 percent of those serving during the 1950s had attended a college or university. Of the Civil War senators studied, 52 percent had reached college in their education and both the Democratic and Republican means stood at 56 percent (See Table 1-4). Western Republicans scored considerably below their eastern colleagues in this respect, and an even greater discrepancy between northern and border-state Democrats was also largely attributable to differences between eastern and western Democrats.

Most senators have been lawyers. Sixty percent of those serving during the years 1789–1800 followed this profession; the proportion had risen above 80 percent by the 1840s. During the first three decades of our national history, farmers comprised 11 percent of the senators, with a slightly higher proportion coming from the southern states. On the average, businessmen were slightly less numerous than farmers in those early years. Thereafter, the number of farmers dropped to less than 5 percent and the proportion of businessmen rose, particularly in the

36. This and other information conerning the general history of senatorial attributes is derived from a preliminary analysis of a machine-readable data set prepared by Carroll R. McKibbin from the information found in the biographical sketches in the *Biographical Directory of the American Congress* and available to researchers through the agency of the Inter-University Consortium for Political and Social Research, Ann Arbor, Michigan.

TABLE 1-4.
Education of Civil War senators (in percent)

| | Only elementary levels | Reached intermediate levels | Reached college |
|---|---|---|---|
| Eastern Republicans (22) | 9 | 23 | 68 |
| Western Republicans (21) | 24 | 33 | 43 |
| Northern Democrats (14) | 29 | 29 | 42 |
| Border Democrats (11) | 18 | 9 | 73 |
| Border Unionists (8) | 50 | 25 | 25 |
| Northern Unionists (1) | | 100 | |
| Republicans (43) | 16 | 28 | 56 |
| Democrats (25) | 24 | 20 | 56 |
| Grand total (77) | 22 | 26 | 52 |

Midwest. Almost 80 percent of the wartime senators were lawyers; in this respect, Republicans fell six points below the Democratic mean and four below the mean of all the war senators (see Tables 1-5 and 1-6). Twenty-one percent of the wartime Republicans were some sort of businessman, but only 12 percent of the Democrats appeared in the business categories of our occupations table. In terms of primary occupation (some senators had more than one), the difference between eastern and western Republicans was negligible. Ironically, lawyers, society's specialists in negotiation, dominated the Senate of the Civil War era to a greater degree than ever before or since. Only 57 percent of the senators of the 1890s had practiced law prior to their election, according to one source.[37]

More dramatic contrasts emerge in a comparison between state represented and state of birth (see Table 1-7). Here, sharp sectional divergence appears because most eastern senators represented the state of their birth, while westerners came from adopted constituencies. But, of course, the contrast was an artifact of the westward movement within an expanding nation. Had some western states been forced to send native sons to Washington, those representatives would have been mere striplings or Native Americans. And the tendency of the western states to send adopted sons was not restricted to those controlled by the Republicans; the Democratic pattern of representation from the West was similar to that found in Republican territory. Although one can speculate that transplantation might somehow produce differences in legislative style or

37. Rothman, *Politics and Power*, p. 115. The McKibbin data suggest that the number of senators who were lawyers in this decade was substantially higher than this. The trend, however, was downward.

TABLE 1–5.

Occupations of Civil War senators

| | Farmer | Lawyer | Other profession | Merchant | Manufacturer | Other business | Craftsman |
|---|---|---|---|---|---|---|---|
| Eastern Republicans | | 16 | 1 | 1 | 3 | 1 | |
| Western Republicans | 1 | 16 | | 2 | 2 | | |
| Northern Democrats | 1 | 10 | | 2 | 1 | | 1 |
| Border Democrats | | 10 | | 1 | | | |
| Border Unionists | | 7 | | | | | |
| Northern Unionists | | 1 | | | | | |
| Republicans | 1 | 32 | 1 | 3 | 5 | 1 | |
| Democrats | 1 | 20 | | 2 | 1 | | 1 |
| Grand total | 2 | 60 | 1 | 6 | 6 | 1 | 1 |

TABLE 1–6.

Occupations by party (in percent)

| | Farmer | Lawyer | Other profession | Merchant | Manufacturer | Other business | Craftsman |
|---|---|---|---|---|---|---|---|
| Republicans | 2 | 74 | 2 | 7 | 12 | 2 | |
| Democrats | 4 | 80 | 1 | 8 | 4 | 1 | 4 |
| All senators | 3 | 78 | 1 | 8 | 8 | 1 | 1 |

TABLE 1-7.

Civil War senators representing state of birth

|  | Number | Percent |
|---|---|---|
| Eastern Republicans | 18 | 82 |
| Western Republicans | 1 | 5 |
| Northern Democrats | 2 | 14 |
| Border Democrats | 6 | 55 |
| Border Unionists | 6 | 75 |
| Northern Unionists |  |  |
| Republicans | 19 | 44 |
| Democrats | 8 | 32 |
| Grand total | 33 | 43 |

mitigate regional disagreement, it is difficult to effect clearcut tests of such propositions.

But surely—some will say—the representatives of a vibrant young party, the Republicans, could be expected to be younger than the Democrats, the frayed defenders of the status quo. Unfortunately for such speculation, Senate Democrats averaged forty-seven years of age as of December 1, 1862, in comparison to the Republican mean of 50 (see Table 1-8). Western Republicans, however, were some five years younger than their eastern colleagues.

If we can consider any institution to be the "political cradle" of the Civil War senators, it was the state legislature. Sixty-seven percent of the group had served in a state legislature, a proportion that would decline thereafter in the history of the United States Senate. A considerable part had served in the state or federal judiciary, the House of Representatives, or in a state executive branch. Only two senators, both

TABLE 1-8.

Mean age of Civil War senators,
December 1, 1862

| Eastern Republicans (22) | 52.5 |
|---|---|
| Western Republicans (21) | 47.6 |
| Northern Democrats (14) | 45.5 |
| Border Democrats (11) | 49.9 |
| Border Unionists (8) | 54.1 |
| Northern Unionists (1) | 52 |
| All Republicans (43) | 50.1 |
| All Democrats (25) | 47.4 |
| Grand mean | 49.7 |

## TABLE 1-9.

Types of public office held by senators prior to election to the Senate

| | No prior office | Municipal | State legislature | State constitutional convention | State executive branch | State or federal judiciary | House of Representatives | Federal executive branch |
|---|---|---|---|---|---|---|---|---|
| | | | | (Number) | | | | |
| Eastern Republicans | 2 | 2 | 15 | 6 | 5 | 7 | 6 | 1 |
| Western Republicans | | 4 | 14 | 1 | 8 | 8 | 7 | |
| Northern Democrats | | 3 | 8 | 2 | 6 | 8 | 6 | 3 |
| Southern Democrats | | 1 | 8 | 2 | 4 | 6 | 4 | 2 |
| Border Unionists | | 3 | 6 | 6 | 1 | 1 | 2 | |
| Northern Unionists | | | 1 | | 1 | 1 | 1 | 1 |
| Republicans | 2 | 6 | 29 | 7 | 13 | 15 | 13 | 1 |
| Democrats | | 4 | 16 | 4 | 10 | 14 | 10 | 5 |
| Grand total | 2 | 13 | 52 | 17 | 25 | 31 | 26 | 7 |
| | | | | (Percent) | | | | |
| Republicans | 5 | 14 | 67 | 16 | 30 | 35 | 30 | 2 |
| Democrats | | 16 | 64 | 16 | 40 | 56 | 40 | 20 |
| Border Unionists | | 38 | 75 | 75 | 13 | 13 | 25 | |
| All groups | 3 | 17 | 68 | 22 | 32 | 40 | 34 | 9 |

TABLE 1-10.
Number of types of prior public office held by individual senators

|                      | 0  | 1 | 2  | 3  | 4  | 5 |
|----------------------|----|---|----|----|----|---|
| (Number)             |    |   |    |    |    |   |
| Eastern Republicans  | 22 | 2 | 7  | 6  | 5  | 2 |
| Western Republicans  | 21 | 0 | 7  | 8  | 5  | 1 |
| Northern Democrats   | 14 |   | 3  | 4  | 4  | 2 | 1 |
| Southern Democrats   | 11 |   | 2  | 6  | 1  | 2 |
| Border Unionists     | 8  |   |    | 4  | 3  | 1 |
| Northern Unionists   | 1  |   |    |    |    |   | 1 |
| Republicans          | 43 | 2 | 14 | 14 | 10 | 3 |
| Democrats            | 25 |   | 5  | 10 | 5  | 4 | 1 |
| Grand total          | 77 | 2 | 19 | 28 | 18 | 8 | 2 |
| (Percent)            |    |   |    |    |    |   |
| Republicans          |    | 5 | 33 | 33 | 23 | 7 |
| Democrats            |    |   | 20 | 40 | 20 | 16 | 4 |
| All senators         |    | 3 | 25 | 36 | 23 | 10 | 3 |

eastern Republicans, Sumner and Cowan, had attained the Senate without holding previous public office at some level of government. Proportionally (as Table 1-9 shows) the Democrats had served in the state executive branch, the judiciary, the House of Representatives, and the executive branch to a greater extent than had the Republicans.

The Democrats also tended to have held more types of office per man than did the Republicans (see Table 1-10). Thirty-eight percent of the Republican senators had held only one office or less; the comparable Democratic figure was 20 percent. A relatively larger proportion of Democrats had held four or five different pre-Senate offices, a finding that apparently reflects the fact that the Democracy had in general been the dominant party in the United States during the previous twenty years. Of course, since the underlying numbers are small, one must not read too much into the results.

Increasingly during the last few years, political historians have emphasized the relation between religion and political behavior in American politics.[38] The religious data collected by American census takers prior to the end of the nineteenth century is sparse and unsatisfactory,

38. Lee Benson initiated this trend in *The Concept of Jacksonian Democracy: New York as a Test Case* (Princeton: Princeton University Press, 1961) and antecedent papers. See Joel H. Silbey, Allan G. Bogue, and William H. Flanigan, *The History of American Electoral Behavior* (Princeton: Princeton University Press, 1978), pp. 3–27 and other introductory sections, and Allan G. Bogue, Jerome Clubb and William H. Flanigan, "The New Political History," *American Behavioral Scientist*, 21 (November/December 1977), 201–20, for a discussion of these developments and relevant bibliographies.

## TABLE 1-11.

### Religious preferences of Civil War senators (in percent)

| | Eastern Republicans (22) | Western Republicans (21) | Republicans (43) | Northern Democrats (14) | Border Democrats (11) | Democrats (25) | Border Unionists (8) | Northern Unionists (1) | Percent of whole |
|---|---|---|---|---|---|---|---|---|---|
| Baptist | 13.6 | 4.8 | 9.3 | 7.1 | | 4.0 | | | 6.5 |
| Christian | | | | | 9.1 | 4.0 | | | 2.6 |
| Congregational | 27.4 | 14.3 | 20.9 | | | | 12.5 | | 11.7 |
| Disciples | | 4.8 | 2.3 | | | | | | 1.3 |
| Episcopal | 31.8 | 4.8 | 18.6 | 64.4 | 45.4 | 56.0 | 25.0 | | 31.1 |
| Methodist | | 23.7 | 11.7 | 7.1 | 9.1 | 8.0 | 25.0 | | 13.0 |
| Presbyterian | 9.1 | 33.4 | 20.9 | 14.3 | 18.2 | 16.0 | 25.0 | 100 | 19.5 |
| Roman Catholic | | 4.8* | | | 9.1 | 4.0 | | | 1.3 |
| Unitarian | 18.1 | | 11.6 | | 9.1 | 4.0 | | | 7.8 |
| Universalist | | 4.8 | 2.3 | | | | | | 1.3 |
| Unknown or unclassified | 4.8 | 4.8 | 2.3 | 7.1 | | 4.0 | 12.5 | | 3.9 |

*Conness was the son of Roman Catholic parents, but his last rites were Unitarian.

and only the task of ferreting out the occupations of senatorial fathers was comparably difficult to that of ascertaining religious preferences. The results, however, did produce the most intriguing relationships discovered in the analysis of biographical data (see Table 1-11). Thirty-one percent of all the senators were Episcopalian in preference. And within that group, the Episcopalians were disproportionately affiliated with the Democracy—56 percent as compared to 19 percent among the Republicans. Conversely, the Republicans were markedly Congregationalist, Presbyterian, and Unitarian, members of denominations with strong doctrinal or organizational interrelations—Republican senators in these religious groups made up 53.5 percent of their party contingent in the Senate in comparison to the 20 percent found among the Democratic senators. Intraparty differences among the Republicans were less striking, although western Republicans were more likely to be Presbyterians or Methodists, while Episcopalians, Congregationalists, and Unitarians were more common in the eastern wing of the party. Translated into a gamma contingency coefficient the relationship between Episcopalianism and Democratic affiliation was a positive .69 (r is a less generous .37). It is surprising to discover that Episcopalians, the members of a high-status but relatively declining religious faith, were more numerous than supporters of other religious denominations in the Civil War Senate. It is less so, perhaps, that the evangelical persuasion should have been associated with Republicans and that ritualists were dominant among the Democrats, but the proportions are unexpected.

The socioeconomic characteristics of the Republican senators of the Civil War Senates do not indicate any striking break with the patterns of the past. The great change from the Thirty-sixth to the Thirty-seventh and Thirty-eighth Senates lies in the transfer of party control and the regional character of the party that took command. But some of the social characteristics of the Republican senators may indeed have been related to behavior *within* the party, and this possibility will be explored in Chapter 4.

# 2

# Committees, Rules,
# and Leaders

Although some of the Civil War senators were relatively inexperienced and all labored in a Senate chamber that was only a few years old,
they also worked within a structure of committees, rules, and leadership
that had been evolving since the first days of the Republic. We must
understand something of the institutional structure of the Senate, the
ways it worked, the attempts that were made to modify it, and the kind of
personal leadership that was exercised in those years. In this chapter we
examine these matters withholding, as we must, discussion of much of
their relevance in controversies between radicals and moderates until we
have identified the radicals in Chapter 3.

"It still sleeps . . . in my committee room," wrote Sumner of an obnoxious resolution, thus implicitly emphasizing the power of the Senate's
standing committees over the subjects discussed and voted upon in
Committee of the Whole and in the Senate. Not only could the committees allow measures to "sleep"; they could report them with nullifying, or
crippling amendments, select a favorite among a number of proposals
on the same subject, or report back adversely. Placement on particular
committees, and especially the opportunity to hold the chair of specific
committees, gave some senators unique opportunities to shape what was
done in particular categories of legislation. Clearly, if we discover that we
can develop useful definitions of radicals and moderates, we may well
also find that their appointment to committees and their role in these
bodies affected policy outcomes in important ways. How were committee
assignments arranged during the Thirty-seventh and Thirty-eighth
Senates?[1]

1. Charles Sumner to Francis Lieber, May 4, 1864, cited in Edward L. Pierce, *Memoir
and Letters of Charles Sumner* (Boston: Roberts Brothers, 1893), 4:193. Two standard works,
George H. Haynes, *The Senate of the United States: Its History and Practice*, 2 vols. (Boston:

The Republican senatorial caucus made the fundamental decisions as to who chaired and who served on the standing committees, acting on the recommendations of a caucus committee. The president or president *pro tempore* of the Senate apparently named the personnel of select and conference committees, and that power could have very important consequences in the development of particular legislation. But the influence of Foot, who was president *pro tempore* recurrently through the Thirty-seventh Congress and during the first session of the Thirty-eighth, went considerably further. In his memorial address on the death of the senator from Vermont, Fessenden remarked, "Often have I known him to insist that his name should be struck from an important committee, in order to replace it with the name of a friend or associate to whom he thought the distinction would be grateful. To him more than any other was assigned the unenviable task of arranging these committees, not only because all confided in his sense of justice, but because of his disinterested magnanimity."[2]

But when Anthony, as chairman of the Republican caucus endeavored to organize the committees at the beginning of the special executive session on March 5, 1863, with the resolution "That the President *pro tempore* be authorized to appoint the standing committees of the Senate for this session, and also the members of joint committees," it was Fessenden who tried to substitute "For the purposes of this session, the standing committees be continued as constituted at the last session of the Senate, and that the President *pro tempore* be authorized to fill vacancies wherever the same may be necessary." Fessenden argued that his motion was in substance the same as that of Anthony's resolution, but did not carry the implication that the president *pro tempore* might "exercise the power of remodeling the committees as he pleases." Sherman, Fessenden's companion on Finance, supported his colleague because he wanted a "clear indication . . . that at the next session . . . we shall reorganize them entirely." We cannot tell the degree to which these statements reflected adherence to broad principle or domestic frictions within the Finance Committee, but after Saulsbury had seized the opportunity to complain of the Republicans' arbitrary refusal to allow the minority to allocate its representatives on committees during the Thirty-seventh

Houghton Mifflin, 1938), and Lauros G. McConachie, *Congressional Committees: A Study of the Origins and Development of Our National and Local Legislative Methods* (New York: Thomas Y. Crowell, 1898), are extremely informative but do not give particular attention to the era of the Civil War.

2. *Proceedings on the Death of Hon. Solomon Foot, including the Addresses delivered in the Senate and House of Representatives on Thursday, April 12, 1866* (Washington: Government Printing Office, 1866), p. 51.

Congress as these gentlemen saw fit, the senators s
thony. In December their colleagues of the Republi
appointed Foster, Sherman, Fessenden, Harlan, and
tee to revise committee assignments at the beginning
of the Thirty-eighth Congress.[3]

There were twenty-two standing Senate or joint con.
at the beginning of the second session of the Thirty-sev
which thirteen were seven-man committees, four had fi       , and
five involved groups of three. The Republicans assigned ᴅemocrats and
Unionists to the committees arbitrarily: two to each of the largest committees and one to smaller. This departed from the practice developed
in the 1840s according to which the minority party was allowed to provide the names for an agreed proportion of committee seats left vacant
by the majority. The entrance of an avowedly independent antislavery
contingent had strained this system for a time, but it prevailed again in
the late 1850s, and the War Democrats considered the Republican action
to be high-handed in the extreme.[4]

New England Republicans chaired eleven of the committees, and the
western Republicans provided eight chairmen recruited from a senatorial party in which there were seventeen easterners and fourteen westerners. Although this apportionment does not suggest extreme imbalance,
there were some disaffected mutterings about the dominance of New
England's representatives in the committee structure.[5] And certainly
imbalance becomes more evident if one considers only the chairmen of
the five committees that could be expected to play the largest role in a
congress obligated to reconstruct the Union by warfare: Foreign Relations, Finance, Military Affairs and the Militia, Naval Affairs, and
Judiciary. Of these chairmen, only Trumbull was a westerner (see Table
2-1). Still, of twenty Republican places on these committees, westerners
held nine in 1862. It is also clear that, in a general way, length of service
or seniority in the chamber dictated the selection of committee chairmen. Every Republican senator who had served more than four years in
the Senate chaired a seven- or five-man committee. It was only when their
length of service was less than three years that men were passed over for
chairmanships and, of those ignored, only Ten Eyck and Wilkinson had

3. *CG*, 37 Cong., 3 sess., 1554. The Chicago *Tribune*, March 6, 1863, noted that Fessenden's action broke a caucus agreement and caused "not a little ill-feeling." Chicago
*Tribune*, December 8, 1863.

4. McConachie, *Congressional Committees*, p. 287.

5. Chicago *Tribune*, March 6, 1863; Springfield *Weekly Republican*, December 19, 1863;
Chicago *Times,* December 21, 1863. The following analysis of committee service is based on
the committee lists taken from the *Senate Journal* of the various sessions of the Thirty-
seventh and Thirty-eighth Congresses.

TABLE 2-1.

Major chairmen and party seniority

| Committee | Chairman | Party rank—continuous Senate service |
|---|---|---|
| Foreign Relations | Sumner | 3 |
| Finance | Fessenden | 4 |
| Military Affairs and Militia | Wilson | 5 |
| Naval Affairs | Hale | 9* |
| Judiciary | Trumbull | 6 |
| Territories | Wade | 1† |
| Claims | Clark | 15† |

*Also served one full term earlier, and was thus the Republican senator with the longest total service.

†Added for purpose of comparison.

served more than two years. If New Englanders did well in obtaining committee chairmanships, that fact was related to a considerable extent to their prior arrival in the Senate.

In the selection of chairmen of particular committees, length of service, previous experience on the committee (specific seniority), constituency characteristics, and personal preference all seem to have played some part. Foot and Wade took their oaths on March 4, 1851 and Sumner on April 24 of that year, and thus these three outranked all their Republican colleagues in continuous service. Foot, however, chaired Buildings and Grounds, while serving as president *pro tempore*. As a member of the majority party, Wade, seemingly, was content to chair the Committee on Territories, maintaining his interest in a subject formerly of deep concern to members of the antislavery party, and also came to chair a most important joint committee—that on the conduct of the war. Sumner assumed the chair of the more prestigious Committee on Foreign Relations, on which he had served as a minority member and junior to William Seward. Both Collamer and Foster had served longer continuously than Hale, chairman of Naval Affairs, although the latter's total senatorial service was greater than theirs. Collamer was from an interior state, which perhaps disqualified him from serving, but Foster represented a maritime constituency. Hale had served on the Naval Affairs Committee previously, however, and perhaps Foster's interests ran in other directions. Despite such qualifications, the chairmen of the major committees shaping the war effort in 1862 were men of relative experience whose previous committee service and other attributes qualified them to assume their assignments. All had served as minority members on these committees during the Thirty-sixth Congress. This was not true of committee chairmen in general, however; during the

TABLE 2-2.
Origins of committee chairmen in Senate: 36 Cong., 1 sess. to 37 Cong., 2 sess.

| Movement pattern | Number |
|---|---|
| Senior Republican advances to chair | 9 |
| Senior Republican leaves Senate floor; junior Republican advances to chair | 2 |
| Senior Republican leaves committee; junior advances to chair | 1 |
| Nonmember Republican assumes chair in preference to remaining Republicans | 2 |
| Nonmember Republican assumes chair; Republican delegation completely reorganized | 7 |
| Democrat remains in chair | 1 |
| | 22 |

second session of the Thirty-seventh, nine committees were entrusted to men who had not been serving on them at the beginning of the long session of the Thirty-sixth Congress (see Table 2-2). Six of these, on the other hand, were small committees; a system of seniority of a kind was in effect within the party delegation and within committees, although not applied invariably.

During the four regular legislative sessions of the Civil War, the personnel of most major committees showed a considerable degree of turnover; Table 2-3 shows this phenomenon in the five major committees and two other seven-man committees that serve as a basis for comparison. Most senators vacated committee seats because they departed from the Senate, in defeat, resignation, or death. The cases of a seat being vacated in which the senator remained in the Senate are of considerable interest, however. Why did holdover senators leave major committees?

Eleven men departed from the five major committees between late

TABLE 2-3.
Major committee circulation, December 2, 1861–March 4, 1865

| Committee | Places | Departures | Left Senate | Remained in Senate |
|---|---|---|---|---|
| Foreign Relations | 7 | 8 | 6 | 2 |
| Finance | 7 | 7 | 5 | 2 |
| Military Affairs | 7 | 4 | 3 | 1 |
| Naval Affairs | 7 | 9 | 5 | 4 |
| Judiciary | 7 | 3 | 1 | 2 |
| Territories | 7 | 4 | 3 | 1 |
| Claims | 7 | 9 | 8 | 1 |
| Totals | 49 | 44 | 31 | 13 |

1861 and March 1865 and remained in the Senate. Two instances involved transfers to other major committees. Collamer left Foreign Relations for Finance at the beginning of the third session of the Thirty-seventh Congress—no doubt a desirable move in view of his well-known interest in banking and his long friendship with Fessenden. Newspaper comment suggests that the other shift involving this committee, that of McDougall from Finance to Foreign Affairs a session later, was engineered by Fessenden, the chairman of Finance. McDougall's insobriety and erratic brilliance accorded little with Fessenden's obsessive diligence, and the eccentric Californian had also opposed the New Englander and the committee's Republican majority on the floor. However, McDougall's destination was not a minor committee, but Foreign Affairs. As a member of the caucus committee that recommended revisions in the standing committees at the beginning of the long session of the Thirty-eighth Congress, Fessenden must have enjoyed some anticipatory pleasure in placing the obstreperous Californian in the hands of Sumner, who had also sorely tried the patience of the senator from Maine on many occasions. In four other instances, senators left one of the five crucial committees when they assumed the chairmanship of other committees. In six of eleven cases, therefore, the departure from one of the "big" committees involved little if any loss of status and, except for McDougall, the men involved probably regarded the move as an improvement in station—since a new chairman, despite the lower status of his committee, now had a committee clerk to lighten his legislative burdens.

But, on five occasions, senators moved to positions on minor committees. Harris left Foreign Relations to accommodate Joseph Wright, who had served in a diplomatic post abroad. James Lane left Military Affairs during the second session of the Thirty-seventh, to sit subsequently on Territories and, in the next Congress, to chair the new Committee on Agriculture. The remaining transfers of this sort all involved Naval Affairs: Foot, senior to all his colleagues but the fiery Wade, departed at the beginning of the Thirty-seventh's third session, moving to Public Lands, perhaps as a welcoming gesture to the new Rhode Island senator, Arnold. A session later, McDougall took a seat on Private Land Claims. This marked a drop in the overall status of his committee assignments, although, as a senator from a state with various interesting and potentially remunerative private land cases, the Californian may have regarded his new seat as an opportunity better to serve his constituents and, perhaps in the future, his own economic interests.

The final case of movement from Naval Affairs was one of the most celebrated incidents in the history of the Civil War congresses. At the beginning of the second session of the Thirty-eighth Congress, the Republican caucus awarded the chair in Naval Affairs to Grimes, placing Hale in Grimes's former spot at the head of the Committee on the District of Columbia. Hale had long been embroiled in conflict with the Secretary of the Navy, and there were allegations that his influence was for hire. We shall return to his story below.

Quite clearly, few of the transfers from the strategic committees were falls from grace, and most were consonant with the positions that some committees were more important than others and that serving on the more prestigious committees was desirable. Yet the movement of hold-over senators also suggests that service on lesser committees might be rewarding, given the perquisites of the chairman and unique constituencies and interests of the senators in general. Although most holdover senators left the major committees for good reasons, senators of senior or middle-range service did not clog the routes to places on them. Table 2-4 shows that many junior men obtained seats on the more important committees; having discussed the meaning of departures from committees, we may usefully examine the arrivals as well.

At the beginning of the first regular session of the Thirty-seventh Congress, men serving in their first congress occupied nineteen of the forty-nine places in the seven committees listed in Table 2-1; of forty-four subsequent entrants from both parties to these committees between December, 1861, and March 4, 1865, twenty were serving in their first session and only four stood in the upper half of the Republicans in terms of service. It was surely no accident that these four joined Finance, Foreign Relations and the Judiciary committees, but only the latter took in no first-term man subsequent to the second session of the Thirty-seventh Congress; other major committees welcomed three or four.

TABLE 2-4.

Committee entry, December 2, 1861–March 4, 1865

| Committee | Senators in their first Congress, December 2, 1861 | Later entry | | |
|---|---|---|---|---|
| | | Upper half length of service | Lower half length of service | Freshmen |
| Foreign Relations | 3 | 1 | 7 | 4 |
| Finance | 3 | 2 | 5 | 3 |
| Military Affairs | 3 | | 4 | 4 |
| Naval Affairs | 2 | | 9 | 3 |
| Judiciary | 2 | 1 | 2 | |
| Territories | 3 | | 4 | 1 |
| Claims | 3 | | 9 | 5 |
| Totals | 19 | 4 | 40 | 20 |

Nor was the contribution of junior men on committees necessarily minor in nature. Sherman rose from the status of freshman on the Finance Committee to become its chairman in less than four years and played a major role in its work from the beginning. Of course the Ohioan brought a record of distinguished service in fiscal affairs from the other house. There is also evidence that when Fessenden screened committee members, he paid more attention to their abilities or judgment than he did to seniority. Whether other chairmen did likewise is uncertain.[6] In any case, the record shows that junior men could indeed aspire to major committee assignments and, during the Civil War congresses, some sort of a Senate chairmanship was within reach of most in the majority. Thirty-one Republican senators provided twenty-one standing committee chairmen in the long session of the Thirty-seventh Congress, leaving only the Library Committee in the hands of the courtly Democrat, Pearce. In the first session of the Thirty-eighth Congress, that chairmanship also passed into Republican hands, and with the reconstitution of two committees abandoned in the late 1850s, Agriculture (March 6, 1863) and Manufactures (February 10, 1864), and the creation of the Pacific Railroad (December 22, 1863), and Mines and Mining (March 8, 1865) committees, twenty-six Republicans could exercise their managerial talents. This burst of committee construction moved the impish Davis to try to amend the Senate rule listing committees, Number 34, by adding a "Committee for the investigation of the transactions of the government in all its departments and offices," to be appointed by the presiding officer and to include a majority "from the senators in ... opposition," including the chairman and "with power to continue its investigations during the recesses" and "to send for persons and papers."[7] The Republicans were neither amused nor interested by this imaginative proposal.

The standing committees did not exhaust the senators' opportunities for influencing policy at the committee level. There was in addition the possibility of serving on ad hoc and conference committees. The strategic importance of some of the latter will become clear in Part II. Of ad hoc committees, the Joint Committee on the Conduct of the War and the Senate's Select Committee on Slavery and Freedmen made unique although controversial contributions to the legislative history of the war. Some committees, as we shall see, were much more concerned with the great issues and controversies of the war than others. The presence of

6. *Memorial Addresses on the Life and Character of William Pitt Fessenden (A Senator from Maine,) Delivered in the Senate and House of Representatives...* (Washington: Government Printing Office, 1870), p. 36. Winfield Scott Kerr, *John Sherman: His Life and Public Services* (Boston: Sherman, French, 1908), 1:133.

7. *Senate Journal* (hereafter *SJ*), 38 Cong., 2 sess., 113.

leading moderates or radicals, or of moderate or radical majorities, on such committees might influence the work of these groups in significant ways and, perhaps, lead disaffected colleagues to develop counterstrategies. We shall discuss such matters further in Chapter 4 and the second part of this book.

The war senators, as we have seen, altered the committee structure somewhat by adding committees. To what degree did they seek to change other aspects of the legislative system? "The rules," intoned Sumner, "are more even than a beautiful machine; they are the very temple of constitutional liberty." The edifice was not so perfect that impatient senators, including Sumner, did not suggest alterations during the war. Perhaps visualizing an avalanche of wartime legislation, Hale moved in January, 1862, to recommend that "no bill, joint resolution, or other subject, be made a special order for a particular day and hour without the concurrence of two thirds of the senators present." He was successful. Some weeks later, however, his colleagues retreated somewhat in their efforts to increase the efficiency of floor proceedings, when they agreed to add state and territorial governors to those categories of individuals admitted to the floor while the chamber was sitting.[8]

During this same session the senators debated Sherman's resolution that proposed to terminate the practice of defining a quorum as a majority of the senators from all of the states (thirty-five senators) whether represented or not, and the New York *Herald* saw the work of the radicals in this maneuver. Not until May 4, 1864, however, did the senators agree on the necessity of this change; henceforth a majority of "the senators duly chosen" would constitute a quorum, although the original motion had proposed the wording, "a majority of the senators duly elected and entitled to seats" and the measure as introduced in 1864, "duly elected and qualified." Although Sumner supported Sherman's motion in 1862, other hotspurs played little part in the debate. Fessenden and Collamer, spoke powerfully for change, and Sherman argued that sickness and departures had reduced the number of senators available to the floor to thirty-seven and noted, "two or three States now might by withdrawing break up a quorum." Foot and Grimes, as well as Foster, opposed the resolution. When the senators approved it on May 4, 1864, Anthony, Doolittle, Foot, Foster, and Grimes left their Republican colleagues to vote against it. A few minutes after the Senate approved Sherman's effort to reduce the size of the quorum, its members ap-

8. *Proceedings on the Death of Hon. Solomon Foot*, p. 63; *CG*, 37 Cong., 2 sess., 240; *SJ*, 37 Cong., 2 sess., 94, 105; *SJ*, 37 Cong., 2 sess., 32, 183. As introduced by Anthony, the latter motion occasioned no discussion in the Senate.

proved Fessenden's resolution providing that the reporter was to list absentees in recording roll calls, a procedure apparently designed to emphasize the delinquency of senators for the benefit of constituents who followed the debates in the *Globe* or in the summaries carried in the newspapers.[9] Although this innovation was also directed against absenteeism, it was not included in the Senate rules *per se*.

Sumner's efforts to force senators to take the more rigorous supplementary oath of office of July 2, 1862, in addition to the usual oath also produced an additional Senate rule. As the Senate proceeded to organize itself in special session on March 4, 1863, following the termination of the third legislative session of the Thirty-seventh Congress, Trumbull pointed out that the oath of July, 1862, had been ignored. On March 5, Sumner submitted a resolution for consideration as an addition to the rules of the Senate. "The oath or affirmation prescribed by Act of Congress of July 2, 1862, to be taken before entering upon the duties of office, shall be taken and subscribed by every senator in open Senate, before entering upon his duties." On the next day, Foot, quietly influential, having been reelected by the legislature of Vermont, expressed his willingness to take the additional oath as did fourteen other senators-elect, including Sumner. When this procedure had been completed, Sumner withdrew his resolution. But Bayard of Delaware did not take the test oath, nor did Richardson of Illinois. Sumner then reintroduced his resolution early in the first regular session of the Thirty-eighth Congress, and his colleagues approved it in somewhat expanded form on January 25, 1864, after considerable discussion and an elaborate defense of his position by Bayard. Both Bayard and Richardson took the extra oath the next morning, but Bayard resigned as a matter of conscience.[10]

In defense of his initial refusal to take it, Bayard argued that the oath of July, 1862, was repugnant to three, and perhaps four, provisions of the Constitution: that defining the qualifications of a senator; the Fifth Amendment, in punishing the individual without due process of law; the second section of the second article, since it nullified the President's authority to pardon; and the restriction on the passage of *ex post facto* laws.[11] He also held that a senator was not a civil officer "within the

9. New York *Herald*, July 10, 1862. See also ibid., May 5, 1864. *SJ*, 37 Cong., 2 sess., 386; 38 Cong., 1 sess., 216; *CG*, 37 Cong., 2 sess., 3021-22, 3189-94, 3280-84 (votes are on 3093 and 3194); 38 Cong., 1 sess., 2050-52, 2082-87 (the vote on Sherman's proposal is on 2087); *SJ*, 38 Cong., 1 sess., 361, 402; *CG*, 38 Cong., 1 sess., 2088-90 (the vote on Fessenden's recommendation is on 2090).

10. *CG*, 37 Cong., 3 sess., 1553-62; 38 Cong., 1 sess., 42, 48-57, 253, 263, 275-81, 290-92, 320-31 (the vote is on 331).

11. Bayard's speech in defense of his course of action appears in *CG*, 38 Cong., 1 sess., *App.* 31-37.

meaning of the Federal Constitution," and therefore not among the categories of individuals touched by the act prescribing the oath of 1862. Why, he queried, should the test oath be exacted from him when it was not demanded of a number of senators elected after the passage of the law who qualified and served during the course of the third session of the Thirty-seventh Congress? Republicans marshaling their own battery of appropriate authorities denied the validity of Bayard's position and asserted that the test oath was essential to barring southern traitors from returning to Congress.

The senators did not accept all the suggestions for revision made by their fellows. Collamer sought unsuccessfully during the first session of the Thirty-seventh Congress to provide that the president *pro tempore* should serve continuously after election until replaced by another senator of the chamber's choice, this procedure to replace the current practice of election for the duration of each absence of the Vice President, including recesses. A decade and half later the senators would acknowledge the wisdom of this suggestion, but they were not amenable to it in July, 1861. Reacting with friendly malice to Republican suggestions to expedite procedures, Rice moved on January 10, 1862, that five dollars be deducted from the pay of senators who did not answer to their names during roll calls, generously exempting those who were absent because of illness or excused by the Senate.[12]

Although his effort to control special orders had won the approval of his colleagues, Hale was unsuccessful in suggesting in early April, 1862, that "the Senate may, at any time during the present rebellion, by a vote of the majority of the members present, fix a time when debate on any matter pending before the Senate shall cease and terminate; and the Senate shall, when the time fixed for terminating debate arrives, proceed to vote without debate on the measure and all amendments pending that may be offered." When the senators turned to this in the morning hour of April 7, the gentleman from New Hampshire remarked that the resolution was well understood and dealt with a matter that had "been discussed a great while." Davis did not believe "that the freedom of debate which is tolerated by the rules of the Senate [had] . . . been so much abused as to make such a change as that at all necessary or proper." More telling, undoubtedly, were similar comments from Collamer, who believed it "uncalled for and unnecessary," and liable to precipitate scrambles for the floor that were "unbecoming the dignity of the body." The morning hour closed without decision, and Hale's suggestion was not discussed formally thereafter in the wartime Senate.[13]

12. *SJ*, 37 Cong., 1 sess., 182; 2 sess., 98.
13. *SJ*, 37 Cong., 2 sess., 370–77; *CG*, 37 Cong., 2 sess., 1557.

Far from restricting debate or making discussion less open, Grimes, in March, 1864, tried to shed more light on the confirmation process and moved an amendment to the rules providing that "all executive nominations shall be submitted to, and considered by the Senate in open session." Routed to the Judiciary Committee, the resolution found few if any friends; Trumbull reported it back several weeks later with the recommendation that it ought not to pass. Late in June, 1864, on the other hand, Wade announced that he would move a resolution enforcing a strict ten-minute limitation on speeches addressed to any particular question for the remainder of the session. He did not, however, carry out his threat. Some days later Pomeroy proposed to amend the Twenty-sixth Rule relative to the reading of bills by adding to the clause "which reading shall be on three different days, unless the Senate unanimously direct otherwise," the further statement, "except on the last day of any session, when bills and joint resolutions may receive their several readings by the vote of the Senate." This too perished with its utterance.[14]

Ben Wade revealed the thinking of the Joint Committee on the Conduct of the War on congressional procedures when he submitted a resolution to add to the Joint Rules on January 21, 1862. It authorized any member of the House or Senate to carry his chamber into secret session by announcing that "the Executive desires immediate action of Congress upon any matter pertaining to the suppression of the present rebellion," and "if the previous question shall not have been ordered," all debate on the proposed measure "shall be limited to five minutes for any member, and the final vote shall be taken before adjournment." During such debates, all external communication was to be made through the president of the Senate or the Speaker of the House; expulsion was to be the fate of any member who broke secrecy, and officers who did so were to be punished as the members of their chamber saw fit. The senators first debated Wade's motion on January 27, and the Ohio senator detected some skepticism among his colleagues. He himself tried to forestall opposition by modifying the restrictions on debate to read, "And shall consider no other matter until such measure shall be disposed of." Senators noted that the Senate already had the power to go into secret session in the Eighteenth Rule of the Senate and to punish their colleagues and officers for disclosure of confidential information (rule of May 10, 1844), that the five-minute restriction was an unfortunate departure (so Sumner said, although others expressed sly gratification),

14. *SJ*, 38 Cong., 1 sess., 256, 309. No debate on Grimes's motion appears in the *Globe; SJ*, 38 Cong., 1 sess., 601; 741. I have not discussed what appears to be a minor effort by Davis to amend Rule 24 as to the ordering of daily Senate business, *SJ*, 38 Cong., 1 sess., 471. Given the mischievous proclivities of the senator from Kentucky, it is possible that it was a "sleeper" with profound implications that are not readily apparent to the historian.

that secrecy was undesirable even in the current crisis (Trumbull and Foster), and that the rule would give one individual undue power to control the agenda. But Fessenden and Chandler pointed out that the new rule provided the House with procedures currently unavailable in that chamber. The latter argued that "it may be necessary . . . that a law should be passed at once to save the Executive from the proclamation of martial law, under which he could perform the very act which he desires to perform in accordance with law." Wade defended the resolution as an effort to "let both bodies have the same rules for the consideration of certain measures," and provide the means for quick and effective coop- eration with the Executive; he proclaimed the desire of his committee to force the government to "move with energy" and castigated colleagues who would "force upon the Executive to usurp powers properly belong- ing to us." As senators, particularly Sumner, sought to amend the resolu- tion to fit their views, Wade despaired and the matter was put aside for the morrow.[15]

When the issue was reached in the morning hour of January 29, Sherman proposed a substitute for his colleague's original motion, de- signed to meet various objections to the implementation procedures of the original, to restore the five-minute rule in modified form, and to allow postponement of the measure on a two-thirds vote. His colleagues returned to the fray and Grimes and Collamer voiced opposition, the latter particularly stressing the invidious distinction that the presump- tion that particular senators had the ear of the President might create. Sherman sought to meet some of Collamer's objections, but Sumner believed that the effort to reintroduce restrictions on debate was unfor- tunate. Hale, on the other hand, was delighted with this feature "since it would do for the chastening of my brother Sumner; and his polished and burning shafts would be more polished and more concentrated if brought down to five minutes." But, after some further ministrations to the measure by Collamer, the senators approved the resolution without a roll call, and it became Number 22 of the Joint Rules.[16]

> 22. When, during the present rebellion, any member of the Senate or
> House of Representatives shall rise and in his place state that the President
> desires the immediate action of Congress upon any matter pertaining to
> the suppression of the present rebellion, the galleries of the house in which
> the statement is made shall be immediately cleared; and after such
> member shall state the action desired by the President, and the reasons for
> immediate action, such house shall determine, without debate, whether the
> proposed measure shall be considered. If decided in the affirmative, de-
> bate shall be confined to the subject-matter, and be limited to five minutes

15. The text of the resolution and the first round of debate appears in *CG*, 37 Cong., 2 sess., 490–94.

16. *CG*, 37 Cong., 2 sess., 534–36.

by any member provided that any member shall be allowed five minutes to explain or oppose any pertinent amendment; and provided that this rule shall not affect the operation of the previous question in the House of Representatives. During such session no communication shall be received or made to or from any person not a member then present, except through the President of the Senate or the Speaker of the House. If any member of the Senate or House of Representatives shall betray, publish, disclose, or reveal any debate, consultation, or proceeding had in such secret session, he shall be expelled; and if committed by an officer of either body, or other person, such punishment shall be inflicted as the body to which he belongs may impose.

Of this measure Hans L. Trefousse has written, "The rule was too stringent to be adopted at that time, but Wade demonstrated clearly that it was victory, not mere party advantage for the radicals, that motivated him."[17] It is not clear whether Trefousse merely ignored the continuation and final outcome of the debate on Wade's rule or whether he considered Rule 22, as adopted, to fall so short of the original as to be unworthy of mention. Wade, however, approved Sherman's substitute and expressed no chagrin at the minor amendments in it. Certainly, by preventing long constitutional disquisitions from border-state senators, the measure indeed seemed to promise some party advantage but, like some other proposals, it was, as we shall see, a reflection of a radical mood and a radical prescription for reform of congressional procedures. The President ignored it, ostensibly at least.

Thus expanded in number from 21 to 22 during the Thirty-seventh Congress, the Joint Rules received additional attention during the sessions of the Thirty-eighth. In December, 1863, Senator Foot brought forward a lengthy revision of the brief and very general first rule dealing with conference committees. In retrospect the specific procedures outlined in Foot's resolution appear businesslike and reasonable, although perhaps overelaborate. But some six months later, Trumbull reported it from the Judiciary Committee with the recommendation that it not pass.[18]

During the second session of the Thirty-eighth Congress the two houses approved still another addition to the Joint Rules when a joint committee submitted a resolution prescribing the methods to be used in "examining" the votes for President and Vice President and in particular detailing the procedures to be followed should "any question . . . arise in regard to counting the votes" certified. In a sense a companion action to a resolution declaring that electors from states that had been part of the

17. Hans L. Trefousse, *Benjamin Franklin Wade: Radical Republican from Ohio* (New York: Twayne, 1963), pp. 163–64.
18. *SJ,* 38 Cong., 1 sess., 31–32, 667.

Confederacy were not eligible to participate in the selection of the President and Vice President, the resolution, under Trumbull's vigilant eye, provoked little comment and became the twenty-third Joint Rule.[19]

Government expenditures increased prodigiously during the Civil War, and lobbying and war-related legal business grew apace. Two incidents involving colleagues forced the senators to establish legal guidelines for congressional behavior. Simmons and his Republican colleagues were put in disarray at the conclusion of the second session of the Thirty-seventh Congress when it became known that he had accepted a fee for assisting constituents to obtain contracts. The senators rushed through a short measure forbidding the practice, and Simmons' resignation spared them the embarrassment of acting on the report from the Judiciary Committee that was prepared in response to Wright's resolution for expulsion. When Hale drew criticism upon himself during the first session of the Thirty-eighth Congress by performing legal services for a New Englander awaiting court martial in Washington on charges of having defrauded the War Department, his senatorial colleagues passed a mild bill defining and forbidding conflicts of interest, but still allowing senators who were lawyers to ply their trade in the Washington courts.[20] Were these cases merely the tip of the iceberg? Some elements of the press believed so. Mark Twain reputedly chose Pomeroy as the model for the corrupt senator of *The Gilded Age.* Was it mere coincidence that Pomeroy's major committee assignments were Public Lands, Pensions, and Claims? An answer to such questions must wait a full-scale study of lobbying in the Civil War era.[21]

Historians who seek to explain legislative outcomes often attempt to identify leaders or cue-givers who particularly shape the final result. Taking his cue from Woodrow Wilson, Lauros G. McConachie emphasized the power of the party caucus chairman, and he extended his listing of such worthies back into the 1840s and 1850s. Significantly, he failed to include the name of such an individual for the years of the Civil War; apparently there was no outstanding leader in this post during those years. However, he suggested that persons fulfilling the function

19. *SJ*, 38 Cong., 2 sess., 139-40; *CG*, 38 Cong., 2 sess., 608.

20. The Wright resolution appears in *CG*, 37 Cong., 2 sess., 3061. Senate Committee *Reports*, 37 Cong., 2 sess., no. 69. The remedial bill was S. 358 and the law appears as Chap. CLXXX, *CG App.*, 37 Cong., 2 sess., 408. Hale's case was reported on by the Judiciary Committee in 38 Cong., 1 sess., United States Senate *Committee Report* 5. The law was Chap. XIX, *CG, App.*, 38 Cong., 1 sess., 177. Hale's most recent biographer discusses the incident: Richard H. Sewell, *John P. Hale and the Politics of Abolition* (Cambridge: Harvard University Press, 1965), pp. 214-17.

21. Springfield *Weekly Republican*, January 2, 1864.

could be identified by the fact that they presented the key procedural motions during the initial stages of a session, such as those governing the organization of the standing committees.[22] What powerful figures does this device unmask in the Senate during the Thirty-seventh and Thirty-eighth Congresses?

Nominally the Democrats still controlled the formal organization of the Senate in March, 1861, and Bright moved the standing committee lists. (He was to be expelled before a year had passed.) In the session of July–August, 1861, Fessenden moved the committees, and his friend Collamer did so at the opening of the second session in December of that year. Anthony performed this function in December, 1862, and would continue to do so throughout the decade. Fessenden's memorandum describing the senatorial effort to recast Lincoln's cabinet during the early weeks of the third session specifically identified Anthony as "our chairman."[23] But Anthony hardly seems to have been a powerful figure during these years, although he became one in the later part of his career. When the senators assembled, after notification by the door keeper, to hold the famous caucus meeting in which they initiated their open war on Seward, Anthony was forced to inquire what the subject of discussion was to be—hardly the act of a real mover and shaker. Nothing in the congressional sources or in newspaper comment of the time suggests that the Republican caucus chairman in the Senate was a figure of great power. Rather, the impression gained is one of a chamber of contending oligarchs or perhaps even of a country debating society in full cry.

If the party caucus chairman was not a focal source of power during the Civil War, did the state legislatures perhaps fiddle a tune to which their senators felt obliged to dance? In an article routinely cited by modern authorities on the Congress, William M. Riker examined the process of instruction by which state legislatures endeavored to participate in the solution of national issues. He concluded that it was a clumsy mechanism, ineffective because refusal to reelect, the most powerful sanction in the hands of the state lawmakers, was insufficient to bring men who served six-year terms to heel. Instruction "lapsed into obscurity" after 1846. Final judgment on these matters must wait until there is a full-scale study of instructional activity in the statehouses during the nineteenth century, but examination of legislative activities in a few states shows that there was effort to instruct the congressional delegations during the war years. If Wisconsin and New York are illustrative, most such efforts ended in reference to the Committee on Federal Rela-

22. McConachie, *Congressional Committees*, pp. 338–39.
23. Francis Fessenden, *Life and Public Services of William Pitt Fessenden: United States Senator from Maine . . .* (Boston: Houghton Mifflin, 1907), 1:231.

tions, in tabling, in indefinite postponement, or with the failure of one chamber to accept the proposition. Occasionally a joint or concurrent resolution of instruction did mature, as in 1862 when both houses of the Wisconsin legislature resolved to request "our Senators and representatives in Congress to oppose the passage of any stamp tax on newspapers." But the following year, a majority of the Committee on Federal Relations of the Wisconsin Senate recommended indefinite postponement of a resolution instructing the state's delegation on the issue of habeas corpus and expressed confidence "in the capacity and disposition of our Representatives in Congress to protect the rights and interests of the people of this state."[24] Legislative instruction must have played an extremely minor role in the formulation of any given senator's responses to the congressional agenda, although memorials and resolutions of instruction directed to emancipation issues or the fugitive slave laws may have fulfilled important partisan objectives in state politics, even when they were not approved for transmittal to Washington. And occasionally, state legislatures did instruct senators during the Civil War.

To what degree did the influence of the committee chairman sway his Republican colleagues in committee and in general? Occasionally in debate, senators acknowledged the influence of chairmen in determining their votes on measures reported from committee. Such statements sometimes provided the setting for a vote running contrary to the chairman's position, and the model in which senators willingly followed the cue of chairmen who were solidly supported by at least their Republican committee colleagues is far from the reality of the Civil War Senate.

Table 2-5 presents an illustrative selection of committee voting behavior, relating to three major measures falling within the province of three eminent Republican chairmen, Fessenden, Trumbull, and Sumner. "Cohesion" refers to the degree to which members of a legislative group vote together and may be measured by subtracting the proportion of dissenters in a vote from the percentage of the group that votes in the majority. A unanimous vote provides a score of 100 and a tie illustrates a case of zero cohesion. Although the Republican committee members achieved more cohesion in the issues summarized in Table 2-5 than did the committees as a whole, the margin was sometimes small, and in the case of the two standing committees of the Thirty-seventh Congress, the level of committee solidarity was rather similar to that of the whole group of Republican senators. Although Sumner appears to have fared better in achieving party cohesion on the Select Committee on Slavery and Freedmen than did Fessenden and Trumbull as the chairmen

24. William H. Riker, "The Senate and American Federalism," *American Political Science Review*, 49 (June 1955), 452–69; Wisconsin Assembly *Journal*, 1862, 175, 275; Wisconsin Senate *Journal*, 1863, 434.

TABLE 2-5.

Committees and cohesion

| Committee and subject | Votes* | Committee members— cohesion | Republican committee members— cohesion | All Republican senators— cohesion |
|---|---|---|---|---|
| Finance (37-2) | | | | |
| Internal revenue | 15 | 41 | 42 | 35 |
| Judiciary (37-2) | | | | |
| Confiscation (S. 151) | 10 | 38 | 41 | 47 |
| Slavery-Freedmen (38-1-2) | | | | |
| Freedmen's bureau | 23 | 45 | 84 | 59 |

*The 15 votes on internal revenue were selected at random; the confiscation votes include all votes on the so-called Trumbull bill; the freedmen's bureau voting extends through two sessions but also includes all votes.

of the Finance and Judiciary committees, this select committee was a very special instrument as we shall see, and despite an overall Republican cohesion level of 59 in the votes on the Freedmen's Bureau, the level was a mere 37 during the second session of the Thirty-eighth Senate when the measure actually passed.

But certainly some senators possessed the ability to shape outcomes to a greater extent than did others of their colleagues, especially in proceedings focused on particular categories of legislation, and many elements were involved in the relative success of particular senators in this respect.[25] A given senator's success in bringing other lawmakers to his point of view might be attributable to his seniority, his committee assignments, the salience of his legislative speciality at a given time, his legislative objectives and style, his personality, energy, and state of health as well as his general reputation in the Senate, party, and nation, or more likely, to combinations of these factors. If the scholar is content to study a few prominent lawmakers, a positional and reputational analysis allows some evaluation of senatorial effectiveness. The contemporary newspapers and biographical data make it possible for us, for instance, to draw some conclusions about the relative legislative contributions of Fessenden, Sumner, and Hale during the Civil War.

Whom would the members of the Thirty-seventh Senate have mentioned most frequently, if asked the identity of their most powerful

25. For a discussion of relevant bibliography and a more extended analysis of power in the Thirty-seventh Senate, see Allan G. Bogue, "Some Dimensions of Power in the Thirty-Seventh Senate," in William O. Aydelotte, Allan G. Bogue, and Robert W. Fogel, *The Dimensions of Quantitative Research in History* (Princeton: Princeton University Press, 1972), pp. 285-318.

colleague? One can make a strong case for William Pitt Fessenden of Maine. In the first place he was the chairman of the Finance Committee, regarded during the middle period of American history as a highly important Senate committee. This was the group which considered the appropriations bills sent to the Senate by the House of Representatives, presenting recommendations for change to the chamber and shaping its discussion of appropriations matters generally. During the generation before the outbreak of the Civil War, the tariff had become a focal point of sectional differences, and the chairman of the Finance Committee was in a strategic position to mediate Senate policy on this issue. The major fiscal problems of the war made the labors of the committee more crucial still. Finance bills had to be considered and passed if the machinery of government was to function.

Individuals may fail to develop the power inherent in their offices or discredit them by laziness, ineptitude, or gaucherie. Neither the *Congressional Globe* nor Fessenden's correspondence suggests that the senator from Maine was of that stripe.[26] The letters to his family tell of unremitting and arduous labor, which brought him to the verge of complete exhaustion. In the columns of the *Globe,* McDougall described him as an intimidating figure while he presided at committee hearings, guarding the Treasury suspiciously from the representatives of special interests who laid their selfish demands before him. Disagreeing with Fessenden as to the basic principles of the Internal Revenue bill, Simmons asserted that if he "agrees to anything, almost everybody else will." Defending one of the interest groups in his state, Harris fumed, "I confess I am surprised at the tenacity with which . . . his views are supported by the Senate."[27]

During the last weeks of the second session of the Thirty-seventh Congress Fessenden's position as Finance chairman gave him a unique opportunity to influence the legislative process. As the session dragged through June and into July, the Democratic senators became increasingly restive, threatening to leave and deprive the Senate of a quorum. In mid-June, Fessenden explained the crucial significance of his role in completing the legislative program of the Republicans: "The tax bill is in the hands of a Com[mittee] of Conference, & will be wound up in a day or two. All my other bills will be wound up, or might be, in two weeks, but there are two or three important measures to be finished, and I must keep one of my bills behind them in order to secure sufficient time for their passage." We see, therefore, in Fessenden a senator who not only

---

26. Unless otherwise noted, letters from Fessenden cited here are in the William Pitt Fessenden papers, Bowdoin College Library, and are quoted with the permission of the Librarian.

27. *CG*, 37 Cong., 2 sess., 2558, 2402, 2467.

occupied a very important committee chairmanship, but a man who understood how to use that position to further the broader legislative designs of his party. Sometimes he was willing to admit that he was uniquely qualified to hold this position, as when he wrote, during the course of the special summer session of this Congress, "there is much in my hands which cannot be so well done by another."[28]

If power may rest in the hands of men in strategic or prestigious positions, the opinions of contemporaries may also guide us to its locus. Fessenden himself provided some testimony on this score when he told of the Maine man who sought his aid in obtaining a place for his son in the Naval academy because a respected friend had told him that the President could refuse Fessenden nothing. "How exceedingly embarrassing it is," he wrote, "to be supposed the possessor of any such power—especially when it does not exist." Yet even in this passage of deprecation he spoke in terms of power, and he had earlier written to one of his sons matter-of-factly, "I have power enough to see that no substantial injustice is done you and will use it, if need be." But it is to Fessenden's respected colleague, Grimes, that we owe the most flattering evaluation of the Maine senator's power—or at least his potential power. Shortly before the beginning of the second session of the Thirty-seventh Congress, Grimes wrote to him: "If you determine to probe the sore spots to the bottom and that right shall be done, we can inaugurate a new order of things and the Country can be saved. You have followers. You can control the Senate—The wicked fear you and will flee before you." Fessenden, in other words, could count on others to follow his lead. Insofar as I can discover, the correspondence of the senators of the Thirty-seventh Congress yields no similar tribute from a fellow lawmaker. And when Fessenden and Charles Sumner clashed during the course of the next Congress, the senator from Maine judged his rival by the criterion that Grimes had used. Sumner "has for followers," wrote Fessenden to another son, "two or three drunken rowdies, and small fry."[29]

Yet Fessenden did not attract the attention of the newspapers during the Thirty-seventh Congress as did outspoken reputed radicals like Benjamin F. Wade and Charles Sumner. Doubtless this reflected the fact that he concentrated his efforts on fiscal and monetary policy—less colorful and contentious matters than confiscation and emancipation, although of key significance to the cause of the Union. Nor did he fancy himself an orator, describing himself during the second session as "leaving all the jabber to others, & being content to work like a dog."[30] As one reads

28. William Pitt Fessenden to Elizabeth F. Warriner, June 15, 29, 1862, July 21, 1861.

29. Ibid., December 15, 1861; William Pitt Fessenden to Francis Fessenden, October 29, 1861; James W. Grimes to William Pitt Fessenden, November 13, 1861; William Pitt Fessenden to William Fessenden, May 7, 1864.

30. William Pitt Fessenden to Elizabeth F. Warriner, February 8, 1862.

the memorial addresses in which the senators paid their last homage to Fessenden, there emerges from the rhetoric and the encomiums a clear picture of his style—perhaps nowhere more clearly than in the rather condescending remarks of Charles Sumner: "As Mr. Fessenden rarely spoke except for business, what he said was restrained in its influence, but it was most effective in this Chamber. Here was his empire and his undisputed throne." Sumner made it clear that this was hardly his conception of the senatorial role, but, then as now, it was the kind of behavior which won the respect of a majority of the members of the Senate. Yet Fessenden was by no means the complete broker in political affairs, a suave or softspoken political manager who built his political capital by doing favors for his colleagues. Many found him austere and stiff-necked, or "cold, reserved, and somewhat aristocratic" as one put it; Senator Justin S. Morrill described him as "holding the formidable power of sarcasm within his compressed lips, it would sometimes escape in sport—quite as often in bitter earnest. This pungency in debate involved him in conflicts, not infrequently with his dearest friends." His ability and his integrity were the qualities that most impressed his colleagues apparently, and Grimes called him "the highest-toned man I ever knew; the purest man I ever knew in public life, and the ablest public man of my day."[31]

The process of decision-making provides other clues to the location of power, although even the best-documented decisions may inspire various explanations. We have Fessenden's own account of the confirmation of Edwin Stanton as Secretary of War, replacing the unfortunate Simon Cameron. The senators were astounded when President Lincoln nominated Simon Cameron as minister to Russia and presented Edwin M. Stanton's name to the Senate. Fessenden explained to his cousin: "It is usual to confirm Cabinet Ministers at once, but I took the responsibility to have the matter laid over for consideration—as I was determined to know what it meant before I acted. . . . Accordingly, I sought and obtained an interview with [Stanton]. . . . If he is a truthful man . . . he is just the man we want. We agreed on every point—the duties of a Secretary of War—the conduct of the War—the Negro question and every thing else." In actuality, Fessenden was not the only senator to interview Stanton before the Senate vote, but surely it was a man of no little power who could thus delay a crucial administration appointment, constitute himself a committee of one, and conduct a hearing on the appointee's qualifications while colleagues awaited his judgment.

But although even recent writers sometimes refer to Fessenden as "the leader" of the Senate Republicans, the literary evidence suggests a need for qualification. Attorney General Edward Bates stigmatized the houses

31. *Memorial Addresses on . . . Fessenden*, pp. 12-13, 30, 64, 43.

of the Thirty-eighth Congress as being "destitute of a *leader*," assemblies where "every little clique and faction aspires to rule," and the senator from Maine was less than universally loved. Trumbull scolded him for his ill-tempered outbursts, and ultimately his dislike of Sumner seems to have become something of an obsession. At the time of his appointment to the Treasury, however, Lincoln characterized him as a "Radical without the petulant and vicious fretfulness of many Radicals."[32]

Sumner had traveled widely in Europe as a young man and spent a considerable period abroad during the convalescence that followed Congressman Preston Brooks's assault upon him.[33] He maintained a correspondence with a number of eminent British figures. To his personal knowledge of European governments and people he added the information gained from his reading over the years in the classics of international law. His selection as chairman of the Senate Committee on Foreign Affairs was quite appropriate. Although the problems of diplomacy were different in many respects from those confronting the congressional leaders who worked to mobilize the men and materials of war, few would argue that they were less significant to the outcome of the struggle. The effort to keep major European powers in a posture of neutrality, despite enflaming incidents and provocative situations, demanded patience and resolution in both the administration and the Senate. Sumner did his share in providing both, particularly during the Trent affair, when his moderate views prevailed despite the sword rattling of more hot-tempered colleagues. Thus we can say that Sumner also held one of the most important chairmanships in the Senate and that on occasion he used it to provide vital leadership. Moreover, in most matters of foreign affairs he cooperated with the President, if not always with the Secretary of State, thus bringing to his advocacy in the Senate the influence of the administration as well as his own prestige and power.

In general, the conduct of foreign affairs roused less intense controversy during the Civil War than did domestic issues. And if recognition of Haiti and Liberia and ratification of the treaty with Great Britain

32. William Pitt Fessenden to Elizabeth F. Warriner, January 19, 1862. Benjamin P. Thomas and Harold M. Hyman, *Stanton: The Life and Times of Lincoln's Secretary of War* (New York: Knopf, 1962), p. 139; Michael Les Benedict, *A Compromise of Principle: Congressional Republicans and Reconstruction, 1863–1869* (New York: Norton, 1974), pp. 83, 39; Howard K. Beale, *The Diary of Edward Bates.* American Historical Association, *Annual Report, 1930,* 4:382; John G. Nicolay and John Hay, *Abraham Lincoln: A History* (New York: Century, 1890), 9:100.

33. Of all the senators of the Thirty-seventh Congress, Charles Sumner has attracted the most biographers. Pierce, *Memoir and Letters of Charles Sumner,* 4, is still useful. David Donald, *Charles Sumner and the Rights of Man* (New York: Knopf, 1970) will stand for some time as a definitive treatment of Sumner's political career during and after the Civil War. I have used the major body of Sumner mss. in the Houghton Library, Harvard University.

barring the international slave trade were sensitive issues, it was their bearing on the status of slavery in the United States that attracted attention, much more than other aspects of the diplomacy involved. This fusion of issues, however, illustrates another aspect of Sumner's senatorial career during the Civil War. He had been the tribune of the antislavery cause; like no other legislator, he was the voice of abolition on the Senate floor. The degree to which the antislavery forces in states other than Massachusetts chose to send their petitions for emancipation or confiscation to Sumner rather than to the senators of their own states is truly surprising, particularly when their own senators had distinguished reputations as foes of the peculiar institution. Sumner tried to attack slavery in every possible way, and his legislative activity carried him into areas of discussion in which his committee chairmanship did not give him special status. The specific motions he made in the Senate during the second session of the Thirty-seventh Senate revealed a very different pattern than did those of Fessenden. With few exceptions, the latter's motions concerned issues within the purview of the chairman of the Finance Committee. Several, relating to taxes on cotton and slaves, did also involve the southern question. By contrast, almost all of Sumner's motions lay outside his major committee assignment.

Contemporary newspaper reporters almost invariably mentioned Sumner when discussing the Senate radicals. In their accounts he was often termed a "leading" radical or linked with Benjamin F. Wade and Zachariah Chandler as "radical leaders." Yet such descriptions may have carried a rather special meaning. Sumner was undoubtedly a leader in that he was an articulate and lucid exponent of particular elements in the ideology of the radical Republicans. Just as the Communist party leadership today includes men who are considered to be uniquely theorists, so in a real sense was Sumner. He marshaled arguments for emancipation with cogency and force, and his statement of the relationship of the rebellious states to the government of the Union was one of the major theories advanced on that difficult subject. But his voluminous correspondence does not contain an authoritative statement comparable to the blunt assurance from Senator Grimes to Fessenden, "You have followers." Nor in his own letters did Sumner articulate the concept of power as did Fessenden on occasion. Unquestionably Sumner was sometimes the despair of more practical legislators. "I do most sincerely hope that Massachusetts will have sense enough to remit him to the vocation for which he was designed—a professor of rhetoric & a lyceum lecturer," wrote Fessenden on the first day of June, 1862.[34]

Legislative style determines the degree to which a lawmaker realizes

34. William Pitt Fessenden to Elizabeth F. Warriner, June 1, 1862.

the legislative power inherent in his seniority and committee assignments. No other senator answered more roll calls than did Sumner
during the Thirty-seventh Senate. He spoke frequently, and many of his
contributions to the *Congressional Globe* were truly orations. He was personally honest and indefatigable in running errands for and fostering
the interests of his constituents. Emerson could say of him, "I think he
has the whitest soul I ever knew," and John Lothrop Motley wrote that
he was "found at his death like an ingot of finest gold" despite "half a
lifetime" in "the fiery furnace of Washington politics." John Sherman
remarked in his eulogy of Sumner, "on all the vital issues . . . he has been
a prominent, conspicuous, and influential advocate of the opinions and
principles represented by the republican party, which have either been
ingrafted in the Constitution of the United States or have controlled the
policy of the Government since 1861." But Sherman also noted, "he
would not yield even on minor points, and would often fight for a phrase
when he endangered a principle. He would sometimes turn his warfare
upon his best friends." Justin Morrill mentioned "his persistency in
pushing his own measures to the front, though to their present hurt or
to the hurt of others." Sumner was "not always a practical statesman,"
admitted George S. Boutwell of Massachusetts in a phrase that others
came close to echoing. He had, said one of his old colleagues in the Senate,
"the egotism of genius and the impatience of fanatical conviction."[35]

Sumner would not have been Sumner had he played the political
broker among his colleagues. He had not, after all, won either local fame
in Boston or national fame in Washington during the 1850s by plying
the arts of conciliation. But, perhaps in rationalization of his own in-
adequacies, he did have a reasoned conception of his legislative role.
During the memorial observances for Fessenden, Sumner maintained,
"without neglect of business, the Senate has become a center from which
to address the country. A seat here is a lofty pulpit with a mighty
sounding-board, and the whole wide-spread people is the congrega-
tion."[36] Probably he believed that he did indeed speak to the "whole
wide-spread people" when he rose in the Senate, and perhaps the victory
of the Republicans and the crumbling power of the slavocracy convinced
him—he who had been a lonely spokesman of the antislavery forces in
the early 1850s in the Senate—that this was indeed the way to move a
nation. The statesman spoke in the Senate to convert the people, and

---

35. *Memorial Addresses on the Life and Character of Charles Sumner, (A Senator of Massachusetts,) Delivered in the Senate and House of Representatives . . . April 27, 1874 with other
Congressional Tributes of Respect* (Washington: Government Printing Office, 1874), pp. 34,
45, 46–47, 23, 14, 97. George W. Curtis, ed., *The Correspondence of John Lothrop Motley* (New
York: Harper, 1889), 2:377.
36. *Memorial Addresses on . . . Fessenden,* p. 12.

they in turn pressed the laggards in Congress to accept the new challenge or replaced them. If this was Sumner's interpretation of the rise of Republicanism, such strategy could attract few of his fellow senators, facing, as they did, the terrible immediacy of the war; they must make decisions now. To some of his colleagues, Sumner's rhetoric perhaps sounded hollow indeed, directed frustratingly past them to their constituents. But Sumner also believed that discussion could change the minds of colleagues, hard set against his wishes, often recounting, according to Senator Allen G. Thurman, instances in which thorough debate had meant the difference between the success and failure of legislative measures.[37]

Another aspect of Sumner's legislative style is worth mentioning. In a legislative chamber where men ostensibly were equals, although such equality, let it be agreed, was modified by membership in the minority or majority party, by length of service and committee assignments, and by personal style, the senator who could mobilize the power of the Executive to his own ends was clearly in a very favorable position. The extent of Abraham Lincoln's influence in Congress is a subject of dispute, but that he did possess power none can deny. Sumner tried diligently to enlist the chief executive in support of his most cherished objectives. He sprinkled his letters to John Bright and to the Duchess of Argyll with allusions to conversations between the President or the cabinet officers and himself. Writing to the duchess in November, 1862, he rejoiced that emancipation was to be won and exclaimed, "How many dreary conversations I have had with the President on this theme, beginning sixteen months ago."[38] As was well known, he developed the habit of staying in Washington for some time after the close of each session, and was thus able to confer with officers of the executive branch after the pressure of congressional business had ended. Remorselessly implacable in debate, Sumner enraged both the opposition and various of his party colleagues, as we shall see, but he was a force in the shaping of much war legislation.

Other senators were obviously very influential men also. As chairman of the Committee on Territories, Benjamin F. Wade of Ohio guided the Senate on subjects that had come particularly to symbolize the sectional divisions within the nation during the 1850s.[39] As chairman of the Joint Committee on the Conduct of the War, he terrorized members of the armed forces and those who thought to assist or serve them. Considerable evidence testifies to his power. But in contrast to such men as Wade,

---

37. *Memorial Addresses on . . . Sumner,* p. 17.

38. Charles Sumner to the Duchess of Argyll, November 17, 1862. See also Sumner to John Bright, December 23, 30, 1861, August 5, 1862, all in Pierce, *Memoir and Letters,* 4:57-59, 83, 108.

39. Trefousse, *Benjamin Franklin Wade,* is the most recent full scale biography of Wade.

Fessenden, and Sumner, let us establish another reference point and briefly discuss a senator who was relatively unsuccessful as a member of the majority party despite long service and high status among its founders.

The election of John P. Hale to the Senate from New Hampshire in 1846 was the most notable political victory of the antislavery forces to that time.[40] Although not reelected in 1853, he returned to the Senate in 1855, and he could claim greater total service in the chamber than any other Republican member of the Thirty-seventh Senate. The Republicans selected him as chairman of the Committee on Naval Affairs. But Hale apparently failed to realize his potential power because of shortcomings in his legislative style. Portraying him with sympathetic objectivity, his most recent biographer describes a man who waged guerrilla warfare against the majority with considerable success while he was a member of the opposition. But as a member of the party in control of the government, he found it difficult, even impossible, to assume a more responsible posture. His biographer called him a maverick, as well as a guerrillist, and the appellations are perhaps too kind. Extremely conscious of his senatorial prerogatives and sensitive to slights, real or imagined, he was exasperated when some of his requests for patronage at the Navy Department were ignored. When he learned that the Secretary, Gideon Welles, had used his brother-in-law to purchase vessels for the department in New York, he excoriated the cabinet member in terms that made his colleagues wince. The chairman of the Senate Committee on Naval Affairs and the Secretary of the Navy convinced themselves of each other's corruption in short order. Hale thereafter expended much of his energy in efforts to expose malfeasance in Welles's department, and in bickering with the Secretary concerning appointments. Hale even carried the quarrel to the point of trying to cut the Secretary's request for iron-clads from twenty to twelve vessels and suggesting that the authorization to have them constructed be given to the President rather than to Welles. These were dubious tactics at a time when the navy was hard pressed to fulfill its obligations. Gideon Welles was delighted when the New York *Tribune* published a story in December, 1863, suggesting that Hale had sold his influence in obtaining the parole of a man under indictment for defrauding the War Department. By that time Welles had already come to depend upon other members of the Committee on Naval Affairs, notably Grimes and Foot, to represent the interests of the navy in the Senate.

Hale's perversity was not restricted to his relations with Gideon Welles. He tried to stampede the Senate into endorsing Captain Charles Wilkes's

40. I have in this account generally followed Richard H. Sewell in *John P. Hale and the Politics of Abolition.*

ill-considered action in removing Confederate envoys from the British vessel *Trent,* thereby embarrassing Sumner and more responsible Republicans. He taunted the supporters of the bill to create a department of agriculture by charging that they were more concerned with the votes of farmers than with the welfare of agriculture.[41] Even if true, the comment must have irked the practical politicians who were more intent on party-building than was Hale. It was a remark apparently typical of the strain of flippancy or even irresponsibility which marked his conduct as a senator.

During the Thirty-eighth Congress, Hale's colleagues placed their evaluation of him on record. Although the Judiciary Committee did not recommend censuring him for unethical practices, it did, as we have seen, report a bill that forbade congressmen to accept fees in return for representing clients in the departments of the government, "other than its judiciary tribunals," and it was passed.[42] More indicative of the dissatisfaction of his colleagues was the suggestion that he might be deprived of his committee chairmanship. The senatorial caucus of Republicans did not take this action in December, 1863, but the following June, New Hampshire legislators rejected Hale's bid for reelection and in December the senators made Grimes of Iowa chairman of the Naval Affairs Committee for the duration of the second session of the Thirty-eighth Congress despite Hale's piteous pleas to be allowed to hold the post until his term expired in March, 1865. Poor "Jack" Hale was not among the group of Republican senators whose stature and power waxed during the war years. His, apparently, was a story of lost opportunities; for him access to power had come too late.

In this examination of the institutional structure of the Civil War Senate we have described features of the committee system, and the changing structure of rules, and have used three notable Republican senators as an introduction to senatorial leadership. Clearly the Republicans of the Thirty-seventh Senate did not start anew, but took control of a well-developed institutional system. They changed it in some respects, and they seriously considered making other alterations in its functioning. Although the system defined some of the obligations and prerogatives of leadership, the personality, style, and objectives of the individual senator were important. After we have investigated the differences in voting behavior among the Republican senators in the next chapter we shall be in a position to examine the connections between such patterns, if any, and the characteristics of individual senators and the institutional structure.

41. Pierce, *Memoir and Letters,* 4:53; *CG,* 37 Cong., 2 sess., 2014.
42. See note 20 above.

# 3

# Radicals and Moderates

In the *Congressional Globe* of the war years, one can easily find affirmations of loyalty to constituency, frank declarations of sectional interest, and the appeals of Republican leaders to their colleagues to shun factionalism and cleave to party. But oratorical flourishes can be deceiving; in the end it was the votes of the representatives and senators that counted. And what do the votes tell us of geographical bloc, of party faction, and of the bonds of party? Let us try to answer this question by first considering the roll calls recorded in the first regular session of the Thirty-seventh Senate—the assembly that first met in the portentous weeks of early December, 1861. Did Allan Nevins aptly describe this body when he wrote, "Parties were in chaos when Congress met, and the session did little to fix firm lines. Radical Republicans, conservative Republicans, War Democrats, Peace Democrats, Lincoln-haters and Lincoln-defenders, made up an assemblage defying clear analysis"?[1]

To analyze the long session of the Thirty-seventh Senate, I initially selected all the substantive votes concerned with the South and its institutions, particularly slavery and confiscation measures; the tariff and the internal revenue bills; legal tenders; the agricultural college bill; the homestead law; the department of agriculture bill; the Pacific railroad act; northern civil liberties and the general conduct of the war; and finally a few important procedural votes that seemed related to some of these measures. Most of these votes fell into one of three broad categories. Eighty-seven dealt with southern issues and racial matters (see Appendix C); 51 emerged from the debate on the Internal Revenue Act of 1862; and the debates on other major economic legislation of

1. Allan Nevins, *The War for the Union, 2: War Becomes Revolution, 1862–1863* (New York: Scribner, 1960), p. 190.

national interest produced 35 votes. During the course of the research the scope of the study was broadened to include 368 roll calls of this session, excluding only those that related to appointments.[2] These votes are the major source for the scholar seeking evidence of patterns in the voting of the thirty-one Republicans, eleven Democrats, five Border Unionists and one northern Unionist who sat in the Senate during most of the second session of the Thirty-seventh Congress.[3]

We can cut our first benchmarks in concise and simple terms. Disagreement between nominal groups, such as parties or regional delegations, can be measured on a scale of zero to 100 (see Appendices A and B). As is explained in the second methodological appendix, a disagreement value of 40 or more was assumed to represent substantial disagreement between groups in the Thirty-seventh Congress, and that standard was maintained subsequently in examining the roll calls of the Thirty-eighth Senate as well. In their voting in 368 roll calls of the second session of the Thirty-seventh Congress, the senators of the Republican and Democratic parties differed by 40 percent, or more, of the total disagreement possible in 161 roll calls. Restating the matter in different terms, a majority of Republicans opposed a majority of Democrats in 180 of the 368 voting divisions, that is, in 49 percent of all these votes. But of the 87 roll calls on southern and related issues in the original selection, 65, or 75 percent, showed a majority of Republicans opposed to a majority of Democrats. We shall return to some of the implications of these figures below.

Since the Democrats and Border Unionists in the Thirty-seventh Senate were few in numbers, widely scattered as to constituency in the case of the Democrats and, in both instances, the disorganized remnants of once-proud parties, it appeared that the purest test of the importance of sectionalism would be given by consideration of the Republican voting patterns alone, and the eastern border of Ohio provided a reasonable boundary between eastern and western Republicans. The oratorical flourishes of sectionalism within the party are apparent in the *Globe*. "We" [of the Northwest], said Senator Grimes, "are the only portion of all the loyal States that feel the effect of this war oppressively.... Whilst men who own the railroads in the Northwest are making fortunes out of this war by the transportation of our produce, we are receiving nothing

2. This included votes in the Senate proper, in Committee of the Whole, and in executive session. Tallies used are those recorded in the *Senate Journal*, supplemented occasionally by those in the *Congressional Globe*.

3. In the Border Unionist category I included five senators of Whig origins from the border states. I have used the term Northern Unionist to describe Senator Joseph A. Wright of Indiana. See his letter to the Indiana State Union Convention, *National Intelligencer*, June 23, 1862. However, Kenneth M. Stampp lists him as a War Democrat in *Indiana Politics during the Civil War* (Indianapolis: Indiana Historical Bureau, 1949), p. 237.

in fact from it."[4] Later in the session, Ten Eyck of New Jersey spoke for the East when he asked: "Now what inducement is there for a Senator from an Atlantic State to vote an appropriation of large sums of money, even in the shape of a loan, to construct a variety of [rail] roads for the advantage of the western States?"[5] In numerical terms, there was substantial sectional disagreement among eastern and western Republican senators in 47 of the 368 votes of the second session.

The sectionalism of East and West appeared most frequently in voting on economic measures of national significance. Only 7 percent of the original selection of 87 roll calls relating to southern issues and race showed substantial sectional disagreement between the eastern and western Republicans, in comparison to 25 percent of the 86 votes linked to major economic legislation. Consideration of all 368 roll calls does not change the generalization.

In voting on southern issues and racial matters, the Republican senators divided on an East-West basis in seven substantive votes, in three procedural votes, and in two roll calls concerning the possibility of expelling Lazarus Powell, senator from Kentucky. Among the votes on major economic legislation we find a division between eastern and western Republicans on eight roll calls during the debates on the internal revenue bill; on eight votes in the discussion of the land-grant college bill; on three concerning greenback issues; on three during the Pacific railroad debates; and in two divisions concerning the tariff. Sectionalism appeared also in three votes relating to the judiciary, three concerning appropriations for the armed forces, and in five roll calls on miscellaneous matters.

Western Republicans ranged themselves against the eastern members of their party most sharply on the land-grant college bill. As noted, eight of the nine roll calls generated in discussion of this bill showed substantial disagreement between East and West; the index of disagreement between the sections ranged from 71 to 85 in the roll calls on the major amendments. In the end both Wisconsin senators and one Republican senator from Iowa, Kansas, and Minnesota voted against the bill. They were joined by Senator Wright, the Northern Unionist from Indiana, whose Republican colleague supported the most severe amendments proposed by the westerners but did not vote on the bill itself.

Indices of party disagreement do not reveal whether the representatives of a section were more united in their approach to certain categories of legislation than were the legislators of another section. But this was indeed the case among the Republican senators of the Thirty-seventh Congress. The average voting agreement among all possible

4. *CG*, 37 Cong., 2 sess., 114.
5. Ibid., 2805.

pairs of western senators, when both were present, was 61 percent, in the roll calls on the major national economic legislation and 59 percent in the votes on the internal revenue bill. In contrast, eastern Republican pairs had mean agreements of 76 to 65 percent. The differences between the two groups of senators would have been greater still if the senators from the middle states were dropped from the comparison. Six New England senators, Clark, Collamer, Fessenden, Foot, Foster, and Morrill, were in particularly strong agreement in the votes on economic legislation. The lowest mean agreement among these men was 73 percent, and Clark and Fessenden voted together in 97 percent of the roll calls on major economic legislation. There was no western group comparable in strength of agreement.

Among the 368 roll calls of the second session, there were 91 in which the cohesion indices of eastern and western Republicans differed by as much as forty points. In 59 of these roll calls it was the easterners who showed the greater solidarity. The western Republicans were more cohesive in voting on only 32 roll calls of this type. Of the 105 votes in this session which were related to economic measures of national interest, 35, or 33 percent, showed a marked difference in the cohesion of eastern and western Republicans. Of 120 roll calls linked to slavery, confiscation, and the general conduct of the war, only 18, or 15 percent, revealed a similar pattern. Thus, economic issues provoked more sectional responses from eastern and western Republicans than did legislation concerned with southern issues, and it is clear also that the eastern Republicans were in greater agreement on the national economic legislation of this Congress than were their western colleagues.

The most striking sectional alignment in Congress during the years before the Civil War had reflected the divergent interests of North and South. During most of the second session of the Thirty-seventh Congress, senators represented five slave states. This group, which included Democrats, former Whigs, and an American, guarded the southern heritage insofar as they considered it appropriate and feasible—which was frequently a good deal further than the Republicans liked. An index of disagreement which compares the voting of the senators from the slave states with that of the senators from the free states shows substantial disagreement on 154 of the 368 roll calls of this session. Sixty-seven of these votes appeared in the original selection of 87 roll calls related to slavery and confiscation legislation. The slave-state delegation was so small that this bloc's voting was sometimes masked by other voting determinants, but the group was of major importance when radical and moderate Republicans disagreed.

Although party lines did shift and blur somewhat during the Civil War, party affiliation is usually easy to identify and there can be little argument among sober persons about the geographical location of a senator's state. But to define a legislator as radical or conservative is a good deal more difficult, and distinguished historians have sometimes contented themselves with merely giving a few outstanding illustrations.[6] No one formal act officially proclaimed that a Republican senator was either a radical or a conservative. No one impartial observer authoritatively ranked all the Republican senators as to their radicalism or lack of it. But perhaps conventional wisdom offers a starting point; according to it, we should expect that radicalism would be most evident in matters relating to race, slavery, and southern issues generally. If in examining such matters we can find no trace of something definable as radicalism, there is not much point in going further.

When we examine a matrix composed of all pair agreements among the senators of the long or second session of the Thirty-seventh Senate in the voting on 87 roll calls relating to southern issues, we find evidence of pronounced clustering among the Republicans, as Table 3-1 shows.

When present and voting, the seven Republican senators whose names stand at the top of the column of names in this table obviously agreed strongly with one another. The next five senators also agreed strongly among themselves but showed considerable less enthusiasm for voting with King, Wilmot, and Co., as the cross agreements in the rectangle show. Of all the Republican senators, Cowan of Pennsylvania agreed least frequently with the Republicans in the top cluster but far more strongly with men such as Collamer and Fessenden, whose voting placed them in the second cluster in Table 3-1. Since the three Republican senators who are most frequently described as radicals—Chandler, Wade, and Sumner—appear in the King-Wilmot cluster, we can argue that this must indeed represent the radical voting nucleus and that the other cluster may properly be considered a nonradical or moderate voting nucleus. Cowan, we should judge, must have been the most conservative of the listed senators in the roll calls under study. The fact that slave-state senators agreed even less with senators such as Wilmot than did Cowan supports that view.

6. Glenn M. Linden pioneered in the quantitative analysis of the roll calls of the Civil War congresses. See: "'Radicals' and Economic Policies: The Senate, 1861–1863," *Journal of Southern History*, 32 (May 1966), 189–99; "'Radicals' and Economic Policies: The House of Representatives, 1861–1873," *Civil War History*, 13 (March 1967), 51–65; "'Radical' Political and Economic Policies: The Senate, 1873–1877," *Civil War History*, 14 (September 1968), 240–49; "A Note on Negro Suffrage and Republican Politics," *Journal of Southern History*, 36 (August 1970), 411–20. His work was published, however, after Edward L. Gambill's article on the Thirty-ninth Senate, "Who Were the Senate Radicals?" *Civil War History*, 11 (September 1965), 237–44, a scaling study. Although Linden's work was an important contribution, it was vulnerable, in theoretical terms at least, to the criticisms of percentage scoring that are developed in Appendix A. His criticism of Gambill's methods in "'Radicals' and Economic Policies: The Senate," pp. 191–94, is invalid. The works cited in note 11 introduce the reader to other viewpoints.

TABLE 3–1.

Clustering among Republican senators on southern issues (in percent)

| | King | Wilmot | Wilkinson | Chandler | Wade | Morrill | Sumner | Collamer | Foster | Anthony | Simmons | Fessenden | Cowan |
|---|---|---|---|---|---|---|---|---|---|---|---|---|---|
| King | | | | | | | | | | | | | |
| Wilmot | 97 | | | | | | | | | | | | |
| Wilkinson | 96 | 98 | | | | | | | | | | | |
| Chandler | 94 | 90 | 91 | | | | | | | | | | |
| Wade | 93 | 93 | 96 | 90 | | | | | | | | | |
| Morrill | 89 | 91 | 94 | 88 | 89 | | | | | | | | |
| Sumner | 89 | 86 | 89 | 90 | 81 | 92 | | | | | | | |
| Collamer | 69 | 63 | 66 | 67 | 74 | 78 | 69 | | | | | | |
| Foster | 68 | 62 | 68 | 69 | 71 | 81 | 72 | 95 | | | | | |
| Anthony | 68 | 64 | 65 | 69 | 72 | 74 | 71 | 92 | 91 | | | | |
| Simmons | 55 | 58 | 59 | 55 | 60 | 74 | 61 | 90 | 91 | 93 | | | |
| Fessenden | 68 | 67 | 68 | 67 | 68 | 85 | 74 | 87 | 90 | 86 | 95 | | |
| Cowan | 42 | 36 | 34 | 46 | 39 | 44 | 48 | 69 | 65 | 77 | 71 | 63 | |

The scaling process makes the relationships still clearer (see Appendix A). From our set of 87 roll calls on southern issues there emerged scalograms containing the following number of roll calls: 52, 7, 7, 5, 4, and 3. Most of the smaller scales were quite strongly correlated with the largest one, suggesting that they were variations of a dominant scale (see Table 3-2). But in two of the small scales, radicals stood adjacent to slave-state senators. These scales, in other words, ranged elements from the ends of the dominant scale against its middle portion.[7] Of the 87 roll calls, nine

7. This is not as peculiar a deviation as might appear initially, since such a scale groups extremist elements from the poles of one scale pattern together in another scaling pattern. In the second arrangement, extremist is still associated with extremist, although the individual bases of the voting decisions are quite different. Whereas the more usual scale ranges individuals along a straight line dimension, as in the following diagram (a generalized depiction of column 1 in Table 3-6), the ends-against-the-middle pattern becomes more comprehensible if we consider that, on occasion, a circle would be a more appropriate representation. Thus the ends of the continuum in the diagram would be joined. A voting majority or minority might be made from any segment of the circumference and might include both Republican radicals and the most committed defenders of slavery from the border states.

Voting continuum, southern issues, 37th Congress, 2d session

| Republican party | | Opposition | |
|---|---|---|---|
| | | Free | Slave |
| Radicals | Moderates | state | state |

required for majority

had no strong scaling relation to other votes. When we examine a skeleton representation of the 52-item scale (Table 3-2) we see that the King-Wilmot cluster is indeed placed at one end of the Republican voting spectrum, that Cowan ranks farthest from the radicals, and that beyond him extend the senators from the slave states.

We could assume that the scale shown in Table 3-2 reveals the definitive ordering of senators along a radical-conservative continuum. But in drawing that conclusion we discard the evidence provided by an additional 35 roll calls. We know that the closer legislators are to one pole or the other of a scale, the more extreme their attitudes are in regard to the proposals under consideration. We know also that the 87 roll calls under study all bore upon southern issues. Why not, therefore, develop a measure that reflects the tendency of the senators to take polar positions in all the scales generated from this particular universe of roll calls, thereby using a good deal more of our evidence? Unfortunately we cannot prepare simple mean position scores for each of our senators because Guttman scales are ordinal rather than interval scales. The senator who appears in scale type 4 in a Guttman scale is not therefore necessarily more opposed to slavery than those in scale type 3 *to exactly the same degree* as are those in scale type 6 when compared to those who occupy the scale type 5 position.

As usual in statistics, there is a way out. There is a simple method of standardizing scale positions by relating them to the total number of senators appearing in the scale (see Appendix A). Legislator scores derived from such a standardized scale can be averaged with the scores of other standardized scales, using the number of roll calls in the various

TABLE 3-2.
Dominant scale: southern issues—37 Senate, 2 session*

| Senator | Party-state | Scale type | 1 Y | 2 Y | 3 N | 4 Y | 5 Y | 6† Y | 1 N | 2 N | 3 Y | 4 N | 5 N | 6 N |
|---|---|---|---|---|---|---|---|---|---|---|---|---|---|---|
| Wilmot | R–Penn. | 6 | o | + | + | + | o | + | | | | | | |
| Wade | R–O. | 6 | + | e | + | + | + | + | | | x | | | |
| King | R–N.Y. | 6 | + | + | + | + | + | + | | | | | | |
| Trumbull | R–Ill. | 6 | + | + | + | + | o | + | | | | | | |
| Wilkinson | R–Minn. | 6 | + | + | + | + | + | + | | | | | | |
| Chandler | R–Mich. | 6 | + | + | + | + | + | + | | | | | | |
| Grimes | R–Ia. | 6 | + | + | + | + | o | + | | | | | | |
| Pomeroy | R–Kan. | 6 | + | + | + | o | + | o | | | | | | |
| Harlan | R–Ia. | 6 | o | o | + | + | + | + | | | | | | |
| Lane, J. H. | R–Kan. | 5 | | + | + | + | + | + | − | | | | | |
| Morrill | R–Me. | 5 | | o | + | + | + | + | − | | | | | |

TABLE 3-2.—*continued*

| Senator | Party–state | Scale type | 1 Y | 2 Y | 3 N | 4 Y | 5 Y | 6† Y | 1 N | 2 N | 3 Y | 4 N | 5 N | 6 N |
|---|---|---|---|---|---|---|---|---|---|---|---|---|---|---|
| Sumner | R–Mass. | 5 | + | + | + | + | + | − | | | | | | |
| Wilson, H. | R–Mass. | 5 | + | + | + | + | + | − | | | | | | |
| Hale | R–N.H. | 5 | o | o | + | + | + | − | | | | | | |
| Clark | R–N.H. | 5 | + | + | + | + | + | − | | | | | | |
| Foot | R–Vt. | 4 | | + | + | + | + | − | − | | | | | |
| Harris | R–N.Y. | 4 | | + | + | + | + | o | − | | | | | |
| Howe | R–Wis. | 3 | | | + | + | + | − | − | − | | | | |
| Simmons | R–R.I. | 3 | | | + | + | + | − | − | − | | | | |
| Lane, H. S. | R–Ind. | 3 | | | o | + | o | − | − | − | | | | |
| Fessenden | R–Me. | 3 | | | + | + | + | − | o | − | | | | |
| Ten Eyck | R–N.J. | 3 | | | + | + | + | − | − | − | | | | |
| Foster | R–Conn. | 3 | | | + | + | + | − | − | − | | | | |
| Sherman | R–O. | 3 | | | + | + | + | − | − | − | | | | |
| Collamer | R–Vt. | 3 | | | + | o | + | o | − | − | | | | |
| Doolittle | R–Wis. | 3 | | | + | + | + | − | − | − | | | | |
| Anthony | R–R.I. | 3 | | | + | + | + | − | − | − | | | | |
| Browning | R–Ill. | 2 | | | | + | + | − | − | − | − | | | |
| Cowan | R–Penn. | 2 | | | | + | + | − | o | − | − | | | |
| Henderson | D–Mo. | 2 | | | | + | + | − | − | − | − | | | |
| Wright | NU–Ind. | 2 | | | | + | e | − | − | − | − | | | x |
| Willey | BU–Va. | 1 | | | | | | o | − | − | − | − | − | |
| Stark | D–Ore. | 1 | | | | | | o | − | − | o | o | − | |
| Saulsbury | D–Del. | 1 | | | | | | o | − | − | o | o | − | |
| Carlile | BU–Va. | 0 | | | | | | | − | − | o | − | − | − |
| Wilson, R. | BU–Mo. | 0 | | | | | | | − | − | − | o | − | − |
| Davis | BU–Ky. | 0 | | | | | | | − | o | − | − | − | − |
| Kennedy | BU–Md. | 0 | | | | | | | o | − | o | − | − | − |
| Powell | D–Ky. | 0 | | | | | | | − | − | − | − | − | − |

*+ may be regarded as an antisouthern vote and − as a status quo or prosouthern vote; a combination of e and x represents a nonpattern vote or error; o designates absence. By convention, legislators are not assigned to a particular scale type if their first response is an absence. In the case of this skeleton scale, however, the senators are fixed in position by other votes; an additional 46 roll calls fit into this scale. The coefficient of reproducibility was .99. Missing senators did not vote in half of the divisions shown here.

†Voting Key:
1. King's amendment to the confiscation bill, S.151, inserting, "Persons in the present insurrection levying war against the United States or adhering to their enemies."
2. Sumner's amendment to S.365, providing for immediate emancipation in the state of West Virginia.
3. Sherman's amendment to S.394, to amend the Militia Act, inserting, "who . . . shall owe service or labor to any person who . . . levied war or has borne arms against the United States."
4. Sumner's motion to amend S.351, supplementary to the Act for Emancipation in the District of Columbia, by inserting, "That in all judicial proceedings . . . there shall be no exclusion of any witness on account of color."
5. Final vote on S.394.
6. Final vote on S.351.

scales to weight the contribution of each scale to the whole.[8] We can ignore the nonscaling roll calls because they apparently reflected unique constituency attitudes or the idiosyncracies of individual lawmakers. In this way we have developed a measure of the tendency of the senators to take polar positions in the various scales that they appear in. And, without straining credibility too much, we can in this research describe the resulting rank-order listings as illustrating a radical-moderate-conservative continuum of attitude on southern issues. This does not mean, of course, that the members of any given scale type reached their voting decisions by exactly the same process of reasoning, or that they necessarily interpreted the meaning of their votes in exactly the same way.[9]

Table 3-3 contrasts the Republican rank order derived from all the scales found in our 87 roll calls with the rank order of the dominant scale. Addition of 26 roll calls to the scaling evidence changed the rank order of the dominant scale in only minor respects. The additional roll-call evidence allows us, however, to rank almost all of the senators, including those who were absent in a considerable number of votes. As a result, the Republicans Dixon and Howard appear in the combined scale ranking, as do four additional Democrats or Border Unionists. Harris of New York fell from seventeenth rank in the single scale to twenty-fifth, and the former Democrat, Wright of Indiana, and McDougall and Rice intrude in the second ranking between Browning and Cowan, the two most conservative Republicans. But when only those Republicans who

8. I am indebted to Aage Clausen for assistance and advice on these problems. See his article, "Measurement Identity in the Longitudinal Analysis of Legislative Voting," *American Political Science Review*, 61 (December 1967), 1020-35.

9. Murray G. Murphey has cautioned, "What the model does is to test the scalability of the universe of items and respondents—to test whether or not one-dimensional orderings of the items and respondents can be assumed, given the response patterns. The model itself has nothing to say about the nature of the variables which determine these orderings. They may, of course, be due to attitudes; but they may be due to length of time in office, or to the income of the legislator, or to his wife's age, or to any one of an infinite set of variables, some of which do and some of which do not involve explicit reference to the perceptual-conceptual system of the culture" (*Our Knowledge of the Historical Past* [Indianapolis: Bobbs-Merrill, 1973], p. 189). Certainly these reservations are well taken, but when scaling across large numbers of items places individuals in relatively the same position in relation to others to whom particular attitudes were very widely attributed, such as Sumner or Chandler, we may, I believe, argue with some confidence that we are dealing with attitudinal continua. Those who take a contrary view in fact have the obligation to show why they believe that the age of a senator's wife or his length of service shaped his voting pattern rather than a relatively consistent set of attitudes. There is not, of course, anything in my conception of these matters that rejects the possibility that constituency pressures or cue-giving processes may influence the voting patterns of the individual senator. In some cases, as we shall see, they surely did. And even if the attitudinal aspect of the scales are rejected, they still stand as *real* artifacts of the voting process, demanding explanation by any historian who seeks to explain the legislative activity of the Civil War.

TABLE 3-3.
Dominant scale rank and ranking across all scales

| Dominant scale ranking | Combined scale score rank | Dominant scale ranking | Combined scale score rank |
|---|---|---|---|
| 1 Wilmot | 1 Wilmot | 24 Sherman | 24 Foster |
| 2 Wade | 2 Wade | 25 Collamer | 25 Harris |
| 3 King | 3 King | 26 Doolittle | 26 Anthony |
| 4 Trumbull | 4 Trumbull | 27 Anthony | 27 Sherman |
| 5 Wilkinson | 5 Wilkinson | 28 Browning | 28 Doolittle |
| 6 Chandler | 6 Chandler | 29 Cowan | 29 Collamer |
| 7 Grimes | 7 Grimes | Party Boundary | |
| 8 Pomeroy | 8 Pomeroy | 30 Henderson | 30 Browning |
| 9 Harlan | 9 Lane, J. H. | 31 Wright | 31 Wright* |
| 10 Lane, J. H. | 10 Morrill | 32 Willey | 32 McDougall† |
| 11 Morrill | 11 Sumner | 33 Stark | 33 Rice† |
| 12 Sumner | 12 Harlan | 34 Saulsbury | 34 Cowan |
| 13 Wilson, H. | 13 Howard | 35 Carlile | 35 Nesmith |
| 14 Hale | 14 Wilson, H. | 36 Wilson, R. | 36 Wilson, R. |
| 15 Clark | 15 Hale | 37 Davis | 37 Carlile |
| 16 Foot | 16 Clark | 38 Kennedy | 38 Davis |
| 17 Harris | 17 Foot | 39 Powell | 39 Stark |
| 18 Howe | 18 Dixon | 40 | 40 Henderson |
| 19 Simmons | 19 Howe | 41 | 41 Latham |
| 20 Lane, H. S. | 20 Simmons | 42 | 42 Willey |
| 21 Fessenden | 21 Lane, H. S. | 43 | 43 Saulsbury |
| 22 Ten Eyck | 22 Fessenden | 44 | 44 Powell |
| 23 Foster | 23 Ten Eyck | 45 | 45 Kennedy |

*Northern Unionist
†Northern Democrat

appear in both lists are considered, the value of gamma calculated as a rank-order correlation coefficient shows correlation between the two rankings of 1. Despite this fact, the knowledge that all relevant scaling roll calls underlie the cross-scale average scores is comforting, and this technique is used, therefore, in constructing comparable legislator rankings for subsequent sessions of Congress.

We can now suggest that Wilkinson of Minnesota was more radical than Foot of Vermont and that the latter was less moderate than Harris of New York, and this is of consequence. It is important also to realize that Republicans were not merely radicals *or* moderates but that senatorial positions on the legislative issues of the war extended across a range of policy options. Division into two groups is useful, however, for research purposes and the matrix of pair agreements on southern and racial issues of the long session of the Thirty-seventh Senate was, therefore, examined for evidence of a structural break where the radical-conservative continuum might be divided. Such a clue allowed a division into a group of seventeen Republican radicals and another group of fourteen nonradicals in the long session of the Thirty-seventh Senate. The agreement of individual senators with the anchor lawmakers in the upper-left-hand corner of the matrix, King and Wilmot, dropped away by one or two percentage points through about one half of the Republican group. But when Henry S. Lane was reached, his agreement scores with the preceding senator were 7 and 9 percentage points below that senator's agreements with King and Wilmot. A gradual rate of decline resumed below. Since literary materials also suggested that the Indiana senator was a moderate, he was assumed to be the marginal nonradical. But absences may distort the result in percentage agreement scoring. Due to his recruiting activities, Dixon missed various votes in which the differences between radicals and moderates were pronounced. The agreement matrix showed him to be in stronger agreement with known radicals than the biographical evidence would have led one to expect. The scales, however, revealed his affinity with moderate colleagues, and he was classified as one. In the scale score summary the cutting point lay between Foot and Dixon, and the members of each group agreed more strongly on the average with members of their group than with senators assigned to the other.

Dividing the Republicans into radicals and moderates by using the scales and cluster blocs found in the original selection of 87 roll calls on slavery and confiscation allows computation of an index of disagreement for each of the 368 roll calls under study. In all there were 58 roll calls in which the disagreement ranged between 40 and 100, or 16 percent of the total of 368 votes. The proportion was much greater among roll calls on southern issues and racial matters, but traces of the pattern were visible in many other roll calls as well. These 58 roll calls highlight the areas of major conflict between moderate and radical Republicans in the Senate during the second session. Although I was initially uncertain that

TABLE 3-4.

Republican radicals and moderates, 37th Senate, 2 session

| Radicals | | Moderates | |
|---|---|---|---|
| Chandler (Mich.) | Morrill (Me.) | Anthony (R.I.) | Foster (Conn.) |
| Clark (N.H.) | Pomeroy (Kan.) | Browning (Ill.) | Harris (N.Y.) |
| Foot (Vt.) | Sumner (Mass.) | Collamer (Vt.) | Howe (Wis.) |
| Grimes (Ia.) | Trumbull (Ill.) | Cowan (Penn.) | H. S. Lane (Ind.) |
| Hale (N.H.) | Wade (O.) | Dixon (Conn.) | Sherman (O.) |
| Harlan (Ia.) | Wilkinson (Minn.) | Doolittle (Wis.) | Simmons (R.I.) |
| Howard (Mich.) | Wilmot (Penn.) | Fessenden (Me.) | Ten Eyck (N.J.) |
| King (N.Y.) | Wilson (Mass.) | | |
| J. H. Lane (Kan.) | | | |

this method of selection was best, later experimentation showed that analysis of the Republican cohesion indices or the use of groups of legislators, constructed by merely breaking the Republican scaling rank order in two, would have produced much the same grouping of roll calls (see Appendix B).

The disagreement indices provide us with some evidence of the duration as well as the intensity of disagreement during the session. Three votes revealed substantial disagreement between radicals and moderates during January, 1862, but 36 occurred during the last six weeks of the session.[10] This is perhaps not surprising, since many legislative measures were in the final stages of perfection during that time. However, every vote in which the index rose to 85 or better occurred in July. Party harmony was obviously in serious jeopardy as the session closed. Although it is tempting to emphasize the confiscation issue and the emancipation of slaves in the District of Columbia in discussing the achievements of Congress during this session, the sharpest disagreement between radicals and moderates did not develop in the roll calls on these measures, but rather when the senators voted on the emancipation clauses of the bills to amend the act calling forth the militia and on Sumner's amendment to provide unlimited emancipation in the new state of West Virginia. On these issues the maximum disagreement provided indices of 100 and 85 respectively. Sumner far surpassed any of his colleagues by offering eleven (19 percent) divisive motions, and the mean disagreement score calculated from the resulting roll calls was 73 in comparison to the overall mean, 58. The senator from Massachusetts was apparently a particular catalyst of radical-moderate disagreement.

We have seen that there were 47 votes that divided Republicans perceptibly on sectional lines and 58 that produced relatively strong disagreement between radicals and nonradicals. Ten votes appear in both categories. Five of those votes are found in the debates on confiscation, of which four related to the effort to substitute the bill drafted by the Select Committee on Confiscation for a House bill (H.R. 471) and the fifth occurred when Sumner endeavored to terminate the debate at one point so that the senators could move into executive session. Sumner provoked another such vote when he moved that his colleagues consider the resolution to expel Senator Stark. Others occurred on motions to approve an explanatory resolution clarifying the status of tea, coffee, and sugar in bond at the time the duties on these commodities were raised by an act of December 24, 1861, and when Powell of Kentucky

10. By months, the number of roll calls reflecting major disagreement between radicals and moderates and the mean levels of disagreement were as follows: January: 3, 47; February: 4, 63; March: 3, 51; April: 7, 47; May: 5, 46; June: 19, 57; July 1–17: 17, 70.

tried to have the senators reject the report of the committee of conference recommending appropriations for the payment of bounty to army volunteers (H.R. 413). Finally Senator Grimes introduced motions concerning restrictions on the rates of the Washington Gas Light Company and relating to adjournment that aligned senators on both an East versus West and radical versus nonradical lines. Most obviously these facts suggest that there was some sectional coloration to the debates on confiscation. The implications of this overlapping will be discussed in the following chapter.

Having examined some of the dimensions of geographical bloc and party faction, we can consider the question whether historians are justified in emphasizing the internecine conflicts of the Republicans or whether they should stress the importance of party and the basic agreement among Republicans.[11] We have seen that eastern and western Republicans differed substantially in 47 roll calls and that radical Republicans similarly opposed moderate Republicans in 58 votes, with some overlap in the categories. Disagreement at a comparable level between Democrats and Republicans occurred in 161 roll calls. In these crude terms, party was indeed more important than factionalism.

We cannot leave the matter here, however. Howard W. Allen and Jerome M. Clubb calculated the number of party votes (party majority ranged against party majority) in the 1187 roll calls of the Senate during the Sixty-first, Sixty-second and Sixty-third Congresses, 1909–1915, when the winds of progressivism were blowing strongly. They found that some 70 percent of the total were party votes. In the second session of the Thirty-seventh Senate the percentage of party votes in the selection of 87 roll calls on slavery and confiscation issues was 75, but this figure drops to 49 percent when all 368 roll calls are considered. Rela-

11. The last generation of Civil War historiography reflects some tendency to downplay the divisiveness of Republican factionalism and to emphasize the common bonds of party. See for example, David Donald, "Devils Facing Zionwards," in Grady McWhiney, ed., *Grant, Lee, Lincoln and the Radicals: Essays on Civil War Leadership* (Evanston: Northwestern University Press, 1964), pp. 72–91; Eric L. McKitrick, "Party Politics and the Union and Confederate War Efforts," in William N. Chambers and Walter D. Burnham, eds., *The American Party Systems: Stages of Political Development* (New York: Oxford University Press, 1967), pp. 117–151; Hans L. Trefousse, *The Radical Republicans: Lincoln's Vanguard for Racial Justice* (New York: Knopf, 1969). But T. Harry Williams, whose *Lincoln and the Radicals* (Madison: University of Wisconsin Press, 1941) is a classic statement of the theme, continued to feel that intraparty conflict was a valid and useful focus. See "Lincoln and the Radicals: An Essay in Civil War History and Historiography," in McWhiney, *Grant, Lee, Lincoln and the Radicals,* pp. 92–117. Williams presented a condensed version of his argument in a new introduction, appearing in the second paperback edition of *Lincoln and the Radicals* (Madison, 1965). See Herman Belz, *Emancipation and Equal Rights: Politics and Constitutionalism in the Civil War Era* (New York: Norton, 1978), for a recent suggestion that disagreement among the Republicans in Congress was relatively unimportant during the Civil War.

TABLE 3-5.
Republican voting cohesion in the Senate*

| Congress | Session | Dates | Cohesion |
|----------|---------|-------|----------|
| Thirty-seventh | 1 | July–August 1861 | 62 |
| Thirty-seventh | 2 | December 1861–July 1862 | 50 |
| Thirty-eighth | 1 | December 1863–July 1864 | 46 |
| Thirty-ninth | 1 | December 1865–July 1866 | 45 |

*All roll calls in each session are used here. In the preparation of this table, cohesion data provided by the Inter-University Consortium for Political and Social Research were used.

tively speaking, party was apparently less significant in the voting of this session than in the Progressive era. On the other hand, "party votes," as a percentage of all Senate votes, represented only 45 percent on the average during the Eighty-fourth through the Eighty-eighth Congresses, 1955–1964.[12]

Over all, mean Republican cohesion in voting in the Senate fell in the major legislative sessions from 1861 through 1866 as Table 3-5 shows. Realignment theory suggests that party cohesion should diminish as the time elapsed since the previous realignment increases, but actually the mean Republican party cohesion in the Senate during the long sessions of the Thirty-seventh and Thirty-eighth Congresses was substantially lower than that found in the congresses between 1869 and 1905. Only three of the eighteen congresses of the latter era reveal lower levels of cohesion among the Republicans than did the assemblies of the Civil War years. The mean cohesion, 1869–1905, was 64.8.[13] Within this perspective, Republican solidarity was relatively low during the war years. Some may argue that party realignment was still under way during the years of the Civil War, as attested by the presence of unaligned Unionists in the Congress. This contention is correct in a sense, but Unionist votes were not used in the tabulation of party votes in Republican cohesion indices. Those who emphasize the unity of Republican lawmakers during the Civil War fly in the face of much evidence to the contrary.

The relative cohesion of the Democrats and the Republicans has

12. Jerome M. Clubb and Howard M. Allen, "Party Loyalty in the United States Senate in the Taft and Wilson Years" (mimeographed, Inter-University Consortium for Political [and Social] Research: Ann Arbor). See particularly pp. 7, 9 and n. 8, p. 28.

13. Jerome M. Clubb and Santa A. Traugott, "Partisan Cleavage and Cohesion in the House of Representatives, 1861–1974," *Journal of Interdisciplinary History*, 7 (Winter 1977), 375–401; William G. Shade et al., "Partisanship in the United States Senate: 1869–1901," ibid., 4 (Autumn 1973), 185–205.

some bearing on the significance of party among the Republicans. Leonard Curry has argued that the Democrats were more cohesive during the Thirty-seventh Congress than were the Republicans.[14] The voting analysis of the second-session Senate supports his conclusion. The mean Democratic cohesion in the original selection of slavery and confiscation votes was 69 and that of the Republicans was 63. In 86 divisions on the major national economic legislation of this session, Democratic cohesion was 66 and that of the Republicans was 38. We have to discount this finding somewhat, however, because the Democratic group was small and absenteeism among its members was much more marked than among the Republicans, even after adjustment is made for the illness of several Democratic senators.

To divide the roll calls of this session into those that show sectionalism, those that illustrate the conflict between radical and moderate Republican, and those that illustrate party differences is to disregard a considerable number of votes. There were 132 roll calls in the long session of the Thirty-seventh Senate on a variety of issues in which Republican cohesion was 60 or below and in which the likeness indices of East against West and of radical versus moderate were quite high. In these divisions, apparently, the idiosyncracies of the individual constituency or senator were asserted or subregional voting patterns became important. Although it is possible to build some scales from these roll calls, the scalograms include a relatively small number of votes, and it is difficult to suggest underlying continua of attitude.

We have examined a cross section of data. It is now time to consider Republican radicalism across a more extended period of time. Table 3-6 displays scale summary scores for the third session of the Thirty-seventh Congress and for the first and second sessions of the Thirty-eighth Congress, based upon the same methods used in analyzing the second session of the Thirty-seventh Congress. Edward Gambill kindly provided his scales based on votes in the first session of the Thirty-ninth Congress, and the column in Table 3-6 ranking the senators of that body is based upon the scales which he believed to reflect the radical-moderate dimension in that Congress as derived from the votes on political reconstruction.[15] We have, therefore, scales and scale summaries derived from the voting of five sessions of Congress available for consideration.

The data underlying the various columns vary somewhat in quality. The second Thirty-seventh, the first Thirty-eighth, and the first Thirty-

14. Leonard P. Curry, "Congressional Democrats: 1861–1863," *Civil War History,* 12 (September 1966), 220–21. See also Jean H. Baker, "A Loyal Opposition: Northern Democrats in the Thirty-Seventh Congress," *Civil War History,* 25 (June 1979), 139–55.

15. Gambill, "Who Were the Senate Radicals?" pp. 237–44.

ninth were long sessions, while the other two were three-month sessions. Customarily, much more emphasis was placed upon budgeting than upon general issues in the short sessions. If radicalism is a complex phenomenon, involving many issues or even, perhaps, a whole set of closely related attitudes, the opportunity for all these attitudes to become obvious was clearly greater in the long general sessions. Similarly, our confidence in the results should be strengthened in proportion to the number of roll calls underlying the columns; by this criterion the findings of columns 1, 2, and 3 deserve most credence and that of column 4, representing only 32 votes, the least. We must remember also that a few places either up or down in a particular summary index may reflect relatively minor differences in voting behavior. Because of absences, the scale positions of some legislators may not be a complete reflection of their legislative positions, since a senator's absences above the conventional limit of 50 percent attendance were disregarded in constructing the basic scales. We can make too much of the distorting influence of absences, but they should not be ignored. In the case of certain legislators, also, absences from particular votes may have reflected a considered position rather than lack of interest, illness, or the pressure of other duties.

As noted, historians have traditionally considered Wade, Sumner, and Chandler to have been the radicals most worthy of note. Our confidence in the rankings is considerably bolstered by discovering that these three ranked high in all the listings. If, on the basis of Senate debate, any two Republicans could have been considered the special *bêtes noires* of the radicals during the second session of the Thirty-seventh Congress, they would surely have been Browning of Illinois and Cowan of Pennsylvania. They were the Republicans who ranked lowest in the summary ranking of that session, separated by Wright of Indiana, a former Democrat who had specifically abjured party for the duration of the war, and the "War Democrats" McDougall and Rice. Cowan ranked lowest of all Republicans in three of the four remaining lists as well, being exceeded in his conservatism during the second session of the Thirty-eighth Senate only by the conservative Republican from New Jersey, Ten Eyck. Stewart of Nevada, who entered the Senate during this session, categorized Cowan in his gossipy and perhaps somewhat malicious autobiography as a Democrat at that time.[16] Five rankings, all of which present either Sumner or Wade as one of the leading radical figures and end the roll of Republicans with either Cowan or Ten Eyck, may reasonably be accepted as having at least appropriate termini. On the other

16. George R. Brown, ed., *Reminiscences of Senator William M. Stewart of Nevada* (New York: Neale Publishing, 1908), p. 202.

TABLE 3-6.

The radical-moderate-conservative continuum in the Senate through five sessions, 1861–66*

| | 2-37 | 2-37 Party-State | 3-37 | 3-37 Party-State | 1-38 | 1-38 Party-State | 2-38 | 2-38 Party-State | 1-39 | 1-39 Party-State |
|---|---|---|---|---|---|---|---|---|---|---|
| 1. | Wilmot | R-Penn. | Sumner | | Lane, J. H. | | Stewart | R-Nev. | Wade | |
| 2. | Wade | R-O. | Wade | | Sumner | | Howard | (T)† | Sumner | |
| 3. | King | R-N.Y. | Wilson, H. | | Morgan | R-N.Y. | Sumner | (T) | Morrill | |
| 4. | Trumbull | R-Ill. | Fessenden | | Wilkinson | | Brown | (T) | Wilson | |
| 5. | Wilkinson | R-Minn. | Chandler | | Pomeroy | | Wilson | (T) | Yates | R-Ill. |
| 6. | Chandler | R-Mich. | Wilkinson | | Clark | | Wade | | Chandler | |
| 7. | Grimes | R-Ia. | Morrill | | Anthony | | Conness | | Fessenden | |
| 8. | Pomeroy | R-Kan. | Pomeroy | | Wilson, H. | | Nye | R-Nev. | Anthony | |
| 9. | Lane, J. H. | R-Kan. | Collamer | | Wade | | Hale | | Pomeroy | |
| 10. | Morrill | R-Me. | Clark | | Howard | | Chandler | | Howe | |
| 11. | Sumner | R-Mass. | Howard | | Ramsey | R-Minn. | Grimes | | Sprague | |
| 12. | Harlan | R-Ia. | King | | Chandler | | Clark | | Howard | |
| 13. | Howard | R-Mich. | Foot | | Conness | R-Cal. | Collamer | | Creswell | R-Md. |
| 14. | Wilson, H. | R-Mass. | Foster | | Dixon | | Anthony | | Trumbull | |
| 15. | Hale | R-N.H. | Lane, J. H. | | Morrill | | Morgan | | Ramsey | R-N.H. |
| 16. | Clark | R-N.H. | Doolittle | | Hale | | Morrill | | Cragin | R-Ia. |
| 17. | Foot | R-Vt. | Harlan | | Sprague | R-R.I. | Foster | | Kirkwood | |
| 18. | Dixon | R-Conn. | Wilmot | | Foot | | Wright | D-N.J. | Conness | |
| 19. | Howe | R-Wis. | Grimes | | Harlan | | Sherman | | Foster | |
| 20. | Simmons | R-R.I. | Trumbull | | Fessenden | | Sprague | | Grimes | |
| 21. | Lane, H. S. | R-Ind. | Dixon | | Sherman | | Foot | | Lane, H. S. | |
| 22. | Fessenden | R-Me. | Sherman | | Harris | R-Mo. | Ramsey | (T) | Edmunds | R-Vt. (T) |
| 23. | Ten Eyck | R-N.J. | Ten Eyck | | Brown | | Harlan | (T) | Harris | (T) |
| 24. | Foster | R-Conn. | Anthony | | Howe | | Lane, J. H. | | Poland | R-Vt. (T) |

| No. | | | | | |
|---|---|---|---|---|---|
| 25. | Harris (R-N.Y.) | Arnold (R-R.I.) | Foster | Farwell (R-Me.) | Brown (R-Ore.) |
| 26. | Anthony (R-R.I.) | Lane, H. S. | Grimes | Pomeroy | Nye |
| 27. | Sherman (R-O.) | Howe | Collamer | Dixon | Stewart |
| 28. | Doolittle (R-Wis.) | Harris | Ten Eyck | Trumbull | Clark |
| 29. | Collamer (R-Vt.) | Cowan | Lane, H. S. (T) | Lane, H. S. (T) | Williams (T) |
| 30. | Browning (R-Ill.) | Hicks | Trumbull (T) | Buckalew (T) | Henderson (T) |
| 31. | Wright (NU-Ind.) | Rice (BU-Md.) | Doolittle | Davis (T) | Morgan |
| 32. | McDougall (D-Cal.) | Willey | Van Winkle (BU-W. Va.) | Powell | Sherman |
| 33. | Rice (D-Minn.) | Henderson (D-Ore.) | Willey | Johnson | Van Winkle |
| 34. | Cowan (R-Penn.) | Harding | Henderson | Henderson | Lane, J. H. (R-Minn.) |
| 35. | Nesmith (D-Ore.) | Nesmith | Harding (D-Md.) | Hendricks | Willey |
| 36. | Wilson, R. (D-Mo.) | Turpie (D-Ind.) | Johnson | Howe | Dixon |
| 37. | Carlile (BU-Va.) | Richardson (D-Ill.) | Cowan | Harris | Doolittle |
| 38. | Davis (BU-Ky.) | Latham | McDougall | Van Winkle | Norton (T) |
| 39. | Stark (D-Ore.) | Davis | Nesmith | Willey | McDougall |
| 40. | Henderson (D-Mo.) | Wilson, R. | Carlile | Doolittle | Hendricks |
| 41. | Latham (D-Cal.) | Saulsbury | Saulsbury (T) | Nesmith | Johnson |
| 42. | Willey (BU-Va.) | Carlile | Buckalew (D-Pa. (T)) | Cowan (T) | Patterson (D-Tenn. (T)) |
| 43. | Saulsbury (D-Del.) | Powell | Riddle (D-Del.) | Richardson (T) | Buckalew |
| 44. | Powell (D-Ky.) | Wall (D-N.J.) | Richardson | Saulsbury | Guthrie (D-Ky.) |
| 45. | Kennedy (BU-Md.) | | Powell (T) | Ten Eyck | Nesmith |
| 46. | | | Davis (T) | | Davis |
| 47. | | | Hendricks (D-Ind.) | | Cowan |
| 48. | | | | | Riddle |
| 49. | | | | | Saulsbury |
| 50. | | | | | Stockton (D-N.J.) |

*Senators who failed to appear in at least one-half of the scales are excluded.

†T designates tie.

hand, Sumner occupies the eleventh place in the ranking of the Thirty-seventh Congress, second session, and Wade appeared in the ninth place in one list. Obviously these men did not agree completely in their voting. If we widen our focus to include senators who did not serve in all five sessions, we discover a remarkable illustration of consistency in Wilkinson who appeared in the fifth, sixth, and fourth spots in the rankings of the Thirty-seventh second, Thirty-seventh third, and Thirty-eighth first sessions. But this committed radical did not record enough votes during the second session of the latter Congress to place him in the scales, and he ended his senatorial service in March, 1865.

When we look for the influence of party in the summary rankings of the scales of the five sessions, we discover that the Republicans invariably occupy one end and the middle of the rankings and that the Democrats and Border Unionists, somewhat fewer in numbers, appear at the opposite end. Not until the second session of the Thirty-eighth Congress was there any considerable mixing at the margin in the lists where Republicans gave way to the opposition. The statistical relationship between successive scale-score rankings among the Republicans and within the chamber is shown in Table 3-7. The correlations between successive rankings of Republicans ranged from .54 to .61, showing that there was indeed a continuing voting structure among the Republicans. However, as the lack of mixing in most of the lists illustrates, that structure was less strong than the ordering provided by party. When the correlation between the legislator rankings in the second and third sessions of the

TABLE 3-7.
Scale-summary correlations: 1861–66*

| | 3–37 | 1–38 | 2–38 | 1–39 |
|---|---|---|---|---|
| 2–37 | .54 / .82 | Republican senators | | |
| 3–37 | | .61 / .87 | | |
| 1–38 | All senators | | .57 / .71 | |
| 2–38 | | | | .59 / .70 |

*The coefficient is Pearson's r and was calculated from the standardized scale-summary rankings. The values of the Republican coefficients are somewhat stronger than those presented in "The Radical Voting Dimension in the U.S. Senate during the Civil War," *Journal of Interdisciplinary History*, 3 (Winter 1973), 461, where a different statistic was used.

Thirty-seventh Congress is recalculated to include the members of the opposition, the coefficient rises from .54 to .82.

To what extent may turnover of personnel have affected the correlations? Is it possible that the appearance of new senators could have changed the rank order, even though the holdovers clung stubbornly to their principles and prejudices? More than 40 percent of the Senate of the second session of the Thirty-seventh Congress had disappeared from the chamber when the chaplain's prayer opened the first session of the Thirty-ninth Senate. But, although the change is impressive in cumulative terms, it was much less so when we consider Republican carryover session by session. Twenty-eight of the thirty-one Republicans of the Thirty-seventh second session appear in the scales of the third session, and illness rather than replacement explains Hale's absence from the scales of the third. Republican carryover in the sessions thereafter was 26, 30, and 27. In no instance, therefore, were the incumbent Republican senators confronted by a large contingent of mavericks, or of a new breed of Republicans whose voting behavior immediately changed the overall pattern of Republican response to the issues of the time. Given the relative numbers involved, there appears to have been ample opportunity for new Republican senators to reinforce their convictions with kindred spirits of either radical or moderate persuasion, or to succumb to socialization at the hands of the Republican veterans. New Republican senators were not narrowly concentrated in the scale-summary lists, but none was highly conservative.

When we look behind the correlation coefficients, we find personal continuities, but we also find evidence of voting behavior that should cause us to treat with some skepticism analyses that seem to freeze the Republicans into dichotomous groups. There was no great variation in the numbers of senators represented in the various scale-summation indices—the forty-four senators listed for the Thirty-seventh third comprised the smallest number and the fifty of the Thirty-ninth first stood as the largest. We do not do great violence to the data, therefore, if we consider a ranking in one scale summary list to be roughly equivalent to a ranking in another. Table 3-8 presents the records of fourteen senators across five sessions chosen to illustrate the various patterns of voting behavior.

Wade and Sumner, we see, stood high in all rankings and had small deviation scores; Fessenden and Trumbull illustrate a very different pattern of behavior. Fessenden voted a moderate position during the second session of the Thirty-seventh, rose to fourth in the rankings of the next session, although absences may have affected his ranking, returned to the twentieth position during the long session of the Thirty-eighth Senate, missed the short session while serving as Secretary of the

TABLE 3–8.

Rank-order polarity scores of selected senators, 37th, 38th, and 39th Congresses, 1861–66

| | 1 | 2 | 3 | 4 | 5 | 6 Mean (Cols. 1–5) | 7 Standard Deviation |
|---|---|---|---|---|---|---|---|
| | 2–37 | 3–27 | 1–38 | 2–38 | 1–39 | | |
| 1. Sumner | 11 | 1 | 2 | 2* | 2 | 3.6 | 3.72 |
| 2. Wade | 2 | 2 | 9 | 6 | 1 | 4 | 3.03 |
| 3. Wilson, H. | 14 | 3 | 8 | 2* | 4 | 6.2 | 4.40 |
| 4. Chandler | 6 | 5† | 12 | 10† | 6 | 7.8 | 2.71 |
| 5. Fessenden | 22 | 4† | 20 | ** | 7† | 13.25 | 7.85 |
| 6. Anthony | 26† | 24 | 7 | 14† | 8 | 15.8 | 7.91 |
| 7. Trumbull | 4 | 20 | 29* | 28 | 14 | 19 | 9.29 |
| 8. Lane, H. S. | 21 | 26 | 29* | 29 | 21 | 25.2 | 3.60 |
| 9. Sherman | 27 | 22 | 21 | 19† | 32 | 24.2 | 4.71 |
| 10. Harris | 25 | 28 | 22 | 37 | 23† | 27 | 5.40 |
| 11. Cowan | 34 | 29 | 37 | 42 | 47† | 37.8 | 6.24 |
| 12. Nesmith | 35† | 35† | 39† | 41 | 45 | 39 | 3.79 |
| 13. Davis | 38 | 39 | 45* | 30 | 46 | 39.6 | 5.75 |
| 14. Saulsbury | 43† | 41 | 41* | 43† | 49† | 43.4 | 2.94 |

*Tie
†Absent from one or more underlying scales
**Serving in Cabinet

Treasury, and stood seventh in the rankings of the long session of the Thirty-ninth Senate. In this latter session he again failed to appear in all scales because of absences. Voting a highly radical position during the second session of the Thirty-seventh Congress, Trumbull appeared in the twentieth, twenty-ninth, and twenty-eighth places in the next three sessions, and then rose to fourteenth place during the Thirty-ninth first. The standard deviations of the scores of Fessenden and Trumbull were 7.85 and 9.29, among the largest of such Republican scores. Although not included in Table 3-8, Grimes of Iowa compiled a voting record that was somewhat similar to Trumbull's. These men were among the six most variable of the senators who served in four or more of our sessions. It is notable that Grimes, Fessenden, and Trumbull were all members of the group of seven "renegade" Republicans who voted against the impeachment of Johnson, and the only three of the seven who served in the Senate as Republicans throughout the time span 1861–66. A fourth renegade, Henderson of Missouri, served in the Thirty-seventh Senate and thereafter, but was initially considered to be a War Democrat. To some degree, perhaps, the earlier voting of Fessenden, Grimes, and Trumbull forecast their behavior at the time of the impeachment.

    Lane of Indiana, Harris, and Sherman were more consistently moderate in their voting behavior, appearing almost invariably below the twentieth place in the rankings. Senator Anthony's voting scores provide another pattern. During the Thirty-seventh Congress he voted well to the moderate side of the Republicans, but thereafter his scores place him close to or among acknowledged radicals. Cowan's record suggests that he was a conservative Republican who became ever more conservative. The remaining senators shown in Table 3-8 were a Democrat from the Pacific Northwest, Nesmith, a Kentucky Unionist and former Whig, Garrett Davis, and a slave-state Democrat, Willard Saulsbury.

The voting behavior of individual senators in relation to that of their colleagues becomes somewhat clearer if we record our findings on graphs. A distinction in legislative behavior between radicals and moderates first became clear in the roll calls of the second session of the Thirty-seventh Congress. Focusing our attention upon the Republicans of that session, we discover that Wade, King, Wilkinson, Chandler, Morrill, Sumner, Howard, Henry Wilson, and Hale never appeared

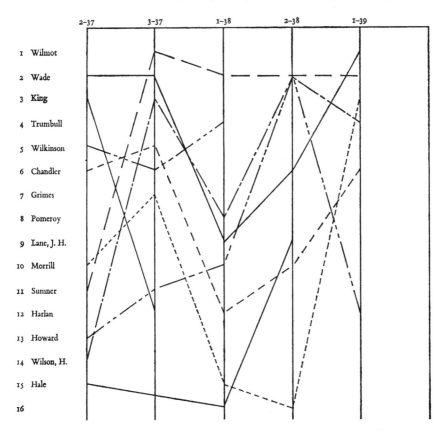

FIGURE 3-1. Consistently radical Republican voting patterns, 1861–66

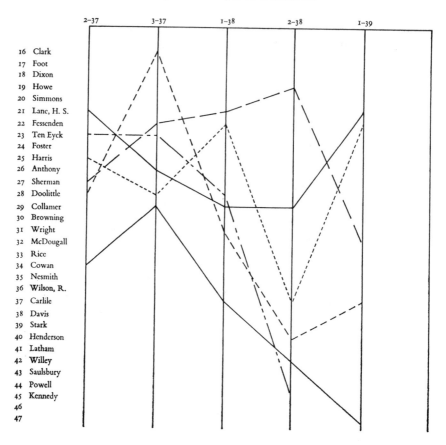

FIGURE 3-2. Consistently moderate Republican voting patterns, 1861–66

below the sixteenth place in the scale summaries of the various sessions in which they served (see Figure 3-1). In other words, our numbers show them invariably among the most radical half of the Republicans. If one is seeking the radical nucleus within the Republican party, these men must be considered the major part of it. Other Republican senators of this session never appeared above the sixteenth rank in the scale summaries in this or in succeeding sessions. These men—H. S. Lane, Ten Eyck, Harris, Sherman, Doolittle, and Cowan—maintained a continuing moderate position within the Republican party (see Figure 3-2). The scale summaries of three other senators, Harlan, Foot, and Foster, show them to have been centrists, their positions falling on either side of the midpoint of the party rankings, although Harlan dropped steadily in the listings (see Figure 3-3). Still other Republicans—the most numerous group—were more variable in their behavior as reflected in the ranking summaries (see Figure 3-4). On one or more occasions, each appeared relatively high in the most radical part of the Republican scale summaries but was either first located or later dropped into the more moderate half. Of these men—Wilmot, Trumbull, Grimes, Pomeroy, J. H. Lane, Clark, Dixon, Howe, Fessenden, Anthony, and Collamer—Anthony clearly became more radical over time, as suggested above. Trumbull, only three places removed from the radical pole in the second session of the Thirty-seventh Congress, ranked twenty-ninth in the Thirty-eighth first but rose to fourteenth in the Thirty-ninth first. Clark, however, appears in the sixteenth place in the Thirty-seventh second, sixth in the Thirty-eighth first, and twentieth in the Thirty-ninth first.

If anyone doubts the persistence of party lines in the Senate during the Civil War, Figure 3-5 should disabuse them. The opposition, Democrats and former Whigs of the border states, also showed considerable variation in behavior, but movement within the group was confined almost solely to the lower part of the scale summaries. Figure 3-6 depicts the behavior of the senators who entered the chamber after the close of

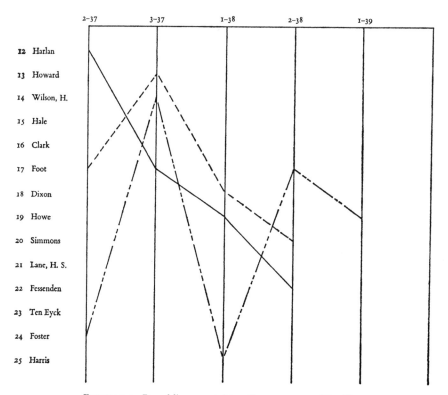

FIGURE 3-3. Republican centrist voting patterns, 1861–66

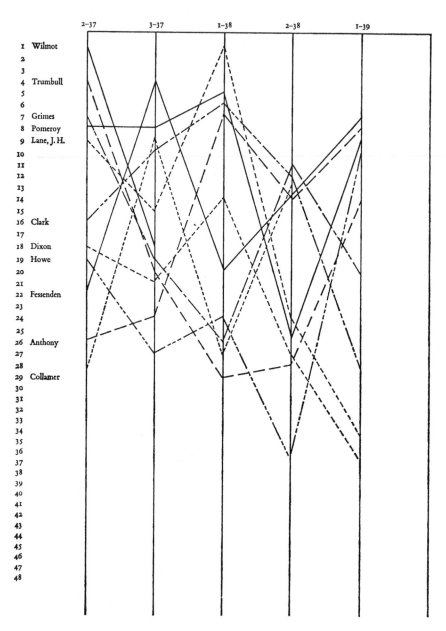

FIGURE 3-4. Unaligned Republican voting patterns, 1861–66

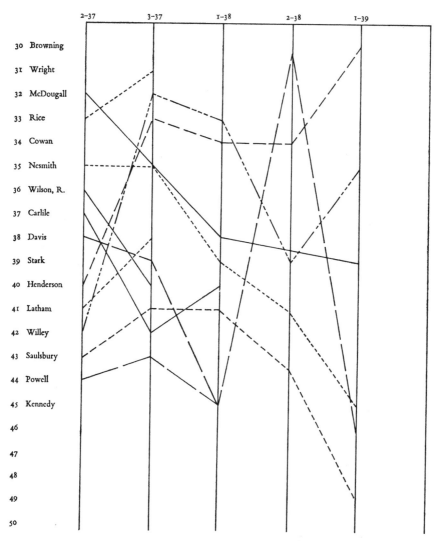

FIGURE 3-5. Voting patterns of the opposition, 1861-66

the Thirty-seventh second and served for more than one term. Of the northern Republicans involved, none fit the pattern of continuing radicalism illustrated in Figure 3-1, although Conness very nearly did. If we consider Conness to be a centrist, there were three of that type among the newcomers. The remaining Republicans who entered the Senate during the later sessions displayed the erratic or variable pattern of Figure 3-4.

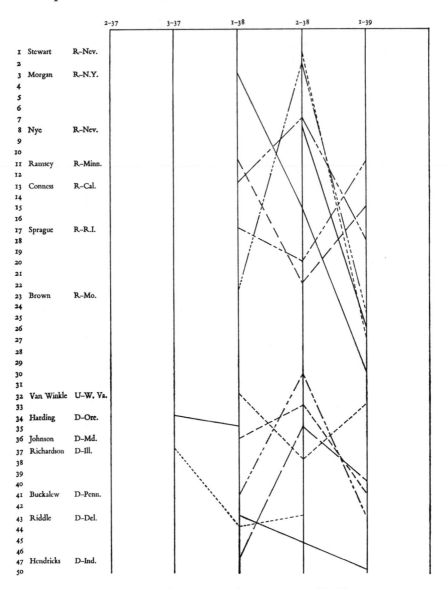

FIGURE 3-6. Voting patterns of new senators, 1862–66

Table 3-5 showed that voting cohesion among the Republican senators was somewhat lower during the first session of the Thirty-eighth Congress than it had been during the long session of the preceding Congress. Did the differences between confirmed radicals and habitual moderates increase or narrow between 1862 and 1864? Scales are not very useful in providing an answer to such a question, but comparison of the levels of agreement between pairs of senators during the second session of the Thirty-seventh Congress and the first session of the Thirty-eighth is instructive.

The various subtables of Tables 3-9 and 3-10 summarize the voting behavior of four senators who were consistently in the more radical half of the Republican voting spectrum during the Civil War and four who were almost always to be found among the moderates when voting behavior is generalized over any substantial number of roll calls. The sets of roll calls underlying the tables are the initial selection of 87 rolls relating to southern issues in the second session of the Thirty-seventh Congress and a similar selection of 82 votes in the first session of the Thirty-eighth plus the roll-call sets in those sessions which reflected substantial disagreement within the party along the radical-moderate continuum. The percentages within the triangles are the means of the agreements between all radical or moderate pairs.

Tables 3-9 and 3-10 suggest that the attitudinal distance between these two small groups remained much the same in the two sessions, despite the progression of time and an obvious change in the character of war-

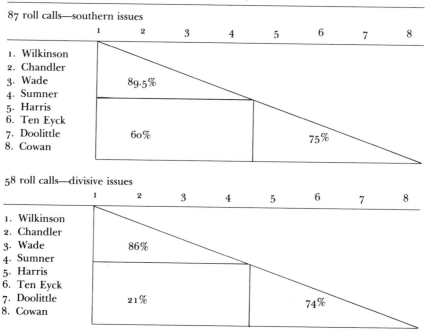

TABLE 3-9.
Radical-moderate agreements: Thirty-seventh Senate, 2 sess.

87 roll calls—southern issues

|     | 1 | 2 | 3 | 4 | 5 | 6 | 7 | 8 |
|-----|---|---|---|---|---|---|---|---|
| 1. Wilkinson |
| 2. Chandler |
| 3. Wade |
| 4. Sumner |
| 5. Harris |
| 6. Ten Eyck |
| 7. Doolittle |
| 8. Cowan |

89.5%

60%

75%

58 roll calls—divisive issues

|     | 1 | 2 | 3 | 4 | 5 | 6 | 7 | 8 |
|-----|---|---|---|---|---|---|---|---|
| 1. Wilkinson |
| 2. Chandler |
| 3. Wade |
| 4. Sumner |
| 5. Harris |
| 6. Ten Eyck |
| 7. Doolittle |
| 8. Cowan |

86%

21%

74%

TABLE 3–10.

Radical-moderate agreements: Thirty-eighth Senate, 1 sess.

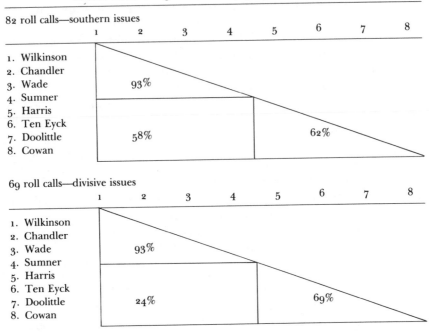

82 roll calls—southern issues

| | 1 | 2 | 3 | 4 | 5 | 6 | 7 | 8 |
|---|---|---|---|---|---|---|---|---|

1. Wilkinson
2. Chandler
3. Wade          93%
4. Sumner
5. Harris
6. Ten Eyck
7. Doolittle     58%                        62%
8. Cowan

69 roll calls—divisive issues

| | 1 | 2 | 3 | 4 | 5 | 6 | 7 | 8 |
|---|---|---|---|---|---|---|---|---|

1. Wilkinson
2. Chandler
3. Wade          93%
4. Sumner
5. Harris
6. Ten Eyck
7. Doolittle     24%                        69%
8. Cowan

time issues. But the solidarity of the radicals apparently also increased somewhat and that of the moderates declined. On southern issues generally, the moderates agreed with each other during 1862 quite substantially more than they did with the radicals, although their cohesion was considerably less than that displayed by those in the other wing of the party. During 1864 the moderates were only a few percentage points more united among themselves on southern issues generally than they were with the radicals. Although internal agreement among the moderates was some 5 percentage points lower in the divisive roll calls of 1864 than in those of 1862 and moderate agreement with the radicals increased a few percentage points during the same time, there still remained a very substantial difference in agreement within and across the groups in the divisive roll calls of 1864. Considerable difference remained between confirmed radicals and moderates, therefore, and by 1864 the radicals were more firmly united and the moderates were somewhat less in agreement than had been the case early in the war. Means, of course, obscure individual differences, and when we examine the complete agreement matrices we see that Harris agreed with the radicals rather substantially more frequently in 1864 than he had in

1862, the scores of Ten Eyck and Doolittle showed only minor changes, and Cowan was definitely less willing to vote with the radicals in 1864 than in 1862. We have already noted that some senators did change their positions relative to their colleagues, but Tables 3-9 and 3-10 suggest that the range of disagreement within the Republican party in the Senate remained substantial.

The relative numbers of roll calls in which substantial East-West and radical-moderate differences appeared during 1861–62 and 1863–64 attest as well to the continuing existence of both dimensions of party disagreement. In the first case eastern Republican senators were ranged against western in roll calls revealing disagreement at the 40 percent level or above in 47 roll calls, and in the latter session, where recruitment policies roused additional sectional animosity, there were 55 such votes. The equivalent numbers of disagreements among Republican radical and moderate senators were 58 and 69. Sumner, as we have seen, surpassed all of his colleagues during 1861–62 in submitting divisive motions, accounting for 19 percent of such roll calls; during 1863–64, this proportion rose to 22 percent.

Clearly, Allan Nevins' suggestion that "parties were in chaos" during the greater part of the working life of the Thirty-seventh Congress requires considerable qualification. No doubt "chaos" did seem an apt description of wartime Washington in general and to some members of the Congress in particular, but when the senators set themselves to the making of policy they did not behave like so many skiffs cut adrift in seas agitated by violent storms. We cannot doubt that they were discomfited by wartime rumors, frustrated and puzzled at times by the course of events, besieged by place-seekers and would-be advisers, and battered by the conflicting counsel of their colleagues and major members of the executive branch. But through it all, their conceptions of their obligations to party, to section, and to their own ideological convictions apparently shaped their legislative behavior in ways that in retrospect were anything but chaotic.

This is not to say, however, that the patterns of behavior displayed by the senators were simple or easy to understand. The time-hallowed dichotomy of radical and conservative is certainly much too simple a chart for anyone who wishes to understand government in wartime Washington in any but the most superficial way. Certainly there was a continuing pattern of legislative behavior that related to such distinctions, and there were senators whose votes in one session predicted their positions relative to their colleagues in the next, but there were also others who changed their positions or whose general actions cannot be accurately classified as belonging to either of two polar types. And to use such terms as "vindictive" or "nonvindictive" to refer to the behavior of legislators on an issue-by-issue basis is also misleading because the practice disregards the fact that some senators were indeed radical or moderate on a wide range of issues, a fact that contemporary usage of such terms surely was intended to reflect. On being confronted with the evidence in this chapter, one graduate student wailed, "But this muddies the water," and indeed for those who seek simplistic answers to complicated historical questions or eras it does just that. But it is also congruent with the common-sense dictum that men and issues change through time. Even in this last respect, however, a word of caution is in order. Change in the position of senators in the scale summaries denotes change in the tendency of individual senators to assume polar positions relative to one another. If, on some grand hypothetical or imaginary index of radicalism, all senators moved toward the radical pole to the same degree, the summary rankings would not reveal it. In the case of an issue such as emancipation, it can indeed be argued that such an underlying shift occurred.

Thus far we have examined the patterns that emerge from analysis of a universe of roll calls that included most of the motions that bore substantively on the South and the problems that it presented to the Congress of the Union, as well as some of the more important procedural votes related to such issues. Some may wish to argue at this point that the substantive issues before the Civil War Senates were of unequal importance and that we should have focused on the major subjects. Would the results have been different? In scaling, those votes were placed together that scaled with the largest number of companion votes in the pool of votes provided by each session, and it would have been more useful, according to this viewpoint, simply to scale the votes on "important" specific issues. This line of argument runs counter to the sound maxim that historians should look at all the available evidence. And we must remember that the senators did not tally votes unless some of their members believed that it was important that they should. Moreover, consideration of reasonably large bodies of evidence is more likely to display basic regularities than analysis of smaller bodies of evidence selected by criteria that perhaps reflect the personal biases of the researcher.

On the other hand, examination of specific instances often clarifies larger patterns, brings out individual examples of behavior that are of interest, and may also place generalized findings in better perspective. This being the case, we have constructed scales of the voting on eight measures or subjects that historians in general have considered to be important: emancipation in the District of Columbia, the confiscation law of 1862, the 1862 Act Amendatory to the Militia Act, assistance for emancipation in Missouri, the Wade-Davis reconstruction bill, repeal of the fugitive slave acts, creation of the freedmen's bureau, and two related matters concerning Louisiana—the questions of counting that "reconstructed" state's presidential votes in the 1864 election and of seating the Louisiana senators. Historians have emphasized the Militia Act of July 17, 1862, less than the other issues selected here, but as we shall see, the debates on that measure opened up aspects of emancipation that were of great significance. Debate and voting on these eight measures extended chronologically from 1862 until the winter of 1865, thus allowing some consideration of the effect of time upon the voting postures of the Republicans.

The votes on all of the eight issues produced usable scales, although only the votes on the Wade-Davis bill scaled together without exception. Usually nonscaling votes related to procedural matters, a voting category allowing greater opportunity for the display of individual idiosyncracy. Most of the scales displayed the usual continuum (or variants of it) in which the slave-state senators stood at one end, northern Democrats stood next adjacent to them, and the Republican moderates appeared next with the radicals standing at the pole opposite the border-state men. Two issues, however, particularly showed the influence of "ends-against-the-middle" behavior in which Republican radicals voted with slave-state senators. These were confiscation and the Louisiana question. The debate on confiscation centered on three bills: S. 151, the Judiciary Committee or Trumbull bill; S. 310, the product of a select committee chaired by Clark of New Hampshire; and H.R. 471, the bill passed by the representatives and considered more satisfactory by radicals than the measure of the select committee. The voting on S. 310 produced a strong ends-against-the-middle pattern that dominated the scale found in the voting on that measure.[17] Traces of such a pattern also appear in two scales found in the Louisiana voting. Issue-by-issue analysis does perhaps emphasize the presence of such deviant voting patterns to a greater extent than does scaling within a broader universe of roll calls, but ends-against-the-middle voting did not go unnoticed when that approach was used, as we have seen.

In contrast to the voting on confiscation, the cleanest scale was pro-

---

17. The fact that two different alignments appeared in the voting on the three major confiscation proposals posed a problem in preparing a summary confiscation measure. In the confiscation summary used in the correlation table, the Republicans who voted with the slave-state senators on S. 310 were given the scores that they would have had if they had been at the Republican pole. The correlations of the confiscation item with the other issue summaries may be regarded, therefore, as somewhat high.

vided by the roll calls on the Act Amendatory to the Militia Act of the second session of the Thirty-seventh Congress, in which ten votes fit together with only two errors and an eleventh division rejected as a "nonscaler" departed from pattern only in five instances. But we must remember that absences provide particular problems in the relatively small scales constructed from the voting on specific measures. Some of the scale scores attribute positions to some senators that they might not have held if they had recorded votes in all divisions. And although analysis across sessions is much more feasible in Senate voting than in the case of the House, where the turnover between the Thirty-seventh and Thirty-eighth chambers was little short of cataclysmic, the membership of the Senate did change somewhat from session to session, and the votes of senators who served only during some sessions affected the placement of senators in all scales.

The interrelations of the eight issues are summarized in Tables 3-11 and 3-12, the first presenting the degree to which the positions of Republican senators were correlated in the scales and the second providing similar coefficients for all the senators. In general the coefficients are higher in the second table as the influence of party and the dichotomy between the northern and southern border senators influenced the voting patterns. The Louisiana scale ranking is an exception to the generalization—that issue obviously created unique disarray among the non-Republicans. As to the Republicans, it is clear that there were basic common elements in the voting structure of the various scales as the analysis in the preceding section of this chapter suggests. If we compare the correlation coefficients in Tables 3-11 and 3-12 with those in Table 3-7, we see that the latter fall comfortably in the central range of values obtained by correlating scale positions derived from the single-issue rankings. This is as it should be and confirms the utility of the summary rankings developed above as general measures of radicalism or non-radicalism.

Four of the issues represented in Tables 3-11 and 3-12 bore directly on the status of slavery: emancipation in the District, the freeing of black soldiers and their families, emancipation in Missouri, and repeal of the fugitive slave laws. Most of the stronger correlations in Table 3-11 are among the scale rankings generated by these issues. The strongest correlation, .82, depicts the relation between the voting on the Militia Amendatory Act of 1862 and the fugitive slave acts repeal in 1864. The weakest relationships among these four items involve the Missouri emancipation proposal.

The two issues that are apparently least related to the emancipation scales were those provided by confiscation (which also included an emancipation feature) and the freedmen's bureau. The weak relation-

TABLE 3-11.
Bill-scale correlations: Republicans

| Year | 1862 | 1862 | 1862 | 1863 | 1864 | 1864 | 1864–65 | 1865 |
|---|---|---|---|---|---|---|---|---|
| Bills | 108 | 151–471 | 384–394 | 634 | 244 | 141–512 | 51 | 126–117 |
| Emancipation, D.C.: S. 108 | | | | | | | | |
| Confiscation: S. 151; S. 310; H.R. 471 | .45 | | | | | | | |
| Militia Act, July 17, 1862: S. 384–394 | .71 | .56 | | | | | | |
| Emancipation, Missouri: H.R. 634 | .40 | .29 | .62 | | | | | |
| Reconstruction: H.R. 244 | .51 | .23 | .61 | .46 | | | | |
| Fugitive slave repeal: S. 141; H.R. 512 | .74 | .37 | .82 | .47 | .65 | | | |
| Freedmen's bureau: H.R. 51 | .34 | .34 | .32 | .39 | .64 | .42 | | |
| Louisiana: H.J.R. 126; S.J.R. 117 | .61 | .51 | .44 | .49 | .31 | .50 | .45 | |

## TABLE 3–12.
### Bill-scale correlations: all senators

| Year | 1862 | 1862 | 1862 | 1863 | 1864 | 1864 | 1864–65 | 1865 |
|---|---|---|---|---|---|---|---|---|
| Bills | 108 | 151–471 | 384–394 | 634 | 244 | 141–512 | 51 | 126–117 |
| Emancipation, D.C.: S. 108 | | | | | | | | |
| Confiscation: S. 151; S. 310; H.R. 471 | .69 | | | | | | | |
| Militia Act, July 17, 1862: S. 384–394 | .81 | .82 | | | | | | |
| Emancipation, Missouri: H.R. 634 | .71 | .67 | .85 | | | | | |
| Reconstruction: H.R. 244 | .69 | .62 | .80 | .70 | | | | |
| Fugitive slave repeal: S. 141; H.R. 512 | .85 | .68 | .89 | .74 | .81 | | | |
| Freedmen's bureau: H.R. 51 | .72 | .68 | .71 | .73 | .80 | .77 | | |
| Louisiana: H.J.R. 126; S.J.R. 117 | .32 | .15 | .10 | .19 | .01 | .21 | .18 | |

ship between those two measures suggests that they represent other variants of the Republican voting pattern. But since the correlations between the freedmen's bureau scale and other rankings in the Thirty-eighth Congress in general are fairly strong, we may also suspect that changes in personnel to some degree explain the break in the level of the coefficients as between 1862–63 and 1864–65. The reconstruction scale correlates respectably with the emancipation measures as well as the freedmen's bureau ranking but it was much less strongly linked to the Louisiana scales which, in turn, generate one of the higher correlations with the voting pattern found in the confiscation roll calls.

The evidence in the correlation matrix suggests a basic antislavery continuum and variants that were revealed in the voting on the freed-men's bureau, the Louisiana issues, confiscation, and the proposal to subsidize emancipation in Missouri. But we must remember that in gen-eral no scales correlated so strongly that there was no opportunity for individual deviancy. Insofar as possible, the bills in Tables 3-11 and 3-12 are arranged in temporal sequence, although the debates on some mea-sures overlapped. If the earlier scale is assumed to be the independent variable, 67 percent of the variance was explained once and slightly more than 50 percent on two other occasions in Table 3-11.[18]

In statistical terms there are basic underlying structures that run through the scales. But how do we relate these to the behavior of indi-vidual senators? If our interest is Republican radicalism, we can make some simple generalizations on the basis of the eight issue scales: Chan-dler, Conness, King, Nye, Stewart, Sumner, Wade, and Wilkinson ap-peared in the more radical half of the Republican voting spectrum when present. Brown, Morgan, Pomeroy, Sprague, Wilmot, and Henry Wilson appear at the radical end in all but one scale ranking. At the other end of the spectrum, Browning, Cowan, Doolittle, Henry S. Lane, Ramsey, Sim-mons, and Ten Eyck appeared invariably as moderates, while Dixon, Foster, Harris, and Howe crossed the Republican median point of these issue scales but once. The alternation of their colleagues across the scale

18. A simple centroid factor analysis confirmed this analysis of Table 3-11. The various scale rankings had raw (unrotated) loadings on the first factor ranging from .58 (confisca-tion) to .86 (Militia Amendatory Act). Emancipation in D.C., the fugitive slave laws repeal, and reconstruction all loaded on this factor at levels above .70. This first factor explained 52 percent of the total variance in the matrix. The Freedmen's Bureau scale loaded most heavily on the second factor (−.43) which explained only 7.4 percent of total variance, and the Louisiana item provided the strongest loading (.38) on the third factor extracted, which in turn accounted for 7.2 percent of the total variance. At this point in the analysis slightly more than 50 percent of the item variance of the confiscation and Missouri emancipation measures was still unexplained, suggesting additional minor idiosyncratic elements in the voting on those measures. Given the data problems involved in analysis in which the actual population changes through time, it is clear that we cannot interpret these findings rigor-ously or make too much of minor patterns.

median points and the deletion and addition of other colleagues from membership account for the major deviations of the scale rankings, one from another.

Analysis of the scales based on specific issues amplifies the information derived from the scales based on the universe of southern issues and racial matters; only Ramsey's positions proved surprising.

# 4

# Connections

In the preceding chapter we examined the tendency of Republicans to take more or less extreme positions in voting on the legislative issues of the war. Clearly the Republican senators differed in these matters and in ways that created persistent voting patterns. The roll calls show that there were radical and moderate Republican senators, although the terms obscure a good deal of complex reality. Was the distinction of importance in the daily life of lawmakers and the chamber? Did moderate live with moderate or radical sit by radical? Were those of either persuasion particularly eager to change the rules of the Senate? To what degree did the disagreements between such men reflect differences in their personal or political backgrounds? How important were such differences in policy-making and to the party of which they were all members?

Students of legislative behavior have periodically investigated the living accommodations of lawmakers and their seating arrangements in the chamber. Roy F. Nichols identified the F Street mess as a major locus of power in the Senate of the mid 1850s. In 1966 James S. Young concluded that the boardinghouse mess was of major importance in shaping the legislative behavior of the members of Congress during the early national period. It has also been argued that the appellation "backbencher" has real meaning in the history of American legislative proceedings.[1] Did the living arrangements or the Senate seating patterns of the Civil War senators reflect moderate or radical inclinations?

1. Roy F. Nichols, "The Kansas-Nebraska Act: A Century of Historiography," *Mississipi Valley Historical Review*, 43 (September 1956), 187–212; James Sterling Young, *The Washington Community, 1800–1828* (New York: Columbia University Press, 1966); Allan G. Bogue and Mark P. Marlaire, "Of Mess and Men: The Boardinghouse and Congressional

The heyday of the boardinghouse had passed by 1860. Although most representatives and senators still rented rooms, somewhat more impersonal hotels or the single rental had eroded the institution developed specifically for the purpose of housing a group of federal lawmakers. The *Congressional Directory* of the second session of the Thirty-seventh Congress shows that Brown's Hotel housed fifteen representatives and two senators and the famous National accommodated nine representatives and three members of the smaller chamber while the Avenue House, Clay's, the Washington House and Willard's Hotel and A. H. Willard's (across the street from the famous hostelry) all housed sizable groups. Mrs. Best, Mrs. Carter, Mrs. Parry, Mrs. Hyatt and others still upheld the tradition of the smaller establishment. But of forty-four senators listed in the *Congressional Directory* of the second session of the Thirty-seventh Congress, only nineteen listed the same accommodation as did colleagues—three groups of three and five pairs. And there was little continuity in such arrangements. Only seven of the forty-four senators still occupied their residence of late 1861 at the beginning of the Thirty-eighth first session, and, of the nineteen senators sharing facilities in December, 1861, apparently only six men (three pairs) were fellow lodgers in 1864, although Grimes and Fessenden continued to live in close adjacency, if not in the same dwelling.[2]

Examination of the composition of the groups in hotels and boardinghouses in the long session of the Thirty-seventh Congress shows that no Republican senator lived under the same roof as did a Democrat or Border Unionist senator. Lest we read too much into these spatial arrangements, California's McDougall chose to live with eight Republican senators at the Willard during the first session of the Thirty-eighth Congress. Hicks and Peter G. Van Winkle, cooperating Unionists, joined five Republican senators at the National in that session, and both Trumbull and the Indiana Democrat, Hendricks, patronized the Avenue House as the Congress began.[3] As for the differences among Republicans, the groupings of the Thirty-seventh hardly suggest that any particular accommodations served as headquarters for moderate or radical forces. Of

Voting, 1821–1842," *American Journal of Political Science*, 19 (May 1975), 207–30; Robert Zemsky, *Merchants, Farmers, and River Gods: An Essay on Eighteenth Century American Politics* (Boston: Gambit, 1971), passim; Zemsky, "The Congressional Game: A Prospectus," *Social Science History*, 1 (Fall 1976), 109. It should be emphasized that this author used the word largely in terms of legislative style and objectives.

2. *Congressional Director*, 37 Cong., 2 sess. (Washington: Postmailer of House of Representatives, 1862, 2d ed.), 46; ibid. (1st ed.), 38 Cong., 1 sess., 68–69.

3. For purposes of analysis we have placed Hicks, Willey, and Van Winkle in the Border Unionist category. *The Tribune Almanac and Political Register for 1864* (New York: The Tribune Association), p. 24, lists them as "unconditional unionists" in its breakdown of party affiliation for this session, using the same type face as that denoting Republican.

those who lived at Clay's, Pomeroy and Wilkinson stood on the radical side of the Republican center and Harlan is properly considered in the center of the party, although standing to a greater extent with the radicals than with the more conservative Republican senators. At the National, Chandler and Hale were joined by the western moderate, Henry S. Lane, while Willard's Hotel accommodated the moderates Foster and Harris as well as the veteran radical Wilmot. Chipman's, Mrs. Carter, and Mr. Price each housed a pair of Republican senators, and certainly in two of the three instances kindred spirits lived in these menages— Grimes and Fessenden at Chipman's, and Doolittle and Cowan at Price's. The degree of overall affinity between Foot and Browning at Mrs. Carter's is less clear, but on the issue of slavery they stood well apart; apparently Doolittle, and perhaps Cowan, moved to Carter's during the session, creating, at most, a small conservative concentration.

Thus no large and solid phalanx of radicals or moderates lived together during the long session of the Thirty-seventh Congress, and although the group at the National Hotel in the first session of the Thirty-eighth had a moderate tone, Chandler and B. Gratz Brown also patronized that famous hostelry. No one has suggested that any group of fellow boarders wielded power in the party during these years equivalent to that attributed to the Democratic F Street mess of the mid-1850s, and this is obviously correct; neither the continuity of living arrangements nor the composition of the groups that existed suggests any such thing.

In some legislative bodies, party leaders and veteran lawmakers sit in the front rows; this pattern has been apparent to some degree in the United States Senate, although some of its members have proudly retained the desks originally assigned to them. The shrunken band in the new Senate chamber in early December, 1861, spread outward from the central aisle in the three-tiered horseshoe of mahogany desks so that vacant places existed at the end of each row on both the Vice President's left and his right.[4] (A truncated fourth row in the rear to the right used in the Thirty-sixth Senate was now unnecessary.) As Hannibal Hamlin looked to the ornate clock above the studded central door at the rear, his

4. The value of the correlation coefficient relating the length of a senator's service and the row in which his desk was located in the Ninety-sixth Congress was .273. See *United States Senate: Ninety-Sixth Congress* (Washington: Government Printing Office, 1979). For information relating to the Thirty-seventh and Thirty-eighth Congresses, see *Congressional Directory*, Thirty-sixth Cong., 2 sess. (1861), chart and key, [i-ii]; ibid., 37 Cong., 3 sess. (1863), opposite title page; ibid., 38 Cong., 1 sess. (1864). Charts were less frequently published in the directories in the Civil War than in those of the 1850s; that of the Thirty-eighth, 1st sess. was obtained from a directory in the Library of Congress Treasure Room. The historian of the Senate has a comprehensive collection but it does not include a chart for the second session of the Thirty-seventh Congress. Comparison of the 1860-61 and 1862-63 charts places the senators in 1862.

fellow Republicans for the most part ranged to the left of the aisle while Democrats and Border Unionists, with one exception, were seated to his right (see Fig. 4-1, the seating chart for the subsequent session, in which the arrangement was very similar). However, several new Republican senators had also taken seats to the right in the middle row between Bayard, who continued to hold his aisle seat, and the courtly Pearce of Maryland, while two others occupied the two desks to the right of the aisle in the back row. The diminutive senator from Kentucky, Garrett Davis, reminded the observers in the balconies of the Whig origins that he shared with many Republicans by occupying a seat in Republican territory, second from the outer end of the middle row, between Howard and Simmons and in front of the scowling Chandler.

During the second session of the Thirty-seventh Congress, none of the chairmen of the more important committees sat in the front row; instead, they formed a kind of nucleus in the middle of the second and third tiers of desks to the left of the aisle, where Fessenden, Foot (president *pro tempore*), Wilson, Wade, and Trumbull sat side by side, and Sumner, Hale, Harlan, and Chandler sat diagonally behind them. Rather than taking seats mainly in the back row, most of the newer Republican senators were arranged around the periphery of the Republical formation, though some filled vacated seats in both the front and rear rows. Howe occupied the outer desk of the front row while Browning sat at the other end, and across the aisle and separated from it by at least one Democrat. Morrill drew the front-row desk second from the aisle on the Republican side. James H. Lane, Pomeroy, and Sherman occupied seats across the aisle in the second tier, while Howard and, in the third session, Arnold, held the other flank; Henry Lane and Harris sat across the aisle in the third row and Cowan and Wilmot, other new senators of this Congress, were interspersed between Doolittle on the aisle, King, and Sumner.

Figures 4-2 and 4-3 show movement from congress to congress on the part of holdover Republicans. In the first session of the Thirty-sixth Congress, Clark, Foster, Anthony, and Wilkinson sat in the front row with southerners occupying the three seats on their left closest to the aisle. With the departure of the "cavaliers," Clark moved over to take the aisle and Morrill, a new senator, sat at his right. Grimes descended from the second tier to sit third from the aisle, and Foster, Anthony, and Wilkinson all shifted one seat to their left, while the new boy, Howe, now occupied the end position formerly held by Wilkinson. Between the Thirty-sixth Congress and the Thirty-seventh, Doolittle moved from the desk next adjacent to the last of those occupied by Republicans in the rear row to replace Seward at the aisle, Ten Eyck shifted from the end to take Doolittle's old place, and Dixon, who enjoyed longer tenure than

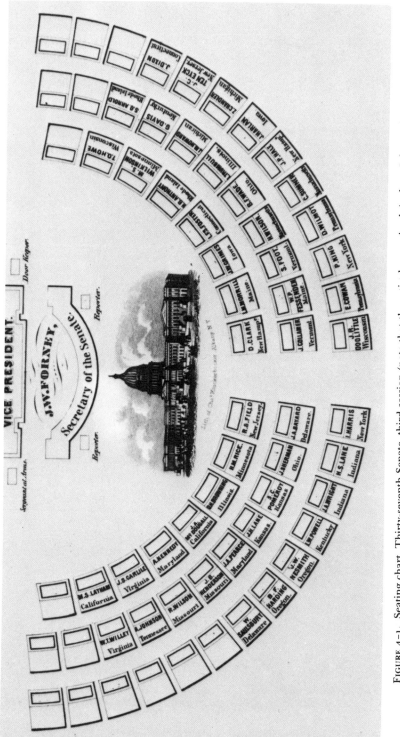

FIGURE 4–1. Seating chart, Thirty-seventh Senate, third session (note that the artist has retained Andrew Johnson in his seat).

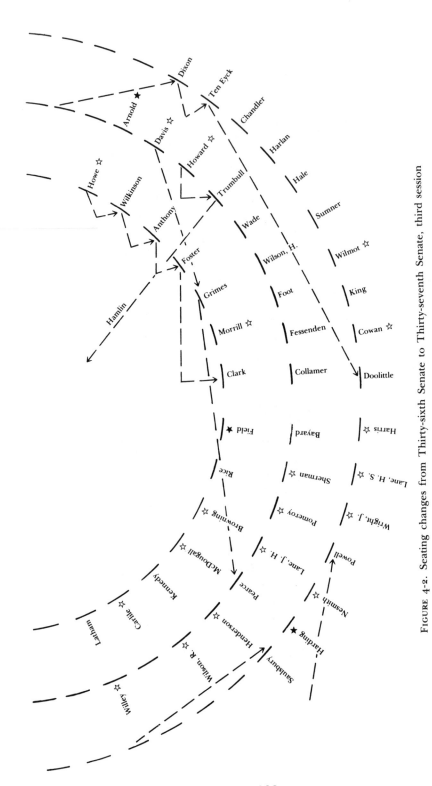

FIGURE 4-2. Seating changes from Thirty-sixth Senate to Thirty-seventh Senate, third session

Movement -----
New member: Thirty-seventh Senate, first or second session ☆
New member: Thirty-seventh Senate, third session ★

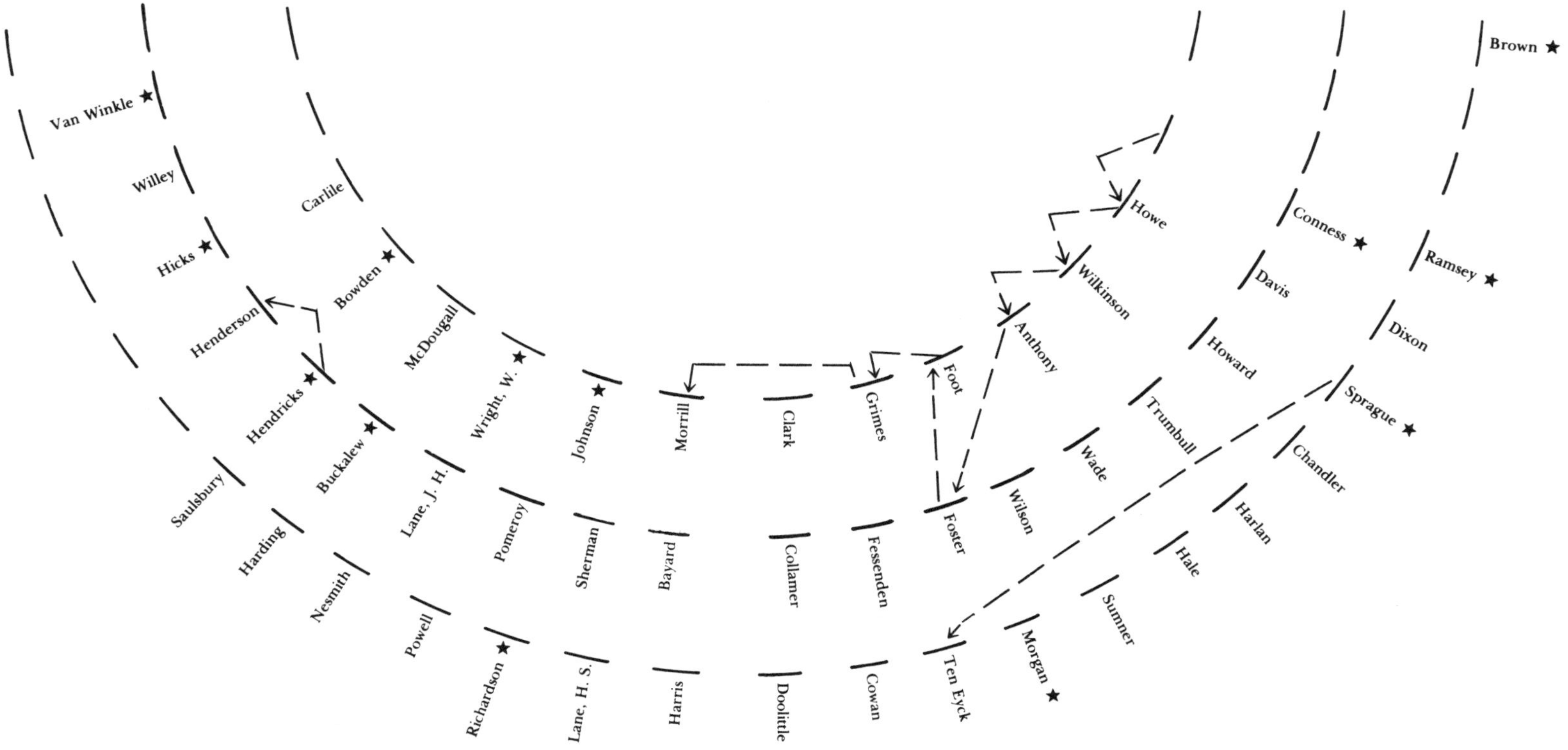

FIGURE 4-3. Seating changes from the Thirty-seventh Senate to Thirty-eighth Senate, first session

Movement ----
New member: Thirty-eighth Senate, first session ★

either of them, moved back from the right side of the second row to take Ten Eyck's former place.

In the rearrangement of seats at the beginning of the Thirty-eighth Congress, Ten Eyck moved to occupy King's vacated desk beside Cowan and surrendered his seat to Sprague; Ramsey and Brown occupied seats on the end of the rear row and Morgan replaced Wilmot. Four new senators therefore took their places in the rear, and Conness accepted the old Simmons-Arnold seat at the end of those occupied in the second row. Other shifting in the second and first rows may have been designated primarily to accommodate Foot, the president *pro tempore,* who descended to the first row while Foster moved back to Foot's former desk. Morrill took the aisle seat vacated by Field and other front-row occupants, with the exception of Clark on the aisle, all moved one seat to the left.

In only one instance in the regular session of the Thirty-seventh Congress did fellow boarders occupy desks adjacent to each other. Doolittle and Cowan not only lived together, they sat together and, since Henry S. Lane and Harris were just across the aisle, the back center seats represented a small concentration of moderate sentiment. When Ten Eyck moved in the next Congress to sit beside Cowan, the group was further enlarged. The radical core occupied the rear and central tiers to the right of the moderate enclave. Undoubtedly there was a certain amount of doctrinal and personal reinforcement implicit in such arrangements, but we strain too much if we read strong significance into them.

The committees of the second session of the Thirty-seventh Congress were, of course, organized before the senators received the opportunity to participate in the roll calls that allow the student to classify them as radicals or moderates. Their previous assignments as well as their current wishes and the preferences and qualifications of their colleagues all played a part in determining their assignments, circumstances that undoubtedly introduced fortuitous elements in the distribution of radicals and nonradicals in the committees. Still, the results were of some importance.[5] On Military Affairs and Naval Affairs there were three Republican radicals and one moderate. Although Sumner was in the chair, moderates predominated on the Committee on Foreign Relations by a ratio of 4 : 2 in the second session and 3 : 2 in the third. Finance tolerated no radicalism whatsoever; four moderate Republicans served there until Bright's expulsion; then the number became five. Judiciary too was, in general, moderate ground, although Trumbull, the chairman, compiled

5. As in Chapter 2, the discussion is based upon the lists of committee assignments found in the various *Senate Journals.*

a radical voting record during the second session and was on occasion at odds with his Republican colleagues on the committee: Foster, Ten Eyck, Cowan, and Harris, all staunchly moderate or, in radical eyes, worse. For the next session a constitutional radical, Howard, replaced Cowan, but by that time Trumbull's radicalism as measured in his reaction to the issues before the chamber was faltering somewhat. The other two committees most strategically placed to strike at slavery were those on the Territories and the District of Columbia and here, during both sessions, radicals predominated by margins of three to two and four to one. Was it mere coincidence that the effective focus of committee activity on reconstruction matters moved from the Judiciary Committee in 1862 to the Committee on Territories during the next Congress? One assumes not. And of course Wade, as chairman of the Joint Committee on the Conduct of the War, resolutely radical in composition, was in a position to introduce legislation bearing on the war effort, which might well have far-reaching impact on southern institutions.

Table 4-1 shows the proportion of motions offered by various senators that were accepted by their colleagues during the long sessions of the Thirty-seventh and Thirty-eighth Congresses. Such success scores are far from being an infallible measure of a lawmaker's legislative power or skill in handling his committee assignments.[6] But those of Browning, Powell, and Davis—all notably outside the mainstream of legislative activity—suggest that this computation does convey some impression of legislative effectiveness. The scores of other senators in the table show that the moderates Fessenden and Doolittle scored somewhat better than did Wade, Wilson, and Sumner. Clark's impressive percentage of successful motions during the Thirty-seventh Congress reflected his activity as chairman of the Select Committee on Confiscation. Although normally radical-centrist in his voting, the New Hampshire senator relied particularly on moderate votes in steering the compromise bill, S. 310, through the chamber. During the session of 1863-64, however, Clark made little effort to shape activity on the floor.

Table 4-1 suggests a number of general conclusions. The radicalism or moderation of the Republican senators had no clear-cut relation to their success in having their wishes prevail during the everyday business in the Senate. Success, or lack of it, in the Thirty-seventh Senate did not guarantee comparable achievement in the next Congress. (Clark offered

6. For a discussion of measures of power or interpersonal influence, see Allan G. Bogue, "Some Dimensions of Power in the Thirty-Seventh Senate" in William O. Aydelotte, Allan G. Bogue and Robert W. Fogel in *The Dimensions of Quantitative Research in History* (Princeton: Princeton University Press, 1972), pp. 285-318, and the works cited there. See also Charles M. Dollar and Richard J. Jensen, *Historian's Guide to Statistics: Quantitative Analysis and Historical Research* (New York: Holt, Rinehart & Winson, 1971), pp. 111-16.

TABLE 4-1.
Motions made

| | 37th, second session | | 38th, first session | |
| --- | --- | --- | --- | --- |
| | Total no. | Percent success | Total no. | Percent success |
| Sumner | 33 | 52 | 31 | 55 |
| Fessenden | 25 | 72 | 33 | 67 |
| Wilson, H. | 17 | 59 | 23 | 65 |
| Hale | 17 | 29 | 14 | 64 |
| Trumbull | 17 | 71 | 11 | 64 |
| Wade | 14 | 64 | 13 | 69 |
| Clark | 13 | 85 | 2 | 50 |
| Doolittle | 10 | 70 | 12 | 50 |
| Browning | 8 | 12 | | |
| Powell | 11 | 45 | 20 | 15 |
| Davis | 18 | 28 | 14 | 21 |

only two motions in the first session of the Thirty-eighth Senate; despite his declining influence, Hale was apparently more successful in that body than he had been during 1861–62.) Sumner's scores fell substantially below those of most chairmen of major committees. On the other hand, by offering a considerable number of motions and supporting them tenaciously, Sumner succeeded in gaining much of what he desired, as we shall see in subsequent chapters. In great degree the statutes of the United States were indeed purged of slavery and prejudice according to his specifications. But seventeen motions won at the expense of offering thirty-three must also have represented seventeen motions won at the cost of much frustration and irritation among his party peers.

Viewed within the perspective of the Senate's institutional structure, Sumner's war on slavery was anomalous. The three committees that had particular relevance to the institution of slavery were those concerned with the Judiciary, Territories, and the District of Columbia. Sumner served on none of them prior to the conclusion of the Civil War—a most amazing circumstance. And surely his request for the establishment of a Select Committee on Slavery and Freedmen in the Thirty-eighth Congress must be viewed in part as an effort to mobilize the kind of support for his views on these matters that a committee, even though only a select one, might provide.[7] But in practical terms the gambit failed, although all the Republicans on this committee were resolutely radical and initially appeared more willing to follow the chairman's lead than was the

7. For a somewhat different interpretation of the committee, see David Donald, *Charles Sumner and the Rights of Man* (New York: Knopf, 1970), pp. 147–52, 173–78, 194–96.

case in some other committees. During the second session of the Thirty-eighth Congress, Sumner's colleagues refused to accept his recommendations for a freedmen's bureau. Sumner's handling of the bureau bill was a debacle (see Chapter 7), and the Judiciary Committee successfully asserted its claims to leadership in matters of constitutional revision. Sumner waged his war on slavery and racial injustice, and other reconstruction issues, in opposition to eminent colleagues and outside the normal framework of the standing committees.

The Joint Committee on the Conduct of the War was the outgrowth of a motion by a radical, Grimes, and served as an instrument of radicals throughout the conflict.[8] But it achieved its influence through exercise of its investigatory power rather than by legislative contributions. In theory, its members could have brought legislative proposals in great number before the houses of the Congress. In fact they brought very few, perhaps because the chairmen of the standing committees were jealous of their prerogatives, or perhaps, because the committee's members found investigation to be a more rewarding activity.

The summary of suggestions for changes in the Senate and joint rules in Chapter 2 shows that the radicals were not alone in trying to change legislative procedures during the course of the Civil War. If motions of the sort introduced by the irrepressible Davis and other opposition men are disregarded as less than serious efforts to reform procedures, Sherman was the most energetic advocate of revising the quorum rule and few can seriously argue that he was an ultra. Votes to postpone and table this measure in July, 1862, however, reveal that the radicals of the second session of the Thirty-seventh Senate supported Sherman's resolution more strongly by some 20 percentage points than did moderates. When the senators approved the resolution on May 4, 1864, Anthony, Doolittle, Foot, Foster, and Grimes left their Republican colleagues to vote against it. Fessenden's motion to record absentees after the quorum was changed was apparently viewed as a moderate solution to the problem of absenteeism. When the votes of the holdovers from the second session of the Thirty-seventh Congress are examined, 78 percent of the moderates, and 55 percent of the radicals supported the suggestion of the senator from Maine. Chandler and Wade, however, were in the opposition.

The most far-reaching proposals for change in the rules did emanate from the radicals. Hale's proposal to limit debate would have changed

8. The classic study is T. Harry Williams, *Lincoln and the Radicals* (Madison: University of Wisconsin Press, 1941). See also Hans L. Trefousse, "The Joint Committee on the Conduct of the War: A Reassessment," *Civil War History*, 10 (March 1964), 5–19, and William W. Pierson, Jr., "The Committee on the Conduct of the Civil War," *American Historical Review*, 23 (April 1918), 550–76.

Senate practice drastically. Wade and his colleague on the Joint Committee, Chandler, led the supporters of Joint Rule 22, providing for secret
discussion and limiting speeches to five minutes on matters that the
President deemed highly urgent. Did Wade visualize himself acting as a
kind of prime minister for the President under these procedures, and
the Joint Committee, perhaps, as a kind of legislative cabinet? The chief
executive proved unwilling to arm that peculiar device, but we should
not dismiss Rule 22 as inconsequential. It is a sketch of how radicals like
Wade believed a wartime senate should conduct its business.

The battle lines within the Republican party in the Senate were never
drawn as closely on matters relating to the rules as on various substantive
issues. But the proceedings suggest that the radicals were more willing to
abandon precedent and to place restrictions on the expression of opinion in the Senate than were their colleagues of moderate temper. The
reluctance of radicals to adjourn both the Thirty-seventh and the
Thirty-eighth Senates showed their desire to emphasize the role of the
Congress in government and their distrust of the executive branch.

The radicals were particularly active also in attempting to purge the
chamber of disloyalty as they defined it. Of eight resolutions for expulsion that senators presented between December, 1861, and early 1864,
radicals submitted seven: Chandler (Breckinridge); Foot (Waldo
Johnson); Wilkinson (Bright, Powell); Sumner (Polk, Stark); and Wilson
(Davis).[9] In addition, Sumner moved to make the oath of office of July 2,
1862, obligatory upon all the senators. After taking the oath in January,
1864, Bayard then resigned in protest on constitutional grounds.[10] "It
was clear," writes Sumner's latest biographer, "that Sumner's objective
was not so much to oust Bayard, whose loyalty nobody questioned, but to
establish a precedent barring leaders in the rebellion from returning to
the Senate."[11] An alternative view is to regard his activity as part of the
harassment of the Democratic and border-state opposition which had
begun long before the passage of the test oath. The use of the oath to
forestall returning traitors need not have involved attempting to deny
Bayard time to prepare his defense as Sumner did.

Historians have paid little attention to the institutional framework
within which the wartime Congress worked. Clearly, in some degree,

9. *CG*, 37 Cong., 2 sess., 9, 36, 89, 126, 891, 1983, and 38 Cong., 1 sess., 139. Joseph
Wright, the Northern Unionist, directed the eighth motion of expulsion at Simmons after
the latter's financial interest in government contracts was revealed (*CG*, 37 Cong., 2 sess.,
3061).

10. *CG*, 37 Cong., 3 sess., 1553–62; 38 Cong., 1 sess., 42, 48–57, 253, 263, 275–81,
290–96, 320–31 (the vote is on p. 331). Bayard's defense appears in the *Appendix*, 31–37.
When Sumner made the matter an issue at the beginning of the Thirty-eighth Congress,
Richardson had not taken the oath either.

11. Donald, *Sumner and the Rights of Man*, p. 182.

radical and moderate senators disagreed about the advisability of changing that structure, and they differed also in the eagerness with which
they monitored the loyalty of their fellows. To some degree, as well, the
disagreements among the various persuasions in the Republican party
affected the legislative process, since some committees were dominated
by radicals and others by moderates.

What of the personal backgrounds of the senators? Were they to some
degree predictive of radical or moderate sentiment or activity? Although
we can rank Republicans by scaling and make a reasonably convincing
case for dividing the group into radicals and nonradicals on the basis of
their votes in a particular session, we have already seen that the behavior
of the senators in one session did not precisely predict their voting in
relation to their colleagues in the following session. This is not surprising; issues change and so do men's understanding of issues. It does
suggest, however, that any effort to discover personal characteristics
invariably associated with radical voting patterns will be inconclusive,
given the fact that some Republicans voted radically at times and on
other occasions assumed a moderate or conservative stance. On the other
hand, enough Republicans consistently appeared in relatively the same
position in the Republican voting spectrum on southern issues to suggest
the existence of a radical-conservative voting structure in the Civil War
Senates. Nine of the Republican senators of the second session of the
Thirty-seventh Congress invariably voted in the most radical half of the
party's voting continuum as long as they served during the Civil War
and, in addition, six appeared consistently in the more conservative half
of the Republican ranks.

In an earlier chapter we tentatively divided the thirty-one Republican
senators serving in the long session of the Thirty-seventh Senate into two
groups consisting of seventeen radicals and fourteen nonradicals. At one
point in my research I tested these groups against Ralph Waldo Emerson's formula for the making of a Free-Soiler. Emerson wrote in his
journal: "The Unitarians, born Unitarians, have a pale, shallow religion;
but the Calvinist, born and reared under his vigorous, ascetic scowling
creed, and then ripened into a Unitarian, becomes powerful. . . . So it is
in politics. A man must have had the broad, audacious Democratic party
for his nursing-mother, and be ripened into a Free-Soiler, to be efficient."[12] When applied to our two groupings of senators, Emerson's
"law" does have some predictive value. Of seven former Democrats

12. Edward W. Emerson and Waldo E. Forbes, *Journals of Ralph Waldo Emerson, 1820–
1876* (Boston: Houghton Mifflin, 1913), 9:407–8. Actually, some of his illustrations are
difficult to fit into his pattern.

among the Republicans, six were radicals, including four of the most radical complexion, and only Doolittle was a moderate. Trumbull, however, was to modify his position thereafter. Of the five former Democrats who entered the Senate during the Thirty-eighth Congress either as Republicans or as Republicans-soon-to-be, Conness voted among the more radical Republicans and Sprague and Brown stood in the center of the party during the first session. By the second session the old slavery issues were pretty well dissipated, and both Brown and Conness took positions on southern issues that placed them well to the radical side. Entering from Nevada, Nye and Stewart stood in the same general area. Sprague, on the other hand, remained in the center of the party. Certainly, however, none of the new Republicans of Democratic origins established reputations as being notably moderate in sentiment. In surveying the political antecedents of the Republican senators, I noticed also that former Whigs who had made some striking commitment to the antislavery cause before 1854 appeared to take more extreme positions in general than those who had made their public commitment in 1854, or thereafter. However, problems of definition render this suggestion somewhat uncertain.

It is tempting to speculate that radicals would come from the states in which the Republican party was most firmly established. On the other hand, the senators generally served for six years, and their views presumably reflected those of their constituencies when they were elected. The fast pace of wartime events may well have put constituency and senator out of step. Regression analysis in which the scale type scores of the senators were correlated with measures of Republican state electoral strength yielded minimal correlation coefficients of .2 or less.[13] It is true that all of the regression lines sloped as predicted by the hypothesis, but simple regression analysis denied that relative party electoral strength in a senator's state was a major predictor of voting behavior.

Was there any relation in general between the sectionalism of East and West and the disagreement between radicals and moderates in the Republican party?[14] We can respond to that question by examining the

13. Two independent variables designed to show the relative strength of the Republicans in each state were used: the proportion of Republican representatives elected in the last election and the proportion of Republican votes cast in that election.

14. See V. Jacque Voegeli, *Free but Not Equal: The Midwest and the Negro during the Civil War* (Chicago: University of Chicago Press, 1967). There has been a good deal of careless reification in using terms such as "sectionalism" or "radicalism" in the explanation of political behavior. But let us suppose we have discovered that all, or at least a majority, of the Democratic members of the national House of Representatives voted alike in the first of two roll calls and were opposed by all or nearly all of the Republicans. In roll call 2, however, most westerners voted together in opposition to most easterners. In such an instance we are justified in saying that party was probably an important voting determinant

TABLE 4-2.

Sections and radicalism*

|  | Radicals | | Moderates | |
|---|---|---|---|---|
| Eastern Republican senators (17) | 8 | 47% | 9 | 53% |
| Western Republican senators (14) | 9 | 64% | 5 | 36% |

*The contingency coefficient gamma = .34. Pearson's r, a more conservative statistic, = .17. The reservations about the use of $X^2$, noted in Table 1-3, are even more relevant here, given the total N, but for those interested: $X^2$ = .89 with one degree of freedom, giving a significance level between .40 and .30.

TABLE 4-3.

Birth and radicalism*

|  | Radicals | | Moderates | |
|---|---|---|---|---|
| Republican senators of eastern birth (26) | 15 | 58% | 11 | 42% |
| Republican senators of western birth (5) | 2 | 40% | 3 | 60% |

*Gamma = .34; r = .13.

division of eastern and western Republican senators between the radical and moderate factions of the party during the second session of the Thirty-seventh Congress. Table 4-2 shows that slightly more than half of the eastern Republicans were moderates and a somewhat larger proportion of western Republicans were radicals. Antislavery sentiment in the West is sometimes linked to eastern origins, and Table 4-3 presents place of birth as a possible variable. But when these relationships are translated into correlation coefficients the results are unimpressive.

For what it is worth, the Republican senator most apt to be extreme in his views on wartime issues was a western senator of eastern origins; seven of the nine senators who fit this description were radicals (78 percent). The senator most apt to be a Republican moderate on the other hand was a western senator of western birth; three out of five, or 60 percent, in this category were moderates. But given the relatively

---

in the first instance and that sectionalism influenced most lawmakers in the second. By this I do not mean that party or sectionalism existed independent of the legislators. Rather, roll call 1 apparently invoked a similar response among those representatives who subscribed to the values and programs of the same political party and roll call 2 presented legislators with a decision in which men who agreed upon the best ways of fostering the welfare of their region voted together. (Granted, the various lawmakers may have arrived at a choice that maintained party solidarity or sectional allegiance by quite different processes of rationalization.)

TABLE 4-4.

Continuing radicals and moderates

| | East | West | Mean age* | Years in Senate* | Con.-Pres.- Unitarian | Bapt.-Epis.- Methodist | Former Democrat | Strong antislavery position pre-1854 |
|---|---|---|---|---|---|---|---|---|
| Core radicals (9) | 5 | 4 | 52.4 | 5.8 | 6 | 2 | 3 | 7 |
| Core moderates (6) | 3 | 3 | 48.6 | 1.6 | 1 | 5 | 1 | 1 |

*December 1, 1862.

small numbers of men involved, the percentage differences that support a sectional interpretation of the disagreement between radicals and moderates are rather small.

We cannot generalize with authority on the basis of groups of nine and six but if certain attributes were found more frequently among those holding radical views than among moderates, they should be revealed by the study of those senators who were consistently radical and those who were consistently moderate during the war. As Table 4-4 shows, regional affiliation could not have been more evenly divided. On the average, four years of age separated the members of the groups but the nonradicals were the younger. Little difference in political experience was revealed, although the moderates had, on the average, held somewhat fewer prior political offices than had the older radicals. The religious preferences of the two groups were somewhat different. The Presbyterian-Congregational-Unitarian rubric covered six of nine radicals and only one moderate. Indeed if we count Wade, notoriously unchurched but a child of stern New England Calvinism, the radical PCU contingent becomes seven rather than six. The moderate group, on the other hand, included two Episcopalians, two Baptists, and a Methodist in addition to Cowan, whose Presbyterian preference was one of the more tenuous affiliations established in this study. One out of three of the radicals had been a democrat; the ratio among the moderates was one out of six. Of the radicals, seven of nine had committed noteworthy acts in opposition to slavery prior to 1854, whereas the biographer of only one out of the six moderates noted similar deeds.

Table 4-4 not only suggests that a religious-cultural foundation underlay Republican factionalism to some degree but indicates also that various political antecedents played some role in these matters—the consistent radicals were to a greater extent veterans of politics at the senatorial level, their radical positions well known presumably in their states. Here, perhaps, the data indicate that the answers to senatorial behavior lay in the constituencies, but in ways seemingly far more complex than any simple reaction to relative party strengths.

As we have seen, the new Republican senators who in earlier times had been Democrats voted on the radical side of the party, or in the center, during the Thirty-eighth Senate. When we add Morgan of New York and Ramsey of Minnesota to the group, we have called the roll of the Republican replacements and reinforcements with the exception of the moderates Arnold and Field, who served only during the third session of the Thirty-seventh. Morgan and Ramsey also fell into position on the radical side of the center, suggesting that the process of circulation must have strengthened the hand of radical spokesmen to a greater extent during the first session of the Thirty-eighth Congress than it reinforced the voices of moderation. The postwar story of some of these men, and also of some longer-established colleagues, was to be rather different, however.

"On coming on any form of organized activity," wrote John Kenneth Galbraith, "—a church, platoon, government bureau, congressional committee, a house of casual pleasure—our first instinct is to inquire who is in charge."[15] Scattered through the Civil War press and the columns of the *Globe* are various allegations or suggestions as to who was indeed in charge in the Civil War congresses—allegedly the radicals in most cases. Such reports were exaggerated, to say the least. In July, 1862, Joseph Wright, the former Democratic governor of Indiana and professed Unionist, told his colleagues: "Sir, the man who can talk about a Republican party, or a Democratic party, or who can talk about anything in this crisis of the country but the best measures to save his country, is unworthy the name of Democrat. There should be no Republican party, no Democratic party now."[16] Did his fellow senators pay heed? They did not. In their voting decisions the senators clearly obeyed the dictates of party to a greater extent than those of any other force. That is, they voted in accord with principles shared with other Republican senators and they tended to follow the lead of committee chairmen or other party leaders, as well as the wishes of the Republican constituencies that they represented.

In general the scale listings and clustering matrices based on the senatorial voting of the Civil War years do separate the Republicans from the Democratic and border-state senators. Nonetheless, the levels

15. John Kenneth Galbraith, *The New Industrial State* (Boston: Houghton Mifflin, 1967), p. 47.
16. *CG,* 37 Cong., 2 sess., 3345.

of cohesion among the Republican senators were substantially lower during these congresses than in most that met during the last forty years of the nineteenth century. Deviation from party-line voting among the Republicans took at least three definable forms: (1) random, in which the senators apparently voted their own personal or constituency positions; (2) sectional, in which discernable numbers of eastern and western Republicans opposed each other, and (3) the radical-versus-moderate alignment. In legislative terms, the latter was surely the most important of the three. More roll calls showed substantial disagreement along the radical-moderate dimension of voting behavior than ranged eastern Republican against western on economic or other issues. Random voting most often appeared in consideration of unimportant or transient matters.

In a sense we create a straw man when we compare the impact of party in voting with that based on the differences between radicals and moderates. The phenomena are of a different order. Underlying the distinctions between ultras and conservatives was a great deal of fundamental agreement on the general principles and objectives of the Republican party. Had this not been so, the party would hardly have been in control of the federal government. The differences between radicals and moderates may best be viewed, perhaps, as disagreements concerning short-run policy objectives, specific legislative measures, and the principles that should govern behavior in such matters. Of course such matters could threaten the long-run consensus and endanger the future of the party. In making decisions on these matters, the number of extreme radicals and of confirmed moderates was sufficient to give opportunities to the fourteen or so opposition senators to influence legislative outcomes materially, or to threaten to do so.

Traces of fundamental social differences, variations in political background, and the influence of institutional factors are tantalizingly discernable in the record of the legislative proceedings of the Senate during the war years. Differences in the social origins of party and bloc members appeared; variations in the past experience of party members were present; regional shadings obtruded in some respects; some moderates sat or lived together, as did some radicals; in general seniority prevailed in the selection of major committee chairmen; party seniors were said to have power and did. To some the imperatives of war were such that the rules of the Senate had to be changed, and they were to some degree. But in all such matters the generalizations must be qualified—there were Episcopalian Republicans; there was little difference in many of the characteristics of senators when viewed across party or region; juniors appeared in the counsels of committees crucially concerned with the war effort; the wishes of the party elders were by no means universally respected on the floor. It was not just radicals who wanted to change the rules to expedite business or whose motions to such ends were accepted. None of the structural elements that we have considered suggests so compulsive a shaping of behavior as to be considered dominant, and many were closely linked to party. Knowledge of all these matters does enhance our comprehension of the behavior of radicals and moderates and policy outcomes. That understanding can be still further enlarged by careful study of the substance of those issues that divided radicals and moderates; that is the objective of Part II of this book.

# Part II

## THE SUBSTANCE OF DISAGREEMENT

★ ★ ★

In many eyes, scale rankings and agreement matrices are dull things, inanimate and crude, hopelessly deficient in portraying the choler, zest, and idiosyncrasies of legislators or in assessing their unique contributions to the legislative process. They are, of course, generalizing devices, and detail is discarded in any attempt at generalization, whether literary or quantitative in nature. But although they tell us nothing of the accuracy with which the individual senator used the chamber's spittoons or his preference in hunting dogs or female companionship, scales, agreement scores, and other tools of the quantitative historian can tell us a great deal about his continuing loyalties and recurring patterns of behavior. These, in turn, point the way for inference and speculation, and sometimes even support hypotheses about the attitudes, ideology, or other sources of motivation that produce such behavior.

Earlier chapters in this book have described the voting structure in which the senators behaved as radicals or moderates and speculated upon the relation of this shifting pattern to senatorial attributes and institutional context. Now it is time to examine divisive issues more closely, to ask what was the substance of the roll calls that brought Sumner's radicalism to the surface or inspired Doolittle to vote in defense of what he considered moderation. What were the conflicting positions that radicals and moderates occupied in discussing these divisive issues and how did they justify them? How did these differences affect the policies that the senators approved? Later we can ask the additional question: what do the issues involved in the roll calls that map the fault lines between Republican radical and Republican moderate suggest to us about the broader meaning and implications of radicalism?

While the war for the Union thundered on, radical and moderate waged a legislative struggle in the houses of the Congress. The battles and skirmishes in that conflict are not all tallied in the roll calls nor documented in the columns of the *Globe*—they were fought in party caucuses and committee, in the rooms of the Willard and the National hotels and in assorted boardinghouses, at the parties of the members of the diplomatic corps, in conversation on the Washington streets and on the sofas along the Senate chamber walls. The burial of bills in committee, seemingly interminable series of motions to postpone, adjourn, and the like in order to forestall other votes, informal agreements to the contrary that speech-making should stop and voting begin, riders attached to "through train" appropriation bills, sudden opportunism following realization that opponents of a measure had scattered on other business—all were part of the legislative process. Unfortunately much of the tactical activity cannot be reconstructed systematically; the roll calls, on the other hand, provide a body of data that was systematically gathered and in which both the articulate and the inarticulate, the leader and the led, recorded his position. The roll calls, of course, are not a complete record of position either; when the senators relaxed their quorum rule in the Thirty-eighth Congress and used the number of state delegations represented in the Union Senate, rather than the number of all states whether loyal or seceded, as in the Thirty-seventh, the absentee list was sometimes formidable. But the legislator who was absent in a particular division was often present when a similar motion was voted on, so absenteeism by no means nullifies roll-call analysis. When roll calls are studied in conjunction with the amplifying information provided in the debates, we do have the basis for analyzing substantive differences between radical and moderate in the Senate more systematically than hitherto has been the case.

As with many matters of method, that by which roll calls were selected as appropriate for analysis leaves some room for argument. The matter is discussed in Appendix B; here I stress only that I have tried to limit my reliance upon both intuition and the insight of other historians in selecting the major issues that separated Republican radical from Republican moderate. After dividing the Republican senators of each of the four regular legislative sessions of the Civil War congresses into radicals and moderates on the basis of scaling and cluster analysis by utilizing the roll calls dealing with southern issues, broadly defined, I then examined all the roll calls of the various sessions and selected for closer consideration every one in which the index of likeness between the two groups was 60 or less on a scale running from 0 to 100, or, stated differently, in which the converse of that measure—the index of disagreement—was 40 or more. The content of the motions producing these roll calls should, I argued, reveal the substance of the differences between radical and moderate as systematically and objectively as it is possible to do. The procedure guided us to 58 roll calls among the votes of the second session of the Thirty-seventh Senate, 18 in the third session, 69 in the first session of the Thirty-eighth, and 23 in the second (see Appendix D). In reading the discussion of these motions it is important to remember that I am not saying, "Because individuals voted yea or nay on the following issues I have proved that they were radical or moderate." Rather, their character as radical or moderate was suggested by my dimensional and grouping analysis. I used the index of disagreement to identify roll calls where the disagreement between Republicans considered as radicals or nonradicals was at a substantial level. Now we shall investigate the substantive meaning of such differences.

Chapters 5–8 contain analysis of the disagreements between radical and moderate Republicans occurring in the roll calls, as these developed in the discussion of various broad categories of legislation, and of the explanations of the issues and of their own acts presented by the senators who took leading roles in the debates. Scrutiny of the senators' own testimony is essential, not only because it offers the formal justification for their behavior but because the emotional content—the wit, the jibes, and the accusations—provides an additional dimension of radical-moderate disagreement, symbolic perhaps of broader and deeper but unspoken disaffections, and substantive in that it unquestionably affected later behavior.

Differences in attitude and action among the Republican senators were recurrent, and individuals frequently took similar positions on several issues or resorted to strategies that they had used before; the narrative in Chapters 5–8, therefore, has at times a somewhat reiterative quality. But since the theme of recurrent and significant disagreement among the Republicans runs counter to the picture of Republican unity which various historians of the last twenty years have emphasized, it is essential that the evidence be marshaled in depth. For the sake of perspective, the evidence is presented within the context of the general development of the various legislative issues, but legislative outcomes are not the primary concern of this study. It aims, rather, to examine a particular kind of recurrent disagreement among the Republican senators and the varied manifestations and results of that factionalism in the lawmaking process.

Other historians have discussed some categories of wartime legislative activity in great detail, but none has systematically noted the various efflorescences of radical-moderate tension in either the House or the Senate, and used them as a guide to analysis even in the case of major measures. Nor has anyone tried to link such phenomena across issues, both major and minor, although doing so is important if we are to understand the federal legislative processes during the Civil War more fully. In Chapter 9 the reader will find consideration of the broader meaning of radical-moderate disagreement, and discussion of two cases in which radical-moderate disagreement appeared when seemingly it might well not have been present.

# 5

# Slaves, Soldiers,
# and Taxes

During the war years, many, if not most, Americans and various senators in particular regarded the problems posed by slavery as somewhat different in meaning and implication from issues related to the status and rights of free blacks. Indeed to some, the distinction was very great, as to Montgomery Blair, who believed during the waning months of the Civil War that race, or, as he put it, "the Negro question," might serve as the fundamental issue in a reorganization of the national parties, now that the institution of slavery was nearing an end.[1] But millions of black men, women, and children were common elements in both the issues of slavery and the issues of race, and the two sets of questions were interrelated in congressional debate and voting. In this chapter we examine three issues or categories of issues which offered the Congress the opportunity of using federal power to strike directly at slavery: emancipation in the District of Columbia, the use of black soldiers, and the taxation of the rights of slave-owners in their bondsmen. Even so, we shall find the problems of slavery and race intertwined. Since perspective is helpful, the senatorial positions in the first great legislative blow at slavery—emancipation in the District—will be developed in more depth than is possible in regard to some later matters, so that this debate can serve as a base point.

Firmly in control of the Thirty-seventh Congress, the Republicans could now, in Fessenden's words, give "something like an indication that the Government of the United States was not bound to the protection of slavery and to the support of it." They should, they believed, "strike it out from the national capital," and they set to the task with high en-

1. Montgomery Blair to Samuel S. L. Barlow, January 13, 1865, Samuel S. L. Barlow Papers, Henry E. Huntington Library, San Marino, Cal.

thusiasm and in agreement that the Congress had exclusive jurisdiction over the District and that there were no constitutional impediments to action.[2] Emancipation of some three thousand slaves in the District of Columbia was only a token gesture in the broader war against the malignant institution, but it would be proof positive that a new era had begun in Washington. In early March, 1862, Senator Morrill reported a bill (S. 108)—originally introduced by Henry Wilson—from the Committee on the District of Columbia to emancipate the slaves of the District and a wide-ranging and sometimes dramatic debate began. Following Bayard's coldly hostile arguments against it on April 3, the senators approved the measure by a straight party vote of 29 to 14.

The stands taken by the Republicans' opponents are not essentially at issue here, but it is helpful to keep them in mind. The Kentuckians, Davis and Powell, plus Bayard, developed a constitutional argument against the District emancipation bill. Supporting their positions with a formidable number of legal references, they maintained that slaves were property and that the individual could not, under the Fifth Amendment, be "deprived of life, liberty, or property without due process of law; nor shall private property be taken for public use without just compensation." By setting an *average* maximum level of compensation for slaves which appraisal commissioners might approve to reimburse slaveholders in the District under the law, the drafters of the bill had abrogated due process, which Powell defined as "judicial process." Nor he argued was this property being taken "for public use."[3]

The requirement of the bill that commissioners approve compensation only to loyal owners also drew fire from Bayard, since it in effect allowed the appraisers to adjudge individuals guilty of treason without trial. Nor, argued Bayard, could the individual who had purchased a slave from an affirmed rebel obtain compensation, no matter how an-

2. *CG*, 37 Cong., 2 sess., 1473. Henry Wilson summarized the congressional proceedings in his *History of the Antislavery Measures of the Thirty-Seventh and Thirty-Eighth United-States Congresses, 1861-64* (Boston: Walker, Wise, 1864), pp. 38-78, and in the *History of the Rise and Fall of the Slave Power in America* (Boston: James R. Osgood, 1872-77), 3:270-84 (this volume was completed by the Reverend Samuel Hunt after Wilson's death). Of the more or less contemporary accounts see also Horace Greeley, *The American Conflict: A History of the Great Rebellion in the United States of America, 1860-65* ... (Hartford: O. D. Case, 1866), 2:258-59. Among more recent accounts see Allan Nevins, *The War for the Union, 2: War Becomes Revolution, 1862-1863* (New York: Scribner, 1960), pp. 93-94; Benjamin Quarles, *Lincoln and the Negro* (New York: Oxford University Press, 1962), pp. 103-4; Leonard P. Curry, *Blueprint for Modern America: Nonmilitary Legislation of the First Civil War Congress* (Nashville: Vanderbilt University Press, 1968), pp. 36-43; Herman Belz, *A New Birth of Freedom: The Republican Party and Freedmen's Rights, 1861 to 1866* (Westport, Conn.: Greenwood Press, 1976), pp. 6-7; Michael J. Kurtz, "Emancipation in the Federal City," *Civil War History*, 24 (September 1978), 250-67.

3. *CG*, 37 Cong., 2 sess., 1523.

cient the transaction nor what the state of the seller's loyalty at the time he made the sale. Such a provision, Bayard argued, constituted a "barbarous violation of every principle of justice." Davis, Powell, and Bayard also maintained that the bill was inexpedient, and distracting Congress as well as demoralizing the populations of the loyal states, and other border-state and Democratic senators agreed. The bill, the critics affirmed, could only exacerbate race relations in the long run by emphasizing the natural antipathy of white and black workers.[4]

Both friends and opponents of the administration believed that the bill could be "improved" in various respects, and among the major suggestions for such improvement were the acceptance of gradual emancipation, the addition of colonization provisions, and submission of the measure to the vote of the residents of the District of Columbia. Wright of Indiana paid particular attention to these matters.

Summary usually does injustice to the participants in congressional debates. The nuances and subtle variation that individuals gave to positions shared in general with other colleagues are often lost in the aggregate. Here we will primarily examine the positions of three Republicans who participated in the emancipation debate and whom the scaling patterns show to have stood in the left wing, in the center, and on the right of the Republican ranks. Slavery, maintained Charles Sumner, was:

> an aggregation of gross pretensions, all of them utterly inadmissible.... First, the pretension of property in man; secondly, the denial of the marriage relation...; thirdly, the denial of the paternal relation; fourthly, the denial of instruction; and fifthly, the appropriation of all the labor of the slave and its fruits by the master.... This fivefold Barbarism, so utterly indefensible in every point, is maintained for the single purpose of compelling labor without wages. Of course such a pretension is founded in force, and in nothing else....
>
> The five-headed Barbarism of slavery, beginning in violence, can have no legal or constitutional existence, unless through positive words expressly authorizing it. As no such positive words can be found in the Constitution, all legislation by Congress supporting slavery must be unconstitutional and void, while it is made still further impossible by positive words of prohibition guarding the liberty of every *person* within the exclusive jurisdiction of Congress.[5]

When pressed by Davis concerning the foundations of his position that "property" in human beings was essentially different from property in things, the radical Morrill took a somewhat different tack from Sumner's. "And God," he intoned, "said unto them ... have dominion over the fish of the sea, and over the fowl of the air, and over every living

4. Ibid., 1524–25.
5. Ibid., 1447, 1449. The speech runs from 1446 to 1451.

thing." Said Morrill, "Man has dominion over things; he has no dominion over persons."[6]

Sumner briefly touched upon the question of whether it was constitutionally proper to appropriate money to free the slaves of the District. That right, he believed, clearly lay within the "exclusive jurisdiction" of Congress over the District, but he preferred to regard payments to slave masters as being ransom rather than compensation. Nor was the future in doubt:

> At the national capital slavery will give way to freedom; but the good work will not stop here. It must proceed. What God and nature decree rebellion cannot arrest. And as the whole wide-spread tyranny begins to tumble, then, above the din of battle, sounding from the sea and echoing along the land, above even the exultations of victory on well-fought fields, will ascend voices of gladness and benediction, swelling from generous hearts wherever civilization bears sway, to commemorate a sacred triumph, whose trophies, instead of tattered banners, will be ransomed slaves.[7]

Fessenden noted that the Maine legislature had recently instructed him to support the dissolution of slavery in the District. He warned senators from the border states against the danger of assuming that the proposals were part of a master plan that in the end would involve unconstitutional action against slavery in the states or, as Davis put it, an effort "to get the head in," intending "to push the monster through" later. But then he stated his general position in words that must have been cold comfort indeed to loyal slaveholders:

> that the Republican party would rejoice to see slavery abolished everywhere, that they would rejoice if it no longer existed, that they feel it to be a blot upon our fair institutions and a curse to the country, there is no doubt. I can answer, for one, that has been my opinion always . . . but, sir, I have held, and I hold to-day . . . that the Congress of the United States, or the people of the United States through the Congress, under the Constitution as it exists now, have no right whatever to touch, by legislation, the institution of slavery in the States where it exists by law. . . . But, sir, I say further, that so far as the people of this country have the power, under the Constitution to weaken the institution of slavery; to deprive it of its force; to subject it, as an institution, to the laws of the land; to take away the political influence which it has wielded in this country, and to render it, so far as they can, a nullity, they have the right to do so, and it is their solemn duty to exercise it.[8]

The voting scales of the second session of the Thirty-seventh Senate show Browning of Illinois to have been one of the most conservative of the Republican senators. In one passage he covered much the same

6. Ibid., 1502–3.
7. Ibid., 1451.
8. Ibid., 1338, 1472.

ground as had Fessenden, but both his tone and his prognosis differed drastically from those of the New Englander. Declaimed Browning:

> While I assert the unqualified and unlimited power of Congress over the entire subject of slavery in the District, and while I further assert that it is the duty of the national Legislature to abolish it in the District, I . . . repeat . . . that it does not justly expose the national Congress to the charge of any intention, however remote, of interfering with the institution of slavery in the States. We disclaim the power to do so, we disclaim the right to do so, and we disclaim the intention to do so. With slavery in the States we have nothing on earth to do. It is a thing of local law. We must let it alone to be managed by them; to be perpetuated and kept forever if they choose to keep it; to be abolished to-morrow if they choose to abolish it; but whether they shall do the one or the other is to be at their own option.[9]

Thus we find striking differences of dimension in the ideas of senators in different positions on the ideological spectrum of the Republican party. Sumner could portray slavery as a barbarism, based on force and subject to attack at will, because no positive endorsement could be found for it in the Constitution. Expressly disregarding slavery in the states during the course of his remarks, he gave little doubt in his soaring conclusion as to his reading of slavery's future. Although much more restrained, Fessenden seemed to call on Republicans to use their considerable ingenuity in devising ways of harming slavery, subject only to the restriction that these be constitutional. Browning, however, flatly disavowed interest in slavery where it existed in the states.

Although the voting scales of the session suggest which senators might have been most willing to endorse each of these statements, the differences among Sumner, Fessenden, and Browning in tone and purpose were not reflected in the voting patterns on the District of Columbia emancipation bill. All the Republican senators agreed that it was their constitutional prerogative to deal with slavery in the District. Nor did constitutional arguments concerning the form of the bill impress them. Neat and incisive though Bayard's summation of such arguments was, his words led no Republican to try and modify the bill to correct what he believed to be constitutional defects. The due-process argument concerning compensation and the fact that a determination of loyalty was to be made without benefit of judge and jury apparently had little weight with them.

When Wright resurrected the sketch of an emancipation bill that Lincoln had drafted in 1848 as a guide to the District of Columbia Committee of the House of Representatives, it was found to include two features lacking in the Senate committee bill: colonization and a provision to

9. Ibid., 1521.

submit the act to the approval of the people of the District. Both these issues caused disagreement among the Republicans. Although Ten Eyck spoke sympathetically of the idea of submitting the emancipation proposal to a vote in the District, Trumbull sniffed, "I should like to inquire what propriety there is in five thousand voters . . . in the District of Columbia, determining for my constituents in Illinois, and his constituents in New Jersey, whether the capital of this great nation shall be in a slaveholding district?"[10] But the moderates Sherman and Ten Eyck cast votes in favor of submission proposals.

The colonization issue provoked even more discord among the Republican senators. Three votes are of particular interest. Sitting in Committee of the Whole on March 24, 1862, the senators considered an amendment to the bill which had been submitted by Davis of Kentucky. It provided, "that all persons liberated under this act shall be colonized out of the limits of the United States, and the sum of $100,000 . . . shall be expended under the direction of the President of the United States for that purpose."[11] By offering this amendment Davis in effect stole a march upon Republicans who favored colonization by making it mandatory, a form that was unacceptable to many within their party.

Doolittle sought to amend the Davis proposal by making colonization voluntary, offering it to "such free people of African descent now residing in said District as may desire to emigrate" and specifying Haiti and Liberia as possible destinations while allowing the President to determine other destinations outside the United States as well. His colleagues approved Doolittle's amendment 23 to 16 (Index of Disagreement: 42), but in its altered form the Davis amendment was lost, 19 to 19 (I.D.: 65), with radicals providing most of the Republican opposition in both cases. In the Senate later, Doolittle moved the amendment again, slightly modified by a provision limiting the emigration subsidy per emigrant to $100 or less, and explained that a number of senators had voted against it earlier in the mistaken belief that it provided for compulsory rather than voluntary colonization. Now the yeas stood at 27 and the nays at 10, with disagreement among the Republicans slightly below 40 percent. Doolittle had, he believed, "*saved* and *carried through* the bill."[12]

Sectional attitudes on race are sometimes emphasized in analysis of Republican voting on colonization.[13] Table 5-1 shows the result when we

10. Ibid., 1517.
11. Ibid., 1333.
12. Ibid.; James R. Doolittle to Mary Doolittle, April 17, 1862. James Rood Doolittle Papers, Wisconsin State Historical Society, Madison, Wisconsin.
13. See Jacque Voegeli, "The Northwest and the Race Issue, 1861–1862," *Mississippi Valley Historical Review*, 50 (September 1963), 244, n. 21, for an illustration of roll-call analysis supporting such interpretation. For general development of the theme see also V. Jacque Voegeli, *Free but Not Equal: The Midwest and the Negro during the Civil War* (Chicago:

TABLE 5-1.

Cohesion and disagreement on colonization amendments

|  | Doolittle Amendment | Davis–Doolittle Amendment Vote 1 | Davis–Doolittle Amendment Vote 2 |
|---|---|---|---|
| Republican Cohesion | 36 | 7 | 24 |
| East-West Disagreement | 31 | 30 | 4 |
| Radical-Moderate Disagreement | 42 | 65 | 36* |

*If Wilkinson's pair is used in the calculation, this value rises to 39. These votes appear in *CG*, 37 Cong., 2 sess., 1333 and 1522–23.

posit a sectional division line along the eastern boundary of Ohio, and consider the votes on the Doolittle and the Davis-Doolittle amendments. Each of the motions provoked considerable disagreement among the Republican senators, particularly the two votes on the Davis-Doolittle amendment. None of the coefficients of East-West disagreement reached a level comparable to that attained when we consider the Republicans as radicals and moderates. This does not mean that there was not racism in the West, but rather that we may have underemphasized its importance in the East, particularly the Middle Atlantic states.

Although the voting patterns on the colonization amendments suggest that we should not overemphasize the role of the West in incorporating a racist dimension in Republican policies, there is no question but that the men who defended colonization most vigorously came from that region.[14] Doolittle put the Davis amendment in a form that a majority of his colleagues found acceptable, and he vigorously advocated colonization on the floor. To be truly free, argued Doolittle, the Negro must have "freedom from the control of a single master" and also freedom from the "presence and domination of a stronger race." The Caucasians

University of Chicago Press, 1967); the note cited above appears as n. 39, p. 33. See also Eugene H. Berwanger, *The Frontier against Slavery: Western Anti-Negro Prejudice and the Slavery Extension Controversy* (Urbana: University of Illinois Press, 1967).

14. Voegeli, "The Northwest and the Race Issue," emphasizes the sectional element. In the most recent general survey of legislative activity in the Thirty-seventh Congress, Leonard Curry more tentatively suggested the importance of sectionalism in these proceedings and cites Voegeli. See Curry, *Blueprint for Modern America*, pp. 36–43, and especially p. 40 and n. 12. I first noted that the roll-call voting showed radical-moderate attitudes to be a better predictor than sectionalism in a paper "Bloc, Party and the Senators of the First Civil War Congress," delivered at the Annual Meeting of the Organization of American Historians, Chicago, April 27, 1967, and this section of that paper later appeared in "Senators, Sectionalism, and the 'Western' Measures of the Republican Party," David M. Ellis et al., *The Frontier in American Development: Essays in Honor of Paul Wallace Gates* (Ithaca: Cornell University Press, 1969). The analysis here has been recast somewhat, but the conclusions are essentially the same.

were destined to dominate the temperate zones and the tropics were the natural realm of the colored man; there, great opportunities awaited American blacks. Doolittle scoffed at the idea that racial antipathy was mere prejudice:

> I know it is sometimes said that the objection which is felt on the point of the white population to living side by side, on a footing of social and civil equality, with the negro race, is mere prejudice. Sir, it has its foundations deeper; it is in the very instincts of our nature, which are stronger and oftentimes truer than reason itself. Men . . . removed above the trials and sympathies of the great mass of laboring men, may reason and theorize about social and political equality between the white and the colored race; but I tell you as a practical fact, it is simply an impossibility.[15]

During the course of the debate on S. 108, Browning submitted a series of amendments that were designed to encourage colonization by raising the average amount of reimbursement in the case of emancipation to $500, half of the sum, however, to be retained in each individual case and paid to the freedman after he had settled in another country. The senator from Illinois was as pessimistic as Doolittle about the future of the black man in the United States:

> We may confer upon them all the legal and political rights we ourselves enjoy, they will still be in our midst a debased and degraded race, incapable of making progress, because they want that best element and best incentive to progress—social equality—which they never can have here. There are repugnances between the two races that forbid and will forever forbid, their admission to social equality; and without social equality they never can attain to a full development of their mental and moral natures, or lift themselves to any tolerable degree of respectable social *status*.[16]

The radical position was quite different. Sumner argued that it was "surely enough for the present to consider slavery at the national capital," and "at some other time" consider emancipation in the states and "whether there is an essential incompatibility between the two races, so that they cannot live together except as master and slave, and whether the freedmen shall be encouraged to exile themselves to other lands or to continue their labor here at home." Wilson of Massachusetts answered the dire prophecies of slave senators, specifically Davis, by arguing that as "a class, the free colored people of this District . . . [were] not worthless, vicious, thriftless, indolent, vagabonds, criminals, paupers." They supported themselves, he pointed out, maintained churches and schools, cared for their ill and dying, and buried "their dead free of public charge." Speaking to another but related issue, Morrill maintained, "Sir,

15. *CG*, 37 Cong., 2 sess., *App.*, 83–84.
16. *CG*, 37 Cong., 2 sess., 1520.

there is no class in this District who care for themselves and for each other as the colored population do."[17]

Rising in protest against the taunts of Davis and Saulsbury, who accused the Republicans of giving equal status to people whom they believed unequal to themselves and whom they themselves would never take in marriage nor welcome to their own communities, Harlan of Iowa met the issue head on. He commented bluntly upon the tendency of gentlemen in the slave states, including former members of the national government, to engage in miscegenation, and announced that he was "disposed to leave ... [the new freedmen] where they now are." They should be treated considerately and left in their familiar surroundings because an "enlightened humanity ... stretches out its arm to protect the feeble." He continued, "here is another feeble people, a race of men that are inferior to us, not equal to us in beauty, not equal to us in symmetry of body, not equal to us possibly in original mental and moral capacities or endowments." Just as American society appoints legal guardians to defend the orphan, "would it not be equally humane to provide for the protection of feeble colored people that have been born in our midst without any fault surely of their own?" Speaking of the District bill, Wilson promised his colleagues that an "act of beneficence like this will be hailed and applauded by the nations, sanctified by justice, humanity and religion, by the approving voice of conscience, and by the blessing of Him who bids us 'break every yoke, undo the heavy burden, and let the oppressed go free.'"[18] Significantly, no Republican, radical or moderate, dwelt upon the glorious future that the new freedmen might expect in the United States.

Efforts to change the status of slaves or free blacks in legislation relating to the armed forces of the Union did not begin auspiciously. On June 16, 1862, Wilson of Massachusetts moved to amend H.R. 423, a naval appropriations bill, by adding a section forbidding the use of slaves in naval installations or at the Naval Academy. The Massachusetts senator offered the amendment without explanation in Committee of the Whole, and his colleagues accepted it without debate, but apparently slaves had been kept as officers' servants or used by local contractors at naval installations in the border states. Powell of Kentucky requested that the senators vote upon Wilson's amendment separately, and this was done. It failed by a vote of 17 yeas and 18 nays. Only twenty-five of the thirty-one Republican senators voted in this division, and thirteen radi-

17. Ibid., 1447, 1352, 1477.
18. Ibid., 1359, 1353.

cals supported Wilson in comparison to three moderates. Seven moderates and the senators from Michigan opposed it (I.D.: 57). Since such slaves were not in the employ of the United States, the constitutional problem is obvious.[19] Other legislation, however, was in train that would have momentous consequences for the blacks.

On July 9, 1862, the senators began to discuss S. 384, "to amend the act calling forth the militia to execute the laws of the Union, suppress insurrections, and repel invasions," of 1795. As originally presented, the bill repealed the clause in the law of 1795 which restricted militia service under the federal government to three months and allowed the President to specify the period of service in his call. Ninety-day men, it was clear by this time, were anachronisms. The managers of the bill, notably Henry Wilson, chairman of the Committee on Military Affairs and the Militia, subsequently merged it with other proposals reforming aspects of army organization and the revised measure, S. 394, won the approval of a majority of the senators. Although Fred A. Shannon, the author of the classic study of the organization and administration of the Union Army, noted that the militia bill "had an easy course in Congress," the debates on S. 384 and S. 394 produced more examples of extremely strong disagreement along the radical-moderate continuum than any other measure discussed in the second session of the Thirty-seventh Congress.[20]

Wilson explained that the military forces needed additional men, and he did not believe that the recruiting system then in effect could do more than replace the losses expected during the next forty days. Fessenden commented to much the same effect. Had that rationale and the basic provisions of the bill been all that was at issue, there would have been

19. Ibid., 2724-25; Wilson did not discuss this resolution in either of his works dealing with the congressional war on the peculiar institution.

20. Wilson, *History of the Antislavery Measures,* pp. 203-17, and *Rise and Fall of the Slave Power,* 3:357-71; Fred A. Shannon, *The Organization and Administration of the Union Army, 1861-1865* (Cleveland: Arthur M. Clark, 1928), 1:275-78. Nevins, *The War for the Union,* 2:145, devoted a short paragraph to "a" bill amending the Militia Act without noting the severe strains that it placed upon Republican solidarity; Curry, *Blueprint for Modern America,* pp. 62-64, briefly discussed the legislative history of S. 384-394 and correctly identified the subject at issue but did not convey the full extent of Republican voting disagreement. For recent interpretive perspectives see Belz, *A New Birth of Freedom,* pp. 21-22 and passim, and Mary F. Berry, *Military Necessity and Civil Rights Policy: Black Citizenship and the Constitution, 1861-1868* (Port Washington, N.Y.: Kennikat Press, 1977), pp. 42-43. The admirable study by Eugene C. Murdock, *One Million Men: The Civil War Draft in the North* (Madison: State Historical Society of Wisconsin, 1971) appropriately notes the act of July only in passing, and the state of the literature suggests that it is time for another frontal assault on the Union Army of the sort attempted by Fred Shannon fifty years ago. Strangely, Dudley T. Cornish, *The Sable Arm: Negro Troops in the Union Army, 1861-1865* (New York: Longmans, Green, 1956), pp. 29, 98-99, does not include the act of July 17, 1862, in his summary of congressional policy.

little debate. But Grimes introduced an amendment providing that color or lineage should in no way lead to exemption from military service and that blacks of appropriate age were to serve thereafter both in the militia and in the volunteers, subject to the authority of the President "to organize them ... according to their race and color, as he shall believe that the public interests may require." In Shannon's eyes, this opened the way for "controversies" on "the extraneous question of freedom for slaves." But in reviewing this development and subsequent reactions to it, the correspondent of the New York *Tribune* concluded that the day was "perhaps the most important in the annals of this Congress."[21]

King asked Grimes to withdraw his proposal in favor of an amendment directed to the same end that he had in hand, and allowed Grimes to modify the substitute in certain respects. Since the conflict between radical and moderate on the militia bill focused solely on efforts to alter the King-Grimes amendment, its provisions are of considerable interest:

> *And be it further enacted,* That the President be, and he is hereby, authorized to receive into the service of the United States, for the purpose of constructing intrenchments or performing camp service, or any other labor, or any war service for which they may be found competent, persons of African descent; and such persons shall be enrolled and organized under such regulations, not inconsistent with the Constitution and laws, as the President may prescribe, and they shall be fed and paid such compensation for their services as they may agree to receive when enrolled.
> *And be it further enacted,* That when any man or boy of African descent shall render any such service as is provided for in the preceding section of this act, he, his mother, and his wife and children shall forever thereafter be free, any law, usage, or custom whatsoever to the contrary notwithstanding.
> *And be it further enacted,* That the provisions of the preceding sections shall be construed so as to apply to and include persons of African descent who may hereafter be called into the service of the United States; and all persons who have been or who may be hereafter enrolled in the service of the United States as volunteers or as militia shall receive the pay and rations of soldiers as now allowed by law according to their respective grades.[22]

The reaction of the slave-state senators to the proposal was predictable. Saulsbury deplored Grimes's original amendment as one in a series of efforts to change the character of the war from one to preserve the Constitution and restore the Union, to one "to elevate the miserable nigger." He denounced the King-Grimes amendment as a "wholesale scheme of emancipation." Moderate on many aspects of southern and war policy, Sherman proclaimed that "the time has arrived when ... the military authorities should be compelled to use all the physical force of

21. *CG,* 37 Cong., 2 sess., 3198; Shannon, *Union Army,* p. 275; New York *Daily Tribune,* July 10, 1862.
22. *CG,* 37 Cong., 2 sess., 3198.

this country to put down the rebellion."[23] Placing the matter in the broader context of war policy, Fessenden supported the use of Negroes in the field because the war must now be fought on "different principles," and the "mode of white kid-glove warfare" abandoned. The soldiers of the Union should fight and not dig ditches and entrenchments. War policy must be changed: "not from any feeling of abolition, not from any feeling of emancipation, not from any of that sort of peculiar sentiment which gentlemen are so fond of attributing to others upon this side of the Chamber and in and out of this Chamber, but from the absolute necessity of the case, from the common sense of the thing." When Fessenden moved, noted the Chicago *Tribune,* "it signifies that the whole glacier has started."[24]

Wilson told his colleagues, "The shovel and the spade and the ax have ruined thousands of the young men of the country, and sent hundreds of them to their graves.... We could have employed thousands of colored men at low rates of wages to do that ditching, and thus save[d] the health, the strength, and the lives of our brave soldiers."[25] On this issue, Rice of Minnesota, a doughface Democrat and confidant of southern congressional leaders during the late 1850s, took common ground with his ultraradical colleague, Wilkinson, deploring the use of Minnesota troops to lay railroad track and in other menial tasks.

Henderson of Missouri precipitated the first divisive vote when he tried to amend the first clause of the King-Grimes amendment by restricting its action to "free" persons of African descent and "also such persons of African descent as may owe service or labor to persons engaged in the rebellion."[26] The effect of this amendment would have been to exempt the slaves of loyal slaveholders from government service; Anthony, Browning, Cowan, and Lane of Indiana voted for the proposal, which failed by a vote of 13 to 22. Only ten moderates had voted, and the four votes they cast in support of Henderson's motion were sufficient to produce an Index of Disagreement of 40, the lowest disagreement score found among the eight divisive votes occurring in the debates on this measure.

Defeated in his first effort, Henderson then moved to add to the amendment's first section the reservation, "That all loyal persons entitled to the service or labor of persons employed under the provisions of this act shall be compensated for the loss of such service." Henderson accepted Hale's suggestion that the clause "by the laws of the State in

23. Ibid., 3198.
24. Ibid., 3200–3201; Chicago *Tribune,* July 14, 1862.
25. *CG,* 37 Cong., 2 sess., 3203.
26. Ibid., 3231.

which the owner of such slave may reside" be inserted after the word
"persons," but refused Sherman's suggestion that the matter of compensation be reserved for a separate section.[27] Of thirteen moderates voting
in the division, only Fessenden, Harris, and Sherman opposed Henderson's second amendment, and it carried by a vote of 20 to 17 (I.D.: 64).

Sherman drew the line between radical and moderate still more sharply when he proposed to amend the second section of the King-Grimes
amendment—that granting freedom to any man or boy of African descent who served the Union and to his mother, wife, and children—by
limiting the action of the section to the bondsmen of "any person, who,
during the present rebellion, has levied war or borne arms against the
United States, or adhered to their enemies by giving them aid and comfort."[28] Slaves of the loyal slave-owners of the border states would not,
therefore, be freed under the action of this law. Sherman's proposal
produced extremely strong disagreement among the Republican
senators. The twelve moderates who voted supported the proposal, and
only Howard left the radicals to join them. The Index of Disagreement
soared to 94, but the moderates with help from the slave-state senators
and free-state Democrats carried the day, 22 to 16.

Browning next moved that the words "his mother, and his wife and
children," should be struck from the second section of the King-Grimes
proposal, as amended by Sherman. Collamer had earlier pointed out
that difficulties might be met in determining the family relationships
specified by the measure, and Browning suggested that the immediate
families of the slaves who were entitled to freedom as a result of service
under the act might actually, in some cases, belong to loyal citizens. To
free such family members would be an unconstitutional invasion of "the
sovereignty of a State," argued the Illinois senator. Lane of Kansas disputed Browning's position scornfully. "I deny," he said, "that this Government cannot take the slaves of the loyal and the disloyal, and that
they are estopped from making any use of them that they choose for the
suppression of this rebellion; and having made use of them . . . it would be
a crime before God to return them to slavery." Browning, with characteristic stubbornness, maintained:

> While gentlemen disclaim any right and power under the Constitution to
> interfere with the institution of slavery in the States, regarded as a legisla-
> tive body and in times of peace, they still assert that in time of war Con-
> gress, by some mysterious operation that no one has explained and no one
> can explain, acquires a power it did not before possess to sweep out the

27. Ibid., 3232.
28. Ibid., 3233–34. Sherman inserted the words "levied war or" subsequent to the first
introduction of this amendment.

institutions of all the States if it chooses to do so; because it can sweep out one under the war power it can sweep out any other.[29]

Late on July 10 the roll was called on Browning's motion, and not a single Republican joined him. But the vote fell short of a quorum and was taken again when the debate began again next day. In this division Anthony, Cowan, Harris, Lane of Indiana, Sherman, and Ten Eyck joined Browning, but his motion was lost in a vote of 17 yeas and 21 nays (I.D.: 58). This was to be the last vote on the provisions of S. 384; on July 14, Wilson of Massachusetts brought S. 394 before his colleagues, assembled in Committee of the Whole.

King described S. 394 as a bill made up "from two or three previous bills." It contained the original provisions of S.384, amended to limit the President's call to nine months, but strengthened in that the President could himself call out the militia when states failed to take appropriate action. It also authorized a substantial increase in the volunteer forces and included sections dealing with judge advocate generals, court martial procedures, military bands, and various other matters. Then followed the basic substance of the original King amendment plus the provision that "persons of African descent" employed under this law should receive ten dollars per month plus one ration, three dollars per month less than the pay of white soldiers.

Significantly, the alterations concerning the service of Negroes that Henderson, Browning, and Sherman had effected in S. 384 had disappeared in the enlarged bill. We cannot, alas, recapture the tone of Sherman's voice as he remarked, "I think by an inadvertence, for the Senator from Massachusetts would not have done it otherwise, he has left out a very important clause in the thirteenth section which was adopted by a deliberate vote of the Senate." The Ohio senator moved to restore the amendment to the King-Grimes proposal that had limited emancipation for war service to the slaves of rebels. James Lane refused to accept Sherman's suggestion that the chamber restore the amended wording. He demanded a division, remarking, "Any price that the Senate choose to give to the loyal master I am ready to vote; but not to remand the man to slavery." On the following day, July 15, Lane announced that he would submit an amendment to the bill promising "just compensation" to loyal citizens whose slaves were freed under the act, if Sherman's amendment was voted down. Sherman retorted that Lane's proposal might cost the government as much as $1,000 when the slave of a loyal man was "employed a single day to carry a single message in the prosecution of this war." Then the Ohio senator went beyond the economics of the matter to argue, "If you adopt the clause as it now stands, you will

29. Ibid., 3235-36.

emancipate all the slaves of this country under the pretense of using them in prosecuting this war. It is unjust, unfair; and I may say further, that it is unmanly to avail yourself of this condition of affairs brought about by rebels, to seize the property of loyal people and deprive them of that property. It will be unjust."[30] Sherman's proposition prevailed by one vote but no radical supported his motion (I.D.: 92). Although believing that the emancipation of families was impractical and not wishing to distinguish between the slaves of loyal and disloyal masters, Harris, alone of the moderates, joined the radical cadre in the division.

With the distinction between the slaves of loyal and disloyal individuals once more grafted in the bill, Browning again moved to strike the words "his mother, and his wife and children" from the emancipation clause. Only six other moderates had been willing to join Browning in this motion on July 11. Although nine Republicans now supported the Browning amendment, it was lost, 17 yeas to 20 nays (I.D.: 75). Browning immediately moved that an additional sentence be added to the emancipation clause, providing, "That the mother, wife, and children of such man or boy of African descent shall not be made free by the operation of this act except where such mother, wife or children owe service or labor to some person who, during the present rebellion, has borne arms against the United States, or adhered to their enemies by giving them aid and comfort."[31] The senators accepted this in a vote of twenty-one to sixteen, with only one moderate, Howe, joining the radicals who were massed solidly against the proposal (I.D.: 92).

When the amendments made in the Committee of the Whole were brought into the Senate, Howard asked for a separate vote on Sherman's amendment. The senators reaffirmed their decision in Committee of the Whole by a vote of twenty-one to fourteen; moderates who voted supported Sherman's amendment and every radical in the division opposed the Ohioan's proposal (I.D.: 100).

Insofar as senate bills 384 and 394 placed additional resources in the hands of the President, they provoked little disagreement among Republicans. The senators of the Republican party were agreed that more men must be brought into the service and that the pool of manpower represented by free blacks and the slaves of rebels in Union-controlled territory must be tapped. The conflict between radical and moderate hung rather on whether the slaves of loyal individuals were to be used; whether, if so, their masters were to be compensated; whether the slaves of loyal individuals were to be emancipated in reward for their service; and whether the immediate families of black soldiers were also to be

30. Ibid., 3322, 3337.
31. Ibid., 3342.

freed if belonging to loyal owners. Setting compensation aside, since it did not become the focus of a vote in the debate on S. 394, the moderate position prevailed in the debate, thanks to votes from the border-state senators. Military service could be a mechanism of emancipation only as punishment for slave-owners' disloyalty. But whatever its shortcomings, and they proved to be considerable, the act of July 17 was a major milestone in the history of Republican party policy and American liberty.

The cause of the black soldiers produced only two votes that appreciably shattered Republican unity during the third session of the Thirty-seventh Congress. On March 2, 1863, the senators considered H.R. 523, to promote the efficiency of the corps of engineers and of the ordnance and quartermaster departments, and for other purposes. Section 8 of this measure provided that forces raised under section 12 of the Act Amendatory to the Militia Act of July 17, 1862, "shall be officered by persons appointed and commissioned by the President, and governed by the rules and articles of war." Section 12 of the act of July 17 authorized the President to raise black troops, but the point of section 8 was unclear on its face and Richardson, the rumpled, tobacco-spewing Democrat who had replaced Browning, slyly moved that it be struck. When Cowan admitted "the object is to officer the negroes," the senator from Illinois congratulated himself, "I did not know but it was meal . . . in the tub, but I thought it likely it was a cat," to the enjoyment of at least some of his audience. Wilson then explained that "a point . . . [had] been raised, whether the President . . . has the power to appoint the officers to command" the black troops, but under the questioning of the Illinois Democrat he denied that it was intended to commission Negroes, although admitting that a few line officers among General Butler's black troops in New Orleans were of that extraction.[32]

Later in the debate Powell moved to attach a specific proviso to section 8, "That no person of African descent shall be commissioned or hold an office in the Army of the United States." With the help of Cowan, Harris, Howe, Lane of Indiana, and Ten Eyck, this was passed in a vote of 18 to 17 (I.D.: 62.5). Lane of Kansas subsequently qualified this restriction by moving that an additional clause be appended to section 8 as amended: "except company officers in companies composed exclusively of persons of African descent." Howe was prepared to support this qualification, but his four companion moderates in the earlier division were now joined by Sherman and Howard in opposition (I.D.: 43). The senators approved Lane's amendment by a margin of two votes, but Wilson, arguing that the House would not accept H.R. 523 if section 8 remained as it was, requested that it be struck. His colleagues agreed in

32. *CG*, 37 Cong., 3 sess., 1441.

an unrecorded vote; when this bill received the President's signature, section 8 dealt with the sanitary preparation of Billy Yank's food.[33]

The black soldier and his problems ranged radical against moderate again during the first session of the Thirty-eighth Congress when Wilson brought S. 41 before his colleagues for discussion on January 2, 1864. Drawn "to promote enlistments in the Army of the United States, and for other purposes," the bill contained provisions that addressed a number of subjects including the duration of enlistments and the pay of chaplains. Two provisions raised the possibility of controversy. The second section equalized the remuneration of black and white soldiers in the same arm of the service in all respects except bounties, and provided that each would receive two months' advance pay immediately after being mustered. Section 3 provided that any slave recruit, his mother, wife, and children, were to be free as soon as he was mustered to the colors—the issue that had provoked intense disagreement among Republicans in the debates on the act of July 17, 1862.

Henderson and Johnson of Maryland opposed section 3—the former offering amendments designed to remove the slave family from the scope of the measure, and the latter arguing that Congress had no constitutional right to take Maryland's slaves without compensation, although it possessed a perfect right to use bondsmen in the army if the circumstances of war dictated. Johnson also elaborated on the difficulties of ascertaining who should be considered a wife under the law. In a long speech of February 2, which Fessenden later reported to have influenced his own thinking on the matter, Sherman urged that emancipation be handled in a general statute, but stressed that the owners of released slaves must be compensated for their loss. The senators deferred consideration of the bill through much of February, and meanwhile the two houses agreed upon the Enrollment Act of February 24, providing in its twenty-fourth section that the slaves of loyal masters who were enrolled under this act were to be henceforth free but that the owner was to be compensated for the loss.[34] Serious discussion of S. 41 did not resume until early March when Brown introduced a substitute for section 3, designed in its first part to write the Emancipation Proclamation freeing the slaves in Confederate territory into law, and declaring, in a second provision, that there should be neither slavery nor involuntary servitude in any of the states or territories of the United States except as punishment for criminal offenses.

Wilson asked Brown to withdraw his proposal and instead offered an

33. Ibid., 1446–47; 37 Cong., 3 sess., *Laws,* Chap. LXXVIII in *CG,* App., 213. Neither Berry, *Military Necessity and Civil Rights Policy,* nor Belz, *A New Birth of Freedom,* nor for that matter, Henry Wilson, mentions this illuminating incident.

34. 38 Cong., 1 sess., *Laws,* Chap. XII in *CG,* App., 142.

amended version of S. 41, proclaiming the wife and children of a slave enlistee to be free as soon as the recruit was mustered. A second section provided that it would be the obligation of the slave-state commissions authorized under the Enrollment Acts of March 3, 1863, and February 24, 1864, to set compensation to loyal masters who lost slaves under the operation of the revised S. 41. Wilkinson was hostile to this provision, proclaiming himself "utterly opposed to . . . paying a 'just compensation' to . . . pretended masters." He was "for setting them free at once." Sherman provided moderate counterpoint, remaining firm in his belief that the senators should "not kill the dog by detachments" but rather "wipe out 'slavery' by a carefully considered amendment of the Constitution," not "by piecemeal."[35] Wilson argued that the measure was essential because owners were selling or mistreating the slave families of enlisted men, and blacks were reluctant to enlist because they were apprehensive about the fate of their families. Thus could the necessities of war be brought to bear on the "domestic" institutions of every loyal slave state.

Other senators believed, like Sherman, that Wilson's bill should be deferred until the Thirteenth Amendment was perfected, and some doubted whether the proposed machinery would work. In deference to the latter group, the Massachusetts senator dropped the provision for payment from the measure. Meanwhile, Conness had recommended that this "important" bill be referred to the Select Committee on Slavery and Freedmen, and Carlile proposed that it go instead to the Judiciary Committee. Since the latter was a standing committee, Carlile's motion took precedence over that of Conness. But the senators, voting on March 21, rejected the gambit as Brown, Fessenden, Foster, Grimes, and Lane of Indiana joined sixteen radicals in opposition, while Cowan, Doolittle, Howe, Ten Eyck, and Trumbull voted with the Democrats and Border Unionists in support of it (I.D.: 50). Was this in part a contest between the two committees over control of legislation relating to slavery? Perhaps, but in the end the senators also refused, in an untallied vote, to commit Wilson's measure to Sumner's committee. On the following day Willey noted that there were:

> several bills before the Senate, each having a special design to accomplish, and all of which have a general purport. The special design of each bill is apparent on its face; but the general object of all these bills, and I am disposed to believe the main object, is the destruction of slavery. Among these bills is one to repeal what is usually called the fugitive slave law. There is another to make persons of color competent witnesses in the Federal courts; and there is also the bill now under consideration more especially.

35. *CG*, 38 Cong., 1 sess., 1178–79.

After an extended explanation of his own position concerning slavery and the Constitution, he called upon his colleagues to support the constitutional amendment prohibiting slavery that the Committee on the Judiciary had reported.[36] Much was still to be heard of the other measures disturbing Willey, but the senators allowed him the last word on S. 41. It was not discussed again.

On February 23, 1864, Senator Wilson called up S. 23, a joint resolution "to equalize the pay of the soldiers of the United States Army." By this time there were some 70,000 blacks in the service of the United States, but pursuant to the act of July, 1862, these Negro soldiers were receiving only ten dollars per month in contrast to the thirteen received by white soldiers. S. 23 provided that "all persons of color who have been or may be mustered into the military service of the United States" would receive "the same uniform, clothing, arms, equipments, camp equipage, rations, medical and hospital attendance, pay, and emoluments, other than bounty, as other soldiers of the regular or volunteer forces of the United States of like arm of the service, during the whole time in which they shall be or shall have been in such service."[37]

Complicating the situation was the fact that Governor John Andrew of Massachusetts claimed that he had raised the Fifty-Fourth and Fifty-Fifth Massachusetts regiments—black volunteer organizations—under the Volunteer Enrollment Act of July, 1861, which made no distinction as to color. Actually, the men of these regiments had not been enrolled until the 1862 act was in effect, but Massachusetts officials had informed them that they would receive the normal wage of volunteer soldiers. The Secretary of War refused to pay the larger sum. Apparently at the suggestion of their officers, the men of the Fifty-Fourth and Fifty-Fifth refused to accept either the wage proffered by the federal government or a supplement tendered by the Massachusetts legislature to make up the difference. Complicating the situation still more, men in a number of other black regiments also claimed to have been told that they would receive the pay of white volunteers, but they clearly had been mustered under the terms of the act of 1862.

S. 23 raised a number of issues. Was the government justified in making retroactive payments, given the condition of the Treasury? The conditions of enlistment of various categories of white soldiers differed; should these also be equalized? Should the gift of freedom be considered as the equivalent of bounty or a certain number of dollars per month? If the government should not make up the deficits in pay to all the blacks, should the members of Congress at least make the increase in pay re-

36. Ibid., 1228–35.
37. Ibid., 632.

troactive for the members of the two Massachusetts regiments, who apparently had received assurance from state officials that they would receive the higher rate of pay? Governor Andrew maintained that he had received permission from Secretary Stanton to give this assurance. But if those regiments received a retroactive raise, why not also include the additional regiments—some fifteen to twenty, according to Senator Wilson—whose members claimed to have been told by recruiting officers that they would be paid thirteen dollars per month?[38] At issue obviously also were those troublesome ethical, philosophical, and political questions that lay at the very heart of the nation's trauma.

Initially, Conness moved to strike out the retroactive feature of the resolution but then withdrew his amendment, fearful of doing injustice to some of the black regiments. He understood, he explained, that Senator Sumner had an amendment ready which would "cover the entire case." The senator from Massachusetts then moved that the following proviso should be attached to the bill:

> *Provided,* With regard to all past services, it shall appear to the satisfaction of the Secretary of War that such persons at the time of being mustered into the service of the United States were led to suppose that in fact they were enlisted under the act of Congress approved July 22, 1861 [*sic*], as volunteers in the army of the United States.[39]

Sumner disavowed any interest in providing retroactive raises for those who were clearly enlisted at a rate of ten dollars per month. But was the matter this simple? Massachusetts had recruited the Fifty-Fourth and Fifty-Fifth regiments from northern states generally, thus drawing on other states to fill the Massachusetts quota. Was the federal government now to reward the Bay State for tapping the manpower of her neighbors with unjustifiable inducements?

Johnson attacked Sumner head on, arguing that there was "no obligation, either legal or moral, upon the Government to pay these men more than the law entitles them to." Grimes took a different tack, arguing against Sumner's attempt to "cover some individual cases in a general

---

38. Henry Wilson describes the issue of pay rather blandly and somewhat misleadingly in *History of the Antislavery Measures,* pp. 293–312, and *Rise and Fall of the Slave Power,* 3:371–79. See also Henry G. Pearson, *The Life of John A. Andrew, Governor of Massachusetts, 1861–1865* (Boston: Houghton Mifflin, 1904), 2:94–121; Cornish, *The Sable Arm,* pp. 184–96; David Donald, *Charles Sumner and the Rights of Man* (New York: Knopf, 1970), p. 160. Herman Belz provides an extremely thoughtful analysis of the equal pay controversy in "Law, Politics, and Race in the Struggle for Equal Pay during the Civil War," *Civil War History,* 22 (September 1976), 197–213. See also Benjamin P. Thomas and Harold M. Hyman, *Stanton: The Life and Times of Lincoln's Secretary of War* (New York: Knopf, 1962), p. 264 and passim. A Massachusetts view from the field is found in Thomas W. Higginson, *Army Life in a Black Regiment* (initially published, Boston: Fields, Osgood, 1870, but used in Beacon reprint, 1962), pp. 280–92.

39. *CG,* 38 Cong., 1 sess., 632.

law." Far better, Grimes suggested, to use special legislation to deal with particular cases. Howe agreed, pointing out that Governor Andrew had acted after the passage of the 1862 act and concluded, "that upon the question of law I think the Senator is mistaken in assuming that there is any legal right vested in these men by any previous legislation of ours to receive more than ten dollars a month." Cowan argued that equity should be first done to the white soldiers who had joined the army for less bounty than was currently being offered, and this long before Negroes entered the service. Collamer attacked the vagueness of the amendment, hanging, as it did, on what the enlistees "were led to believe," although he criticized the way in which the matter had been handled by the War Department.[40] The senators rejected Sumner's amendment without a division.

Later in the discussion of S. 23, Sumner returned to the problem of the Massachusetts regiments and, basing his action upon Collamer's earlier remarks, he moved an amendment as follows:

> *Provided,* That in all cases of past service, where it shall appear to the satisfaction of the Secretary of War by the actual papers of enlistment, that such persons were enlisted as volunteers under the act of July, 1861, the pay promised by that act shall be allowed from the commencement of such service.[41]

Collamer promptly disavowed the action taken in his name, arguing that the matter should be handled by special act rather than by engrafting it in a general law. The motion failed, 16 yeas and 21 nays (I.D.: 69). Of moderates voting, only Foster and Ten Eyck supported Sumner, and Foot and Harlan were the only radicals to oppose him. The senators accepted a somewhat modified version of this amendment on February 25; the vote showed a mere nineteen senators in support and eighteen opposed, and revealed that moderates' support for the formula was still less enthusiastic than that of the radicals. But on February 29 the senators accepted Grimes' motion to refer S. 23 back to committee, and discussion of the issue of equal pay for black soldiers focused on S. 145, "a bill to equalize the pay of soldiers in the United States Army," introduced by Wilson on March 2.

When S. 145 appeared to be stalled in the House Committee on Military Affairs some weeks later, Wilson, to the frustration of Fessenden, inserted its equalization provisions in the army appropriations bill. It was in this measure that they finally became law, so written as to have retroactive effect from January 1, 1864, for all black soldiers. But this victory was neither easy nor complete. The Senate provisions had prom-

40. Ibid., 633–34, 637.
41. Ibid., 641.

ised "all persons of color" the pay and clothing pledged to them on entry into the service by individuals acting under the authority of the War Department. But various members of the House opposed this commitment because they believed it would benefit primarily regiments raised under the aegis of Massachusetts. No fewer than three conference committees were required to conciliate the conflicting views, and the final formula impressed Sumner as being "the little end of nothing."[42]

As Howe, chairman of the Senate managers in the third conference committee, put it to the Senate, "if you insist upon a law now putting all colored troops from the time of their enlistment upon the footing and upon the pay of white soldiers, you cannot carry the bill through both Houses," nor, alternatively, was it possible, he explained, to carry through "a provision paying only colored troops who have been promised a special rate of pay to the exclusion of those . . . who have not been enlisted under a special contract."[43] Reflecting such realities, the Army Appropriation Act of June 15, 1864, provided that black soldiers who had been free on April 19, 1861, were entitled to full pay from the date of their enlistments and instructed the Attorney General to rule on related questions of law—a prospective opinion that was expected to endorse such equalization. The colonels of the Fifty-Fourth and Fifty-Fifth Massachusetts regiments offered a somewhat disingenuous oath to their troops that allowed them to certify their complete muster rolls as having been "free" on April 19, 1861, and these men received their retroactive pay in October, 1864. In early March, 1865, Congress capitulated and provided retroactive equalizations to "any regiment of colored troops," mustered "under any assurance by the President or the Secretary of War," that its privates and noncommissioned officers "should be paid the same as other troops of the same arm of the service."[44]

In part, these events in the Senate during the winter and spring of 1864 apparently reflected irritation at Sumner's efforts on behalf of equal rights, and suspicion that the Yankee sharpers of Massachusetts were self-righteously gratifying their puritanical egos while filling their quota of enlisted men at the expense of other states. Although Governor Andrew's biographer and the modern historian of black troops depict the critics of the Massachusetts position as despicably perverse, and injustice was certainly done to a large number of black soldiers, it is also less than accurate to make Congress as a whole, or moderate Republicans in particular, the scapegoats. The most recent student of the controversy views it appropriately as one in which "law, politics, and

42. Ibid., 2852. Howe embellished this to "little end of nothing whittled down," p. 2879.
43. Ibid., 2852.
44. 38 Cong., 1 sess., *Laws,* Chap. CXXIV, Sec. 2–5 in *CG,* App., 178–79, and 38 Cong., 2 sess., *Laws,* Chap. LXXIX, sec. 5 in *CG,* App., 134.

race . . . interacted in an unusual way." This incident surely provides a fine example of negative cue-giving in the political realm and, once the initial skirmishing had ended in the debate on S. 23, there were no marked differences in radical and moderate voting patterns on the question in the Senate.[45]

On June 29, 1864, Wilson of Massachusetts brought up H.R. 549, to further "regulate and provide for the enrolling and calling out the national forces," before his colleagues in Committee of the Whole. This bill provided for various changes in the system of recruiting volunteers and draftees then in force; section 3 provided that a state governor might send recruiting agents into any of the rebellious states to raise men to help fill the quota of his state.

Brown of Missouri announced that he and some other members of the Committee on Military Affairs believed that such a measure "if passed in its present shape," would "be fatal to the military system of the United States."[46] The bill would perhaps serve to recruit colored troops, but more expensively than the laws then in force, since it raised the three-year bounty from $100 to $400. The increase in bounties would not produce many additional white volunteers and would be a tremendous drain on the treasury. H.R. 549 would provide a "sham system, that simply encourages substitutes hired or caught or brought from the southern States." The measure would destroy "the harmony and the confidence" between the eastern and western States. He explained:

> The people of the West will feel that it is an injustice; they will feel that it is no longer a common cause; they will feel as if the gauntlet had been thrown down by the eastern or *capital* States to this effect, that the war if fought out at all must be fought out by their money and what it will fetch by colored soldiers alone, and not by their sons and brothers; and I tell you when that gauntlet is thrown down the men of the West will not stand to any such distribution of the burdens of this conflict.

Brown moved to strike section 3 of the bill but shortly withdrew his motion in deference to Sherman's desire to replace the offensive section with one directing the President to send federal recruiting officers into the South to recruit, according to the existing law, volunteers who would

45. Cornish, *The Sable Arm*, pp. 184–96; Pearson, *John A. Andrew*, 2:94–121; Belz, "Law, Politics and Race," p. 197. Belz perhaps makes too much of the distinction between radicals and moderates in these matters. For instance, in reference to the Militia Act of July 17, 1863, he argues (p. 210, and n. 56) that "conservative Republicans who wished to restrict blacks to camp labor" supported an amendment to strike the section allowing Negroes to perform "any military or naval service." But the vote on this amendment given on a page cited by Belz (*CG*, 37 Cong., 2 sess., 3231) shows that only Cowan of the moderate or conservative Republicans supported it.

46. *CG*, 38 Cong., 1 sess., 3378, 3381.

be eligible for the same rate of pay, bounties, and pensions as other troops in the service of the United States. Although Wilson argued that individual or state recruiters had been more effective than federal officers, Grimes supported Brown, arguing that section 3 was an "inhuman provision." Ten Eyck took the floor to maintain, "I fear if the loyal, patriotic white men of this country are to be left at home in the pursuit of their lawful money-making business and the battle is to be finally fought by colored men exclusively, that battle which we expected to have been won will be lost and our credit and our character sullied forever."[47] Sherman's amendment was accepted without a division. Criticism of H.R. 549 continued, however, and Grimes finally moved that the Senate substitute its own bill, hitherto ignored by the House of Representatives. His colleagues approved the gambit, and later agreed to various additional clauses. And so the debate ended with Wilson predicting gloomily that the night's work would come to nothing.

In a broad sense Wilson was correct, because the House refused to accept the Senate amendments and called for a committee of conference. The report of the committee came before the senators on July 2, containing twenty-five recommendations. Most important, the managers suggested that the Senate recede from its amendment substituting its own bill, and accept H.R. 549 with various amendments. Of significance among the additional recommendations was number 16, closing Arkansas, Tennessee, and Louisiana to the state recruiters—some solace to those who had originally opposed section 3, as was a reduction in the period of time allowed state recruiters in the South. But in the debate on the report, four votes produced radical-moderate disagreement at the 40 percent level or above. The senators refused to agree to the report by a vote of 16 yeas and 18 nays (I.D.: 44), and approved Sherman's motion requesting a further conference, 28 yeas and 8 nays, with six radicals opposed (I.D.: 40). But after more rather acrimonious discussion, Wilson explained that the members of the House of Representatives "had put together the repeal of the commutation clause [allowing individuals to purchase exemption] and the reduction of the time and the liberty to enlist men in the rebel States, and they would not separate them, and that any attempt to do so would be a defeat of the measure by a decisive majority."[48] After the senators had agreed to reconsider the vote on the call for a new conference, Conness asked that a vote instead be taken on reconsideration of the vote rejecting the committee report. Seventeen Republicans rallied behind him and seventeen senators opposed the proposal; the motion carried, 18 to 17. The senators then approved the committee report by the same margin. Minor changes in

47. Ibid., 3382, 3384.
48. Ibid., 3487.

the voting alignment raised the disagreement score from 49 on the reconsideration motion to 69 on the roll call on the committee report. So passed "An Act further to regulate ... the enrolling and calling out the National Forces."

In the three most closely contested roll calls dealing with the recommendations of the select committee, Cowan, Doolittle, Harris, Howe, Lane of Indiana, Sherman, Ten Eyck, and Trumbull voted against H.R. 549, although not all were present for each vote. Significantly, a disproportionate number of moderates were absent for these roll calls, as was the case with some other roll calls that produced substantial radical-moderate conflict during this session. Grimes and Brown had spoken against southern recruitment, but they did not vote against the committee findings. Although East-West disagreement scores of 30 and 37 percent did develop on two of the four votes discussed here, radical-moderate scores were of greater magnitude. Apparently this issue tapped the anti-Negro or racist dimension of Republican moderation more strongly than it did sectional loyalties. And with this measure, the black soldier's role in dividing radical and moderate Republican senators ceased to be of major importance.

During the second session of the Thirty-seventh Congress, the representatives and senators perfected an elaborate system of taxation. Marshall's famous maxim, "the power to tax involves the power to destroy," was not lost on Sumner at least, and on Friday, May 28, he offered a new section to the internal revenue bill (H.R. 312), providing "that any person who shall claim the service or labor for life of any other person under the laws of any State shall pay, on account of such person so claimed, the sum of ten dollars." Fessenden informed Sumner that the Committee on Finance had agreed upon an amendment to the same end which "would be drawn with more care than that," but the senator from Massachusetts explained that he was following the "precedent of the Constitution, which taxes slaves imported at ten dollars." Actually section 9 of Article I of that document merely provided that Congress *might* impose a tax or duty on slaves imported, "not exceeding ten dollars for each person." Sumner's tax, he explained, was not a capitation tax, which would have to be levied in proportion to the population of all states. Rather, it was a "tax on a person who claims the service or labor of another for life, proportioned to the extent of his claim. In other words, ... *a tax on a claim of property.*" Such a levy, explained Sumner, in no way endorsed the morality of the institution nor gave it any "sanction."[49]

---

49. See Sidney Ratner, *American Taxation: Its History as a Social Force in Democracy* (New York: Norton, 1942), pp. 57-99 for a general account of taxation during the Civil War.

Sumner saw no inconsistency, he maintained, in arguing that slaves should have all the rights of "persons" under the Constitution, on the one hand, while at the same time proposing that the master's claim to property in the slave should be taxed, because "by an unquestionable rule of interpretation, applicable to the Constitution, every word is to be construed *in favor of liberty,* so as most to promote liberty. . . . But while insisting upon every such presumption, it does not follow that the counter-claim shall not be taxed. . . . Freedom is to be enlarged in every way possible, whether by encouraging the slave or discouraging the master." The tax, Sumner continued, "is easy to levy. It is profitable. And so far as it exerts an influence, it must be a discouragement to an offensive wrong, which is the parent of our present troubles, and the occasion of all this taxation."[50]

Sherman immediately took the floor in opposition to Sumner's amendment. "The persons . . . commonly called slaves," he argued, were "persons and not property within the meaning of the Constitution. . . . Taxes upon persons must be assessed in a different mode. You cannot levy a poll tax under the Constitution of the United States except it apply to all persons, and be duly apportioned." The senator from Ohio also maintained that the tax was inexpedient in that it would be collected only from the "loyal men" of the border states, "those who are suffering most from this war." He pointed out that there was not "a single article of property, personal or real, taxed by this bill. . . . The theory of the bill is to put a tax upon luxuries, or rather upon the process of making them, upon manufactures, upon certain productions of nature, upon certain employments of life, upon receipts of corporations, and upon certain stamps."[51] Far more appropriate therefore, he believed, would be a tax on cotton, thus far favored in the House but spurned in the Senate, no doubt to the great relief of some Massachusetts manufacturers.

At this point in the debate, Fessenden explained that the Committee on Finance had struck out the cotton tax and had agreed that a slave tax should be offered. Simmons then read the provision that he had drawn on behalf of the committee, and Sumner accepted it with some modification in place of his original amendment. Now the proposal read:

> That an annual tax of five dollars shall be paid by every person or persons, corporation, or society, for and on account of the service or labor of every

The Internal Revenue Act and its implications are briefly described on pp. 73–77. Ratner makes no reference to the incidents described here, nor did Harry E. Smith, *The United States Federal Internal Tax History from 1861 to 1871* (Boston: Houghton Mifflin, 1914). See, however, Milton M. McPherson, "Federal Taxes on Cotton, 1862–1868" (Ph.D. diss., University of Alabama, 1970). *CG,* 37 Cong., 2 sess., 2401.

50. *CG,* 37 Cong., 2 sess., 2401–2.
51. Ibid., 2402.

other person between the ages of ten and sixty-five years, whose service or labor, for a term of years or for life, is claimed to be owned by such first-mentioned person or persons, corporation, or society, whether in a fiduciary capacity, or otherwise, under and by virtue of the laws or customs of any State; and said annual tax shall be levied and collected of the person or persons, corporation, or society, making such claim, and of their goods, chattels, or lands, as is hereinbefore provided; but in no case shall the person or persons whose service or labor is so claimed, or their service or labor, be sold for the purpose of collecting said tax; *Provided,* That this tax shall not apply to service due to parents."

After presenting this proposal, which also reached apprentices in northern states, Sumner noted Sherman's objections. His colleague from Ohio, he pointed out, had voted to tax "auctioneers, lawyers, jugglers, and slaughterers of cattle"—here the Massachusetts senator accepted Sherman's interjection that the tax was on their employments—and in his proposal, he continued blandly, "we propose to tax the employment of the slave-master, that is all. It is the business of the slave-master to make the slave work. . . . He is an auctioneer of human rights, a broker of human labor; a juggler of human sufferings and human sympathies; I might say a slaughterer of human hopes; and, sir, if the Senator from Ohio can tax an auctioneer, or a broker, or a juggler, or a slaughterer of cattle," why not, asked Sumner, tax "the special form of these vocations which all concur in the slave-master?"[52]

As was to be expected, Sherman found Sumner no more convincing in his second explanation than in his first and suggested that the amendment was an effort "to gratify a feeling of resentment against a class of persons who are not here." He moved to substitute a provision imposing a tax of one cent a pound on all cotton held "on and after the 1st day of July, 1862," and excepting manufacturers' inventories of that date. King and Howe interjected their opposition to this tactic, maintaining that both levies were desirable.[53]

Fessenden took the floor to explain that his viewpoint was financial, "the very driest point of view in which it can be looked at—as a mere question of dollars and cents." There was no question of constitutionality in his mind, he told his colleagues:

Whether you call it by its name of slavery, or whether you call it by any other name, it makes no difference. I see no sort of objection to it. I cannot conceive that it is a capitation tax in any sense of the word. We do not lay the tax, as the Senator of Massachusetts said, on the slave. We do not select a person, we do not select a class of persons as such, to be taxed; but we select persons having under the laws peculiar privileges which are pecuniary benefits, and result as such, and are understood as such. Those

52. Ibid., 2403.
53. Ibid., 2403-4.

privileges are as proper subjects of taxation as anything else that is a privilege and results in pecuniary benefit.[54]

There was, as Sherman had admitted, precedent for taxing slaves. In Fessenden's view the slaves were untaxed property, which should bear a just proportion of the costs of the war. He believed that a two-dollar tax per slave was equitable and proposed to amend Sumner's amendment to that effect, if Sherman would withdraw his proposition. That senator, however, requested a division and saw his amendment defeated, yeas 15, nays 22 (I.D.: 22).

Sumner's proposal disturbed various Republicans, including some normally considered to have been radicals. Although the positions of Sumner, Sherman, and Fessenden defined the major parameters of the debates, other statements and exchanges were also enlightening. Pomeroy argued that slaves must be taxed on a three-fifths basis if considered as persons. If, instead, the tax was on the claim to use slave labor, why not tax the labor of domestic animals? Nor would he support the tax if it was to be viewed primarily as punishment. Clark then suggested that Pomeroy might regard the tax as one on the income from slave labor, only to have Sherman point out that such an interpretation meant that this particular form of income would be twice taxed. Cowan argued that the wording of the proposition was a patent attempt to evade the Constitution's requirement that capitation or other direct taxes must be laid in proportion to the last enumeration or census; in reality, he asserted, this was a capitation tax on the slave, plain and simple. Ten Eyck and Browning agreed and the latter also detected a covert attack on the institution of slavery in the states. The capitation-tax provision had been placed in the Constitution, such men declared, specifically to protect slaves from taxation, and they pointed out that abolition speakers had long made much of that very fact. Browning chided Sumner for arguing that a cotton tax was illegal because it was in effect an export tax and forbidden by the Constitution, only to propose an unconstitutional direct tax on slaves.

Fessenden's proposal to reduce the amount of the tax from five dollars to two passed by a vote of 28 to 10 (I.D.: 40). King, Pomeroy, Trumbull Wilmot, and Wilson joined Sumner in opposing it, although Pomeroy's vote may actually have been directed against the principle of the proposition rather than representing support of the five-dollar tax. When the senators voted on the amended motion, Fessenden, Howe, and Simmons, moderate members of the Committee on Finance, were joined by Anthony, another moderate, and ten radicals in voting yea (I.D.: 46). But twenty-two nay votes carried the day and the amendment failed.

54. Ibid., 2406.

On June 4, 5, and 6, the senators once more discussed the troublesome subjects of slaves and cotton, as the actions of the senators in Committee of the Whole were considered in the Senate. As pursued by Wilson and Chandler, the rhetorical discussion of the cotton-tax provision developed overtones of East against West. Seeking to have the matter compromised by agreement on a half-cent tax on each pound of cotton, a scheme previously tried and defeated, Sherman moved that the earlier vote on the subject be reconsidered. His colleagues accepted the motion by a vote of 24 to 15 (I.D.: 45). In the new vote on the one-half-cent amendment, the chamber voted 30 yea and 10 nay. Seven radicals and Ten Eyck opposed both the motion to reconsider and the amendment, but Hale, Howard, and Lane of Indiana switched their votes to yea in the second division and the disagreement score in that tally was only 39.5. Neither vote showed disagreement of any consequence between eastern and western Republicans.

Subsequently Sumner returned to the subject of taxing slaves or slaveholders, by proposing to add a new section to the internal revenue bill:

> that every person claiming the services or labor of any other person as a slave shall pay a tax of two dollars on account of every person so claimed; but in no case shall any person so claimed be sold for the purpose of collecting the tax.

This wording, it should be noted, exempted the northern manager of apprentice labor from the provisions of the clause. The vote supported the proposition, 19 to 16 (I.D.: 42). But the matter was not ended; on June 6, Anthony moved to reconsider the vote that had laid a tax of two dollars on slaves, announcing that he did so at the request of other senators. There now ensued a burst of rather sharp debate in which Sumner and Trumbull once more avowed the constitutionality of the measure, and Doolittle affirmed that it was a poll tax, despite the ingenuity with which its champions defended it. It was, he maintained, both unconstitutional and inexpedient. The debate became acerbic as Trumbull accused him of repeating a "misstatement in a loud voice and emphatic manner." Proud of his speaking style and admitting that he spoke in "clear and distinct" tones, "perhaps easily heard," Doolittle maintained that he was not aware of having spoken in "any very loud voice."[55]

Surprisingly enough, Hale, and more predictably, Browning and Cowan lumbered into the field to attack the Sumner amendment, and a bitter exchange occurred when Cowan affirmed his determination to be dogmatic in defense of the Constitution. Wade interjected, "All but the

55. Ibid., 2587, 2599.

'matic,'" and then took the floor to castigate the senator from Pennsylvania. He saw, he said, no necessity "for any Senator coming forward with renewed protestations of devotion and fidelity to the Constitution of the United States." He continued:

> I do not deny that a man has a right to take a seat on this floor, and—if he sees fit to do it—become the mere advocate, the watch-dog for traitors in the field.... But, sir let not such a one rise here and criticise my course, and much less get up and reproach, as he has, the Senate of the United States, and put on airs as though a gentleman from the wilds of Pennsylvania should come into the Senate of the United States, and in the middle of his first session, reproach the Senate for the course they had taken....
>
> As to the Senator from Pennsylvania, you cannot get a negro anywhere that he will touch, even across a ten acre lot. He is guarded at all points; he bristles like a porcupine whenever it is proposed to touch the institution of slavery anywhere. Can you tax their cotton? No, says the Senator. Can you confiscate their property? Horrible! Sir, a man may be a watch-dog for that institution on this floor, if he chooses; he has a right to be; but he ought to be content with his occupation.

Though he was indeed young, inexperienced, and from "the wilds of Pennsylvania," Cowan was anything but cowed by the vitriolic language of the senator from Ohio. He had not understood, he remarked, "that age or length of service would sanctify folly, or that it would give character to billingsgate that might well be the envy of a fishwoman of Alexandria." He had "resisted projects which . . . were mischievous as questions of policy," and "other projects which" he believed "were unlawful as against the Constitution."[56] He expressed no regrets. In the voting too, Cowan was to have the better of Wade. The motion to reconsider was accepted by a vote of 22 to 18 (I.D.: 61), and despite an amendment from the House exempting slaves under ten or over sixty years of age from its operation, the Sumner amendment could find only seventeen supporters as compared to twenty-three in opposition (I.D.: 54).

The three votes on the final version of the Sumner amendment did not reflect major shifting of position within the Republican party. Sixteen Republicans (twelve radicals and four moderates) voted for Sumner's amendment when he introduced it, opposed reconsideration, and supported it in the final vote. Eight moderate Republicans and two radicals, Hale and Wilson, made common clause with the Democrats and slave-state senators against it. Only Rice, a Democrat, shifted from initial support of the amendment to opposition; absences account for the other differences in the alignment on these three votes. Whether motivated by constitutional scruples or sympathy for the plight of the border states, a majority of moderates balked when their colleagues proposed to direct

56. Ibid., 2603-5.

the taxing power uniquely at slave owners. When the Internal Revenue Act became law on July 1, 1862, it included a tax on cotton, somewhat more innocuous than Sherman's proposal, but it did not touch the slave, outcomes ignored by most of Sumner's biographers.

A general discussion of the broader meanings of the differences between radicals and moderates will appear in Chapter 9, after most of the divisive voting has been reviewed. But the debates on District emancipation, on issues relating to black soldiers, and on the taxation of individuals as slave owners attune one to various characteristics of the senatorial legislative process. Quite obviously the differences in position among the Republicans were neither random nor in general capricious; they meant something to the men involved and they were recurrent, as the tallies of radical and moderate dissent show. Although the oratory covered much ground and its foundations might range from simple expediency to the hoariest of constitutional maxims, it was advanced in earnest. And one should not, if the evidence in this chapter is illustrative, expect that either radicals or moderates would carry the day completely on issues where strong differences appeared. Although relatively small in numbers, the border-state and Democratic cadres were sufficient to wield a balance of power at such times. On occasion also, these senators could affect the substance of legislation, as the Davis colonization amendment showed. Policy-making in the Civil War Senate was complex, and the significance of particular measures far different on reexamination from what one might expect. Symbolically a great victory for emancipation, the District Act revealed the softness of Republican rapprochement on race; though he represented a far more divisive issue than is normally suggested, the black soldier was to fill the decimated ranks of Union armies and offer the most practical approach to emancipation; the taxation of slave owners would become linked to the needs of cotton manufacturers in Massachusetts.

# 6

# Emancipation and "Human" Rights

No Republican questioned the constitutional right of Congress to abolish slavery in the District of Columbia, but emancipation linked to miliary service and the use of taxation to harass slaveholders in the loyal border regions induced qualms in moderate minds, as we have seen. But the war years also provided the representatives and senators with the opportunity to deal more generally with slavery in regions where it had long existed and where the Republicans had admitted that the federal government had no authority to interfere.

As the second session of the Thirty-seventh Congress drew to a close in mid-July, 1862, the senators debated and finally passed S. 365, "providing for the admission of the State of West Virginia into the Union," a bill affecting Virginia counties in which some ten thousand slaves resided.[1] As the bill came before the Senate, it provided that the delegates to the West Virginia constitutional convention should place a provision

1. For general accounts of congressional efforts to establish West Virginia as an independent state see: Granville D. Hall, *The Rending of Virginia: A History* (Chicago: Mayer & Miller, 1902), pp. 457–70; William P. Willey, *An Inside View of the Formation of the State of West Virginia. With Character Sketches of the Pioneers in that Movement* (Wheeling: News Publishing, 1901), pp. 98–118; Charles H. Ambler, *Waitman Thomas Willey, Orator, Churchman, Humanitarian....* (Huntington, W. Va.: Standard Printing & Publishing, 1954), pp. 75–106; George E. Moore, *A Banner in the Hills: West Virginia's Statehood* (New York: Appleton-Century-Crofts, 1963), pp. 195–207; Richard O. Curry, *A House Divided: A Study of Statehood Politics and the Copperhead Movement in West Virginia* (Pittsburgh: University of Pittsburgh Press, 1964), pp. 69–105; Leonard P. Curry, *Blueprint for Modern America: Nonmilitary Legislation of the First Civil War Congress* (Nashville: Vanderbilt University Press, 1968), pp. 48–52. For a recent review of the issues involved in the creation of West Virginia from Lincoln's point of view, see Dallas S. Shaffer, "Lincoln and the 'Vast Question' of West Virginia," *West Virginia History*, 32 (January 1971), 86–100. This author sees the radicals as providing the driving force for admission in the Congress.

in the constitution pledging that "the children of all slaves born within the limits of said State shall be free . . . from and after the 4th day of July, 1863." Sumner moved to replace this clause prescribing a system of gradual emancipation by substituting the "Jeffersonian" wording of the Ordinance of 1787 as follows: "Within the limits of said State there shall be neither slavery nor involuntary servitude, otherwise than in the punishment of crime whereof the party shall be duly convicted." A solid phalanx of eleven radicals supported the motion, but they were overwhelmed by the votes of twenty-four of their colleagues (I.D.: 85). Among the twenty-four were the radicals Foot and Wade, and the Ohioan admitted that the vote he had just given "was . . . very harsh and unsavory." But the proposition, Wade explained, was "inharmonious and inconsistent with the real purpose we all had in view in admitting this new State."[2]

In order to mollify opposition sentiment, Senator Willey proposed different phrasing, drawing particularly upon wording that had been developed in the House of Representatives. Wade then moved that slaves who were under the age of twenty-one at the time of the creation of the new state should be freed upon reaching that age, and his motion was accepted without a recorded tally. Lane of Kansas subsequently succeeded in having this provision altered to provide that slaves under the age of ten would be freed upon reaching their twenty-first birthday, and those who were over ten years of age and under twenty-one would be emancipated upon reaching the age of twenty-five. When the bill moved from Committee of the Whole to the Senate, Sumner again proposed to substitute his amendment in place of the gradual emancipation provisions. Rather pompously, Lane told him that he proposed "to legislate upon the subject of slavery as upon all other subjects, practically," and said that he had assurances that the House would reject the Senate version if it contained the Jeffersonian provision and that the people of West Virginia certainly would reject it.[3] Sumner, remarkably, resisted the temptation to chastise Lane's effrontery or to question his claims to practical statesmanship, and abandoned his efforts. No doubt all the Republicans, with the possible exception of Cowan and Browning, would have liked to emancipate the slaves of West Virginia immediately. The moderates, however, were realistic enough to see that an effort to do so would have jeopardized both the cooperation of West Virginians and the statehood movement.

2. *CG*, 37 Cong., 2 sess., 2942, 3308. "Sigma" reported in the Cincinnati *Daily Commercial*, July 15, 1862, that Wade's major presentation on behalf of the admission bill "clinched" its passage, an interpretation of the value of congressional debate that runs counter to that of many modern analysts.

3. *CG*, 37 Cong., 2 sess., 3316.

At Lincoln's suggestion and with some grumbling, Republicans of both chambers had approved a resolution in March and April, 1862, pledging assistance to states willing to abolish slavery voluntarily: "That the United States ought to cooperate with any State which may adopt the gradual abolishment of slavery, giving to such State pecuniary aid to be used by such State in its discretion to compensate for the inconvenience, public and private, produced by such change of systems." In July the President went so far as to send a model bill to this end to Capitol Hill and, during the final session of the Thirty-seventh Congress, compensated emancipation received serious attention on the floors of both houses. Specifically at issue in the Senate was H.R. 634, "giving aid to the State of Missouri for the purpose of securing the abolishment of slavery." Described by Harris as the most important measure presented to the Senate during the current session, it provoked wide-ranging discussion of the status of slavery in Missouri and the border states, its constitutional implications, and the powers and obligations of the Congress.[4] Since the resolution of the previous session was a direct outgrowth of presidential initiative, the policies of the President were, in effect, also under review.

Representative John W. Noell of Missouri had steered H.R. 634 through the House and, as approved there, the measure had the following major features; the Congress would provide $10 million to Missouri to assist in the immediate emancipation of the slaves there; there was to be no reimbursement for slaves brought into the state after the passage of the act, and none who had "given aid or comfort" to the rebellion were to receive compensation. The United States would be expected to "employ all reasonable means for the deportation" of the freedmen.[5]

---

4. Ibid., 592. Henry Wilson, *History of the Antislavery Measures of the Thirty-Seventh and Thirty-Eighth United States Congresses, 1861–1864* (Boston: Walker, Wise, 1864), pp. 224–48 and *History of the Rise and Fall of the Slave Power in America* (Boston: James R. Osgood, 1872–77), 3:301–19; John G. Nicolay and John Hay, *Abraham Lincoln: A History* (New York: Century, 1890), 6:395–97. Modern historians have not devoted much attention to the congressional aspects of compensated emancipation in the Congress during 1863, but see James G. Randall, *Constitutional Problems under Lincoln* (New York: Appleton, 1926), pp. 366–70. However, Randall was little concerned with this issue in *Lincoln the President: Midstream* (New York: Dodd, Mead, 1952); Allan Nevins mentioned the subject in *The War for the Union 2: War Becomes Revolution, 1862–1863* (New York: Scribner, 1960), pp. 91–94, 114–18, but in little detail. See, however, Curry, *Blueprint for Modern America*, pp. 44–48, 52–55. William E. Parrish, *Turbulent Partnership: Missouri and the Union, 1861–1865* (Columbia: University of Missouri Press, 1963), pp. 123–48, discusses the emancipation movement in Missouri and briefly touches upon the activity in the United States Congress, emphasizing the failure of Henderson and Noell to agree on specifics and the recalcitrance of the remainder of the Missouri delegation. See also his later *A History of Missouri, 3:1860 to 1875* (Columbia: University of Missouri Press, 1973), passim. *CG*, 37 Cong., 3 sess., 761, gives the Harris comment.

5. *CG*, 37 Cong., 3 sess., 589; see also 587.

The members of the Senate Judiciary Committee found these provisions inadequate to the task at hand and produced an amendment designed to replace everything in H.R. 634 after the enacting clause. Henderson succeeded in bringing this before his colleagues on January 16, 1863.

Very similar to a bill that Henderson had introduced in the Senate, the committee amendment changed the description of Missouri's obligations under the act somewhat and pledged federal bonds to the amount of $20 million to "compensate for the inconvenience produced by ... [the] change of system," provided that the state act of emancipation was adopted within eighteen months after passage of the federal act, and provided also that the institution was terminated not later than July 4, 1876. In aggregate, the value of the bonds must not total more than $300 per slave freed in the state, and individuals freed under the Confiscation Act of July 17, 1862, were not to figure in such calculations. If emancipation was carried through before July 4, 1865, the President would tender all of the bonds to Missouri immediately, but if the institution terminated after that date, the bonds would be paid in four equal installments, spread over the period between the passage of the act and actual elimination of slavery, thus introducing the possibility of gradual emancipation. Missourians might enact additional laws concerning slavery subsequent to their initial act, provided that these did not conflict with the federal measure or if such state enactments were designed to shorten the existence of the institution still further.[6]

But Henderson proposed to amend the substitute in certain respects. His amendments reflected his conviction that there was considerable desire among his fellow senators for a measure that would terminate slavery in Missouri in the very near future, that there were actually more slaves there than some congressmen believed, thus making immediate emancipation more expensive than supporters of the Noell bill had expected, and that some of his senatorial colleagues were concerned at the price tag. A scheme of gradual emancipation, he believed, would be less expensive than immediate termination. Henderson therefore proposed that Missouri approve its termination plan within twelve months and receive $20 million in bonds, provided that the state's slaves were freed before July 4, 1865, and only $10 million in assistance for later action. That pill was to be sweetened, however, by extending the termination date of gradual emancipation from 1876 to 1885. Detailed consideration of the Judiciary Committee amendment began with discussion of Henderson's recommendations.

Events justified the Missouri senator's reading of the situation. There was little doubt among Republicans that Congress had a perfect right

6. Ibid., 351.

under the war power to pass such a measure, "with a view to the more speedy and effectual suppression of the rebellion," as Fessenden, one of the more dubious party members, put it. But the Republican senators definitely disagreed as to both the amount of aid appropriate and the proper length of time that Missouri should be given to eliminate its system of bondage. Fessenden added a somewhat different dimension to the debate by arguing that the Judiciary Committee had weakened its amendment by discarding the words, "good, valid and constitutional," used in the Noell bill's description of the emancipation act expected from the Missouri legislature.[7] Subsequently Fessenden also questioned the degree to which the Congress was bound by the resolution of the previous session, and Collamer seems to have shared Fessenden's reservations in these matters. Finally, despairing of solving these problems on the floor, Harris moved on January 30 that the Senate amendment be referred back to the Judiciary Committee along with a substitute proposed by Wilson of Massachusetts.

The revised amendment returned to the floor on February 7. Now Missouri's action must be "valid and constitutional" and taken within twelve months of the passage of the federal act. The maximum value of the federal bonds to be tendered was placed at $20 million, and no part of that sum was to be used in freeing slaves taken into Missouri after passage of the federal law, nor to apply to slaves already or subsequently freed under the Confiscation Act of 1862. But unless "full and perfect manumission" had been achieved by July 4, 1865, Missouri was to receive bonds in the amount of $10 million only. The institution of slavery in Missouri must in any case end no later than July 4, 1876.[8]

When the bill returned, Democrats such as Richardson of Illinois and the slave-state senators excoriated measures in which the federal government interfered with the domestic institutions of states, and scoffed at the concept of a "war power." Turpie explained, "India rubber has had some reputation heretofore for being elastic; gold and silver for being malleable and ductile; but, sir, they must yield to this war power in all those qualities. Why, sir, it 'Lives through all life, extends through all extent, Spreads undivided, operates unspent.'" The opposition deplored the decision of the Republicans to make war on slavery a party objective under the guise of waging a more efficient war against rebellion; Richardson wished the President home in Illinois, and Davis derided him because he had forgotten his "whole magazine of anecdotes, old and new, fresh and stale, pointed and pointless" during the famous

7. Ibid., 589, 593.
8. Ibid., 776.

conference in which he had urged emancipation on the border-state delegations.[9] Now, the opposition supported various amendments proposed by Henderson's colleague, Wilson, who demanded that the voters of Missouri should express themselves on any emancipation plan developed by state authorities. Henderson argued, meanwhile, that the specific details of Missouri's course should be left to the Missourians, rather than laid down by the Congress.

Republicans participated little in this part of the debate, although Collamer briefly complained on February 7, "The resolution was that we would aid the States. Now the demand is not made upon us to aid Missouri; it is to do the whole thing out and out; and yet it is claimed under that resolution. I do not think that is exactly a fair claim." But Sumner, who apparently was unwell during the early stages of the debate on H.R. 634, roused himself to move that 1876 should be replaced by 1864, finding it "simply ridiculous" that action rooted in the war power should be translated into a proposition to end slavery in Missouri "ten years from now, or twenty years from now." This was on February 7, and when the Senate returned to the bill on the 12th there was an agreement in effect, arrived at a "few evenings ago," to refrain from floor discussion. Sumner, however, maintained that he was not a party to the agreement and mounted a last-ditch fight for immediate emancipation. "Whatever is done as a war measure must be immediate, or it will cease to have this character. If made prospective, it will not be a war measure," he insisted.[10] But he failed to carry a majority with him in his efforts.

Disagreement indices of 40 or more appeared in three votes during the course of the debate on the Missouri bill. These included the vote on Henderson's motion to insert 1885 rather than 1876 in the Judiciary Committee's original amendment. The motion was lost 16 to 22 but eight Republican moderates supported Henderson, as did Morrill and James Lane (I.D.: 53). In the following vote the radicals, however, failed to rally sufficient strength to sustain Clark's effort to limit Missouri's remuneration to $10 million, as seven moderates plus a few radicals joined the Democrats and border-state men (I.D.: 46). The third divisive vote occurred very late in the debate, when Sumner moved that the valuation of slaves to be used in calculating the amount of remuneration owing to Missouri be reduced from $300 to $200. He succeded in a vote of 19 to 17, with eight moderates on the losing side (I.D.: 47).[11] Muting the

9. Ibid., 785, 797.
10. Ibid., 795, 901, 902.
11. Sumner's effort on February 7 to set the emancipation date on July 4, 1864, produced a vote that scored 37 on the disagreement index. *CG*, 37 Cong., 3 sess., 795 and 800.

distinctions of the previous session most noticeably, in these and other votes, was the fact that Fessenden and Collamer tended consistently to vote the radical position. On two of the three most divisive votes, Lane of Kansas and Morrill, on the other hand, were to be found voting with a majority of the moderates.

Although the senators were sufficiently united to send the amended bill back to the House of Representatives, the members of that body failed to act upon it before the end of the session. Evaluating the situation in Congress, a Missouri paper noted the obstacles to the measure: "the great outlay of money" envisaged; "perplexity" as to the precise sums needed; "the unwillingness of the radicals to put their professed philanthropy to the cash test"; and "differences in regard to the details of any plan."[12] There is no question, however, that the moderates in general were more supportive of the President's hopes than the radicals.

During the Thirty-eighth Congress, Sumner spent much effort endeavoring to purify the federal statute books of all content recognizing any right of property of man in his fellow man—endeavors that were sometimes more significant as symbolic gestures than as substantive legislative contributions.

On February 29, 1864, he reported a bill from the Select Committee on Slavery and Freedmen to repeal all laws for the "rendition of fugitives from service or labor" (S. 141). On March 18 he tried to make it the special order of the day for the following Tuesday. Now occurred the first vote on the bill, and eighteen of his colleagues supported him while twenty opposed his motion, including nine Republicans, most of them moderates (I.D.: 67). Clark, a centrist, although usually more radical than moderate, and Collamer explained that they had voted against the proposal because they preferred first to debate Trumbull's joint resolution proposing a constitutional amendment to abolish the institution of slavery. Finally, after trying "at least a dozen times to get it up," the Bay State senator succeeded and his colleagues considered S. 141, a brief measure that repealed "all acts of Congress, or parts of acts, providing for the rendition of fugitives from service or labor." Sumner disavowed intent to discuss the measure; it was, he said, "perfectly plain. . . . Like a diagram . . . like the multiplication table . . . like the ten commandments."[13]

12. St. Louis *Tri-Weekly Missouri Republican*, February 3, 1863, as quoted in Bill R. Lee, "Missouri's Fight over Emancipation in 1863," *Missouri Historical Review*, 45 (April 1951), 266–67. The Springfield *Weekly Republican*, March 7, 1863, noted the "indifference of many of the republicans," and the New York *Herald*, March 2, 1863, charged that "a large portion of the republicans have no earnestness in the matter." Both papers agreed that many Republicans objected to compensating slaveholders.

13. Wilson, *History of the Antislavery Measures*, pp. 273–92, and *Rise and Fall of the Slave*

Senator Hendricks was no less convinced, however, that the pledge in the Constitution to provide such a law should be honored until slavery was abolished by constitutional amendment. Sherman took the floor to state that the Fugitive Slave Law of 1850 was unconstitutional in his opinion, but that he believed it inexpedient to repeal the law of 1793. He wished, he said, to give the southerners, "the few that are left who have the right to enforce the Constitution against us, their constitutional rights fully and fairly." The courts, he added, had found the 1793 law to be valid and constitutional. Sumner immediately disagreed, maintaining that the Supreme Court had found it unconstitutional in *Prigg* v. *Pennsylvania* and that Judge Joseph Story, in developing his opinion, had noted that the law had not been attacked on the grounds that it denied "a trial by jury in a case of human freedom," a matter which that jurist considered to be "an open question." Noting that the law had been framed by the "founders of this Government," Sherman moved to amend the bill by adding the words: "except the act approved February 12, 1793, entitled 'An act respecting fugitives from justice and persons escaping from the service of their masters.'"[14]

Before the vote, the able Reverdy Johnson of Maryland argued that the Constitution, as it stood, required Congress to provide legislation governing the return of slaves. He denied that Justice Story believed that the act of 1793 was unconstitutional, pointing out that the *Prigg* ruling held that the law of 1793 was unconstitutional only insofar as it required the cooperation of the states. The laws by this time were actually inoperative, and he could see nothing to be gained from the measure except, perhaps, some honor for the Republican party and the creation of "unpleasant feeling" among southerners of the loyal border states, or among unionists in the Confederacy. Although the constitutional implications of the bill were as clear as the multiplication table to Sumner, Johnson suggested that the issue had also been clear to those framers of the Constitution who served in the Congress that approved the Fugitive

*Power*, 3:394–402; Edward L. Pierce, *Memoir and Letters of Charles Sumner* (Boston: Roberts Brothers, 1893), 4:175–77; David Donald, *Charles Sumner and the Rights of Man* (New York: Knopf, 1970), pp. 153–61.

14. See Joseph C. Burke, "What Did the Prigg Decision Really Decide?" *Pennsylvania Magazine of History and Biography*, 93 (January 1969), 73–85, for a recent discussion of the meaning of the Prigg decision. If Burke is correct, Sumner was wrong in his contention that the justices found the law of 1793 to be unconstitutional. But note also Paul Finkelman, "Prigg v. Pennsylvania and Northern State Courts: Anti-Slavery Uses of a Pro-Slavery Decision," *Civil War History*, 25 (March 1979), 5–35. *CG*, Cong., 1 sess., 1710. Winfield S. Kerr, *John Sherman: His Life and Public Services* (Boston: Sherman, French, 1908), 1:189, marvels that Sherman "rendered such important service" and "acted with such consummate ability" in the "widely separated fields of . . . slavery and finance," but cannily omitted further details of his contributions in the congressional war on slavery. *CG*, 38 Cong., 1 sess., 1710.

Slave Law of 1793. He summed up Sumner's approach to the Constitution: "The Constitution recently, first, construed with reference to the principles to be found in the Declaration of Independence, and secondly, construed by itself through very many of the clauses which relate to personal freedom, has been held to be so inconsistent with slavery that an act of this description cannot be maintained as valid." Sumner, according to Johnson, held that the constitutional clause concerning the rendition of fugitives was intended to reach only fleeing apprentices. The senator from Massachusetts interjected to admit that the authors of the clause had indeed meant that it should apply to slaves. However, "according to all just rules of interpretation . . . the language they employed cannot be interpreted to mean slavery; for according to those rules slavery cannot stand on inference. It requires," he said, "a positive text to sustain it." Although Johnson maintained that "the question between the honorable member from Massachusetts and myself, and between him and Washington and every member of the Convention, all the State Legislatures, every State court, every district court of the United States, and the Supreme Court of the United States, with Marshall at their head, is whether the term, 'held to service,' as used in what is called the fugitive slave clause, embraces slaves," Sumner argued that the whole clause must be construed together and when this was done, he argued, contract was implied. But slavery dealt in things, not persons; slavery knew no contract, nor could service or labor be "due" from a slave.[15]

After Johnson had proven to his satisfaction that the term "other persons" elsewhere in the Constitution could not be made to fit anyone other than slaves, Sumner renounced his pledge against speaking to the bill and replied to Sherman and Johnson. The senator from Ohio was reminded that he was warmly cherishing a bill that allowed a "fellowman" to be "hurried before a magistrate and doomed to slavery without a trial by jury." To Johnson he reiterated his interpretation of the fugitive slave clause of the Constitution:

> I insist that, whatever may have been the original intention of the framers of that clause, they did not succeed in making it cover fugitive slaves. . . . There is a rule of interpretation which the Senator will not call in question. Where any language is open to two constructions, one favorable and the other odious, *that which is odious must be rejected.* . . . The rule is unquestionable and the authorities are ample. . . . In its application to apprentices, redemptioners, and the like, . . . [the clause] is exhausted, so that it cannot be made to cover a slave without offending against the rule which requires us to adopt the construction which is the least odious. And sir, if we go further and scan nicely the language of the clause, we shall find that

15. *CG*, 38 Cong., 1 sess., 1711–12.

the words employed are all applicable to a relation of *contract* or *debt*, and not to a relation founded on *force*. The clause is applicable to a "person," and not to a *thing*, and this "person" is to be surrendered on the claim of the person to whom his service or labor may be *due*. But clearly no labor or service can be *due* from a slave to a master. The whole pretension is an absurdity. . . . But the Senator dwelt especially on the words "held to service or labor in one State *under the laws thereof,*" and triumphantly insisted that slaves were included under this language. Here again he is mistaken. Apprentices and redemptioners were held under "laws"; but I need not remind the Senator of the admission repeatedly made on this floor by Mr. Mason, that there were no "laws" for slavery in any slave State; at least, that none could be produced. Besides, as a jurist, the Senator cannot have forgotten the ancient truth that injustice cannot be "law" but is always to be regarded as an "abuse" or a "violence," even though expressed in the form of "law". . . . No ingenuity of honest effort can make the words that the Senator cites or any others in that clause sanction slavery and the hunting of slaves. In order to proceed with his argument the Senator must begin by setting aside those commanding rules of interpretation which are binding on him as on myself. If, where words are susceptible of two significations, one favorable and the other odious, the former only can be taken, then must the Senator restrain this clause to that signification which is not odious. And again, if every word is always to be construed so as most to favor liberty, then must the Senator follow implicitly this rule. But these two rules make it impossible to torture this clause into any *odious* or *tyrannical* signification.[16]

Granville Sharp, Sumner pointed out, was not disheartened when the bar rejected his position that slavery could not exist in England, for "he knew well that there was no statute of limitations against principles; and, better still, that principles must finally prevail over precedents." He deplored the ignominy that the institution brought upon Americans in foreign nations and concluded: "Slavery has struck at the national life. Let us strike back wherever we can hit it, and above all let us purify the statute-book, so that there shall be nothing in it out of which this wrong can derive any support. In the discharge of this duty, all fugitive acts should be repealed. The argument against one is good against all." Their major statements made, Sumner and Johnson sparred with each other a little longer, and Johnson's irony played about Sumner like sheet lightning on a hot summer evening. Why, he asked, bother to repeal laws which used the constitutional terminology "persons," since the senator from Massachusetts was sure that the word did not mean slaves? Sumner replied that the Supreme Court might not accept that interpretation. But, rejoined the Maryland senator, how could the august members of the Supreme Court fail to accept a position clear as the multiplication table? Nay, more, Sumner had said that his view was "as imperative as

16. Ibid., 1712–13.

anything to be found in the decalogue." At this point Sumner interrupted to point out that the decalogue forbade stealing, adultery, and
coveting the wife of a neighbor—all sins that were integral to slavery as
practiced in the United States. Southerners, thought Johnson, might
interpret Sumner's desire to take the slave from his master as a sin
against the decalogue also.[17] Eleven Republicans supported Sherman's
amendment and fifteen opposed it. Democratic and border-state votes
helped carry the proposal, with the final tally standing 24 yea and 17 nay
(I.D.: 70).

The next day Foster took the floor in opposition to the bill. He reviewed the circumstances in which the Fugitive Slave Law of 1793 was
passed and pledged to stand by the position then taken by the distinguished senator from his state. Repeal would hardly set the Union right
in the eyes of the world, since European opinion favored the Confeder-
ates to a distressing degree. Reviewing the clauses of the Constitution
that were said to refer to slaves, he concluded that they did indeed refer
to that category of individuals. He would support the amended bill on
the grounds that the act of 1793 was constitutional and obligatory under
the Constitution. "If the honorable Senator cannot find anything in the
Constitution or the law of 1793 which are any impediments or restraints
upon him, I trust that he will realize that others may," and again he
remarked:

> Our political salvation is in the Constitution. Let men think or say what
> they will; let them imagine that exigencies or so-called necessities may arise
> where we had better step aside from the Constitution, we delude ourselves
> if we think we can abandon that instrument and go on to victory. The path
> of glory is here the path of duty, the path of the Constitution; and di-
> vergence from it is dangerous.

Argued "with great calmness and logical force," Foster's speech reportedly produced "a profound sensation . . . among the radicals."[18] Later,
Conness urged that the Senate lay Sumner's bill aside until the next
week, since the Sherman amendment had made the bill unsatisfactory
both to him and to various other original supporters of the measure. S.
141 did not appear on the floor again.

In the late afternoon of June 21, 1864, Sumner moved that the Senate
proceed to the consideration of H.R. 512, a bill repealing the fugitive
slave laws. Following a protest from Hendricks, Doolittle argued against
taking up the measure on the grounds that the hour was late, that there
would be no positive outcome, and that other questions of "actual pressing importance" must be considered on the following day. Sumner af-

17. Ibid., 1713–14.
18. Ibid., 1749; Springfield *Weekly Republican,* May 7, 1864, and New York *Herald,* April
21, 1864.

firmed that he knew of none who wished to discuss the bill "unless it is the senator from Wisconsin himself, if he proposes to make a plea for slave-hunting." Doolittle remarked sarcastically that he bowed to the senator from Massachusetts who was "learned, learned beyond comparison. I sometimes almost fear that he is so learned that he has lost all practical sense." He noted that Senator Davis wished to speak on the bill and possibly some Republicans, although not the senator from Wisconsin. He summed up his own position:

> I am of the opinion that upon the Constitution as it originally stood, independent of the construction made by courts and others, it did not belong to Congress at all to pass any laws upon this subject; but there are a great many gentlemen on this side of the Chamber who believe that under the Constitution as it stands, and by the decisions of the courts as they are made, they are under obligations and the obligations of their oaths, that there should be some kind of law to enforce that provision of the Constitution of the United States. Does the Senator from Massachusetts as a friend of those gentlemen, associated with them politically, desire to press them to the point of either voting what upon their oaths they have sworn they will not do, or to break with him?

Doolittle, responded Sumner, failed "to see the requirements of his country at this hour; he fails to see what is due to the civilization of the age; and in that respect he shows a want of practical sense in the highest degree."[19]

Of the Republicans, only Doolittle and Hale opposed discussion of H.R. 512, the latter arguing that naval affairs should have priority. Although Davis spoke in opposition at some length, other opponents from the slave-holding states contented themselves for the most part by supporting procedural delays. During consideration of the measure on June 21, 22, and 23, five roll calls revealed substantial conflict within the Republican party. Four of these were concerned with procedural matters: "to proceed to consideration of H.R. 512," "to proceed with consideration," to adjourn, and to proceed to the consideration of executive business (I.D.: 45, 60, 50, 49). The fifth vote was on Johnson's unsuccessful amendment to H.R. 512, providing that the act of 1793 was not to be affected (I.D.: 46). But on June 28 the President was able to sign the bill; an era surely had ended.

The major outline of the disagreement between radicals and moderates can be most economically reviewed by comparing three votes: one of April 19 when the Sherman amendment to S. 141 was adopted; one of June 22, when the senators refused to discuss H.R. 512, preferring to deal with other business; and the roll call on the Johnson amendment of June 23, when the senators refused to delete reference to the act of 1793

19. *CG*, 38 Cong., 1 sess., 3128.

from H.R. 512. On April 19, ten moderates and one radical joined
Democrats and border-state senators to make a majority; on June 22,
eight moderates and two radicals joined Democrats and border-state
senators to defeat twelve radicals and two moderates; and on the following day only five moderates rallied in support of the Johnson amendment. This voting trend did not, however, reflect much movement of the
moderates into the Sumner camp. Of the ten moderates who supported
the Sherman amendment in April, only Howe voted against the Johnson
amendment. Cowan, Harris, Lane of Indiana, Ten Eyck, and Trumbull
fought to preserve the act of 1793 in both divisions, and Collamer,
Doolittle, Foster, and Sherman were absent during the roll call of June
23. Since all four of these men were present for other roll calls on that
day, we can reasonably assume they salved their consciences by absenting
themselves, although Johnson's amendment would still have failed by
two votes had they supported it. In the vote on the bill, following the
defeat of Johnson's amendment, only Cowan of the Republican moderates dared to vote against it, but Collamer, Doolittle, Foster, and Sherman were still recorded as absent. In this episode, we again see the
willingness of Sumner and other radicals to embarrass more moderate
colleagues on issues which would, in the final analysis, have little practical effect.

On June 24, 1864, as Sherman was leading debate on H.R. 527, the
civil appropriation bill, Sumner offered an additional section as an
amendment:

> *And be it further enacted,* That sections eight and nine of the act entitled "An
> act to prohibit the importation of slaves into any port or place within the
> jurisdiction of the United States from and after the 1st day of January, in
> the year of our Lord 1808," which said sections undertake to regulate the
> coastwise slave trade, are hereby repealed.[20]

These sections provided that slaves should not be carried in the coastwise
trade in ships of less than forty tons burthen and prescribed various
regulations to which individuals shipping slaves must conform, particularly designed to protect free blacks from being carried into slavery.

Sherman immediately protested that Sumner was encumbering an
appropriation bill with "a matter . . . in no way connected with the appropriations in the bill." He hoped that his colleagues would keep the bill
free from "these disputed, extraneous, political questions." No whit
abashed, Sumner argued that an appropriation bill was like a "through
train" and although "its special office" was "to appropriate money, yet it

20. *CG*, 38 Cong., 1 sess., 3235. Wilson, *History of the Antislavery Measures*, pp. 362–66,
and *Rise and Fall of the Slave Power*, 3:354–56. Pierce, *Sumner*, 4:177; Donald, *Sumner and
the Rights of Man*, pp. 153, 161.

may carry any propositions required by the public good." Almost all appropriation bills carried "passengers" of this sort, he argued, and mentioned Hale's amendment banishing the lash from the navy, and Grimes's successful attempt to eliminate the naval grog ration. But Sherman responded that riders should not be attached to appropriation bills unless they bore some direct relation to an allocation provided in them; this had been the case both times when Hale and Grimes succeeded in changing naval policies. In contrast, said he, here was a "matter wholly extraneous . . . dragged and lugged in here without any pertinency whatever; an amendment which, if adopted, will tend to embarrass the passage of this bill, will create political controversies."[21]

Johnson of Maryland argued that Sumner's proposal would not remedy the situation. Rather, if it passed, traders would then be able to transport slaves in vessels of less than forty tons burthen without any regulations protective of the bondsmen whatsoever. Hendricks was less interested in constitutional implications and far more bitter, hailing the amendment as one in a series of measures wiping out "all the positions assumed by our fathers touching the relations of these States," and proving that the initial assurances of the Republicans that they sought only to restore the Union were false. In deference to Johnson's line of argument, Sumner perfected his amendment adding the words "and the coastwise slave trade is prohibited forever."[22]

Responding to the kind of crisis that "occasionally" made him feel it his "personal duty" to speak, Collamer refuted Sumner's contentions, expressed at other times in the Senate, that certain constitutional clauses did not really refer to slaves, and that, although the Founding Fathers had meant to refer to slaves, they had failed to make their meaning clear. Such arguments were "a quibble, an equivocation, pettifogging." But as for the subject before the chamber at that time, he believed that attempts to "deal with slaves, who are persons under the Constitution and our laws, as articles of merchandise in any form under any regulations of trade whatever, are unconstitutional. . . . Therefore, inasmuch as the sections of the law to which our attention is now called and which it is proposed to repeal are of that character and attempt to deal with the subject as of that character, I say repeal them." In rebuttal, Johnson inquired how Congress had found the power to regulate the admission of slaves into the Territories if not under the interstate commerce clause, and deplored the time wasted in considering the Sumner amendment—perhaps to be more still, depending on the action of the members of the House:

21. *CG*, 38 Cong., 1 sess., 3235.
22. Ibid., 3236–37.

Suppose they dispose of it differently from us by rejecting the amendment, then the bill comes back here and the honorable member from Massachusetts will at once be found upon his feet again trying once more to strike that last blow at slavery—which I thought by the by, he said the other night he had done when he got the fugitive slave law repealed—which he is so very anxious to strike that he may stand in that respect as he is entitled to stand, not only fair in the opinion of his particular constituents, but fair in the estimation of the world where slavery is held in so much detestation.[23]

With this the senators adjourned.

Collamer addressed Sumner's amendment once again on the following day and discoursed upon *Groves* v. *Slaughter*. He remarked, after reading at length from the decision in which the justices found that a state did indeed have the right to bar the admission of slaves into its territory: "The great point in the case is that they are, as Judge McLean says, persons, not property, not articles of commerce and trade, and therefore do not fall within this delegated power that is given to Congress. I say, therefore, that the sections of the law of 1807 which it is proposed to repeal ought to be repealed, because they attempt to regulate it."[24] But then the elderly gentleman from Vermont pointed out that the additional clause that Sumner had added to his amendment was an attempt to exercise the federal interstate commerce power in regulating the slave trade and rendered the amendment unacceptable to him. Twelve radicals and one moderate supported Sumner's proposal; six moderates and one radical opposed it, as it was lost by a vote of 13 yeas and 20 nays (I.D.: 78). Six radicals and six moderates were absent. But the indomitable senator from Massachusetts offered his amendment again when H.R. 527 was reported to the Senate, and the moderate Doolittle announced his intention of voting for the bill since several other extraneous matters had been incorporated in it. Sumner's amendment now passed easily, but H. S. Lane, Sherman, and Trumbull voted against it, and Collamer, Cowan, Foster, Grimes, and Hale were recorded as absent.

As we have seen, the Republican senators disagreed—at times very "earnestly"—in their approach to the institution of slavery. Such differences of opinion were not random; rather the senators *tended* to distribute themselves along a radical-moderate-conservative continuum. Issues involving the status of free blacks produced similar arguments, recrimination, and divisive roll calls. Sumner's efforts to pluck "the twigs and leaves of the Upas" which he was "at the same time trying to uproot" frequently aligned Republican radicals against Republican moderates. This was also the case in discussion and voting about the rights and status

23. Ibid., 3237–38.
24. Ibid., 3256.

of free blacks. Constitutional historians of the Civil War have weighed the hostility of Republicans toward the Supreme Court, described their reorganization of that body and federal judicial districts in 1862, and noted their tendencies to place additional responsibilities in the federal courts at the expense of state tribunals.[25] But such historians have in general paid little attention to the efforts to harmonize state and federal judicial procedures that occurred during the war. Sumner, however, was quick to try and put such measures to his own purposes.

On July 3, 1862, Foster successfully moved to take up S. 113 for consideration, describing it as a "little bill . . . in regard to legal proceedings," which would not "occupy time or create division." For the original wording of the measure, Foster, representing the Committee on the Judiciary, proposed to substitute:

> That the laws of the several States, except where the Constitution, treaties, or statutes of the United States shall otherwise require or provide, shall be regarded as rules of decision in all trials at common law in the courts of the United States, in cases where they apply; also in all trials in equity in all States having courts of equity, either separate from courts of law or where the courts of law are vested with equity powers.

This was a restatement, with some expansion, of section 34 of the Judiciary Act of 1789. In Committee of the Whole, Sumner moved immediately to add an additional sentence, "And there shall be no exclusion of any witness on account of color."[26] Foster lamented the action, which, he predicted, would produce debate and delay other measures that he had in hand. Sumner, however, was determined to press his amendment, and Collamer, Harris, and Howe joined eleven radicals in support of it in the division. Twenty-one senators, however, voted against it, including three radicals and nine moderates (I.D.: 54).

After Foster had successfully proposed another amendment to S. 113, it moved to the Senate floor for action. Sumner immediately returned to

---

25. New York *Daily Tribune,* February 10, 1864. For a short but useful overview of Republican attitudes toward the Supreme Court during this period, see Stanley I. Kutler, *Judicial Power and Reconstruction Politics* (Chicago: University of Chicago Press, 1968), pp. 7–29. Harold M. Hyman, *A More Perfect Union: The Impact of the Civil War and Reconstruction on the Constitution* (New York: Knopf, 1973), has numerous references to the roles of the state and federal courts. For a concise statement of Republican policies, see William M. Wiecek, "The Reconstruction of Federal Judicial Power, 1863–1875," *American Journal of Legal History,* 13 (October 1969), 333–59. Kermit L. Hall, "The Civil War Era as a Crucible for Nationalizing the Lower Federal Courts," *Prologue,* 7 (Fall 1975), 177–86, qualifies the revisionist views of Kutler, Wiecek, and Hyman but does not discuss S. 113 and H.R. 390, which seemingly support his emphasis on the conservative nature of Republican policy. Senator Dixon, Foster's moderate colleague from Connecticut, was the original sponsor of S. 113 in a form that also covered admiralty law. See Springfield *Weekly Republican,* March 5, 1864, for an extended examination of the measures discussed here.

26. *CG,* 37 Cong., 2 sess., 3098.

the issue raised by his amendment, arguing that the senators were proposing to make a category of individuals "incompetent on account of
color," as witnesses in the courts of the United States. He chided Hale for
opposing his amendment and termed the Senate's decision "melancholy,
disastrous, discreditable." Now there ensued a three-cornered exchange
between Sumner, Hale, and Davis of Kentucky, who had argued that this
bill was highly necessary in his state. Both Hale and Davis argued that
Sumner was raising an issue of no practical significance. The New
Hampshire senator pointed out that the Supreme Court had ruled that
Negroes were not citizens and were therefore barred from the federal
courts; he had himself gone to the root of the problem earlier in the
session, he reminded the senators, by proposing to abolish the high
tribunal. Davis argued that cases involving blacks were almost invariably
of the sort taken into state courts and maintained that black witnesses
were indeed allowed to testify in the state courts of Kentucky. There was
no need he said, "for sticking the perpetual, the all-pervading, the
everywhere-to-be-found, the ever-in-the-way negro to this bill." But in
Sumner's mind the bill would allow state precedents to rule that barred
the Negro as a witness in southern states. He offered his proposition
again as a proviso, "*Provided,* that there shall be no exclusion of any
witness on account of color."[27] At King's suggestion, the Senate then
moved to consider executive business, and the bill made no further
appearance on the floor during the session.

But the issue was joined again when Foster called up H.R. 390, "in
relation to the competency of witnesses in trials of equity and admiralty,"
on July 15. The Committee on the Judiciary proposed to amend this bill
so that its first section would read, "That the laws of the State in which
the court shall be held shall be the rules of decision as to the competency
of witnesses in the courts of the United States, in trials at common law, in
equity and admiralty."[28] In this clause, therefore, the House bill overlapped the provisions of the Senate bill considered on July 3, but also
applied to admiralty courts.

Early in the amending process, Sumner introduced the amendment of
July 3, forbidding the exclusion of any witness on account of color.
Wilkinson and Howard rushed to Sumner's support, arguing that the
credibility of the testimony offered by a witness should be the crucial
factor in judicial process, rather than the alleged competency of a witness based on such an extraneous matter as color. Foster maintained in
rebuttal that various states denied the witness stand to atheists, and
summarized his position:

27. Ibid., 3099, 3101.
28. Ibid., 3354.

It is competent for every State to fix its own rules for itself, and that the independence of each State of every other State requires that they should be protected in that right of making their own laws. Nobody questions it as regards their own tribunals. The only question is, whether, after they have made a law controlling their own State tribunals, we, sitting as the Legislature of the country, shall establish in the courts of the United States sitting in those several States, a rule at variance with and contradictory to, the laws thus established within the States.[29]

Sumner rose, proclaiming that he held the Declaration of Independence in his hand, and reminding his hearers that it began with the words "We hold these truths to be self-evident: that all men are created equal." He continued:

The gentleman from Connecticut, representing the Judiciary Committee of the Senate of the United States, proposes to establish as a rule of evidence in the United States courts that men are not equal. . . . To ingraft into the legislation of the United States, in defiance of the Declaration of Independence, the practical principle that all men are not equal. . . . He undertakes to regulate the competency of witnesses here by the voice of Congress, and gravely asks us to enact that witnesses shall be incompetent to testify on account of color. This proposition is not made openly, but under the guise that the local laws of States shall in all cases prevail in the national courts. Can the Senator forget the character of these local laws: how instinct with barbarism they are; what a shame and scandal they are . . . and will he now recognize such a scandal and shame and give them new effect? . . . The State courts . . . are beyond our control; but let the United States courts which are within our control be brought at last within the pale of civilization.

After some further interchange, Foster—no doubt with some satisfaction—sprang the trap. He explained that in trying admiralty suits in United States courts in Boston, Sumner's friend, the district attorney of Massachusetts, bound by federal practice, could not "examine a party or any one having an interest in the cause." This bill was "to enable him to do it. The court of the United States sitting there as a court of equity," could not "permit the examination of the parties without this law."[30]

Trumbull, chairman of the Judiciary Committee, supported Foster, arguing that the bill was merely a proposal "to adopt, in the different States of the Union in the United States courts, the same rules of evidence that are adopted in the State courts," a practice hitherto at the discretion of the judges concerned.[31] This, in Trumbull's view, was a desirable change, and he deplored the effort to read additional significance into it. Of the moderates, only Howe voted with the thirteen radicals who

29. Ibid., 3355.
30. Ibid., 3356–57.
31. Ibid., 3357.

supported Sumner's amendment. Twenty-three senators rallied against it (I.D.: 72), and subsequently the bill passed and was approved. Not all Republican wartime legislation on the judiciary had a nationalizing effect.

As the debate progressed on the civil appropriations bill during the first session of the Thirty-eighth Congress, Sumner fixed his sights upon the third section which appropriated $100,000 to be used in the apprehension of individuals who attempted to counterfeit United States currency or securities and proposed to add the following: "*Provided, That in the courts of the United States there shall be no exclusion of any witness on account of color.*"[32] Having been chastised by Sherman the evening before for encumbering appropriations with irrelevant matter, he pointed out in some triumph that his amendment did indeed relate to the clause amended, since a counterfeiter might well choose to use "colored accomplices," secure in the knowledge that in some states they would not be allowed to testify against him. And he summarized the earlier arguments in behalf of this provision.

Sherman remarked that the debate on an "irrelevant matter" (Sumner's amendment concerning the coastal slave trade) during the previous evening, when the thermometer rose to 93, had exhausted everyone. He inquired whether the amendment now offered had not been brought to a vote on earlier bills. Sumner noted that it had prevailed in the District of Columbia bill but his efforts to add it to other measures had thus far failed. However, he added, it was incorporated in measures pending both from his Select Committee on Slavery and Freedmen and in a bill reported by Collamer from the Committee on Post Offices and Post Roads. Sherman responded, "I beseech the Senator from Massachusetts not to load down this, the last of the general appropriation bills, with amendments that are likely to create discussion or controversy between the two Houses."[33]

Sumner was obdurate, "I believe," he said, "it is always time to do an act of justice. . . . I plead for it now as essential to the administration of justice." The reaction of slave-state and Democratic senators was predictable. Carlile knew of nothing, he said, more likely to outrage public sentiment in a slave state than the knowledge that property had been confiscated on Negro testimony, and argued that blacks could hardly be expected to provide useful evidence. Saulsbury expatiated upon the incompetence of Negro testimony. More effective was Buckalew's effort to limit the amendment by adding the clause "or in civil actions because he is a party to, or interested in, the issue tried." This was accepted by the

32. *CG*, 38 Cong., 1 sess., 3259.
33. Ibid., 3260.

senators over Sumner's protest. As altered, the Sumner amendment was passed by a vote of 22 yeas and 16 nays (I.D.: 44), and so reads in the laws of that session. Seventeen radicals and five moderates stood in the majority. Four moderates opposed the amendment and an additional four were recorded as absent, in comparison to two radical absentees.[34]

On February 9, 1863, during the third session of the Thirty-seventh Congress, Morrill brought H.R. 468 before the Senate on behalf of the Committee on the District of Columbia. Referred to subsequently as a "little twopenny railroad bill," this measure conferred authority on the ill-fated Alexandria and Washington Railroad Company to extend its track from the south end of the Potomac Bridge to the Baltimore and Ohio Depot, acquiring real estate and building such structures as were necessary or appropriate to the project. Admittedly minor in nature, the bill produced a sharp exchange between Morrill and Clark as to whether the measure should be considered at the expense of more important legislation.[35]

Differences along the radical-moderate continuum developed in the debate when Sumner proposed to add the provision "that no person shall be excluded from the cars on account of color," citing "a new illustration . . . of the barbarism left . . . from slavery: that an aged colored person had been excluded" recently "from the cars and dropped in the snow and mud." No doubt with common-law doctrines in mind, Howe inquired as to whether the company, a common carrier, was not liable under the law as it stood, should it refuse to carry any individual who offered the proper fare. Legally, Sumner agreed, this was so, but "wherever slavery is in question, human rights are constantly disregarded . . . principles of law . . . constantly set aside," making it "the duty of Congress to interfere, and specifically declare them." When Howe inquired as to whether the amendment would not be a "reenactment of the existing law?" Sumner responded, "That was said precisely about the Wilmot proviso."[36] The vote was 19 yea and 18 nay (I.D.: 50). In terms of votes cast, the number of dissenting Republicans was small, including only Howe, Anthony, Cowan, and Lane of Indiana, but they were half of the moderates voting and the issue was to reappear in the next Congress.

34. Ibid., 3260–61. Apparently, it is this amendment to the Civil Appropriations Act of 1864 (approved July 2) that Harold M. Hyman refers to as follows: "Pressures deriving from these insights resulted (July 4, 1864) in a statute of Sumner's inspiration admitting Negroes' testimony in national courts" (*A More Perfect Union*, p. 272).

35. The quotation appears in *CG*, 37 Cong., 3 sess., 1328. See Constance M. Green, *Washington: Village and Capital, 1800–1878* (Princeton: Princeton University Press, 1962), passim for references to the wartime role of this railroad. *CG*, 37 Cong., 3 sess., 1330.

36. *CG*, 37 Cong., 3 sess., 1329. Wilson, *History of the Antislavery Measures*, pp. 371–76, and *Rise and Fall of the Slave Power*, 3:505–15; Pierce, *Sumner*, 4:179–81.

On March 16, 1864, Senator Morrill of the Committee on the District of Columbia brought before the chamber S. 54, a bill to incorporate the Metropolitan Railroad Company, a street railroad.[37] After the senators had considered the committee amendments and several presented by Ten Eyck, Sumner moved to add *"Provided,* That there shall be no regulations excluding any persons from any car on account of color."

Saulsbury immediately rose to the bait and proclaimed that the use of segregated cars was completely analogous to the practice of distinguishing first-class accommodations aboard ships or providing emigrant cars, cars for gentlemen, or for gentlemen and ladies, and smoking cars on railroads. Only in the case of the colored surgeon, Dr. Alexander T. Augusta, had any incident resulted from the practice on the street railroad then in service. "The men," he said, "who so persistently attempt on all occasions to introduce measures which in their very nature are calculated to bring about social and political equality among the races, and which are seized hold of by the subordinate race and cause them to believe that that is the intent and meaning of our legislation, are not the true friends of that subordinate race." God, he maintained, made both the "great oak" and the "humble sapling," and he concluded, "If in the providence of God it shall ever happen (which I pray may never be) that the majestic columns which now support this Capitol shall fall in ruin and destruction, upon the cenotaph of a once great nation will be inscribed this epitaph: 'Here lie thirty million white men, women, and children, who lost their liberties in trying to equalize with themselves four million negroes.'"[38]

Johnson reiterated the position taken by the Committee on the District of Columbia when the company had been accused of discrimination on an earlier occasion. There was no legal basis for excluding blacks from particular cars in the District; legislation forbidding such practice was unnecessary. If any black wished to complain of discrimination, the courts stood open. Sumner, Johnson alleged, had initially accepted that conclusion without complaint. As to Saulsbury's argument, companies did provide first- and second-class accommodations but there was "nothing in that fact which" showed "any right to distinguish as between different descriptions of passengers ... willing to comply with the terms required of them in order to be transported on any one of the classes of cars which the company" determined to run. Nor was there any police power inherent in such companies which should allow them to make such distinctions. There was no need, therefore, to pass Sumner's amend-

37. Some discussion of the street railways of Washington is found in Wilhelmus B. Bryan, *A History of the National Capital from Its Foundation through the Period of the Adoption of the Organic Act* (New York: Macmillan, 1916), 2:363–66, 491–92, 530–31, 616–17.

38. *CG,* 38 Cong., 1 sess., 1141–42.

ment; that senator might "just as well . . . propose to pass a law providing that these black men and black women shall have the same right to visit the presidential mansion on public occasions as the white men and the white women." Johnson was willing to pass all the laws necessary to provide that blacks "be protected in life and property."[39] Those who had been in slavery, at least, were not prepared for more, he believed.

Sumner acknowledged Johnson's "nimbleness of speech" but argued that his provision had been applied to another railroad company in Washington and that it had not produced trouble or complaint. Moreover, discrimination in such matters did patently exist. The courts were not, after all, the answer for "a poor, humble person," because of the expense and delay involved. In situations such as this, declaratory acts reaffirming current law and practice were quite appropriate, he believed. Morrill took the floor, incensed by Saulsbury's contention that "the whole question of the regulation of the intercourse or relations between the races had better be left to the gentlemanly instincts of the superior race and the principles of Christianity." The church, except—as Foster interjected—the church South, had fostered emancipation, responded Morrill; "the gentlemanly instincts of the superior race" on the other hand, had produced half a million mulattoes in a population of four million blacks. He would not, said Morrill, have spoken if Saulsbury's assault on the bill had not emphasized that some people shared the senator's sentiments and would try to exclude blacks from some cars. That being the case, he intended to vote for the amendment although it merely reenacted "the general law of the District."[40] Fourteen radicals and five moderates voted for the amendment; but Doolittle, Harris, Lane of Indiana, Sherman, Ten Eyck, and Trumbull voted with eleven Democrats and Border Unionists in opposition (I.D.: 56).

Another engagement in Sumner's war against segregated railway cars began on June 21, 1864, when Senator Grimes brought up H.R. 495, a bill to amend the act amending the charter of the Washington and Georgetown Railroad and providing for various changes in the corporation's practices and in the service that it provided. Sumner moved to supplement the first section of the bill by adding "*And provided further, That there shall be no exclusion of any person from any car on account of color.*"[41] He explained that such a provision appeared in the charters of the F Street and Alexandria railroads and that his amendment would make the three roads equal in that respect. Apparently the Washington and Georgetown Railroad had designated some of its cars for whites and

39. Ibid., 1156–57.
40. Ibid., 1158, 1160.
41. Ibid., 3131.

others for colored passengers. Conductors frequently forced Negroes seeking access to cars reserved for whites to ride on the open front platform with the driver, irrespective of their dress, sex, or social stature. When told that the company had no right under its charter to make such distinctions or refuse service to anyone, blacks explained to Sumner that they were too poor to bring the matter into the courts. In offering this amendment, Sumner was trying to make the obligations of the company explicit.

Predictably, slave-state senators and Democrats took exception to the Sumner amendment. But Sherman argued that inserting provisions apt to "excite . . . public hostility" in street railroad company charters would discourage the development of local transportation facilities. Trumbull recalled the days when the slave power "sometimes passed laws and put into them provisions that were offensive, for the very purpose . . . of offending the people of the North." Certain clauses in the Fugitive Slave Law of 1850 particularly illustrated this tendency, and he exhorted, "let us not fall into the same error that the advocates of slavery fell into. . . . The law now is that this company has no authority to exclude a person on account of color." When Sumner admitted that he believed that to be the law, Trumbull challenged him, "Then why do you want to repeat it? So as to make it offensive to somebody? So as to make it distasteful to somebody?" He urged Sumner to tell him of "any right secured to the colored man by this provision that he [did] not have without it."[42] There was, he would say later, no practical object in the amendment.

Also predictably, Sumner disliked Trumbull's illustration. Did the Illinois senator not well know he asked, "that everything introduced into the fugitive slave bill was in the interest of slavery and contrary to every sentiment of humanity, and that it was intended to give offense? The proposition now moved" was "just in the opposite sense; it" was "to sustain the principles of humanity, to uphold human rights and human equality, and with no purpose of offense." Wilson rallied to Sumner's defense, determined, as he said, to "protect the rights of the poor and the lowly, trodden under the heel of power," and Grimes joined Trumbull in arguing the futility of reenacting what the law already provided.[43] In Committee of the Whole, seven moderates made common cause with the opposition to defeat the twelve radicals and two moderates who supported the Sumner amendment (I.D.: 78). When the bill passed into the Senate, Sumner again moved his amendment and this time emerged victorious by a vote of 17 to 16 (I.D.: 80). The difference in result is

42. Ibid., 3131–32.
43. Ibid., 3132.

explained almost solely in terms of absenteeism. In the vote in the Senate, Doolittle and Van Winkle, previously absent, joined the opposition, but Davis and Hendricks did not vote. Three of Sumner's supporters in the Committee of the Whole were also absent in the Senate vote, but six additional radicals voted with the Massachusetts senator to provide the winning margin.

On March 30, 1864, Wade initiated discussion of H.R. 15, providing a temporary government for the Territory of Montana, involving a region then part of Idaho Territory. Wilkinson moved immediately to amend the clause defining the suffrage of electors in the first election by striking the words "white male inhabitant," and substituting "male citizen of the United States and those who have declared their intention to become such." Reverdy Johnson pointed out that the alteration was apparently designed to open the franchise of the territory to blacks as well as whites. None, he said, would seriously contend that those who had been in slavery from birth were "intelligent enough or likely to become intelligent enough at once to exercise the right of suffrage."[44] No Republican spoke against the amendment, but Cowan, Lane of Indiana, Sherman, Ten Eyck, and Trumbull joined Democrats and border-state senators in voting against it, while fifteen radicals and seven moderates united to pass it, by a vote of 22 yeas to 17 nays (I.D.: 42).

As the bill moved into the Senate from Committee of the Whole, Saulsbury and Johnson brought the discussion back to the Wilkinson amendment. The former opposed "giving to this subordinate race any such privileges," and the latter argued that a person of African descent was not a citizen of the United States according to the Dred Scott decision.[45] Wilkinson must adopt different wording if he indeed wished to give Negroes the vote in Montana. Johnson and Sumner then became embroiled in a lengthy colloquy as to whether the Dred Scott case had indeed disgraced the country or the court, and as to the quality of the jurisprudence involved. This concluded, the Senate approved the bill by a division of 29 to 8; no Republican voted against it.

The House of Representatives refused to agree to the Senate amendments; the Senate held firm, requesting a committee of conference, and the Vice President appointed Wade, Lane of Kansas, and Sprague to be the Senate managers. One of the provisions of the conference committee's report recommended that the House accept the Wilkinson amendment. The representatives asked for a further conference and in their

44. Ibid., 1346; See Clark C. Spence, *Territorial Politics and Government in Montana, 1864–89* (Urbana: University of Illinois Press, 1975), pp. 13–15, for a recent scholarly treatment of the Wilkinson amendment.

45. *CG*, 38 Cong., 1 sess., 1362.

resolution on the matter provided that "said committee be instructed to agree to no report which authorizes any others than free white male citizens, and those who have declared their intention to become such, to vote." Wade described this gambit as "very unusual," indeed, "perfectly novel"; Sherman termed it "rather unmannerly"; and Fessenden argued that asking for an open conference committee would involve "getting down on our knees." The senators declined to agree to a committee of conference "in the manner asked for."[46] The House then asked for a free conference. At this point in the proceedings considerable discussion of the Wilkinson amendment occurred in the Senate.

There were, the senators noted, actually two matters involved in the amendment. The original bill had extended suffrage rights in the first territorial election to "free white male inhabitants above the age of twenty-one years," who had resided in the territory for thirty days prior to the balloting. There were Canadian fur traders in the territory who did not intend to become citizens, and other Canadians might arrive in the meantime who were uninterested in becoming citizens. Second, there was the issue of Negro suffrage. The Wilkinson amendment dealt with both issues. Doolittle and Trumbull argued that Negro suffrage was a mere abstraction; since there were no blacks in the territory, the legislation was of no "practical" utility. Trumbull spoke with particular vigor—Wilkinson would later say with bitterness—"The effect is simply to agitate and get up a question where there is nothing practical for it to work upon. The very first Legislature that meets in this Territory, according to the very provisions of this bill, will fix the right of suffrage." With some sarcasm he compared Negro suffrage to woman suffrage and continued:

> If we have done anything to weaken the power of the patriotic people to put down the rebellion, it has been by assuming action which the exigencies of the country did not require. We have a great work to do to save the country, save the Constitution, save constitutional liberty. We want the arms and the help of all the people of the loyal States. We want to get up no divisions about whether women's rights should prevail, or about establishing for a temporary purpose in some far-off Territory a principle that is to alienate and divide loyal men and friends of the Government. . . . It is of a piece with another declaration that I have heard sometimes in this Chamber . . . and that was that it mattered not whether a thing was constitutional or not. Sir, this Government cannot be saved, constitutional liberty cannot be saved, unless we save it under the Constitution. . . . How is it that there is an opposition in the northern States? On what is it based? It is under the pretence that the Government in its effort to put down this rebellion has usurped authority, has assumed to itself powers not warranted by the Constitution. I think these charges are not always just. I know they are

46. Ibid., 1639-40.

not; most frequently they are unjust. But I would avoid, if I could, the appearance of a violation of the Constitution.

To Wilkinson's query as to whether his amendment violated the Constitution, Trumbull replied that it did not, but he added:

> It is a needless provision here; it is of a temporary character; and the only effect of it is to make divisions in the North and among loyal men, and I regret exceedingly that the proposition has been thrust into Congress to go before the people and be discussed upon the stump. Why agitate the question during the summer as we go home among the people whether a colored man shall have a right to vote at the first election in Montana, where there is not a colored man? Shall that be the question to be discussed, instead of the vital one of appealing to the patriotism of the land to rally around the standard of the country and put down this wicked rebellion?[47]

In defense of his proposal Wilkinson emphasized that his amendment would bar hostile foreigners from exercising the franchise in the first Montana election. Although "a large army of black men" was fighting gallantly for the Union, the senator from Illinois wanted "a discrimination made against those men in direct terms in a bill in which we are called upon to define the qualifications of voters." Wilkinson was, he said, "opposed to being governed any longer by that wicked pro-slavery prejudice that has ruled in the Congress of the United States for more than thirty years, and is to-day exerting an influence over the minds of many of our Republican members which it ought not to exert, and which they ought to tread upon and spit upon here in this Congress and always hereafter."[48]

Hendricks twitted Wilkinson by pointing out that the Negro had no vote in Wilkinson's own state, nor in most of the states of the Northwest. Wilkinson was not conferring a "substantial right" upon the Negro, said the Indiana senator, merely asserting a "sentiment," and Hendricks wished to emphasize the implications of the act. "When the Senate says by its vote that [the Negro] ought to be a voter in Montana, the Senate says that he ought to be a voter in Indiana and in the States . . . and I desire the people of the country to understand that distinct proposition."[49]

Speaking before a gallery that shouted its approval, Doolittle argued that the issue of Negro suffrage in the territories and in the District of

47. Ibid., 1705–06.
48. Ibid., 1744–45. The New York *Herald*, April 26, 1864, claimed that Wilkinson severely damaged his case by arguing that a black Montanan had been in wealthy circumstances at the time of his recent death, only to have it revealed that this wealth consisted of "an unworked claim of speculative value" and that the man had been in debt to most of his acquaintances.
49. *CG*, 38 Cong., 1 sess., 1745.

Columbia need not be settled at this time; it was one that encouraged divisiveness and would embitter the presidential canvass. There were no Negroes in Montana, but unscrupulous politicians might manipulate an Indian vote there. He opposed a category of suffrage that was a mere abstraction, because "all history teaches us that upon mere abstractions, which have no practical application, sometimes the fiercest and most bitter controversies arise, whether in the religious, the political, or even in the scientific world." He urged the senators to "seek first, last, and all the time to do nothing, to engage in nothing, to say nothing but that which gives force to our armies, or raises the money to sustain them." The Montana suffrage amendment was one of a class of measures that tended to "distract the public mind and divide the hearts and energies of loyal men." Sumner particularly brought them forward, and Doolittle regretted the tendency of the press to misunderstand his opposition to legislative activity of this kind.[50]

In a final comment, Wilkinson summarized the issue as he saw it: "shall the Senate recede from its amendment and allow everybody to vote in Montana, allow men to be elected to the Territorial Legislature who owe no military service or allegiance to the United States, and exclude these men who do owe allegiance, and who are fighting for their country?" The senators then agreed to a new conference, and the Vice President appointed Wilkinson, Morrill, and Buckalew to be the Senate managers. On May 19, Morrill submitted the conference report and the suffrage was now given to "all citizens of the United States, and those who have declared their intention to become such, and who are otherwise described and qualified under the fifth section of the act of Congress providing for a temporary government for the Territory of Idaho approved March 3, 1863."[51] Insertion of the word "first" elsewhere emphasized that only the first election was involved. Under Sumner's questioning, Morrill admitted that the new wording provided "white suffrage," while remedying the defect in the original bill that allowed individuals who had no intention of becoming United States citizens to vote, provided that they had resided in the territory for thirty days prior to the election.

Moved, according to his most recent biographer, by opposition to "any action which even indirectly or inadvertently might serve as a precedent for readmitting the Southern states under their ante-bellum leadership," Sumner urged the Senate to stand firm in its original position. "Which shall adhere," he asked, "the side that is right or the side that is wrong?"

50. Ibid., 1843–44.
51. Ibid., 1846, 2347.

He believed, he said, "that the statement of [the original] principle at this moment [was] more important than the bill."[52]

Morrill defended the committee recommendation, arguing that the Wilkinson amendment was of no "practical importance," since the first legislature would set its own suffrage qualifications, and that it was desirable to organize the territory. When two legislative branches, both desiring the same object, found themselves at loggerheads, was it not desirable that the initiating branch should be given its way? Particularly so in this case, he believed, because both branches agreed to exactly this disposition of the same question in organizing the Idaho Territory a year earlier. Wade supported Morrill; none was more opposed to discriminatory suffrage than he, but "I never legislate or act in reference to mere shadows. Gentlemen may call them principle or not principle. . . . I cannot be bluffed off by the mere form or shadow of a thing." Others joined the debate but the major points had been made. In summary, Sumner quoted General Grant, "I will fight on this line to the end," and maintained, "There is no line which is better than that of human rights. While fighting on that line I cannot err. There is no pertinacity which can be too great. There is no ardor which is not respectable."[53]

The senators accepted the recommendation of the conference committee by a vote of 26 yeas and 13 nays (I.D.: 56). Eight moderates and six radicals were in the majority. Of those who, in general, voted a moderate pattern during this session, only Grimes was found among the thirteen Republicans in opposition. Minnesota's radical apostle, Wilkinson, did not participate in discussion of the final committee report, and voted to approve it. Did the Montana decision compromise the possibility that black suffrage would be accepted as a basic element in reconstruction? Perhaps, but if so it is strange that such outspoken men as Sumner and Wilkinson did not emphasize that issue in the debate. By this time the analogy between the territorial process and reconstruction was apparently less popular among the senators than formerly. And the situation in Montana was hardly comparable to that prevailing in occupied areas of the Confederacy. This was true also of the District of Columbia, but the discussion of black suffrage there, a few days later, probably gives us a better reading of the intent of the Republican senators in the spring of 1864 than does their handling of the Wilkinson amendment.

On May 24, 1864, five days after the senators had put the Montana

---

52. Donald, *Sumner and the Rights of Man*, p. 180; *CG*, 38 Cong., 1 sess., 2348.

53. *CG*, 38 Cong., 1 sess., 2348, 2351. Michael Les Benedict, *A Compromise of Principle: Congressional Republicans and Reconstruction, 1863–1869* (New York: Norton, 1974), pp. 78–79, emphasizes the relation between Montana suffrage and reconstruction.

suffrage amendment to rest, Wade reported a joint resolution from the Committee on the District of Columbia, S.57, explaining that there was an "immediate necessity" for its passage. The resolution amended the voter registration procedures of the city of Washington prior to the June election there. As interpreted by the incumbent attorney of the corporation, voters must have registered six months prior to an election in order to be eligible to vote. But a former officer had interpreted the law differently and allowed various residents to vote without prior enrollment. The decision of the current corporation attorney disfranchised numbers of long-time Washington residents, and the joint resolution provided procedures under which persons who had resided in Washington for at least a year previous to the election might register, subject to the "other qualifications of an elector now required." "I think there is no objection to it," remarked Wade, but his endorsement did not deter Sumner. On May 26, he fixed his attention on the phrase "the other qualifications of an elector," and remarked "I presume if we go back to the original charter we shall find it is that qualification which . . . is the tail of slavery, that discrimination of color left to us unhappily by the former presence of slavery in the national capital." He moved to amend the joint resolution by adding: "*Provided*, that there shall be no exclusion of any person from the register on account of color."[54]

Wade responded that the joint resolution was not designed to deal with suffrage in general. There was pending another measure (altering the Washington city charter) that dealt specifically with voting qualifications, and the issue raised by Sumner could most appropriately be considered in relation to that bill. Wade maintained:

> I am as strenuous an advocate for the right of voting for colored people as the Senator from Massachusetts; and whenever a case can be made where that question can be tested, I shall endeavor to make myself known and understood upon it, if I have not already done so. I do not, however, think it is incumbent upon us to insist upon it all the time whenever the question may be raised in any possible shape. We know that it is impracticable to act upon it now. . . . The permanent law is before us and can be acted upon hereafter.

Sumner, however, was unimpressed. He returned to the charge, arguing:

> If white persons are kept out of their rights, so are colored persons; and I would ask my friend from Ohio which has been kept out the longest? I am for securing the rights of both, to the end that we may have at last in the national capital *equality before the law*. . . . We are Senators of the United States, bound to consider the whole country in all its extent, and to do

---

54. *CG*, 38 Cong., 1 sess., 2436, 2486. This issue had been before the Senate in different circumstances earlier in the month (see below).

nothing here which shall do mischief elsewhere. Especially are we held not to yield to any local pressure, or to any imagined local interests, and thus forget the cause of justice.... Adopting again the language of General Grant, "I propose to fight it out on this line, if it takes all summer."[55]

In rebuttal, Morrill retorted, "some things may be done, and other things cannot be done; and no Senator knows better than the honorable Senator that this is precisely one of those things which at this moment cannot be done," a reference apparently to the state of opinion in the House. Then Harlan moved to change the word "person" in Sumner's amendment to "persons," adding "and who have borne arms in the military service of the United States, and have been honorably discharged therefrom." His colleagues accepted this without splitting along radical-moderate lines. Although concerned lest the joint resolution allow transients to vote, Willey ridiculed Sumner's position remarking: "It seems to me utterly incongruous and improper to be fighting on this little line all summer. Why, sir, it is the Senator from Massachusetts that is hanging on to the tail, and the tip end of the tail of slavery whenever he can get hold of it." The order of the day pushed S. 57 aside as Wade fulminated, "If we offered the ten commandments here, there would be a thousand propositions to amend, probably ... and the final vote would be very uncertain."[56]

Several days later the senators accepted Sumner's amendment as amended without a division. It now read: "*Provided,* That there shall be no exclusion of any persons from the register on account of color who have borne arms in the military service of the United States and have been honorably discharged therefrom." Since the provision was now far less general than originally, Sumner proposed to add a new clause, based in part on wording devised by Morrill for use elsewhere:

And provided further, That all persons, without distinction of color, who shall, within the year next preceding the election, have paid a tax on any estate, or been assessed with a part of the revenue of said District, or been exempt from taxation having taxable estate, and who can read and write with facility, shall enjoy the privilege of an elector. But no person now entitled to vote in the said District, continuing to reside therein, shall be disfranchised hereby.

55. Ibid., 2486, 2512.
56. Ibid., 2512. Harlan's amendment was by no means the first attempt in American history to introduce military service suffrage; see Chilton Williamson, *American Suffrage: From Property to Democracy, 1760–1860* (Princeton: Princeton University Press, 1960), passim. Massachusetts voters approved a constitutional literacy provision in their constitution in 1857 but did not abolish the taxation requirement already in force. See Commonwealth of Massachusetts, *Manual for the Use of the General Court: Containing the Rules and Orders of the Two Branches* ... (Boston: William White, 1858), p. 92, and *The General Statutes of the Commonwealth of Massachusetts* (Boston: William White, 1860), p. 56.

Sumner read a harrowing account of a fatal beating that a Tennessee slaveholder had recently inflicted on a female slave, an action attributable to the "odious discrimination of color." Let not his colleagues recognize a similar discrimination of color in their actions; there was involved "a question of human rights everywhere throughout this country, involving the national character and its good name forevermore," and not "simply the question of a few voters more or less in this District."[57] When the vote occurred on Sumner's additional amendment, only the senator from Massachusetts and seven other radicals voted yea (I.D.: 57). The resolution then moved to the Senate, and the senators voted on Sumner's original amendment as altered to apply only to colored veterans with honorable discharges. That too was lost, yeas 18 and nays 20 (I.D.: 56.5). Cowan, Grimes, Lane of Indiana, Ten Eyck, Trumbull, and the radical Morrill joined with Democrats and border-state senators to defeat the motion. Foster, Howe, and Sherman of the moderates had supported it in company with fifteen radicals.

There is no reference to distinctions of color in the resolution as it appears in the *Laws* of the Thirty-eighth Congress, and we have in this debate another instance in which Sumner, on grounds of principle, pushed beyond the tolerance of more moderate colleagues. For that matter, he exceeded the tolerance of radicals too; both Morrill and Wade, as members of the Committee on the District of Columbia, opposed his amendments on the floor.[58] Wade, however, was absent for the two roll calls that showed substantial disagreement between radicals and moderates. The voting on S. 57 suggests also that the Republican senators may have moved less far toward unrestricted black suffrage than some have believed the Montana voting to show.

Sumner's hopes for establishing a freedmen's bureau also brought moderates into collision with their radical brethren. Acting in his capacity as Chairman of the Select Committee on Slavery and Freedmen during the first session of the Thirty-eighth Congress, the Massachusetts senator tried to move a bill creating such an agency through the Senate. Proceedings focussed on a House measure, H.R. 51, for which Sumner proposed to substitute his own S. 227. The voting in the Senate did not reveal marked differences between Republican radicals and moderates,

---

57. *CG*, 38 Cong., 1 sess., 2543–44.
58. 38 Cong., 1 sess., *Laws*, 265–66; Donald, *Sumner and the Rights of Man*, p. 181. Wade's most recent biographer does not mention this exchange, although he notes the Ohio senator's introduction of a Negro franchise bill in the next Congress: Hans L. Trefousse, *Benjamin Franklin Wade: Radical Republican from Ohio* (New York: Twayne, 1963), p. 263.

although Sumner's unsuccessful effort to remove a Willey amendment that would have allowed resettlement in the old free states, and an attempt to place the bureau under the War Department rather than under the Treasury, produced suggestions of such conflict.[59] Nor did eastern Republicans differ markedly from western in their reactions to the various terms of the bill. But the chambers did not reconcile their differences on the bureau bill during the first session of the Thirty-eighth Congress. Sumner served on a conference committee that worked to achieve agreement during the early weeks of the second session, and the senators considered its report on February 10, 1865. This report, it developed, was irregular in that it proposed that the houses accept new substance, rather than merely recommending that their members accept or recede from particular amendments, passages, or clauses.

Davis protested the committee's willingness to write its own law and argued that section 12, making civilian officers of the bureau subject to court martial, contravened the provision in the Fifth Amendment directing that citizens other than members of the armed services must not "be held to answer for a capital, or otherwise infamous crime, unless on a presentment or indictment of a grand jury." He noted with relish that this clause had originated in Massachusetts, "that enlightened and patriotic State, but now how deplorably fallen."[60] Opposition was to be expected from such as Davis, and Hendricks who supported him, but Hale too found section 12 unsatisfactory on constitutional grounds, and Grimes felt it necessary to explain "why I shall sever from many friends with whom I usually act on this occasion." The bill created an independent department, contrary to the provisions of the bills proposed by both houses. The Secretary of War, Grimes believed, should supervise the extension of assistance to refugees and indigents. And why, he asked, should the work of the bureau apply only to the states in rebellion since there were at least twelve thousand colored refugees in the city of Washington? He did not believe that blacks alone should have the aban-

59. Wilson, *History of the Antislavery Measures*, pp. 328–36, and *Rise and Fall of the Slave Power in America*, 3:480–85; Pierce, *Sumner*, 4:177–78; Donald, *Sumner and the Rights of Man*, pp. 174–78, 194–95; George R. Bentley, *A History of the Freedmen's Bureau* (Philadelphia: University of Pennsylvania, 1955), pp. 1–49. The latter author sees the bureau as the outgrowth of the economic imperialism of New England, while Pierce attributes Grimes's opposition to ill feeling generated by Sumner's opposition to the latter's support of a policy of granting letters of *marque* and reprisal. See also LaWanda Cox, "The Promise of Land for the Freedmen," *Mississippi Valley Historical Review*, 45 (December 1958), 413–40; and Louis S. Gerteis, "Salmon P. Chase, Radicalism, and the Politics of Emancipation, 1861–1864," *Journal of American History*, 60 (June 1973), 42–62. *CG*, 38 Cong., 1 sess., 3337. The first vote actually generated an index of disagreement in the low 40 percent range, but only six moderates voted. The second produced an I.D. of 30.

60. *CG*, 38 Cong., 2 sess., 786.

doned lands of rebels assigned to them, as provided in the bill. What of the "white refugees and the white Union people . . . in exactly as destitute a condition as these colored men?"

Grimes's major concern was with the ninth section, which provided "That whenever the Commissioner cannot otherwise employ any of the freedmen who may come under his care, he shall, as far as practicable, make provision for them with humane and suitable persons at a just compensation for their services." "As a friend of the emancipated slave," Grimes was unwilling "to place such unlimited power over him in the hands of anybody." A short bill then under final consideration in the House was much more attractive to Grimes than the conference committee's measure, and Lane of Indiana later took the same position. The House bill, providing for the establishment of a bureau for the relief of freedmen and refugees in the War Department, succinctly outlined the organization of the agency and provided that the President might assign the abandoned lands and tenements of rebels for the temporary use of these categories of individuals as well as direct the issuance of provisions, clothing, and fuel to them. For these various reasons, Grimes pronounced himself prepared to vote against the "bill in behalf of freedmen" now before the Senate.[61]

Although he expected to vote to accept the conference report, Pomeroy feared the appearance of permanence that the bureau bill displayed, running counter, as it did, to his conviction that the freedmen would very rapidly be able to look after themselves. "All," he believed, that "the exigencies of the case demand is some temporary expedient for a year or two." He was followed by Sprague, who believed that the measure was unnecessary if the freedmen could be assured the ballot. Henderson criticized the size and powers of the administrative apparatus provided by the committee. Here was slavery's tutelage revivified, and when Lane of Indiana tossed him the word "overseers," he seized it enthusiastically, affirming, moreover, that the senator from Massachusetts was "building up the machinery of a vast system of fraud and oppression throughout the southern States."[62]

An article in the Boston *Commonwealth,* under the head line "Down with the 'D,'" helped to bring Hale back into the lists. The author counseled the antislavery senators "who had any scruples on this subject" that they might be safe in following the counsel of his "distinguished friend from Massachusetts." But Hale complained, "When he asks me to neglect my own kith and kin to legislate for the exclusive protection and benefit of colored men he goes a little further than I am willing to go."

61. Ibid., 958–59.
62. Ibid., 960, 963.

Although recording his "adhesion" to the bill, Morrill was uncertain whether it really provided much practical assistance to the freedmen that could not be provided under existing law.[63]

In various interjections and in one longer statement, Sumner defended the committee proposal. The bill, he argued, was "substantially" the same as that approved by the Senate, differing only in that the agency would be a separate bureau or department, rather than being allocated to the War or Treasury departments. Rebutting the criticism that section 9 would return the freedmen to slavery, Sumner called the attention of a skeptical Grimes to the clause in the fourth section that read, "And every such freedman shall be treated in all respects as a free man, with all proper remedies in courts of justice, and no power or control shall be exercised with regard to him except in conformity with law," which he argued would govern section 9. Doolittle had added the clause to the bill subjecting civilian employees of the bureau to military justice during the previous session. Why now was it to be picked upon as unconstitutional?[64]

Was it not a "strange complaint" that the measure was "too favorable to the freedmen" and too little was being done for the whites, when the war had grown out of the generations of injustice done to the blacks? In the process of this argument, Sumner declared that Grimes was trying to kill the bill, that he was opposed to it "now ... as ... at the beginning," and thundered, "Sir, I am in earnest. ... Even emancipation is not enough. You must see to it that it is not evaded or nullified." This line of response led Grimes to remark quickly, "It was hardly necessary ... for the Senator ... to round out his polished periods, to be inaccurate," reminding Sumner that he had indeed voted for the original Senate measure. He was, he assured his colleagues, "as much in earnest as the Senator from Massachusetts." Of the Republican senators, only Cowan had not endorsed the objectives of the bureau bill of the previous session in the final vote on it, complained Sumner. Now the proposal was "assailed as few measures ever before have been assailed, and all arguments, constitutional, political, personal, have been brought into debate," as his colleagues caught "a tone from the worst days of the olden time, when slavery filled this Chamber with its voice." None could accuse the Republican senators of being a harmonious "band of brothers," at this juncture. The course of Hale, Lane, Grimes, and Henderson was, gloated the New York *Herald,* "quite refreshing."[65]

At this stage of the proceedings, the report of the conference committee could not be amended; ostensibly, this was the senators' problem,

63. Ibid., 984, 988.
64. Ibid., 959, 987–88; the text of the bill appears on pp. 766–67.
65. Ibid., 961–62, 989; New York *Herald,* February 23, 1865.

regardless of their deeper motivations—racism, perversity, honest concern for refugees, freedmen, or whatever. If they approved the report, they accepted a bill that differed in vital respects, or so a majority maintained, from the measure that they had sent to the other house. So they rejected it and sent the matter back once more to conference committee. The new conference committee, chaired by Wilson, returned a much shorter bill, authorizing a bureau of refugees, freedmen, and abandoned lands in the War Department, its duties similar to those specified in the earlier version, but unclouded by the language that the senators had found odious. Loyal refugees now also fell under the authority of the bureau, land might be leased for three years, rather than one, in tracts not to exceed forty acres, and a qualified suggestion of eventual purchase was included. As chairman of the Senate managers, Wilson called the report up on March 2 and requested an immediate vote, but some senators asked for more time in which to consider the new version, and factional disagreement appeared in motions to adjourn without action. Wilson finally agreed that the report should be held over, and on the following day the senators agreed to it without a division. Not only had they rejected Sumner's handiwork, they had turned to his own colleague from Massachusetts to effect a final solution![66]

For comparative purposes, since the debates of the second session of the Thirty-eighth Senate provide a relatively small number of roll calls and since the major focus of debate was moving perceptibly toward reconstruction issues, I calculated disagreement indices for those roll calls on the basis both of the voting in the first session and of that in the second. While H.R. 51 was on the floor, five motions revealed disagree-

66. If Sumner viewed the select committee as a device for strengthening his hand in matters relative to slavery and the freedmen, as seems extremely reasonable, the passage of the freedmen's bureau bill was a debacle indeed. Not only was Wilson the chairman of the Senate managers on the final conference committee, but his senatorial colleagues had approved a highly irritating amendment from Willey (see above, p. 213), who also served on the second conference committee from which issued an acceptable report, in contrast to that of the first conference committee on which Sumner had served. Indeed Charles H. Ambler (*Willey*, p. 113) argues, "In its final form the bill was, in part, Willey's creation." If so, it was a bitter pill to Sumner who had, so Willey charged, called the West Virginian a slave-hunter in a speech delivered in New York City. The regional racist dimension of the freedmen's bureau vote has sometimes been emphasized. Cox, "The Promise of Land for the Freedmen," wrote on p. 438: "A decisive number of the Republican senators who voted against the bill on Februry 22, 1865, were from the agrarian Northwest. There is no evidence to prove beyond doubt that in rejecting the proposal they were mindful of the prejudice of race so widespread among their constituents; yet such a conclusion appears to be a reasonable one." This may well be true, but the suggestion that the senators from the Northwest differed substantially from their party colleagues from other regions in voting against the bill because their constituencies were peculiarly subject to racism is unwarranted. When we use the eastern boundary of Ohio to divide the Republican senators into eastern and western groups, the index of disagreement on this vote stands at 5, a negligible coefficient.

ment of some magnitude between radicals and moderates. Three of these were motions to adjourn (I.D. 1-38: 53, 48, 69; 2-38: 68, 33, 25), another offered the option of postponing discussion (I.D. 1-38: 34; 2-38: 44), and the fifth was the vote to agree to the report of the first committee of conference (I.D. 1-38: 70; 2-38: 60).

Significantly, factional disagreement among the Republicans did not appear insofar as the central purpose of the Thirteenth Amendment was concerned, but one vote involving that measure during the first session of the Thirty-eighth Congress was divisive. On April 7, 1864, Hendricks and Henderson spoke to the measure (S. Joint Resolution 16), and Wilson requested an executive session at the conclusion of the Missourian's speech. Sumner announced that he wished to discuss the amendment resolution, but given his colleagues' desire for an executive session, preferred to do so at one o'clock on the following day. Doolittle urged immediate action on S. 16, and Trumbull expressed mild exasperation at his inability to bring the resolution to a vote. Howard intervened to request the "usual courtesy" for Sumner, but Sherman pointed out that Sumner would have ample opportunity to talk about slavery in the future. All but two of the radicals present supported Wilson's motion to proceed to executive business, while seven moderates opposed it (I.D.: 45).[67] The vote revealed Sumner's disenchantment with the substance of the amendment and the strategy that it reflected. Although they were willing to give him the opportunity to discuss alternatives, the senators did not prove willing to reject the Judiciary Committee's reliance on the wording of the Northwest Ordinance and accept Sumner's formula based on equality of individuals before the law. His suggestions were rebuffed without substantial factional disagreement.

In this chapter we have sketched the disagreements of the senators in considering emancipation in West Virginia and Missouri, the repeal of the fugitive slave laws and the coastal slave trade regulations, efforts to insure the rights of blacks to stand witness in federal courts, to share equally in the benefits of rail transport in the District, and to vote there, as well as in Montana's first territorial election, and the struggle to provide a freedmen's bureau. Clearly, Sumner dominates the narrative of this chapter, although he was not always successful in his designs. Constitutional disagreement was important, particularly in consideration of the repeal of the fugitive slave laws and the coastal slave trade regulations, and differences concerning the constitutional balance between

67. *CG*, 38 Cong., 1 sess., 1465. For a concise but comprehensive summary of the background of the Thirteenth Amendment and its implications, see Herman Belz, *A New Birth of Freedom: The Republican Party and Freedmen's Rights, 1861 to 1866* (Westport, Conn.: Greenwood Press, 1976), pp. 113-37.

state and federal powers underlay other Republican discord. But it is also clear that the senators differed over the political wisdom and practical implications of Sumner's proposals and perhaps reacted negatively as well to Sumner's style and personality. As colleagues had predicted, the Thirteenth Amendment rendered much of Sumner's activity during the Thirty-eighth Congress redundant; some of his achievements in detail were washed away through application of a general formula, but the memory of a good deal of recrimination must have remained.

Browning—a man of questionable judgment and obviously no radical, but hardly one to lie maliciously either—recorded a conversation about Sumner with Collamer, Foot, Senator Fessenden, and the latter's brother, Congressman Tom Fessenden, that took place on the train to Washington, before the third session of the Thirty-seventh Congress. They all agreed, he noted, "in characterizing him as cowardly, mean, malignant, tyranical [sic], hypocritical, and cringing . . . to . . . aristocracy."[68] Sometimes radicals such as Wade and Morrill also found Sumner's tactics unacceptable; the former surely had the Massachusetts senator in mind when he proclaimed that he himself did not legislate "in reference to mere shadows."[69] From our vantage, we can agree with admiration that the senator from Massachusetts "understood the importance attached to precedent, that he opposed any racial discrimination, however fleeting and insignificant, and that he firmly believed in the principle of racial equality."[70] We should also understand that he could at times be a serious threat to Republican party unity and frustratingly obstructive.

68. Theodore C. Pease and James G. Randall, eds., *The Diary of Orville Hickman Browning: I. 1850–1864* (Springfield: Illinois State Historical Library, *Collections*, 20, 1925), p. 588.
69. *CG*, 38 Cong., 1 sess., 2348.
70. From adviser's report to Cornell University Press.

# 7

# Punishment and Rehabilitation

When the senators attacked slavery or reinforced the civil rights of free blacks, they struck directly or indirectly at secessionist southerners. None could doubt that the status of white southerners would be far different in a reconstructed Union if their former bondsmen were free and equal before the law. But in every session of the war congresses, the senators debated other types of measures that affected the status of southerners, either as property holders or as participants in the political process. In discussion of some of these measures too, Republicans aligned themselves as radicals and moderates.

The senators discussed confiscation more thoroughly and over a longer period of time than any other subject during the long session of the Thirty-seventh Congress. Involving also the question of emancipation, the discussion of confiscation generated approximately one fifth of the roll calls that reflected substantial disagreement between radical and moderate Republicans in the second session. During its early weeks, the senators referred six bills and a joint resolution, as well as other matter on the subject, to the Judiciary Committee. On January 15, 1862, Trumbull requested that the committee be discharged of its obligations to consider these documents further and reported S. 151 "to confiscate the property and free the slaves of rebels."[1] Considered to be Trumbull's

1. *CG*, 37 Cong., 2 sess., 334, 942. See: James G. Randall, *The Confiscation of Property during the Civil War* (Indianapolis: Mutual Printing and Lithographing, 1913), pp. 7–12 and passim, and Randall, *Constitutional Problems under Lincoln* (New York: Appleton, 1926), pp. 275–315; Harold M. Hyman, *A More Perfect Union: The Impact of the Civil War and Reconstruction on the Constitution* (New York: Knopf, 1973), pp. 177–81 and 228–29; John Syrett, "The Confiscation Acts: Efforts at Reconstruction during the Civil War" (Ph.D. diss., University of Wisconsin–Madison, 1971), pp. 1–92; Leonard P. Curry, *Blueprint for Modern America: Nonmilitary Legislation of the First Civil War Congress* (Nashville: Vanderbilt University Press, 1968), pp. 75–100 and passim. Duke Frederick, "The Second Confiscation Act: A Chapter of Civil War Politics" (Ph.D. diss., University of Chicago, 1966), includes an interesting effort to define factional affiliation by roll-call analysis.

bill, S. 151 had provoked keen discussion within the Judiciary Committee, and Ten Eyck later explained that only his vote had allowed it to reach the floor. Its history in the Senate was stormy. During the early days of May its supporters were defending it desperately against the efforts of other Republicans to "perfect" it, and on May 6 a frustrated Trumbull saw the majority of the Senate support Clark's motion to refer it and the major amendments to a select committee.

Section 1 of S. 151 declared forfeit the real and personal property of individuals "who shall during the present rebellion, be found in arms against the United States, or giving aid and comfort to said rebellion," whether that property be in the North or in the rebellious southern states. The next section declared the slaves of such individuals to be free, and anyone trying to prove ownership of bondsmen thereafter must prove that he had been loyal to the United States. The President was authorized to colonize abroad those blacks who were freed under the law's provisions, should they so desire. Two sections instructed the President to use military or civil officers to confiscate property in districts "beyond the reach of civil process in the ordinary course of judicial proceedings by reason of . . . rebellion," as often as in his opinion military necessity or the safety, interest, and welfare of the United States required. Such officers were expected to make full reports and to deposit the proceeds from the sale, rental, or other use of confiscated property in the United States Treasury. In a final section of the bill, Trumbull dealt with the property of rebels situated in loyal states or districts. In such cases "proceedings *in rem*," were to be instituted in the appropriate district court of the United States, these actions to "conform, as nearly as may be, to proceedings in prize cases, or to cases of forfeiture arising under the revenue laws." Property taken in such action was to be sold and the returns deposited in the Treasury.[2]

In brief comments on the bill, Trumbull stressed that it was an effort to reach the property of rebels who were themselves beyond the reach of judicial process. It did not "profess or intend to touch the property of any traitor who . . . [could] be reached by judicial process," and it forfeited, "all the property, real and personal." He argued that the procedures of his bill fell outside the scope of the constitutional provision forbidding the property of traitors to be forfeited beyond their lifetimes. Legal authorities generally agreed that the people of one nation might seize the property of the people of another when the two were at war with each other. The forces of the Union were at war with the rebels. "We may treat them as traitors, and we may treat them as enemies, and we have the right of both, belligerent and sovereign," he argued. Nor, he

2. *CG*, 37 Cong., 2 sess., 942.

maintained, was this a bill of attainder, and as such forbidden by the Constitution, since it did "not corrupt the blood of the party." He defended S. 151 in general terms as a measure that would make the rebels pay part of the costs of the war. "It is just and right," said he, "that the men who have instigated the war, pay the expenses."[3]

Of all the Republicans, Cowan was to prove most conservative in his approach to the constitutional issues of the war. A formidable debater, he believed that S. 151 and its main provisions were "unnecessary, impolitic, inexpedient, and unconstitutional, and," he added, "utterly and totally useless," serving only to make southerners more bitter and obdurate in their course. The bill also, he argued, was in "direct conflict with the Constitution of the United States," and the war was being fought "solely for the Constitution, and for the ends, aims, and purposes sanctioned by it, and for no others." The southerners were traitors; their property could not be forfeited for longer than they lived. Under the Fifth Amendment also, they were entitled to judicial process. Trumbull's bill "attempted to deprive a large class of persons of all their estates and property, without any arrest, without any presentment by a grand jury, without any trial by a petit jury, without, indeed, any trial at all in any court." Although not a bill of attainder in that it inflicted capital punishment or corrupted the blood of offenders, its punitive provisions made it a bill "of pains and penalties" and on the same principle. Nor did the bill distinguish between "the wily traitor and his simple dupe." Its provisions, he argued, seemed to verify the southern slander that the Republicans proposed to "meddle with slaves or slavery in the slave States." Finally, Cowan maintained that S. 151 was a legislative invasion of the President's prerogatives as commander-in-chief, which gave him full power to order confiscation on whatever scale he deemed necessary to win the war. Cowan was "content" to "confide it" to the President and his advisers, "as . . . all other duties devolved upon them by the laws and the Constitution."[4] On March 10, Browning agreed at length.

Morrill, Howard, Wade, and other radicals amplified the radical arguments in support of S. 151, and Trumbull himself returned to its defense because of "the fierceness" with which it had been assailed and "misrepresentations . . . unintentional of course." The critics exaggerated in claiming that it struck "at all the property of every kind and character of all the citizens of the seceded States with scarcely an exception." Rather it "would not probably reach the property of one in ten of the *rebels*," since it would apply only to rebels who persisted in their support of the South after the passage of the bill and it would affect only

3. Ibid., 942–44.
4. Ibid., 1050–53.

those who were beyond the reach of Union judicial processes. Cowan and Browning were inconsistent in their criticism, he contended, because they themselves were willing to have the Executive exercise equally sweeping rights of confiscation in his capacity as commander-in-chief. Their emphasis on the powers of the President was designed only to defeat the bill; they were sure that the President would never exercise his prerogatives if left to his own devices. If the Fifth Amendment must apply and due process prevail in the seizure of property, it should equally apply in the taking of life, but none argued, Trumbull pointed out, that the soldiers of the Union could not kill the enemy. Nor could his bill be categorized as an act of attainder, because it would not "touch the property of any one whose life has been taken or who can be brought to trial for his crimes."[5]

Trumbull maintained that "there is not a syllable in the Constitution conferring on the President war powers." When Congress raised armies and navies of which the President was commander-in-chief, he could "only govern and regulate them as Congress shall direct," because, argued the senator from Illinois, "the Constitution says, 'Congress shall have power to make rules for the government and regulation of the land and naval forces.'" It had always been the practice of Congress "to control the President in his government of the Army," as the Articles of War showed. Would the bill "make the rebels desperate, and unite the South as one man against the Union?" Surely not the loyal people in the South and, moreover, "not to confiscate the property of rebels [was] to encourage future rebellions."

Trumbull agreed with Cowan that Congress under the Constitution had no power to "interfere with slavery in the States." But slaves, he maintained, would obtain their freedom under this bill only if rebels persisted in rebellious activity after its passage. Such emancipation would be by the "voluntary act" of the "rebel master." He continued:

> It so happens, in the providence of God, that most of those who own slaves are now in arms against the Government. This gives to the Government the power to destroy them and all they possess if necessary to suppress the rebellion; and Congress is vested by the Constitution with the discretion of determining what means shall be used to accomplish the object. . . . Such an opportunity to strike a blow for freedom seldom occurs as that now presented to the American Congress.[6]

But Trumbull's colleagues deferred action on S. 151, and on April 11 the Illinois senator greeted Sumner's effort to go into executive session with "That is the way the bill is shoved off every day." In further ex-

5. Ibid., 1557, 1559.
6. Ibid., 1559, 1561–62.

change he maintained, "I know . . . there are very many in the Senate opposed to this bill, possibly a majority opposed to any bill of this character. I know that those gentlemen are prepared with speeches, and have been for weeks . . . and do not intend speaking until we bring the bill to a position where they will have to speak."[7] Procedural votes which would delay action on the confiscation bill attracted strong support from the northern Democrats and the slave-state senators. But votes of this nature on both April 10 and April 24 showed substantial disagreement between radicals and moderates as well (I.D.: 44, 43).

As the debates on S. 151 continued, it became clear that all Republicans were willing to admit that the right to confiscate southern property rested in the government of the United States. But in which branch? Beyond this question, the issues involved matters of degree and incidence, means, expediency, and the plans of emancipation and colonization to be included in such a measure. No other Republican could accept the position of Browning and Cowan *in toto*. But the Trumbull bill was also unacceptable to more moderate Republicans, and Harris, and Sherman, and Collamer developed substitute bills, proferred as amendments.

Desiring "simple, moderate, constitutional confiscation," Sherman also prepared amendments designed to perfect Trumbull's measure. If these could be engrafted in S. 151, he proposed to withdraw his substitute. Very important was his proposal (somewhat similar to Harris') to specify various categories of southerners to which Trumbull's bill would apply: military officers; major office-holders of the Confederacy; persons who after the passage of the act filled military or civil offices in which they were required under the Confederate constitution to take an oath of loyalty to that document; United States office-holders who after the passage of the law took up arms against the United States; and persons who, holding property in the loyal states and territories, should thereafter assist or give aid and comfort to the rebellion. King endeavored to vitiate this amendment by adding a final catchall category to it of "persons in the present insurrection levying war against the United States or adhering to their enemies, giving them aid and comfort," that would in effect have restored the more sweeping coverage of S. 151.[8] Both the vote on King's amendment to Sherman's amendment, which was lost, and the vote by which the latter was engrafted in the bill revealed substantial disagreement between radicals and moderates (I.D.: 47, 47). Sherman proposed to hold confiscated property, except when perishable, until federal proceedings *in rem* could be instituted. If the

7. Ibid., 1627.
8. Ibid., 1785, 1813.

designation of categories of southerners, the emphasis on judicial process, and his emancipation proposal, involving a sixty-day warning period, were essentially moderate in tone, the final clauses, authorizing the President to place freedmen under arms, were considerably less so.

Before the votes on King's amendment were taken, Collamer addressed his colleagues. Both Collamer's analysis of S. 151 and the major features of his own bill are of some interest, particularly since the latter appealed to moderate Republicans. He believed that the task ahead was twofold. "The insurrection by force . . . must be put down by force. . . . No treatment can apply to it but that of phlebotomy," he said. But "the other branch of duty" demanded "an endeavor to restore this Government." This task to him involved restoration of the state governments. But the processes must be constitutional:

> When [the Constitution] . . . provided, for instance, that you should not pass any attainder bill, that you should not take away any man's property without due process of law, that no man should be punished unless it was on conviction by a jury, that no man should be twice punished for the same offense—prohibitions of this kind are prohibitions to everybody and they were put in to prevent Congress doing such things when they wanted to do them.

Collamer gently ridiculed "proceedings *in rem*" as a concept with a "vast deal of *hocus pocus* in it," designed to circumvent the constitutional limitations against depriving men of property without due process of law. Their introduction here was sophistry. Proceedings *in rem*, he explained were used in prize or admiralty courts, where "an instrument of wrong," such as the smuggler's goods, could be distinguished. The concept, in his opinion, did not fit this case. "When we legislate for that people as our people in common with the rest of our citizens," he continued, "we must allow to them all the rights and privileges, immunities and protections that the Constitution gives to citizens of the Union."[9]

Collamer had concluded, he said, that the "doctrine about the relative rights and privileges of belligerents to each other" was "utterly inapplicable to the present condition of things." If southerners were to be regarded as belligerents, the "property in the land remains in the individuals who owned it before." And if southerners *were* belligerents they must be recognized as "a coequal power." He concluded, "this legislating for that people as bound by the laws that we here make, and at the same time legislating for them as enemies and belligerents not bound by the laws we make, is to my mind utterly inconsistent, utterly irreconcilable."[10] If confiscation was a military necessity, Collamer believed that

9. Ibid., 1808–09.
10. Ibid., 1810.

decisions concerning it rightfully belonged to the President and his generals. S. 151 was too sweeping; titles sold under its provisions could stand only if two regiments were assigned to protect every plantation.

Collamer then considered the emancipation provision of S. 151 and was "strongly apprehensive," he said, "that the more particular friends of this bill regard that as *the* bill." No explanations, "however ingenious, and all sophistry, however plausible," could convince the independent observer that such emancipation was anything but repudiation of the Republicans' oft-repeated assurances that they would not meddle with slavery as it existed in the states.[11]

The senator from Vermont believed that his substitute bill provided a realistic and constitutional approach to the problem of punishing southerners and restoring local southern institutions. The first section prescribed substantial fines and prison terms as an alternative to execution in the punishment of treason. The slaves of all convicted under the law were to be declared free. The President was authorized to instruct commissioners to seize the real and personal property of rebels (excepting slaves) as he deemed it necessary, and hold the property until judicial proceedings could be brought against its owners. Such assets, presumably, would provide the substance of their fines if they were convicted. Provisions in the bill emphasized the President's power of pardon and amnesty. In areas which the President had "declared in a state of insurrection," the chief executive could, after six months, "if in his opinion it is necessary to the successful suppression of said insurrection, by proclamation to fix and appoint a day when all persons holden to service or labor" should be free, if their masters continued to wage rebellion or give aid to it beyond the date he had proclaimed. A final section provided, as in S. 151, that agents seeking to reestablish ownership of a slave must prove that they and the alleged owner had been loyal to the United States during the "period of insurrection or rebellion."[12]

As major amendments to S. 151, or substitutes, were touted and others rumored, Cowan moved on April 30 that the various confiscation measures be referred to a select committee. He specifically disavowed any desire to chair the committee, as the normal procedures of the chamber dictated, but Wade denounced the motion as the work of "an enemy" of the bill. In a similar mood, Trumbull reported that Cowan had fought S. 151 in the Judiciary Committee "with all the power that he could exert." Although Browning, Collamer, Doolittle, Fessenden, Foster, and Howe joined Cowan in supporting his proposal, the radicals carried the day and the motion was defeated (I.D.: 54).

11. Ibid., 1811–12.
12. Ibid., 1814.

A week later the senators were still struggling with the confiscation bill, and Anthony's motion to postpone discussion, despite its status as special order of the day on May 6, failed (I.D.: 50). Wilson's substitute for the Collamer bill was under discussion and in Clark's mind this went "a good way towards harmonizing some of the differences in the minds of the senators." But despairing of perfecting a satisfactory bill upon the floor, the New Hampshire senator moved that S. 151 and the related proposals be referred to a select committee. Wade fumed that it was "most evident" that the Senate lacked a majority "favorable to an efficient bill of confiscation." But a majority of Republicans supported referral (I.D.: 35). In his distress, Trumbull refused to serve on the select committee; of its members only Harlan, Sherman, and Wilson could be "depended on for anything thorough," sniffed the Chicago Tribune.[13]

Until early May, when S. 151 was entrusted to the tender mercies of a select committee of seven, six roll calls occurred in which radicals and moderates showed themselves to be in substantial disagreement. Four of these can serve only as specific evidence of lack of interest in the issue, of general hostility to Trumbull's bill, or the belief of moderates that other issues were more pressing than confiscation, since they occurred in divisions involving legislative procedures and priorities. Two concerned the categories of people to whom confiscation was to apply, and these revealed that radicals wished to apply confiscation broadly and moderates wished to be more selective.

The debates on S. 151 also suggest that radicals, in addition, wished to treat rebels both as treasonous citizens and as enemies of the country, while moderates were unwilling to dispense with constitutional safeguards of due process. Radicals wished to punish and despoil; some moderates feared action that might forever alienate southerners, whatever the outcome in the field. Some moderates believed also that the emancipation provisions of some proposals abrogated the longtime pledges of the Republican party. They differed also with the radicals in their interpretation of the war powers under the Constitution, some moderates being willing to leave initiative, administrative, and tactical decisions in the hands of the chief executive, while radicals envisioned a much more restricted role for him. More specifically, some moderates insisted that no property should be confiscated without judicial processes, that, of these, *in rem* proceedings were inappropriate, that distinctions should be made among categories of southerners, and that the principle of using warning periods prior to punitive action should be adopted in certain instances.

On May 16, Clark, as chairman of the Select Committee on Confisca-

13. Ibid., 1878, 1883, 1954, 1957; Chicago Tribune, May 15, 1862.

tion, successfully moved consideration of his committee's bill, S. 310, "to suppress insurrection, and to punish treason and rebellion, and for other purposes." In discussion preliminary to a vote on the question, Henderson noted that it was rather a bill "changing the punishment of treason, and forfeiting the property of the convicted rebel." Howard termed it "a clear and distinct renunciation of the principle and right of confiscating the property of rebels."[14]

The major provisions of S. 310 provided that the penalty for treason committed in the future might be either death or, at the discretion of the court, imprisonment and a substantial fine. In either case, the slaves of the traitor were to be declared free. A second section defined disloyal action which would render individuals liable to forfeiture of personal property and to forfeiture of life interest in real estate. The slaves of the guilty were to go free, and the latter were to be forever barred from holding office under the United States government. Section 5 of the committee bill authorized the President to have marshals or commissioners "seize and sequester" all the property "of such persons as shall have been actively and notoriously engaged in said rebellion and especially" that of the five categories of individuals designated in the amended S. 151. Such seizure was to secure the appearance of an offender at his trial. Government officers were not to seize slaves under this clause, but a government lien was to attach to the slaves of the offenders until the decision of the court, and no sale of bondsmen was to be recognized after the commission of the crime. Forfeited property—apart from slaves—was to be levied on as payment of the fines of those found guilty in judicial proceedings, and it or the proceeds of its sale would be returned to those who were discharged by the courts as innocent. Should the owner of sequestered property "flee from justice so that he cannot be brought to trial," the court in which proceedings had begun was authorized to declare the property forever forfeit and the fugitive's slaves to be free.

When he believed it "necessary and proper for a speedy and successful termination of the present rebellion," the President could, at his option, order proceedings *in rem* brought against personal property seized by the army or navy in order that it be confiscated. If the court should find that it had belonged "to a person engaged in rebellion, or [who has] so given aid and comfort thereto," it was to be forfeited to the United States. Similarly, should the President deem it necessary for the suppression of the rebellion, he might issue a proclamation ordering rebels to lay down their arms and return to their allegiance, and warning them that their slaves would be considered free if they themselves were found in

14. *CG*, 37 Cong., 2 sess., 2163–65.

arms or giving aid and 'comfort to the rebellion thirty days thereafter. A fugitive slave clause, a colonization section, and a provision authorizing the President to enroll Negro troops appeared in much the same form as in earlier proposals. The last two clauses of the bill reiterated the pardoning and amnesty power of the President and provided that the courts of the United States should have full power to do all things necessary to put the provisions of the law into effect.[15]

In framing S. 310, the members of the select committee obviously struggled to conciliate "confiscation" and due process. Slaves were to be freed only as a means of punishing their masters for crime or failure to appear for trial, or when rebels disregarded a presidential proclamation calling upon them to return to their allegiance by the end of a stated time period. Proceedings *in rem* were to apply only to personal property and be invoked at the option of the President in connection with his obligation to suppress the rebellion.

Clark explained that the members of the select committee had desired "to harmonize the various shades of opinion and the various plans," and to present something to the Senate which they thought might be passed. Harmony was not the result; the orchestration of the ensuing debates was to be tumultuous, discordant, and interspersed with sour notes. Trumbull immediately tried to strike the first section of the bill as an unconstitutional redefinition of the punishment for treason. Wade and Howard charged that the first two sections prescribed different penalties for the same offense, and the latter "greatly" doubted whether Congress had "power thus to seize upon a man's real estate and sell it under an execution in satisfaction of a fine under a conviction of treason."[16] When Trumbull's motion came to a vote, he was joined by Howard, Wade, Wilkinson, Wilmot, and five senators from the border states (I.D.: 33).

Howard then moved to strike the second section from the bill and summarized the radical position as he saw it:

> A certain portion of the Senate have been anxious to see an act of confiscation passed by which the property of these atrocious and wanton rebels could be seized upon, and confiscated and used for the purpose of aiding and assisting the loyal people of the United States in effecting the restoration of peace, and the reign of the Constitution. We have looked upon it, I have looked upon it as a measure of war, as a military measure, taking the clear distinction which ever exists in all human societies between a state of war and a state of peace. In reply to our urgent arguments upon this subject, in reply to our solicitations made to our brethren in this Chamber, to pass such an act for the purpose of crippling, humbling, and subduing the enemy, we are met habitually, daily, with the reply that it is not permitted by the Constitution. . . . When, if there ever was an occasion for a

15. Ibid., 2989–90.
16. Ibid., 2165, 2170.

severe, exemplary, and speedy punishment of treason by the highest possible penalty, this is that occasion, a very respected select committee of this body bring into the Senate a bill, not to subdue the rebels, not to prosecute this war, but to mitigate and lessen the penalty of treason, which, as established by our fathers, was death by the halter.[17]

To shore up the second section, Clark added the penalty of imprisonment, not to exceed ten years, which might be prescribed either as an additional or an alternative punishment to the forfeiture of property already provided by that part of the measure.

The senators returned to the consideration of S. 310 on May 19, and Sumner obtained the floor to "simplify" the discussion. His simplification was to take eight pages of the *Congressional Globe* and several hours of the time of those who sat through it. The watchword in this instance, he believed, must be "indemnity for the past and security for the future," and the question "transcendent" in importance must be considered "in the various lights of *jurisprudence,* of *history* and of *policy*." None could deny, "whatever . . . the doubts . . . or . . . finespun constitutional theories," that the raging struggle was both "*de facto* rebellion" and "*de facto* war." "The persons now arrayed for the overthrow of the Government of the United States" were "unquestionably criminals, subject to all the penalties of rebellion, which is of course treason." They were also, Sumner argued, "unquestionably enemies, exposed to all the incidents of war, with its penalties, seizures, contributions, confiscations, captures, and prizes." Then he developed the rights of the government in each instance, discussing the constitutional principles that bore upon the treatment of criminals and the rights of war that belonged to independent states. The names of Marshall, Livingston, Tilghman, Sprague, Grotius, Story, Blackstone, Hallam, Vattel, Bynkershoek, Wheaton, Manning, and other eminent authorities slipped effortlessly from his lips, not to mention an account of the activities of Mountstuart Elphinstone in his capacity of commissioner of Poonah. He found ample grounds for all that he and others of like mind wished to do, including seizure of "Pretended property of an enemy in slaves" and their emancipation.[18] He examined confiscation in historical perspective, beginning with Ahab's seizure of the vineyard of Naboth, and listing eighty-eight confiscation statutes passed by the states during the American Revolution.

As he neared his conclusion, Sumner invoked the image of the earnest man, which was part of the stock rhetoric of the session and particularly of the radicals.

Are you in earnest to strike this rebellion with all the force sanctioned by the rights of war, or do you refuse to use anything beyond the peaceful

17. Ibid., 2172–73.
18. Ibid., 2188–89, 2192.

process of municipal law? . . . If you are not in earnest against this rebellion now arrayed in war, if you are content to *seem* to act without acting, to *seem* to strike without striking, in short, *to seem* rather than *to be,* you will pass a new penal statute, and nothing more.

If his colleagues were truly in earnest, he averred, they would not hesitate "to employ all the acknowledged rights of war calculated" to end the conflict. "Two transcendent powers," he argued, had "already been exercised without a murmur: first, to raise armies, and secondly, to raise money. These were essential to the end. But there is another power," he continued, "without which, I fear, the end will escape us. It is that of confiscation and liberation, and this power is just as constitutional as the other two. The occasion for its exercise is found in the same terrible necessity."[19]

In conclusion, Sumner argued, "*every rebel who voluntarily becomes an enemy is as completely responsible in all his property, whether real or personal, as a hostile Government or Prince.*" Briefly he injected a mollifying note, eschewing "any sentiment of hate or any suggestion of vengeance." But, he said:

the tallest poppies must drop. For the conspirators, who organized this great crime and let slip the dogs of war, there can be no penalty too great. They should be not only punished to the extent of our power, but they should be stripped of all means of influence, so that should their lives be spared, they may be doomed to wear them out in poverty, if not in exile. To this end their property must be taken. But their poor deluded followers may be safely pardoned.

He pictured a time when the extensive plantations of the rebel leaders would be broken up, so that they could "never be again the nurseries of conspiracy or disaffection." And "partitioned into small estates," they would "afford homes to many . . . now homeless. . . . Poor neighbors, . . . so long dupes and victims, will become independent possessors of the soil. Brave soldiers who have left their northern skies to fight the battles of their country, resting at last from their victories and changing their swords into ploughshares, will fill the land with northern industry and northern principles." Finally he returned to his text, "indemnity for the past and security for the future," and summed up his solution as "strike down the leaders of the rebellion and lift up the slaves."[20]

After the senators considered amendments from Davis and Henderson on May 19, Wilson of Massachusetts tried to insert the requirement that the President issue a proclamation, calling upon rebels immediately to lay down their arms on pain of seeing their slaves freed, and this

19. Ibid., 2195.
20. Ibid., 2196.

precipitated an exchange of arguments with Cowan. As the chamber seemed to move once more toward adjournment without finishing the bill, Fessenden took the floor in exasperation, arguing that a decided majority of the select committee had been "in favor of a stringent measure." He suggested that Trumbull was trying to "find all the fault you can with the bill here, beat it down if possible, and have nothing" in order to obtain a bill satisfactory to him. He deplored the delaying tactics of Wilson and Cowan. The measure, he argued, *was* a "stringent bill"; his colleagues should accept it with amendment only in details. These comments brought Wade to his feet, raging at being "lectured and scolded." The Trumbull bill had actually "met the approbation of a majority of the Republican members of the Senate." But "those that stood opposed to a vigorous bill" had joined "with the enemies of all confiscation" and referred it to the select committee. The new bill contained the same basic principles as S. 151, but "in homeopathic doses." He continued, the "vigorous measure was referred to the committee, emasculated, rendered null, weakened, destroyed, and when they bring in another we are lectured because we want to amend it." Fessenden was not himself willing to concede anything.[21]

He regretted that he had provoked the wrath "of the distinguished chairman of the committee on the conduct of the war, who seems to have imagined, ever since he was thus appointed, that he not only had the war under his control, but the Senate, too." After more verbal fencing as to his own position, and those of colleagues, Fessenden became sharply personal:

> Certain gentlemen on this floor seem to think that they are the representatives of all righteousness; that unless we take their opinions we are sure to be wrong, and are threatened with an appeal to the people; that they are the only men who want to put down the rebellion, the only men who have any correct idea of how it shall be done, and that if anybody differs from them he is either a fool or a knave. . . . Sir, has the country no friends upon this floor except the gentlemen who wish to go further than the majority of the Senate can go on the subject?

Wade sought to continue the exchange, but Clark interrupted with the plea the senators act "as practical legislators, and not . . . make an exhibition of" themselves.[22] Although Wade's motion for adjournment was defeated (I.D.: 42), Clark failed to bring the bill to a vote on the evening of May 19.

On the morrow, even Clark's patience snapped when Trumbull demanded to know why debate on the confiscation bill should be limited.

21. Ibid., 2202-3.
22. Ibid., 2203-4.

He exclaimed: "Sir, I do not wonder that those men, like the Senator from Illinois, who mean to defeat a measure of this kind, should make that inquiry, because I am aware that there is a systematic and organized attempt here to defeat a mild measure of confiscation in the hope of pressing through one that suits certain Senators." Trumbull, in turn, accused Clark and those who were "egging him on to night sessions to obtain a vote" of being responsible for the delay. Although the Judiciary Committee bill had been very close to a vote, the senators from Massachusetts, Clark, and others had decided that the conflicting proposals should be harmonized in a select committee. But now, he charged, "not one of the earnest friends of confiscation who voted for the committee is for the bill reported by the committee." He doubted that it satisfied Clark either, but the latter had "yielded up his own views to some extent" when he "went into hodge-pot with . . . opponents of confiscation."[23]

Clark found Trumbull's remarks "offensive and discourteous"; he had opposed Cowan's effort to refer S. 151, but detected the hope of harmonizing various proposals in Wilson's amendment and moved referral for that purpose. Nor did he, the senator from New Hampshire told Trumbull, like to have it suggested that he was "the advocate of treason or of traitors" simply because he "still regarded the Constitution." He concluded: "It may be that many of the friends of earnest confiscation, as the Senator calls them, disagree with the bill of the committee. I have yielded something; but let me tell that Senator I infinitely prefer the bill reported by the committee to his bill which took from men, women, and children, property without the scintilla of a trial even *in rem*."[24]

When pressed by Fessenden, Sumner admitted at this point that he preferred to go ahead with discussion of the bill for raising internal revenue and wait until the confiscation bill of the House of Representatives came to the Senate. "We have got to that point," remarked Fessenden, "where the friends, the peculiar friends of confiscation, the gentlemen who are appealing to the country and covertly threatening to expose others to the country, do not want to act on this bill."[25] Agreeing, Chandler moved that further consideration of the confiscation measure be postponed for a week. But soon the roll was instead called on Trumbull's motion to adjourn; yeas 24, nays 12 (I.D.: 53).

Clark and other supporters of S. 310 consented to have it set aside while the senators debated the tax bill. But this done, the senators moved to discussion of the Pacific railroad bill. While they were still debating this measure on June 19, Trumbull reported the House bill on confiscation, H.R. 471, from the Judiciary Committee and announced that he

23. Ibid., 2226.
24. Ibid., 2227–28.
25. Ibid., 2228.

would move consideration as soon as possible. But after the senators passed the railroad bill during the evening of June 20, Clark seized the floor and moved to take up S. 310. Sumner protested, arguing that H.R. 471 had already passed one house while S. 310 still must be passed by both, a situation which would perhaps prevent final action on confiscation. Trumbull went further; there were "fifteen or twenty Senators probably who" were "opposed to any scheme of confiscation whatever," he charged. He implied that some Republicans were sufficiently opposed to either S. 310 or the House bill that they would vote with the bitter opponents of confiscation and defeat any motion to substitute one bill for the other as an amendment. Since most such recalcitrant Republicans would, in the end, no doubt support a confiscation bill, the decision as to whether S. 310 or H.R. 471 reached the floor first was vital to the kind of confiscation bill that was ultimately accepted. The "proper and parliamentary course," he argued was to consider the House bill first. Sherman agreed that "the question of taking up the bill is the question that will probably decide the fate of the measure."[26] The radicals won their point in this procedural matter; H.R. 471 was called up. But Clark promptly moved to amend by substituting S. 310, the bill of the select committee.

Containing no provisions relating to slavery, H.R. 471 bore upon all the other forms of personal and real property that rebellious southerners possessed, and provided for "confiscating the property [of leading classes] of rebels by action directly upon the property," as in the original Judiciary Committee proposal.[27] The discretionary power of the President, so emphasized in S. 310, was missing in H.R. 471. At this very time, a second House bill, designed to free the slaves of the rebels, lay ready for the consideration of the senators. The separation of confiscation and emancipation in these bills appears to have been a clever stratagem to isolate opposition to the two policies. But given the history of the House measures in the Senate, we cannot estimate the number of Republicans who were willing to support confiscation of property as a punishment for treasonous southerners, while opposing emancipation as a means to the same end.

With the House bill and Clark's amendment before them, various senators wished to express themselves. Browning refuted Sumner's speech of simplification, reiterating that the right to exercise the extraordinary powers of war rested in the President. In a forceful speech Howard argued that the judicial mechanism developed in the select committee bill was actually unconstitutional. Bitter exchanges

26. Ibid., 2842–43.
27. Ibid., 2972.

punctuated the oratory, and when Trumbull fulminated at the President's appointment of a military governor in South Carolina, Dixon declared him "unmasked . . . as an opponent of this Administration."[28] Wilkinson bluntly instructed Browning and Cowan to go home and meditate over the graves of the fallen soldiers of their states.

After Browning had chastized Wilkinson, Clark called for a vote on his motion to amend, but Sumner moved to amend the amendment (S. 310) by adding to the matter bearing on the courts, the words "And in all proceedings under this act there shall be no exclusion of any witness on account of color." The select committee had omitted this clause in an effort to be conciliatory, noted Clark, and it was unwise to add it now. Howe and thirteen radicals supported Sumner's motion in Committee of the Whole (I.D.: 79). There was yet to be a good deal of recrimination and bickering about whether majority sentiment among Republicans favored a strong bill and about Wade's definition of the supporters of the House bill as the "earnest, up and down, through thick and thin Republicans," and the opponents as "weak brethren." Again Fessenden rebuked the irrepressible Wade. Finally, the presiding officer was able to ask the Senate if it would agree to the amendment of the bill which had occurred in Committee of the Whole, and the Republican vote was distributed as before (I.D.: 67). Now came the roll call on the bill itself, and Chandler interjected that the bill was not "worth one stiver," and was "utterly worthless."[29] Of the Republicans, he, Howard, and Browning voted nay in a roll call of 28 yeas and 13 nays.

On July 8, Clark reported that the House had refused to accept the Senate amendment to H.R. 471; he moved that the Senate insist upon its amendment and ask for a committee of conference. Sherman promptly moved that the Senate recede from its amendment and was supported by eleven radicals and both Indiana senators (I.D.: 68). In the end, only Lane of Indiana, Trumbull, and Wilkinson opposed Clark's motion. The conference committee combined features of S. 310 and the original H.R. 471, but most radicals still found the result unsatisfactory. Their frustrations were compounded when they learned that they must forestall the President's veto by passing a joint resolution explaining, among other things, that proceedings under the confiscation act would not "work a forfeiture of the real estate of" offenders beyond their natural lives.[30]

28. Ibid., 2973.
29. Ibid., 2995, 3002–6.
30. Ibid., 3374. Of the Republicans, only Browning and Cowan opposed the conference report. But Grimes, Harlan, H. S. Lane, Trumbull, Wade, Wilkinson, and Wilmot opposed the non-forfeiture-beyond-natural-life amendment to the joint resolution (I.D.: 34).

The debates on confiscation were wide-ranging and, indeed, swept completely beyond the subject at times. Were the rebels to be regarded as traitors, or national enemies, or both? Was the constitutional definition of treason adequate to the case or should other degrees of disloyalty be acknowledged and punished? How broadly was punishment to be applied?—was the leader to be distinguished from his humble dupe? Must Congress establish appropriate judicial processes for confiscation, or could it simply authorize confiscation of property as a reasonable act of war? But if the latter, was not Congress encroaching on the prerogatives of the commander-in-chief and the executive branch of the government? And to what extent could emancipation be imposed as punishment for disloyalty? Such were the questions that divided radical and moderate Republicans in their approach to confiscation.

Neither the hopes of the most ardent advocates of the Confiscation Act nor the fears of its opponents were to be realized. The New York Herald forecast that a "good jurist" would probably be able to "drive through it with a two horse team," but so little used was it that no judge needed to try.[31] The broader importance of the confiscation issue in the history of the Republican party and Civil War policy-making lies in the fact that it served as a focal point of radical-moderate disagreement, strained relations between Congress and President, and influenced the latter's thinking in drafting and issuing the Preliminary Emancipation Proclamation.

Never again would a Congress wrestle so resolutely with issues related to southern property-holding as in the debate on confiscation during the second session of the Thirty-seventh. But in succeeding sessions the subject produced a couple of votes that tended to align radicals against moderates. On February 27, 1863, Chandler brought S. 544 before the Committee of the Whole, a bill designed "to provide for the collection of abandoned property, for the purchase of staples and for the prevention of frauds in insurrectionary districts within the United States." This bill authorized the Secretary of the Treasury to appoint agents empowered to take over abandoned or captured rebel property within the Union lines and also purchase southern staples and forward such property to places designated by the Secretary for sale at public auction, except that needed for public purposes where acquired. Agents might also seize property "coming within the lines of the United States from within the insurrectionary districts" through the activities of individuals who were not authorized agents of the Treasury Department.[32] The bill trans-

31. New York Herald, July 18, 1862.

32. CG, 37 Cong., 3 sess., 1330–31. For general discussions see Randall, Confiscation of Property, pp. 39–43; A. Sellew Roberts' pathbreaking article, "The Federal Government

ferred jurisdiction of these matters from the War Department to Treasury because of the widespread belief that military officers were lining their pockets by dealing in captured rebel property.

Although Republican cohesion was low on a number of votes in the debate on S. 544, only one produced the radical-moderate dichotomy in noticeable strength. This occurred when Grimes tried to exempt "property of any description captured by the naval forces of the United States." The senator from Iowa believed that the bill jeopardized the navy's long-established right to take prizes. He agreed that "something ought to be done," but felt that it should not be "accomplished by overturning all the laws in regard to prizes . . . which were a part of your contract with your officers and your men when they went out to fight your battles."[33] In the minority with Chandler in this vote were seven other radicals plus Ten Eyck and Davis (I.D.: 42).

Chandler later persuaded his colleagues to erase the Grimes amendment but Collamer, Doolittle, and particularly Clark "tomahawked" the bill, in Morrill's words. Arguing that remedy for the existing evils was already in the statute books, they found the support to delete the clauses of S. 544 that allowed Treasury agents to buy southern staples. In the end, Chandler characterized the result as "utterly worthless," and continued bitterly, "The Senate have [sic] deliberately voted that it desires the present state of things to go on, or that our generals shall become demoralized by plunder, that thieves shall take possession of this vast amount of property, and divide it among themselves."[34] Early in the debate Clark and Chandler had jousted jocularly about the relative merits of lawyer and merchant legislators; the lawyer, Clark, prevailed when the modified bill became law in early March, 1863.

Time and his colleagues vindicated Chandler; in July, 1864, the Treasury Department obtained the right to buy southern products. But in the waning hours of the second session of the Thirty-eighth Congress, the senators debated H.R. 805, eliminating section 8 of the act of July 2, 1864, allowing the Secretary of the Treasury to appoint agents to buy products of states "declared in insurrection."[35] Now senators alleged that

and Confederate Cotton," *American Historical Review*, 32 (January 1927), 262–75, does not investigate congressional policy-making. But see J. W. Schuckers, *The Life and Public Services of Salmon Portland Chase: United States Senator and Governor of Ohio; Secretary of the Treasury, and Chief Justice of the United States* (New York: Appleton, 1874), pp. 317–29, and Sister Mary Karl George, *Zachariah Chandler: A Political Biography* (East Lansing: Michigan State University Press, 1969), p. 75.

33. *CG*, 37 Cong., 3 sess., 1332.
34. Ibid., 1340, 1435.
35. *CG*, 38 Cong., 1 sess., 1349; Ludwell H. Johnson, "Contraband Trade during the Last Year of the Civil War," *Mississippi Valley Historical Review*, 49 (March 1963), 635–52, particularly pp. 635–41.

irregularities had developed under Treasury administration of such purchasing. Chandler, however, argued that the present administration was an improvement over the conditions prevailing before July, 1864, when the navy and army were gathering cotton in ways that demoralized both military efficiency and the character of numerous senior officers. After Wilson had modified the measure in the interests of his cotton-manufacturing constituents, Sumner proposed to eliminate a clause protecting contracts under which delivery had been received and to limit the activity of Treasury agents to areas within the lines of the Union forces. Other senators maintained this to be the law already, but Sumner pressed his amendment to a vote and obtained enough support from Republicans and the opposition to carry the field in Committee of the Whole (I.D.: 1-38: 9; 2-38: 42). His amendment failed in the Senate, however, and the bill too was ill fated; Lincoln maintained the murky commercial intercourse policies of the administration by using the pocket veto.

Members of the current generation of specialists in the history of the Civil War have emphasized that reconstruction was a process that began virtually with the outbreak of the conflict and that the policies developed in the council chambers of Washington, events in the field, and the growth of public opinion almost immediately rendered it impossible to restore the South as it had been before the election of 1860. The point is worth emphasis, but, as some contemporaries used the term during the war, "reconstruction" primarily involved reestablishment of satisfactory relations between the southern state governments and the federal government and did not necessarily connote the reorganization of society in the South. Even in this restricted sense, Americans both within and without the Congress began to think about ways of reconstructing the Union as soon as the states began to secede.[36] It is also true, however,

36. Although the perspective is judicious in various respects, Eben G. Scott, *Reconstruction during the Civil War in the United States of America* (Boston: Houghton Mifflin, 1895) will appear dated and shallow to the modern student, but the emphasis on developments prior to Appomatox is a forecast of work after 1960. Charles H. McCarthy, *Lincoln's Plan of Reconstruction* (New York: McClure, Phillips, 1901), is more interesting and devotes pp. 190–384 to the issues considered here. William B. Hesseltine, *Lincoln's Plan of Reconstruction* (Tuscaloosa, Ala.: Confederate Publishing, 1960) deals with the Wade-Davis bill succinctly, pp. 95–120, but does not consider the Harris bill. Currently, the most authoritative work is Herman Belz, *Reconstructing the Union: Theory and Policy during the Civil War* (Ithaca: Cornell University Press, 1969). See also Harold M. Hyman, ed., *New Frontiers of the American Reconstruction* (Urbana: University of Illinois Press, 1966), particularly his own contribution, pp. 1–39, and *The Radical Republicans and Reconstruction, 1861–1870* (Indianapolis: Bobbs-Merrill, 1967), especially pp. xvii–lxviii. Michael Les Benedict, *A Compromise of Principle: Congressional Republicans and Reconstruction, 1863–1869* (New York: Norton, 1974), emphasizes the breadth of Republican support for the Wade-Davis bill. John Syrett reflects the tendency to define "reconstruction" broadly in the title of his

that the members of the Thirty-seventh Senate spent little time in debating such matters on the floor.

Sumner presented his resolutions "declaratory of the relations between the United States and the territory once occupied by certain States, and now usurped by pretended Governments without constitutional or legal right," on February 11, 1862. In the first of the nine resolutions, Sumner developed the theory of territorial reversion; the rebellious states now to be "under the exclusive jurisdiction of Congress as other territory," the "State being" having ceased to exist. The following seven resolutions maintained that the institution of slavery in such territory was now illegal and proclaimed the obligation of the United States to implement a policy of freedom there. Resolution 9 charged the Congress with the obligation of establishing "republican forms of government under the Constitution" in the territory formerly occupied by the seceded states. Clearly, Sumner's resolutions were much more a manifesto against slavery and an affirmation of the civil rights of free men, irrespective of color, than a prescription for governmental reconstruction, but the formulas so briefly outlined were to be of great importance in the thinking of congressmen.[37]

Sumner himself moved that the resolutions be tabled. Six moderates and two radical Republicans opposed this motion as well as seven members of the opposition, these men apparently preferring that the resolutions go to the Committee of the Judiciary. The senators did not debate the Sumner resolutions formally during the remainder of the session although some, notably Dixon, tried to counter the constitutional doctrines involved in them during the course of debate on other measures. But when the President named military governors in Tennessee and North Carolina, members of the Congress became restive. Although Hale had reported early in the session that the Committee on Territories was considering measures relating to such matters, the bill eventually considered by the senators in early July, 1862, emerged from the Committee on the Judiciary. This was S. 200, "to establish provisional governments in certain cases," introduced initially by Harris of New York.

S. 200 authorized the President to establish temporary governments which, in some respects, were reminiscent of the governments found in the first stage of territorial evolution under the terms of the Northwest Ordinance and other early territorial organic acts. The major officers in

dissertation, "The Confiscation Acts: Efforts at Reconstruction during the Civil War." Distinctions between "restoration" and "reconstruction" are appropriately made, but so confirmed a Peace Democrat as James A. Bayard used the latter word at a very early date. See James A. Bayard, Jr. to Samuel L. M. Barlow, February 17, 1861, S. L. M. Barlow Papers, Henry E. Huntington Library, San Marino, Cal.

37. *CG*, 37 Cong., 2 sess., 736–37.

such governments were to be a governor and three judges, who were to serve as the nuclei of the executive and judicial branches; governor and judges together were to serve as a legislature. Governments established by presidential proclamation under the law were to operate for no longer than three months after the beginning of the session of Congress "next succeeding the termination of the insurrection." Harris suggested that the constitutional justification for establishing such governments lay in the clause guaranteeing a republican form of government to the states of the Union.[38]

When Harris submitted various Judiciary Committee amendments to the bill in Committee of the Whole, Sumner objected to the insertion of the provision, "And not interfering with the laws and institutions existing in such State at the time its authorities assumed to array the same against the Government of the United States further than shall be necessary to carry into effect the provisions of this act," and read excerpts from the Code of North Carolina that he considered unconscionable. He moved to strike "laws and institutions" and insert "constitution." The dismayed Harris maintained that:

> The object of the bill is not to change the legislation of the States. It is to establish a temporary government, to execute the constitution and laws of the rebel States during the interval that may occur between the time when the rebellion shall be suppressed, and when those States shall be able to reorganize themselves and shall be restored to their proper position in the Union. The bill contemplates a simple, efficient, temporary government.[39]

Amending the measure to specify that the executive would enforce the laws of the United States mollified Sumner so that he withdrew his amendment, but Trumbull, Ten Eyck, Powell, Davis, Wilkinson, and Cowan sallied into the lists determined either to strengthen or to obliterate S. 200. The bill would, thought Ten Eyck, reduce the southern states to a territorial condition, thereby fundamentally changing the status of "States of this Union," and thereby acknowledging "at least the power, if not the right, of secession." The debate reached its nadir when Chandler seized the floor to charge that either Lincoln or McClellan was criminally responsible for the recent unfortunate experiences of the Army of the Potomac.[40] At the urging of Doolittle and Sumner, Harris moved that further consideration of the bill be postponed until the next day at noon, when it would be the special order of the day. The motion failed, yeas 17 and nays 20 (I.D.: 66). Eight moderates and one radical voted to make S. 200 the order of the day on the morrow but fourteen radicals and three moderates foiled them with support from Stark, Wilson of Missouri, and

38. Ibid., 843, 3138, 3141–42.
39. Ibid., 3139.
40. Ibid., 3140, 3149.

Wright. Carlile immediately moved indefinite postponement; with this the question, the debate sputtered on until executive business intervened. The senators did not debate the Harris bill again.

Although the Harris bill was merely one of a number of measures before the Thirty-seventh Congress that directly addressed reconstruction, it moved the furthest in the legislative process. The discussion filled a mere fourteen pages of the *Globe* and generated only one vote. That roll call, however, showed that a temperate reconstruction measure, sponsored by a moderate Republican but appearing in part to use the territorial formula, had fewer friends than enemies in the Senate.[41]

After cataloguing important achievements of the first session of the Thirty-eighth Congress, Allan Nevins wrote, "They received little attention, however, in comparison with one topic that dominated the attention of the session from its opening until adjournment on July 4, 1864—Reconstruction." But in this Congress there was no great Senate debate on reconstruction that thundered on intermittently through several months, as did the great debate over confiscation in 1862. Although he reported it from his Committee on the Territories in late May, 1864, Senator Wade did not try to bring the House bill on reconstruction before his colleagues until June 29. Failing, 5 yea and 28 nay, he moved on the next day that all prior orders be postponed, so that the senators could take up H.R. 244, "to guarantee to certain States whose governments have been usurped or overthrown, a republican form of government." This was the Wade-Davis bill, the congressional alternative to the executive reconstruction already under way.[42] Senator Cowan maintained that the chamber should instead finish considering the bill to reimburse the state of Pennsylvania for expenses incurred in calling out

41. A more radical measure introduced in the House by James M. Ashley was tabled in March with minimal debate after emerging from a sharply divided Committee on the Territories. Herman Belz analyzes the "territorialization" measures of the Thirty-seventh Congress in considerable detail and suggests that the Harris bill was a "moderate alternative," taking a middle ground between radical territorialization and Lincoln's "conservative policy of military government," that might have averted later conflict between Congress and the President. See *Reconstructing the Union*, p. 97, and for the full discussion, pp. 66–99.

42. Allan Nevins, *The War for the Union, 3: The Organized War, 1863–1864* (New York: Scribner, 1971), p. 454. *CG*, 38 Cong., 1 sess., 3407. According to Belz, Wade preferred to postpone debate pending the results of the Baltimore convention and the effort to win passage of the Thirteenth Amendment in the House (*Reconstructing the Union*, p. 213). Although the outcome of both did, as Belz suggests, emphasize the importance of passing the reconstruction measure, because the selection of Johnson, a provisional governor, as vice presidential nominee seemed an endorsement of presidential reconstruction, and the amendment failed of passage, historians of reconstruction do not make it clear why it would not have been useful to press the bill forward anyway. Belz, *Reconstructing the Union*, pp. 198–243, presents a thoughtful discussion of the implications of this bill and the congressional proceedings that produced it. For a discussion of Wade's role, see Mary Land, "Ben Wade," in Kenneth W. Wheeler, ed., *For the Union: Ohio Leaders in the Civil War* (Columbus: Ohio State University Press, 1968), pp. 206–15; Hans L. Trefousse, *Benjamin*

its militia during the Gettysburg campaign. The senators rejected Wade's motion by a vote of 11 yeas and 17 nays (I.D.: 68).

On July 1, the senators began to discuss H.R. 244. This elaborate piece of legislation prescribed the methods by which loyal governments were to be instituted in Confederate states after armed resistance to the Union had ceased. It empowered the President to appoint military governors for each such state with the advice and consent of the Senate and required that a majority of white male citizens take an oath of loyalty to the United States as an essential preliminary to a constitutional convention called by the provisional governor. Other sections of the bill prescribed election procedures and limited the franchise in the election of delegates, as well as the field of candidates, to loyal white male citizens who had neither held civil office under the Confederacy nor borne arms against the United States. The convention delegates must declare the submission of their state to the Constitution and laws of the United States and incorporate provisions in the new state constitution to disbar permanently the holders of major Confederate military or civil office from either voting in the elections for the legislature and the governor or from holding either office. They must prohibit involuntary servitude, guarantee the freedom of all persons in the state, and repudiate Confederate and state war debts. After a provisional governor had certified that a majority of the votes cast from the state electorate, as defined by the Wade-Davis bill, had been in support of the new constitution, the President, with the approval of Congress, was to proclaim the new government to be the constitutional government of the state. At this point, the reconstructed state might elect United States representatives, senators, and presidential electors.

Should a convention refuse to accept the conditions imposed by the law, the governor was authorized to dissolve it and call another when the President decided that conditions were more favorable. In the interim, the provisional governor was authorized to enforce all federal and state laws in effect "when the State government was overthrown by the rebellion" (jurors were to have the same qualifications as the convention electors), and to provide for the collection and disbursement of taxes. The final sections of H.R. 244 declared all slaves in the states to be free and provided punishment for persons attempting to hold others in involuntary servitude contrary to the provisions of this law. Of the committee amendments, the most interesting dealt with the franchise and struck

---

*Franklin Wade: Radical Republican from Ohio* (New York: Twayne, 1963), pp. 218-32, is a judicious modern treatment that interprets Wade's maneuver as a skillful prelude to a major political blunder, the Manifesto. Albert G. Riddle, *The Life of Benjamin F. Wade* (Cleveland: William W. Williams, 1886), pp. 257-58, treats the Wade-Davis bill with signal brevity.

the word "white" before the word "male," making a portion of the second section of the bill read: "and enroll all male citizens of the United States." Although he had agreed to this amendment in committee, by the time it reached the floor Wade believed that it would "sacrifice the bill"; he recommended that it not be accepted.[43] Lane of Kansas demanded a vote on the question, but could rally only Brown, Morgan, Pomeroy, and Sumner in opposition to Wade's position.

When the bill was opened to amendment from the floor, Brown promptly moved substitute wording, initially formulated by Collamer, for everything after the enacting clause in the bill:

> That when the inhabitants of any State have been declared in a state of insurrection against the United States by proclamation of the President, by force and virtue of the act entitled "An act further to provide for the collection of duties on imports, and for other purposes," approved July 13, 1861, they shall be, and are hereby declared to be, incapable of casting any vote for electors of President or Vice President of the United States, or of electing Senators or Representatives in Congress, until said insurrection in said State is suppressed or abandoned and said inhabitants have returned to their obedience to the Government of the United States, nor until such return to obedience shall be declared by proclamation of the President, issued by virtue of an act of Congress, hereafter to be passed, authorizing the same.

Brown argued that there was not enough time left in the session to give Wade's bill the discussion that it deserved, and to amend sections of the measure that he believed should be changed. His amendment, this "prince of radicals" maintained, provided "all the security which can be asked in regard to the exercise of electoral privileges in these districts. That is the necessity of the hour." In other words, presidential electors from states of the Confederacy were not to participate in the presidential election of 1864. Brown proposed, "to leave the matter of reconstruction to a later day when events shall have perhaps altered some of the relations in which these districts now stand to us." The "attitude" in the Confederacy was not as yet "sufficiently distinct and sufficiently developed to justify" decisions upon "the work of reconstruction."[44]

Wade thereupon made the only extended defense of the bill in the Senate that appears in the *Congressional Globe;* it occupies less than five columns. He stressed the labor that members of the House had lavished

43. *CG*, 38 Cong., 1 sess., 3449.

44. Ibid., 3449; The biographer of B. Gratz Brown notes the contrast between his stand on the Wade-Davis bill and other issues where his course won the approbation of the radicals: Norma L. Peterson, *Freedom and Franchise: The Political Career of B. Gratz Brown* (Columbia: University of Missouri Press, 1965), pp. 139-41, 143-44. She has not discovered any explanation of Brown's motives in pressing his amendment other than those that he himself advanced in defending it. See pp. 130, 143 for references to Brown as Missouri's "prince of radicals."

on the bill and the fact that its provisions could be readily understood by all. He warned, "The question will be asked of every man who goes out to canvass during the coming election, 'What do you propose to do with these seceded States in regard to their coming back?'" During the session, Congress had refused to accept representatives from some conquered southern states. "Political opponents will say," he predicted, "'It is your deliberate purpose to subdue these people, to subjugate them, to tyrannize over them, and never to let them come back into the Union on equal terms with the other States; when they have in form made a free constitution and elected Senators according to the forms of law.'"[45] Brown's amendment did not provide adequate answers to questions such as these, he argued; H.R. 244 did so.

Adjusting the status of the seceded states was the responsibility of the Congress, maintained Wade. The President's plan to allow states to reenter the Union "when one tenth of the population" had taken an oath of loyalty was "absurd," as well as "most anti-republican, anomalous, and entirely subversive of the great principles" underlying the state and federal governments. H.R. 244 was not based on the assumption that the state governments were "lost, obliterated, blotted out" or "reduced to the condition of Territories," but rather on the constitutional provision that "the Federal government shall guaranty to every State a Republican form of government." In discussing the specific provisions of the bill, Wade paid particular attention to the requirement that the southern states must renounce slavery as a condition of reentry:

> This terrible revolution has . . . grown out of the institution of slavery alone. . . . Would we then, in guaranteeing a republican form of government, suffer it to be mixed up with anomalous elements calculated to immediately destroy what we set up? . . . Therefore this bill has taken special pains to say that the new government shall, in its constitution, proclaim emancipation as a condition upon which it shall be permitted to come into the Union.
>
> There was a time when a precedent like this would have been deemed unconstitutional. . . . But in the light of our present experience I ask any man who is a lover of peace and who intends to make a constitution that shall live forever . . . saying nothing of slavery in any other than a political point of view, would it be safe, would it be wise for us in admitting States back into this Union to permit them to come with the very element that had carried them out, with the very seeds of destruction which had destroyed them already?[46]

Yielding on occasion for other business, charged with "dodging" by Wade, subjected to catechism by Clark and heckling by Wilkinson, Carlile of Virginia tried to argue the case of the loyal slave states against the

45. CG, 38 Cong., 1 sess., 3449–50.
46. Ibid., 3450.

Wade-Davis bill.[47] To guarantee a republican form of government to the loyal people of the southern states, in his opinion, was to guarantee them the form of government which they had enjoyed prior to the outbreak of hostilities; the additional requirements of H.R. 244 were unconstitutional.

Before the yeas and nays could be taken on Brown's amendment, Wade and Brown had a brief exchange in which the senator from Ohio denounced the latter's proposal as a "mere negation" and emphasized that a vote in favor of it was a vote in opposition to the House bill. Brown, however, would not "sustain" a reconstruction bill "which leaves out of that reconstruction nearly all the loyal element in those States by disfranchising and leaving them out of account." But Wade termed Brown's solution a "miserable dodge," a "negation," an "amendment that asserts no principle." To his consternation, Brown's amendment carried by a vote of 17 to 16 (I.D.: 86). Brown, Cowan, Doolittle, Grimes, H. S. Lane, and Trumbull joined Democrats and border-state men in supporting it. Of the sixteen in opposition, only Sherman is usually considered to have been a moderate Republican. Of ten Republican absentees, only Howard and Foot had shown themselves to be consistently radical in earlier sessions.

Sumner promptly offered an additional section to the revised bill,

> *And be it further enacted,* That the proclamation of emancipation issued by the President of the United States on the 1st day of January, 1863, so far as the same declares that the slaves in certain designated States and portions of States thenceforward should be free, is hereby adopted and enacted as a statute of the United States, and as a rule and article for the government of the military and naval forces thereof.

He ingeniously defended the amendment as an attempt to bring emancipation under the rule of Congress, just as Brown's amendment was an effort in part to bring "all those activities tending toward reconstruction . . . under the rule of Congress." Both Brown and Hale objected that his proposal was out of place and the Missourian noted, "It is perfectly possible to unite two measures, each of which commands a majority in itself, and yet which combined cannot by any possibility get a majority; and that is just the proposition . . . here."[48] Ten Republicans supported Sumner's proposition, while eight moderates were joined by Hale and Sprague in the opposition, which mustered 21 votes (I.D.: 85). Now the chamber considered the amended bill, and the senators approved it by a vote of 20 to 13. Harlan, Pomeroy, and Sprague added their votes to

47. Ibid., 345–54.
48. Ibid., 3460–61.

those of six moderates voting in the majority, and Sherman and Ten Eyck joined eleven radicals in the opposition (I.D.: 54).

The amended H.R. 244 was carried to the House, which on the next day, July 2, disagreed with the Senate amendment and asked for a committee of conference. Late in the afternoon, Wade got H.R. 244 before his colleagues and moved that the senators recede from their amendment, although Henry Winter Davis, drafter of the bill, had little hope that the strategy would succeed.[49] By a vote of 18 to 14 the senators present supported him and the Wade-Davis bill had survived the ministrations of the legislators (I.D.: 57). Only three of the more consistently moderate Republicans—Harris, Howe, and Sherman—supported Wade's motion. But the President used his pocket veto on the bill despite Chandler's urgent plea to the contrary, as Lincoln sat signing bills at the Capitol during the waning hours of the session.

If any of the senators or leading correspondents left a truly illuminating discussion of these events, modern historians have failed to find it. Why did four Republican senators recant in their support of the Brown amendment? Had various moderate Republicans and opposition senators succumbed to apathy, the temptation to seek tea or stronger sustenance, or were they really voting with their feet? Fessenden's most recent biographer noted that the Maine senator considered the Wade-Davis bill to be "a dangerously radical abuse of power," indeed unconstitutional because of the emancipation provision. He "absented himself from the roll call" and was joined by sixteen of his moderate colleagues. Early in their proceedings on July 1, the senators had provisionally confirmed Lincoln's nomination of Fessenden to the position of Secretary of the Treasury, and the latter spent much of that day and the next agonizing over whether or not to refuse the post. He was present in the Senate chamber during the late afternoon of July 2, but brief discussions of a bill regulating the carriage of steamship passengers and of recessing prior to the evening session intervened before Wade got H.R. 244 before his colleagues. Did Fessenden leave to avoid voting, or to wrestle further with his conscience about the Treasury, or merely to go to dinner? The circumstances cloud not only his motives but those of various colleagues.

Of the absentees, three were radicals, seven were Republican moderates in terms of that session's voting, and another seven were opposition or border-state senators. At least six of the absentees had already requested permission to be absent in order to leave for home, including Brown himself, and of others in that category only Howard was a radical. It seems safe to say that only a handful, if that, of senators tried deliber-

---

49. Hesseltine, *Lincoln's Plan of Reconstruction*, p. 118.

ately to avoid voting and that the success of Wade's maneuver probably reflected the confusion found at the end of a session in a chamber girding itself for a late sitting. Certainly as Table 7-1 shows, the Republican senators were anything but unanimous in supporting the Wade-Davis bill.[50] Raging in frustration at the President's inaction, Wade and Davis published their famous manifesto denouncing him, and this sulphurous document drew considerably more comment from the press than had the Senate debate on H.R. 244.

In the second session of the Thirty-eighth Congress, the senators once more confronted the exasperating problems of reconstruction, although efforts to recast the Wade-Davis bill centered in the House. On February 1, Trumbull asked for discussion of H.R. 126, a joint resolution providing that no state of the Confederacy was entitled to representation in the Electoral College chosen in 1864. A preamble explained that "the inhabitants and local authorities of" eleven designated southern states had "rebelled against the Government of the United States, and . . . continued in a state of armed rebellion for more than three years, and were in said state of armed rebellion on the 8th day of November, 1864." The Judiciary Committee proposed to strike out the reference to the "continued" armed rebellion and the contention that the states were in that same state on November 8, 1864, substituting the wording, "And were in such state of rebellion on the 8th day of November 1864, that no valid election for President and Vice President of the United States . . . was held therein on said day."[51]

Ten Eyck moved to strike Louisiana—the particular target of the

50. Charles A. Jellison, *Fessenden of Maine: Civil War Senator* (Syracuse: Syracuse University Press, 1962), p. 175; Fessenden's agony is described particularly in Francis Fessenden, *Life and Public Services of William Pitt Fessenden: United States Senator from Maine 1854–1864, Secretary of the Treasury 1864–1865, United States Senator from Maine 1865–1869* (Boston: Houghton Mifflin, 1907), 1: 315–25. The *Biographical Directory of the American Congress, 1774–1961* (Washington: Government Printing Office, 1961), p. 179, states erroneously that Fessenden resigned his Senate seat on July 1; he was provisionally confirmed by his colleagues on that day but participated in a number of roll calls on July 2. Belz, *Reconstructing the Union*, pp. 212–25, infers that absence implied approval of the bill in at least some instances. This may be true but it is doubtful that it was the general rule.

51. *CG*, 38 Cong., 2 sess., 533. See Belz, *Reconstructing the Union*, passim for general background. On p. 269 he notes the congressional action on this resolution as a blow to executive reconstruction but does not discuss the positions of the senators. For a succinct account of the Louisiana background, see Fred Harvey Harrington, *Fighting Politician: Major General N. P. Banks* (Philadelphia: University of Pennsylvania Press, 1948), pp. 140–50. More recent studies are: Joe Gray Taylor, *Louisiana Reconstructed: 1863–1877* (Baton Rouge: Louisiana State University Press, 1974), and Peyton McCrary, *Abraham Lincoln and Reconstruction: The Louisiana Experiment* (Princeton: Princeton University Press, 1978). Pages 212–36 of the latter are particularly useful. See also Scott, *Reconstruction during the Civil War*, pp. 317–89; McCarthy, *Lincoln's Plan of Reconstruction*, pp. 314–83.

TABLE 7-1.

Republican voting patterns on two Brown amendment votes and Wade motion to recede*

---

*Support Brown amendment; oppose Wade motion:*  Doolittle, H. S. Lane, Trumbull

*Support Brown amendment; support Wade motion:*†  Harlan, Harris, Pomeroy, Sprague

*Support Brown amendment; absent on Wade motion:*  Brown, Cowan, Grimes

*Oppose Brown amendment; absent on Wade motion:*  Hale, Morrill

*Oppose Brown amendment; oppose Wade motion:*  Ten Eyck

*Absent on Brown amendment; support Wade motion:*  Anthony, Foot, Howe

*Absent on all three votes:*  Collamer, Dixon, Fessenden, Foster, Howard

*Oppose Brown amendment; support Wade motion:*  Chandler, Clark, Conness, J. H. Lane, Morgan, Ramsey, Sherman, Sumner, Wade, Wilkinson, Wilson

---

*At Trumbull's request, a third vote on the Brown amendment was taken. Three senators opposed it.

†This category further subdivides into three categories: Harris was absent in the Committee of the Whole vote on the Brown amendment and Pomeroy and Sprague both voted a nay, yea, yea pattern.

resolution—from the list of states in the preamble. After discussion, Collamer gave notice that he proposed to submit an amendment in more general terms as a substitute for the resolution:

> That the people of no State, the inhabitants whereof have been declared in a state of insurrection by virtue of the fifth section of the act entitled "An act further to provide for the collection of duties on imports, and for other purposes," approved July 13, 1861, shall be regarded as empowered to elect electors of President and Vice President of the United States until said condition of insurrection shall cease and be so declared by virtue of a law of the United States.

He also decided to expand his amendment, adding, "Nor shall any vote cast by any such electors elected by the votes of the inhabitants of any such State, or the Legislature thereof, be received or counted." Later, the elderly gentleman from Vermont further revised his wording by inserting, "or until they shall be represented in both Houses of Congress," at the end of his original proposal and immediately precedent to the supplementary sentence.[52]

Harris also offered a substitute resolution which stated the following premises: that the loyal inhabitants of Louisiana and Tennessee had established a government in response to the proclamation of the President on December 8, 1863, in good faith, that presidential electors had been named under the aegis of these governments, that doubts existed as to the validity of that action, and that the votes of such electors would

---

52. *CG*, 38 Cong., 2 sess., 552–53, 582.

not affect the electoral outcome. It was, therefore, inexpedient to determine the validity of the Louisiana and Tennessee electoral votes; the result of the electoral count was to be announced both counting and excluding these votes, "such result being the same in either case."[53]

These, then, were the substantive elements on which the senators focused their attention in the debate on Louisiana's electoral votes. Time was short; the electoral votes of the states were to be opened and counted on February 8, one week from the day on which Trumbull brought H.R. 126 before his colleagues. The implications of the outcome might be momentous. To reject the Louisiana electoral votes would severely compromise President Lincoln's reconstruction efforts. More immediately, action in this instance might serve as precedent in determining whether the congressional delegation representing Louisiana, and perhaps that from Arkansas, should be admitted later in the session. Such delegations might well swell the opposition forces in the Congress. Each senator, on the other hand, must also have felt that the decision would either reinforce or threaten his personal interpretation of the constitutional relations between the states and the Union.

In a relatively dispassionate introductory summary of the issues, Trumbull suggested that there could be no election "according to the laws and Constitution of the United States" in Louisiana when much of the state "was overrun by the enemy, and the legal voters had no opportunity to vote one way or another." Pursuant to law, the President had declared Louisiana to be in a state of insurrection and Congress had not changed that situation. Electoral votes ought not to be accepted from the Bayou State until Congress took remedial action. Later Trumbull admitted that he himself would have preferred to omit the preamble of the resolution but was prepared to support the alternative wording of the Committee of the Judiciary.[54]

The advocates of H.R. 126 belittled the number of Louisiana voters who participated in the elections, and pictured the loyal state government there as a puny puppet created by the United States military, utterly dependent on General Banks for survival. In 1856 a paralyzing blizzard had delayed the choosing of presidential electors in Wisconsin beyond the appointed day, and the chair ruled that the Badger State's votes were to be disregarded; when the decision to lay them aside was challenged, Senator James M. Mason led an exodus of southern senators, indignant that the ruling was questioned. The Louisiana case was more dangerous, thought some, and Hale even saw implications in it

53. Ibid., 579.
54. Ibid., 535.

"fraught with the consequences of revolution." Howard and Wade, however, made the most arresting statements in support of the resolution. The southern states, argued Howard, were in insurrection and would continue so until Congress acted, "revoking and annulling the proclamation issued under the act of 1861." He would never consent, he thundered, "to admit . . . a State, a majority of whose people are hostile and unfriendly to the Government of my country. I prefer to hold them in tutelage . . . one year . . . even twenty years."[55]

Wade's statement was even more belligerent and provocative. He was, he said, "exceedingly jealous of military power," and would never "consent that a people predominated over by a hostile military power shall found an American republican state." The southern communities should be left until there was "at least reasonable evidence to show that a majority of them are loyal, and in a condition to maintain a free republican government of their own." Wade railed against the President for "vetoing" the Wade-Davis bill and derided Lincoln's plan as "the most absurd and impracticable that ever haunted the imagination of a statesman." "Let us settle now and forever," he snarled, "the principle that the President of the United States cannot . . . improvise by military force a Legislature, and call it the power of a State in such sort as to count that semblance in his favor as a fact." He maintained that no Union man in the Senate would have consented to counting southern electoral votes if that action would have elected McClellan. He challenged any such senator to "rise and tell me that he would have permitted these counterfeits, these disloyal States . . . to select a president for us."[56] Although Sherman supported the resolution because he believed the responsibility for making the decision on Louisiana's votes should not be laid solely on the Vice President, who must open the certificates, the junior senator from Ohio maintained that to support it did not necessarily imply censure of the President. But to Wade the two issues were clearly inseparable.

As in most such disputes, the supporters of the resolution probably differed somewhat in the constitutional basis of their positions. Hale invoked the "necessary and proper" clause. More generally held, apparently, was the position that Congress had authorized the President to proclaim the southern states in rebellion in the Tariff Act of July 13, 1861, and must take equivalent action to bring them back. But it was left for Collamer—usually moderate in his views—to state the most elegant rationalization of congressional intervention in the process of counting

55. Ibid., 549, 554.
56. Ibid., 559–60.

the electoral returns. Arguing that general principles should prevail, Collamer found his justification in the guarantee clause of the Constitution, as well as in the "necessary and proper" clause. The guarantee section provided "for the security of all the States of the Union." To assure a republican form of government to the people of all the states, Congress might do whatever was needed, he suggested, to insure that the states formerly in rebellion would not rise again, even to requiring the southern states to destroy slavery before "again exercising their franchise as integral members of this Union," thereby enabling "the Union to continue and exist." "It would be a strange thing," Collamer said, "if it were not true that this nation, in ending a civil . . . war, could close it . . . by securing . . . at least some security for future peace."[57] The electoral votes of the rebel states should not be counted until the Congress was satisfied that such guarantees had been extracted.

Most Republicans who opposed H.R. 126 had established their credentials as moderates in previous sessions. Ten Eyck, Harris, Doolittle, Howe, Cowan, and Lane of Indiana were in this category, but they were joined in their struggle by both Kansas senators and Harlan, as well as by Nathan A. Farwell, Fessenden's replacement. In this instance, however, the advocates of restraint lost three men who frequently took moderate positions during the Thirty-eighth Congress; Trumbull, Collamer, and Sherman voted with the radicals.

In their arguments against the resolution, moderates covered a lot of ground. The southern states were still in the Union, maintained Ten Eyck, their legitimate governments merely "in abeyance." When loyal southerners had set their governments "in action anew" and revolving in their "old orbits," he would feel it his duty to "extend to them all the privileges and all the rights which the loyal people of a loyal State are entitled to at the hands of their sister States."[58] No formal congressional action was required. Howe believed that the statutes of the United States authorized the loyal people of Louisiana to vote. Harris maintained that the constitutional issues involved were extremely serious and it was both unnecessary and inexpedient to go deeply into them at this time. In addition, the proposed preamble was untrue in so far as it applied to Louisiana, Tennessee, and Arkansas.

Moderates also maintained that a high proportion of eligible Louisianans had voted and that the electorate was by no means in the pocket of the military, although they granted that some members of the armed forces had been allowed to vote. The relative proportion of

57. Ibid., 591–92.
58. Ibid., 535.

Louisianans involved did not matter, argued Cowan; rather it was the fact that they were loyal. What better base on which to erect a new government than on the foundation of the loyal residents? Harris, again, could not "find in the provisions of the Constitution any authority for Congress to pass a law . . . excluding any votes . . . returned to the Vice President." The procedures of the electoral convocation were laid down in the Constitution, Doolittle argued, and needed no further elaboration at the hands of the Congress. He was willing to give the "Government all the power . . . conferred upon it by the Constitution, and not . . . more." The country was "too large . . . covers too many and too varied interests, to endure the establishment of the doctrine that this is one consolidated empire." He continued, "the President of the Senate alone counts the votes, or it is the body over which he presides, having a power over his decision by appeal in the final resort, to decide the question." By passing H.R. 126, Congress would invade the domain of the executive branch, although Doolittle admitted the powers of the House to rule on its own membership. The doctrine that the erring states were out of the Union was "one huge, infernal, constitutional lie." It was a strange spectacle, he observed, to see Wade and Powell of Kentucky united to support the resolution. Veritably, Pilate and Herod had come together to "attack the Administration" and "see if they could crucify the free State of Louisiana." This unusual, although not unprecedented alliance, inspired jocular repartee as to which senator was playing which biblical role. We have examined Wade's position; Powell stigmatized the administration's Louisiana policy as a violation of "the fundamental principle of constitutional and civil liberty."[59]

Disagreement scores based on the voting patterns of both the first and second sessions of the Thirty-eighth Senate show that five votes generated substantial differences of opinion between Republican radicals and moderates during the debate on H.R. 126. These included Lane of Indiana's motion to postpone the House resolution indefinitely (I.D.: 1:57; 2:57), and Harris' proposal to substitute a more innocuous formula in place of Collamer's amendment (I.D. 1:43; 2:56). The three remaining roll calls revealed disagreement in terms of the voting structure of the second session but not of the first. In this category fell Ten Eyck's motion to delete the word "Louisiana" from the preamble of the resolution (I.D. 1:27; 2:75), the effort of Lane of Kansas to strike the preamble completely (I.D. 1:34; 2:64), and the final vote in the Senate on the resolution (I.D. 1:35; 2:46). Although the radicals were joined by a few members of the opposition, the latter would have carried the day for the

59. Ibid., 548, 550, 578, 581.

moderates in only one of the five roll calls if they had reversed their votes. To such senators from the border states the provisional governments were mere sham.

Undoubtedly the practical political implications of accepting the resolution were no more lost upon the moderates than upon the radicals. It did repudiate the President's policy of reconstruction, and its application to Louisiana would stand as a precedent in the decision to come, concerning the seating of that state's congressional delegation. Doolittle even saw Louisiana's vote as essential in obtaining the requisite number of states to approve the Thirteenth Amendment, and a similar perception perhaps underlay the opposition of some border-state men. Trumbull's wry summation at a late point in the debate was an oversimplification:

> We have had everything brought into the debate. The Administration has been defended when nobody has assailed it. Pontius Pilate and Herod have been assailed and defended. We have had a general discussion about reconstruction, and an excited debate upon a question which it seems to me should have called for no excitement; and all I have to say to the Senate now is to appeal to its members that . . . they will not crucify us here by bringing in all these extraneous circumstances and prolonging this debate.

When the President signed H.R. 126 on February 8, 1865, he appended a brief message to the members of the Congress. Theirs was the power under the Twelfth Amendment, he noted, to reject "all electoral votes deemed by them to be illegal." The Executive had no right to interfere in the electoral canvass or count, but Lincoln also denied that in signing the measure he had "expressed any opinion on the recitals of the preamble, or any judgment of his own upon the subject of the resolution." "He reads us a lecture, virtually," protested Reverdy Johnson, and called for a clear-cut policy of presidential approval or disapproval in such matters.[60] His Republican colleagues laid the message on the table silently, but with varying degrees of sullenness.

Consideration of seating the Louisiana delegation during the winter of 1865 was peculiarly entwined with discussion of a measure enigmatically entitled "A bill to regulate commerce among the several States" (H.R. 307), which Chandler had unsuccessfully moved to consider in the closing days of the first session (I.D.: 56). Both the constitutional implications of its provisions and the broader parliamentary strategy of its friends linked H.R. 307 to the Louisiana resolution (S. 117). Designed to seat that state's congressional delegation and return its government to

60. Ibid., 582, 711.

full participation in the Union, the latter measure produced the "most exciting" struggle of the session, according to the Boston *Journal,* and carried the mind of the New York *Herald*'s reporter back to the excesses of the debate on the Lecompton constitution.[61]

When the senators began to debate H.R. 307, on January 16, 1865, this measure was deceptively simple in form, providing only:

> That every railroad company in the United States whose road is operated by steam, its successors and assigns, be, and is hereby, authorized to carry upon and over its road, connections, boats, bridges, and ferries, all freight, property, mails, passengers, troops, and Government supplies on their way from any State to another State, and to receive compensation therefor.[62]

Actually the bill's advocates hoped to break the monopoly of through railroad traffic from New York to Philadelphia that the Camden and Amboy Railroad Company enjoyed under a charter obtained from New Jersey some thirty-five years previously. This was Sumner's bill, and he denounced the transit duty of ten cents per through passenger and

---

61. Boston *Daily Journal,* February 28, 1865; New York *Herald,* February 27, 1865.

62. *CG,* 38 Cong., 2 sess., 814. The summary on p. 270 gives a slightly different wording of the operational verb. The "Camden and Amboy" bills are most fully discussed by David F. Trask, who has provided a detailed account of the general background, the legislative history of the measures, and the constitutional issues involved ("Charles Sumner and the New Jersey Railroad Monopoly during the Civil War," *Proceedings of the New Jersey Historical Society,* 75 [October 1957], 259–75). However, he does not discuss the relation between this issue and either the Louisiana question or ratification of the Thirteenth Amendment. As the events were recounted by Nicolay and Hay, Representative Ashley tried unsuccessfully to persuade Lincoln to urge Sumner that he should defer consideration of the railroad bill in the Senate in return for the votes or absence of New Jersey Democrats at the time of the House vote on the amendment. Albert D. Riddle gave a more detailed account of bargains with several Democrats, and George W. Julian referred enigmatically in his memoirs to negotiations, "the particulars of which never reached the public." Randall and Current, as well as Donald handle these matters rather gingerly but the latter describes the account in Riddle as "erroneous." And in identifying the railroad involved as located in Pennsylvania and alleging that Sumner did not report the railroad bill in that session, Riddle certainly was incorrect or misleading. Strangely enough, none of the modern historians cited here report examination of the behavior of the New Jersey delegation on the House vote on the amendment. One of the five New Jersey members, identified in the *Biographical Directory of the American Congress* as a Republican, voted yea; a Constitutional Union man and a Democrat voted nay; and two Democrats were reported as "not voting." One of the latter was Andrew Jackson Rogers, an attorney, identified by Trask as "one of the principal Camden and Amboy agents in Washington" (p. 267). The votes of the New Jersey delegation are therefore consonant with the hypothesis that in some way Representative Ashley had managed to arrange a *quid pro quo.* As the vote turned out, the two absentees from New Jersey could have appeared and voted nay and the constitutional two thirds would still have been retained; two additional defections from the absentee list into the nay category would have defeated the amendment at that session. See: John G. Nicolay and John Hay, *Abraham Lincoln: A History* (New York: Century, 1890), 10:84–85; Albert G. Riddle, *Recollections of War Times: Reminiscences of Men and Events in Washington, 1860–1865* (New York: Putnam, 1895), pp. 324–25; James G. Randall and Richard N. Current, *Lincoln the President: Last Full Measure* (New York: Dodd, Mead, 1955), p. 310; David Donald, *Charles Sumner and the Rights of Man* (New York: Knopf, 1970), p. 194, n.9.

fifteen cents per ton of merchandise shipped across the state that the railroad company collected on behalf of the treasury of New Jersey as "tribute." An earlier version of the bill had specifically authorized two other New Jersey roads, the Camden and Atlantic and the Raritan and Delaware Bay, to unite in providing competitive through service, an arrangement denied those companies both in the C. & A.'s charter and by judicial decision. Now, in H.R. 307, the issue was reduced ostensibly to general principles, but the focus of the debate still remained on New Jersey.

The constitutional issues discussed by participants in the debate on H.R. 307 were highly important in industrializing America and also of particular concern to those interested in the development of reconstruction policy, since they involved the boundaries of state powers and federal prerogatives. "Public convenience and the Union itself in its beneficent powers" stood, Sumner declaimed, "on the one side. Public inconvenience and all the discord of intolerable State pretensions on the other side." In their remarks, the senators ranged from the implications of the commerce power and, the right of the federal government to establish post roads and raise and support armies—argued particularly by Sumner—to the countervailing rights of sovereign states to order their own domestic concerns, explained in greatest detail by Ten Eyck. In the process, Hale inquired as to which of the two cities, New York or Philadelphia, should be considered the "Heavenly City" and which should be designated the "City of Destruction," if New Jersey was indeed the "Valley of Humiliation" suggested by Sumner. He also wondered why "the patriotic gentlemen" of that "losing concern," the Raritan and Delaware Bay Railroad Company, who "could not pay dividends on their stock or interest on their bonds," had not enlisted the eloquence of Sumner at an earlier date. Saulsbury somberly proclaimed that there was "corruption foul and damnable in the whole thing."[63]

On February 22, Trumbull demurred when Chandler proposed to continue discussion of H.R. 307, arguing that it was high time to consider seating the gentlemen who claimed to be entitled to represent Louisiana in Congress. The Committee of the Judiciary, he explained, had prepared a joint resolution recommending that the "existing State organization in Louisiana be recognized as the legitimate State organization."[64] But Chandler prevailed and the discussion of the tribulations of New Jersey and of passengers on the Camden and Amboy ground on. Not so on the morrow, February 23, however; despite the plaints of

63. *CG*, 38 Cong., 2 sess., 790, 793–94, 1008.
64. Ibid., 990; Horace White, *The Life of Lyman Trumbull* (Boston: Houghton Mifflin, 1913), pp. 231–34; Mark M. Krug, *Lyman Trumbull: Conservative Radical* (New York: A. S. Barnes, 1965), 224–25.

Chandler, Sumner, and Howard, the senators voted to begin discussing the legitimacy of the Louisiana government, no doubt to the great relief of the directors of the Camden and Amboy (I.D. 1:70; 2:31). Chandler again tried to have the New Jersey bill considered in preference to the Louisiana resolution on the following day but failed (I.D. 1:41; 2:45.5). If the leading supporters of the railroad measure were using it, in part, to shunt the Louisiana issue aside, their colleagues would have no more of it.

S. 117 provided:

> That the United States do hereby recognize the government of the State of Louisiana, inaugurated under and by the convention which assembled on the 6th day of April, A.D. 1864, at the city of New Orleans, as the legitimate government of said State, entitled to the guarantee and all other rights of a State government under the constitution of the United States.

Although constrained by the limited amount of time left in the session, the debate on this simple statement was intense and sometimes bitter.[65] We shall consider only the major Republican positions, and to facilitate this I have to a degree consolidated the arguments of the various participants.

Among the Republican opponents of this resolution, Howard developed his position at length, arguing, "A State of the Union or a State in the Union is . . . a people yielding obedience to the laws of the Union, that is, the acts of Congress and the national treaties." Loyalty was the final test "in solving the question, what is a State in the Union?" If, by overt acts, a State had shown a want of this, it was "no longer in the Union *de facto*." Having subdued rebel states, the United States might rule them as "conquered country" for a time until the revival of allegiance, order, and loyalty. They could not be converted into territories, but determining the duration of military occupation was the prerogative of the federal government. During occupation, the people possessed no political privileges under the Constitution except the right to protection. Terminating this condition—"the establishment of provisional governments, the quieting of the rebellious province and the reestablishment of legitimate authority over it," pertained to "the law-giving power of the nation. . . . Lodged in Congress and not in the President." Howard opposed the President's 10 percent plan because such a minority could not sustain its own government and because government by a minority was an "evil example and inconsistent with the genius of American liberty." The Louisiana government represented only some eight thousand voters in a state where the voting population numbered more than fifty

---

65. *CG*, 38 Cong., 2 sess., 1011. Belz, *Reconstructing the Union*, pp. 269–76, briefly discusses the senatorial debate and its implications.

thousand in 1860. It was a "mockery of a government"; a "king of shreds and patches, this mistletoe State *regime* that falls to the earth the moment it ceases to cling around tbe flag-staff of the national forces." He called on the members of Congress to "take the subject of readmission into their own hands" and "perform the plain duty of providing provisional governments for States occupied by our armies," and "say to them 'Return to the ways of peace, revere the Government of your fathers . . . retire to your homes, renew your oath to your old Government, and commence with us a reinvigorated national life.' "[66]

Sumner put his views before the Senate in a series of amendments and in a running exchange of comment and retort with the advocates of S. 117. The senator from Massachusetts presented the first of his amendments as a substitute for the Judiciary Committee's measure. Representatives or senators from an insurrectionary state were to be seated in Congress only after the President had proclaimed that armed hostility to the United States had ceased there, the people of the state had adopted a constitution "not repugnant to the Constitution and laws of the United States," and Congress had by law declared the state to be entitled to representation in the national legislature. This being rejected, Sumner gave notice on February 25 that he proposed to introduce a more elaborate substitute measure, involving nine separate resolutions, which: affirmed the right of Congress to "reestablish by Act of Congress republican governments" in rebellious states, under the guarantee clause; specified that reconstruction "must be performed by the United States, represented by the President and both Houses of Congress"; maintained that in defining a "republican form of government" the Constitution should be construed in terms of the principles of the Declaration of Independence; called for the vote for all loyal people and equality before the law as well as safeguards to prevent "rebels now in arms" from perverting such rights in the future; denied that governments founded on military power were republican, affirming that Congress should not recognize such governments (as in Louisiana) both on that ground and because they made the military authority supreme over the civil; repudiated "oligarchical class" governments sustained by national support as "not competent . . . to discharge the duties and execute the powers of a State"; and concluded by affirming that both expediency and the Constitution required that black soldiers be given the ballot. Sumner asked that this amendment be printed and his colleagues agreed, but he did not move it thereafter, presumably because he accomplished his objectives without having to do so.[67]

66. *CG*, 38 Cong., 2 sess., 1092–95.
67. Ibid., 1011, 1091.

Meanwhile, in the give and take of debate, he contended that the Louisiana government was not truly republican in nature because it did not give the franchise to adult male blacks; it was an "oligarchy of a skin." And he wrangled and quibbled with colleagues about whether Massachusetts could commit an act of injustice, the details of the Missouri Compromise, and what President Washington had meant when he referred to "the consolidation of our Union." In the afternoon of February 25, Sumner moved to add a proviso to S. 117, that "within the State there shall be no denial of the electoral franchise, or of any other rights on account of color or race, but all persons shall be equal before the law." It was on this amendment, and on Henderson's amendment to it that the words "or sex" be added, that the evening debate of February 25 finally bogged down in a series of procedural motions advanced by Sumner and his allies.[68]

Of those supporting the administration, Henderson made the most elaborate statement in favor of the resolution, although Reverdy Johnson frustrated some Democratic colleagues by speaking powerfully in its behalf. Henderson asserted that the seceded states were still part of the Union and could claim the rights of nonseceded states, including all those customarily regarded as belonging to the state governments. He believed that it was improper for the federal government to invade spheres reserved to the states to a greater extent than that required by the necessities of war. Citizens in rebellion lose their rights as such within the Union and, when that occurred in a state, the loyal minority constituted the state and should govern it. In the case of Louisiana, the key questions, as he saw them, were "is the constitution the will of the loyal men qualified to act?" And, second, "is it republican in form?"[69] The answer was affirmative in both instances and Congress should therefore recognize the Louisiana government, and that of Arkansas as well when the time came to decide that case.

Henderson also considered Sumner's contention that Louisiana's government would be republican in form only if it provided Negro suffrage. The Missouri senator suggested that constitutions denying the vote to women were similarly deficient and later pounced on the literacy requirement in the constitution of Massachusetts which, he claimed, would have excluded "nearly every negro in Louisiana" if applied there.[70]

Usually radical in sympathy, Clark supported the Louisiana resolution, arguing that the Union men of Louisiana "ought not to be deprived of the right of voting because the rebels did wrong." If indeed their government was "a very feeble power," all the more reason why Con-

68. Ibid., 1068–69, 1098–99, 1103.
69. Ibid., 1070.
70. Ibid., 1097.

gress, obligated under the guarantee power and the constitutional clause pledging assistance against domestic violence, should nurture and protect it.[71]

Doolittle contended that Louisiana's vote would be needed in the ratification of the Thirteenth Amendment—an argument strenuously denied by Howard—and denounced Powell and Sumner as the nether and upper millstones of the opposition to the free state of Louisiana. He berated Sumner and other obstructionist radicals as "five men claiming to usurp an authority over the action of the friends of the Administration," and took exception to Sumner's condescending assurance to Foster "that a little more study ... would enable him to vote with more intelligence." "What arrogance, what assumed superiority on the part of one man over his equals ... to say that he is prepared to vote, but that other senators are not ... because they do not agree with him." But the people, Doolittle maintained, were in earnest and so was he "earnest in what I do, and earnest in what I say and in what I feel."[72]

In getting S. 117 to the floor, Trumbull had described it as a question of privilege since the right of the Louisiana delegation to take their seats depended on the outcome; beyond that he had said little. When Sumner argued that absent senators should be given an opportunity to speak and that there should be no final vote, therefore, on the evening of February 25, Trumbull denounced him. Sumner, he said, was "in a combination ... of a fraction of the Senate to delay the important business of the country. ... Associating with those whom he so often denounces." His fury rising, Trumbull demanded, "Does he hold in his hand the Senate of the United States, that, in his omnipotence, he is to say when votes shall be taken and public measures shall be passed?"[73] In a calmer vein, he appealed for a vote.

But Sumner was apparently unperturbed. He accused Trumbull of utilizing parliamentary tactics in seeking a vote on the resolution like those used by Stephen A. Douglas in managing the Kansas-Nebraska bill. As for Doolittle, that gentleman "was especially happy when attacking" him and a man to whom "anything for freedom is dangerous." Lacking the votes to defeat S. 117, Sumner and a little group of radicals and members of the opposition found obstructive tactics to be an effective weapon and the clock a powerful ally. Trumbull did not succeed in getting a vote on the resolution and the measure perished. Sumner's "little band," fumed the Springfield *Weekly Republican*, were "maddened republicans and drunken democrats" and proclaimed that it was "a dis-

71. Ibid., 1101–2.
72. Ibid., 1107, 1109–10.
73. Ibid., 1107.

grace to any legislative body" to allow such filibustering to thwart it.[74]

The Bay State senator could count himself the victor, but his opponents enjoyed some slight solace. In the dying minutes of the session, Chandler and Sumner asked for a vote on H.R. 307, the Camden and Amboy bill. Since there was no time to send bills to the House of Representatives, to amend would be to kill. His colleagues quickly accepted Wilson's amendment proposing, among other provisions, that no citizen of the United States be excluded from travel on railroad or navigable water in the United States by state law or municipal ordinance, amid laughter at Hale's addition of "nor from any meeting-houses, churches, or hotels." Clark tried to go still further by attempting to bring the citizens "of any other country" under the protection of the measure. He was admonished for trying to amend the bill while an amendment was pending. Nesmith's suggestion that the bill then be referred to the Committee on the Conduct of the War was narrowly defeated by the margin of one vote. When Morrill, amid chuckles at his threat to make a speech and not give Sumner time for response, moved indefinite postponement, the motion failed. But the subject was swept away after a final exchange of barbs by Chandler and Hale as the chamber swelled with "a distinguished and brilliant assemblage" in preparation for the ceremony of administering the oath to the Vice President-elect.[75]

During the discussion of S. 117, six votes occurred that produced disagreement scores of 46 to 60 when the scale ranking of the second session is used to divide radicals and moderates, but index numbers ranging from 19 to 36 when the factional ranking of the previous session serves as the basis for computation. Five of the votes were procedural in nature: to lay on the table, to postpone, and to adjourn. The sixth occurred when Sumner moved his first substitute for the resolution of the Committee on the Judiciary. Brown, Conness, Grimes, Howard, Sprague, Stewart, and Wade rallied to his support in this roll call. In all, eleven Republican senators cast votes with Sumner at some point during the series of divisive roll calls, following the decision to debate the Louisiana resolution and preceding Sherman's motion to discuss the internal revenue bill instead on February 27. But Brown, Chandler, Howard, Sumner, Wade, and Wilson, supported by a handful of the opposition senators, forced a majority of their colleagues to adjourn in frustration on Saturday night, February 25.

74. Ibid., 1110; Springfield *Weekly Republican*, March 4, 18, 1865. See Nicolay and Hay, *Abraham Lincoln*, 9: 454–56, for an early rendering of the ultra filibuster, and Donald, *Sumner and the Rights of Man*, pp. 196–205, for a modern account, sympathetic to the senator from the Bay State.

75. *CG*, 38 Cong., 2 sess., 1393–94.

Chapter 7 has reviewed the action of the Senate in considering the Confiscation Act of 1862, the general reconstruction bills, the southern electoral votes resolution, the Louisiana recognition resolution, and several minor measures of related interest within the context of radical-moderate disagreement. Clearly the senators found great and troublesome constitutional implications in these matters—far more so than in most other major issues of the war. But when the historian examines the *Congressional Globe* he can only be amazed at the comparatively brief time that they devoted to debate of the general reconstruction bills. Either there were strategic decisions made or inertial forces were present within the Congress concerning this subject that historians have not yet explored in full. The intertwining of the Louisiana recognition resolution and the bill to regulate commerce emphasized, although perhaps inadvertently, the broader implications of action affecting state-federal relations; constitutional principles or formulas invoked in the southern case might have northern implications and some Republican senators, at least, understood that fact very well.

But is it perhaps turning history on its head to view Sumner's positions on both reconstruction and the New Jersey monopoly as flowing naturally from a commitment to strengthening federal powers at the expense of state prerogatives? Did he take a hard line on New Jersey to strengthen the precedents for a tough reconstruction policy? Such a reading seems unduly strained; the willingness of the senator from Massachusetts to buttress federal authority was apparent in discussion of too many other nonsouthern issues during the whole course of the war, some of which are discussed in subsequent chapters.

# 8

# Courts, Border States, and Self-Control

Many of the measures discussed in the preceding chapters have attracted a good deal of attention from earlier historians of the Civil War. But other issues often considered of lesser importance also arrayed the Republican senators along radical and moderate lines. Because it is essential that we understand the full range of such controversy, this chapter considers a number of such matters relating to the nature and functioning of the system of courts, to certain questions of particular interest to loyal southerners, and to issues of governance and control within the Senate.

In the years before they won control of the national government, Republicans were bitterly critical of the Dred Scott decision and the justices who produced it. During the course of the Thirty-seventh Congress, Hale proposed that the Supreme Court be abolished, but his colleagues were uninterested in so drastic a step. No proposal concerning the Supreme Court divided the Republican senators repeatedly along radical-moderate lines in their voting—not even when, toward the end of the second session of the Thirty-eighth Congress, Trumbull introduced H.R. 748 to provide funds to commission a bust of the late Chief Justice Taney and Sumner fulminated against the idea that "an emancipated country should make a bust" of a man who was "to be hooted down the page of history."[1] But in various debates relating to the system of courts and judicial practices in the United States, radical Republicans and moderates did align themselves against each other in some strength and these instances merit discussion. The rights of blacks to take the witness stand, an issue in various legislative exchanges and votes, might

1. *CG*, 38 Cong., 2 sess., 1012. For comment on the attitude of Hale's colleagues see Cincinnati *Daily Commercial*, December 13, 1861.

also be considered in this section but that subject has been discussed in a different context.

In late January, 1862, the Senate returned to H.R. 89, "fixing the circuits of the Supreme Court of the United States." Wade introduced an amendment to change the territorial boundaries of the various circuits that the committee on the Judiciary had recommended, and Grimes in turn moved to amend that part of Wade's proposal which delimited the sixth, seventh, eighth, and ninth circuits. The Ohio senator's amendment ran:

> the districts of Louisiana, Texas, Arkansas and Tennessee, shall constitute the sixth circuit; the districts of Ohio and Kentucky shall constitute the seventh circuit; the districts of Indiana, Michigan, Wisconsin and Minnesota, shall constitute the eighth circuit; the districts of Illinois, Missouri, Kansas and Iowa, shall constitute the ninth circuit.

Grimes proposed to change this wording to:

> the districts of Louisiana, Texas, Arkansas, Kentucky, and Tennessee, shall constitute the sixth circuit; the districts of Ohio and Michigan shall constitute the seventh circuit; the districts of Indiana, Illinois, and Wisconsin shall constitute the eighth circuit; the districts of Missouri, Kansas, Iowa, and Minnesota shall constitute the ninth circuit.[2]

In a brief statement the Iowa senator mainly tried to defend his arrangement of states in the ninth circuit. Although such a circuit would be less densely populated than others, population was increasing rapidly there, considerable distances were involved, and the four states had greatly simplified their codes and adopted an almost uniform system of pleading, differing from that in more easterly states. Ten radicals supported the Grimes amendment and ten moderates opposed it (I.D.: 54).

There were vacancies on the Court and the evidence suggests that the boundary changes were, in part, a response to regional pressures within the Republican party and a judge-making exercise in which the judicial ambitions of Doolittle, Browning, Noah M. Swayne, and others inspired the senators to support district boundaries that would enhance the prospects of their favorites. In this particular roll call the moderation or radicalism of potential candidates may well explain the factional alignment. In the Judiciary Act of 1862, Grimes did indeed win a trans-Mississippi circuit and the Iowan Samuel H. Miller gained the seat on the Supreme Court that went with it. Although Browning and Doolittle coveted the eighth circuit, Lincoln ultimately frustrated them by appointing his circuit-riding friend and supporter David Davis. Browning's opposition to "the most important Republican measures," suggested the

2. *CG*, 38 Cong., 2 sess., 469.

New York *Tribune,* made him "the Jonah of the bill, everybody trying to throw him overboard."[3]

Of more interest to both contemporaries and historians were the issues involved in the President's policy of suspending the writ of habeas corpus in various areas of the country during the early stages of the war and arrests made under the direction of the secretaries of State and War. Did the Congress or the Executive possess the power to suspend the writ? How best to justify the President's past actions and provide a satisfactory formula for the future? How should political prisoners be discharged? During the special summer session of 1861, Henry Wilson presented a joint resolution declaring Lincoln's emergency measures during the spring of 1861 to be as legal as though performed under instructions from the Congress, and Trumbull presented a bill to suppress insurrection and sedition (S.33). Trumbull's measure authorized the military to disregard the writ in regions that the President had proclaimed to be in a state of insurrection or "actual rebellion," and prescribed various relevant procedures, including the requirement of a loyalty oath in certain cases. But the senators disagreed and settled for a rather equivocal amendment to an appropriation bill (S.72), approving the President's emergency military acts but not specifically mentioning habeas corpus.[4]

3. New York *Daily Tribune,* July 14, 1862; see also Springfield *Weekly Republican,* December 21, 1861, and Chicago *Tribune,* February 1, 1862. For secondary accounts see Charles G. Haines and Foster H. Sherwood, *The Role of the Supreme Court in American Government and Politics, 1789-1864* (Los Angeles: University of California Press, 1957), 2:444-54; Stanley I. Kutler, *Judicial Power and Reconstruction Politics* (Chicago: University of Chicago Press, 1968), pp. 1-29; Kermit L. Hall, "The Civil War Era as a Crucible for Nationalizing the Lower Federal Courts," *Prologue,* 7 (Fall 1975), 177-86. Marvin R. Cain, *Lincoln's Attorney General: Edward Bates of Missouri* (Columbia: University of Missouri Press, 1965), pp. 182-88, discusses the act of 1862 from the Attorney General's stand point, and David M. Silver, *Lincoln's Supreme Court* (Urbana: University of Illinois Press, 1956), provides a great deal of useful background.

4. George C. Sellery, *Lincoln's Suspension of Habeas Corpus as Viewed by Congress* (Madison: Bulletin of the University of Wisconsin History Series, I:3, 1907), 217-83, provides the bills' histories in meticulous detail. Senator Grimes explained the failure of Wilson's resolutions concerning habeas corpus in the special session in a letter to A. C. Barnes, September 16, 1861, published in William Salter, *The Life of James W. Grimes: Governor of Iowa, 1854-1858; A Senator of the United States, 1859-1869* (New York: Appleton, 1876), pp. 150-52. There were, he argued, problems in the draughtsmanship and insufficient time to amend them without unanimous consent. This of course glosses over differences of opinion among the senators. Trumbull's particular role is given in Horace White, *The Life of Lyman Trumbull* (Boston: Houghton Mifflin, 1913), pp. 195-203, and Mark M. Krug, *Lyman Trumbull: Conservative Radical* (New York: A. S. Barnes, 1965), pp. 191-94. Some detail is challengeable in both. James G. Randall, *Constitutional Problems under Lincoln* rev. ed. (Urbana: University of Illinois Press, 1964), pp. 118-214 deals with the congressional level rather incidentally while developing the broader constitutional story. See also Harold M. Hyman, *A More Perfect Union: The Impact of the Civil War and Reconstruction on the Constitution* (New York: Knopf, 1973), pp. 245-62, for a heavily documented account.

When the regular session of the Thirty-seventh Congress opened in December, Trumbull shocked some of his colleagues by introducing a resolution calling on the Secretary of State to report arrests under his authority in the loyal states and to explain their legal basis. He precipitated a day of debate that reminded some veteran observers of the time of Webster, Clay, and Calhoun, or so one newspaper correspondent reported.[5] During this session, H.R. 362 arrived in the Senate "to provide for the discharge of state prisoners and others," specifically authorizing the President to suspend the writ of habeas corpus when the public safety required it because of rebellion or invasion, as well as outlining discharge procedures for loyal prisoners. Despite Trumbull's support, this measure failed to pass during the second session. Although there was disagreement among the Republican senators on these matters, voting did not sharply reflect the cleavage between moderates and radicals. Trumbull, for example, opposed the motion to refer his resolution to the Judiciary Committee but the radical-moderate index only reached 30 in that roll call.

In late January of the third session of this Congress, the senator from Illinois brought up Thaddeus Stevens' bill, H.R. 591. This measure would "indemnify the President and other persons for suspending the writ of habeas corpus and acts done in pursuance thereof." The bill was a rather straightforward document acknowledging the President's actions and the fact that various arrests and imprisonments had been made as a result, as well as admitting that there was disagreement as to where the authority to suspend the writ actually lay. The actions taken by the President were to stand, officers of the executive branch and others involved were indemnified and discharged of obligation for their acts, and proceedings brought, or to be brought, against them were to be discharged and rendered void. A final section gave the President authority to suspend the right of habeas corpus as the public safety required during the rebellion. The members of the Senate Judiciary Committee recommended that their colleagues substitute S. 457 for the Stevens bill. The Senate measure was drawn by Collamer on the model of an 1815 law passed to protect government officials against suits arising from enforcement of the Non-Intercourse Act. The law of 1815 permitted defendants being sued for their part in arresting or imprisoning the

---

There is some tendency in the body of work cited in this note to ignore Collamer's contribution to the development of the habeas corpus legislation in the Senate: William M. Wiecek, "The Reconstruction of Federal Judicial Power, 1863–1875" (M.A. thesis, University of Wisconsin, 1967), pp. 44–89, 230–40, surveys the background of the Habeas Corpus Act of 1863 as well as describing the post-1863 developments. See also Cain, *Lincoln's Attorney General,* pp. 189–96, 262–68.

5. "Perley" [Ben Perley Poore] in the Boston *Morning Journal,* December 12, 1862.

plaintiffs, or for related acts, to have the case transferred to the appropriate federal circuit court. In cases of "reasonable or probable cause," or palpable good faith, on the part of the defendant, the court was to certify to that fact, and executions were to be issued or proceedings continued, subject only to particular limitations prescribed. Should the circuit court judgment be adverse to the defendant, he was assured of the right of appeal on writ of error to the Supreme Court; actions of the sort under consideration must be brought within two years after the arrest, imprisonment, trespass, or wrong was made or committed.[6]

The border-state senators used this debate to challenge the constitutionality of Lincoln's proclamations on emancipation, as well as those prescribing the use of martial law, court martial, and military commissions. Davis termed them "imperial edicts," and Saulsbury, rendered audacious by strong spirits, so vilified the President and was so obstructive that the chair had him escorted from the chamber by the sergeant-at-arms. Collamer dismissed the constitutional purity of senators like Powell as holding "that though a man may desire to save the drowning honor of his country, he must not presume upon the guilty familiarity of pulling it up by the locks."[7] No indication of notable differences of opinion between radical and moderate Republicans appeared until Sherman tried to amend the Senate bill in Committee of the Whole by adding a clause requiring that, in those areas where the normal judicial processes were in effect, civilians who were in custody ten days after the passage of the law on a charge of aiding the enemy or obstructing the execution of laws or military orders must be specifically charged in writing in the appropriate U.S. district court. If H.R. 591 was passed, these procedures were to be followed within ten days in all future cases of arrest on similar grounds. The judge of the court involved might then discharge, hold to bail, or remand to custody, as he believed the interests of public safety dictated. Trumbull deplored this amendment; it would open up an area of controversy that the Judiciary Committee amendment avoided.

Sherman did not defend his proposal at length, but when Fessenden charged that "it would defeat all action by the Government entirely," he denied that it would "impair the efficiency of the power of the President." Rather, if it had been the law a year earlier, it "would have saved us all the troubles we had in Ohio, growing out of military arrests, ... and ... would have relieved us from all the opprobrium, perhaps unjustly heaped on the authorities for these military arrests." His amendment lost in a 20–20 vote when first offered in Committee of the

6. *CG*, 37 Cong., 3 sess., 529–30.
7. Ibid., 532, 536.

Whole (I.D.: 32). Sherman offered the proposal again in the Senate, somewhat "modified . . . at the suggestion of one or two Senators," so as to delete the reference to individuals currently in custody.[8] Wilson further modified Sherman's amendment by successfully proposing that the period in which action must be filed be extended from ten to thirty days. In that form it passed by a 22 to 17 margin, with a preponderance of moderates in favor and only two of the radicals supporting it (I.D.: 50). Changes from the earlier alignment involved the appearance of Arnold, Dixon, and Doolittle in support of Sherman's position, while Lane of Kansas also moved in the same direction. Clearly the radicals in this instance supported the more repressive policy and Collamer, Fessenden, Foster, and Ten Eyck voted with them.

Meanwhile, the senators had deferred sustained consideration of H.R. 362, and it was not until February 19 that they began to discuss a somewhat revised version, prepared by Trumbull. This bill, of course, outlined the process by which innocent prisoners were to be discharged but these procedures safeguarded the government more elaborately than did Sherman's amendment, calling on the secretaries to provide lists of prisoners as an initial step. The senators approved the bill some days later but the representatives did not act upon it in that form. They did, however, refuse to accept the amended H.R. 591 and asked for a committee of conference. The members, including Trumbull and Collamer, endeavored to combine the amended H.R. 591 and H.R. 362 with some additional matter designed to satisfy the representatives, and the exhausted senators approved this hybrid creation before breakfast on the morning of March 3, 1863, thanks to the unorthodox style of Pomeroy as presiding officer. It entered the statutes as an "Act relating to Habeas Corpus, and regulating Judicial Proceedings in certain cases." The act did not contain Sherman's amendment, but, rather, the more circuitous delivery procedures of H.R. 362.

Despite its importance and its long legislative history the habeas corpus issue produced only one vote that sharply aligned radical against moderate. There were other votes in the debates that showed low cohesion among the Republicans but the disagreements apparently cut across radical-moderate alignment. Although radicals called for all-out war, they were unwilling to give the President full leeway. Moderates favored giving him freedom of action but also, on occasion, proclaimed their strong devotion to constitutional safeguards.[9]

The senators clashed again on matters of judicial procedure during

8. Ibid., 551, 554.
9. For instance, Collamer moved to strike the jail delivery clauses from H.R. 362 on February 23, 1863. The Republican index of cohesion was only 28 but the radical-moderate index of disagreement was a mere 23. *CG*, 37 Cong., 3 sess., 1207.

February, 1865. On February 3, Wilson asked his colleagues to take up S. 408, a measure supplementary to the enlistment laws and bearing specifically on the procedures of the draft that was to take place in mid-month. Section 3 provided that recruiting agents, substitute brokers, or others who knowingly effected the enlistment of insane or intoxicated individuals or deserters, or deprived a volunteer or substitute of local, state, or federal bounties due to him should, "upon conviction by any court martial or military commission," be fined to a maximum amount of $1000 or jailed for no more than two years, or suffer both penalties. In opposition, Hale emphasized the difficulty of deciding whether an individual was insane or intoxicated and noted that conviction in military court was a matter of majority decision. "Such questions legitimately belong to the civil tribunals," he thought. Cowan maintained that individuals who were tried for the offenses specified in section 3 were clearly entitled to the protections outlined in the Fifth and Sixth Amendments of the Constitution. Howard strenuously defended section 3, arguing that the wording in the Fifth Amendment, "except in cases arising in the land or naval forces, or in the militia, when in actual service in time of war or public danger" justified his position that substitute brokers and the like might be tried in military courts, where their cases would be handled with dispatch. Cowan, he alleged, had disregarded the military exception in the Fifth Amendment (which was untrue unless Cowan edited his remarks in the *Globe*). The Pennsylvanian replied that the Fifth-Amendment phrasing applied to individuals *in service* and not to civilians who rendered incidental assistance in the enlistment process. Howard's interpretation, he remarked, "would be a capital joke if it was not in earnest."[10]

Later, Cowan proposed to amend section 3 by striking "martial or military commission," and providing that the relevant passage should read "shall upon conviction in any court of the United States having competent jurisdiction." Conness rose to stress the excessive delays involved in civil justice, and Howard expanded his interpretation of the Fifth Amendment, which in his mind "was intended to be sufficiently broad to protect the military and naval service of the United States, and to punish all persons offending against it, all persons obstructing it, all persons intentionally damaging it, or injuring it in any respect whatever." If indeed civilians providing services to the military were subject

10. *CG*, 38 Cong., 2 sess., 572, 611–12, 615; the measure discussed was actually a substitute, proferred by the Committee on Military Affairs. For general background see Fred A. Shannon, *The Organization and Administration of the Union Army, 1861–1865* (Cleveland: Arthur H. Clark, 1928), 2:49–102; Randall, *Constitutional Problems*, pp. 239–74; Eugene C. Murdock, *One Million Men: The Civil War Draft in the North* (Madison: Wisconsin State Historical Society, 1971), pp. 255–304.

to military law, responded Cowan, "the whole population is involved, then the military swallows up entirely the civil, and we are cut loose from all the safeguards of the Constitution and all those which the common law throws around us."[11] Although Cowan's stock was not high in the Republican party, his view carried the day, 29 to 14 (I.D. 1-38: 33.5; 2-38: 71).

Critics pronounced one measure relating to the judiciary to be a Republican purge. On February 18, 1863, S. 359 came before the Senate in Committee of the Whole, a bill "remodeling the courts of the District of Columbia," drafted by Senator Harris and under his guidance.[12] It abolished the existing circuit court, district court, and criminal court of the District involving, in all, four judges, and established a single court in which four justices would hold circuit, district, or criminal and equity proceedings as needed. The present system, according to Harris, had evolved haphazardly during the course of sixty years and needed overhaul. Since the judge of the criminal court had died and another of the current judges was, in effect, superannuated, a new system could be begun with minimal disruption to the judicial personnel.

The border-state senators detected more sinister motivation underlying this law. It would turn out incumbent judges and allow a Republican President to appoint new ones. Davis argued that the justices of the District of Columbia courts held their office on good behavior under the Constitution and that to displace them by legislating their benches from beneath them was to act unconstitutionally. Harris denied that this was his intent, but admitted that he believed that one of the judges should not be placed upon the reorganized court. Wilson of Massachusetts was blunter. He opined that Judge William M. Merrick's heart was "sweltering with treason."[13] It was not on such matters, however, that factional division arose in the Republican ranks during the debates on this bill.

Rather, discussion developed when Grimes proposed an additional clause providing that the President be authorized to appoint a warden of the jail for the county of Washington. This man would assume duties heretofore performed by or under the direction of the marshal of the District of Columbia, Ward Lamon, an Illinois friend of Lincoln's. Grimes had criticized Lamon severely in the past because he had allowed

11. *CG*, 38 Cong., 2 sess., 631–32.

12. *CG*, 37 Cong., 3 sess., 1049. See: Walter S. Cox, "Efforts to Obtain a Code of Laws for the District of Columbia," *Records of the Columbia Historical Society*, 3 (1900), 115–35; Wilhelmus B. Bryan, *A History of the National Capital: From Its Foundation through the Period of the Adoption of the Organic Act* (New York: Macmillan, 1916), 2:435-42, 517–22. Describing the new system of the Civil War, Cox wrote (p. 127), "A new judicial system was established, of which the principal author was a Senator from New York, without the least consultation with the people or the legal profession of the District."

13. *CG*, 37 Cong., 3 sess., 1139.

slaveholders to incarcerate their bondsmen in jail while slavery was still
legal in the District. Powell labeled the amendment a "lick at the marshal," and remarked that he thought it "manifestly improper, in the radical crusade that is being made against the judges, to embrace the marshal."[14] The amendment failed but eight other radicals voted for it, in
addition to Grimes, while of the more moderate persuasion, only Foster
came to the Iowan's support (I.D.: 47.5). A final amendment proposed
by Trumbull attaching authorization for the codification of the District
laws—a measure approved by the previous session but unimplemented—
also produced modest opposition from the moderates as four of them
voted against it while no radical opposed (I.D.: 44). Given the small
number of moderates in opposition, we cannot make much of the vote,
but codification clearly could open the way for attacks on the southern
legal system in the District.

A curious thread of factional dissent ran through the voting on various matters related to the United States Court of Claims. Trumbull
succeeded in bringing H.R. 226, to reorganize the Court of Claims,
before the Senate for discussion on January 12, 1863, arousing Hale who
roared that "the national life" was "trembling in the balance," and that
the Senate had "something else to do besides passing bankrupt bills and
Court of Claims bills." The Court of Claims, he fulminated, was merely
"a safe retreat for lame ducks," which, since its creation, had unfortunately been Democratic fowl only. In this bill, Hale detected an effort to
"put in some on the other side who have had to retreat before the face of
popular condemnation." But the senators proceeded to consider the bill
to amend the Court of Claims Act of 1855, motivated mainly, according
to more charitable authorities, by the belief that the war would produce
such a flood of claims that the current system would be inadequate.[15]

At the time, the Court of Claims ruled on claims against the government, but the Congress regarded its findings as advisory only. H.R. 226
provided that the number of judges was to be increased from three to

14. Ibid.; Salter, *Life of James W. Grimes,* pp. 163–68, prints excerpts from the *Globe* in
which the Iowa senator reviewed his differences with Lamon, but the author does not refer
to this incident.

15. *CG,* 37 Cong., 3 sess., 271. There is no definitive history of the Court of Claims at
this writing. The best review of its background and history to 1875 is found in Wiecek,
"The Reconstruction of Federal Judicial Power," pp. 138–81, 255–62. This is the foundation of Wiecek, "The Origin of the United States Court of Claims," *Administrative Law
Review,* 20 (Spring 1968), 387–406. William A. Richardson, "History, Jurisdiction, and
Practice of the Court of Claims of the United States," *Southern Law Review,* 7 (February
1882), 781–811, is an early effort by one of the justices to describe the tribunal's development. See Felix Frankfurter and James M. Landis, *The Business of the Supreme Court: A Study
in the Federal Judicial System* (New York: Macmillan, 1927), for the interpretation that the
revision of 1863 was made in anticipation of larger numbers of claims.

five, of whom one would serve as chief justice. In addition to changing the rules of pleading before the court, the bill provided that its decisions were to be final, subject to appeal to the Supreme Court. The latter provision drastically changed the prevailing practice, under which the Congress reviewed the decisions of the court and accepted or rejected them as its members saw fit.

Trumbull believed that the bill, as the Judiciary Committee proposed to amend it, would considerably improve the handling of claims against the United States stemming from contracts. He admitted that the Congress almost never approved claims that the court adjudged to be without merit but the senators and representatives by no means approved all those found to be in order. Trumbull believed that the court was able to review the evidence involved in claims cases more thoroughly than could the legislators and that congressional review was sometimes capricious, ineffective, and unfair. The bill, he suggested, would make the court "efficient and give some character to its decisions." Hale ultimately blurted out that the bill was in part designed to displace the Democrat, Edward G. Loring, from his position as chief justice of the Court of Claims, "a side-blow . . . unjust and ungenerous," and, added Fessenden, "unchristian!" But Trumbull invited both sides of the Senate chamber to turn their attention to the bill, since it did "not affect the politics of the country," but was "one in which . . . all alike [are] interested."[16]

Fessenden sharply opposed the idea of giving away "our whole jurisdiction over the claims against the Government, to put it in the hands of a court established by ourselves, at a period when we know that claims must accumulate upon us by and by." He believed that congressmen had been "unanimously or nearly so" agreed in 1855 "that Congress could in no event part with the power which it held over claims against the Government in that particular, and could in no event put the Treasury of the United States into the hands of a court or any tribunal whatever, except those who were the proper guardians of it."[17] Although Trumbull argued vigorously that the houses of Congress might except certain claims in the process of providing the court's general appropriation, Fessenden tried in Committee of the Whole to strike the provisions, that made the Court's decisions not subject to congressional review. Hamlin of Maine, presiding in his role as Vice President, broke a tie vote, 20 to 20 (I.D.: 42.5), by voting against his state's senior senator. Fessenden tried again in the Senate, but failed, as only 15 senators rallied to his cause (I.D.: 36).

Moderates usually supported the Trumbull position and radicals in general grouped behind Fessenden in these roll calls. As chairman of the

16. *CG*, 37 Cong., 3 sess., 303, 427, 304.
17. Ibid., 304.

Finance Committee, he was particularly sensitive to efforts to weaken the power that Congress enjoyed over the purse. But radicals, we suspect, were concerned not only with maintaining the powers of Congress but tried on occasion to expand them in areas where they were shared with other branches or agencies of the government. As passed, H.R. 226 was a milestone in the development of the powers of the Court of Claims and the additional places it made available allowed Lincoln to provide a safe haven for an old Illinois friend, Ebenezer Peck, and a defeated senator, David Wilmot.

Division between radicals and moderates sometimes occurred in the discussion of particular claims. On February 15 and 17, 1864, the senators discussed and finally voted on Foster's motion to refer S. 92, for the relief of Albert Brown, to the Court of Claims. At the request of government officers, a New Hampshire wagon-maker, Albert Brown, accepted a contract in 1861, under which he manufactured one hundred army wagons within sixty days. A government inspector checked the work while in progress and approved the wagons as they were completed. But when the wagons reached Perryville, Maryland, Captain Charles G. Sawtelle of the Quartermaster Department inspected them and declared them to be unsatisfactory. The army refused to approve payment to Brown and eventually the railroad company that had carried the wagons sold them to meet the freight bill.[18]

The wagon-maker presented his claim for payment to the Senate during 1863 and, on the recommendation of the Committee on Claims, that body passed a relief bill in his favor. The representatives failed to act upon the bill, however, and Brown submitted his plea for relief once again to the Senate when it convened in the Thirty-eighth Congress. Although the Committee on Claims recommended that the claim be honored, Foster maintained that it should more properly go to the Court of Claims. Howe, Clark, and Hale spoke at some length against Foster's motion to that effect, maintaining that the Senate could, under the law, consider claims against the government. The bill had failed in the previous session only through lack of time. The injustice done to Brown was so flagrant, they believed, that he should receive immediate consideration, rather than suffering additional delays and the costs of counsel.

Foster argued against making exceptions under the law passed during the previous session requiring claims of this type to be referred to the Court of Claims. Many other meritorious claims were pending against the government; Congress could clearly not consider all of them. Nesmith rose to the defense of Sawtelle, whose character he believed had been impugned, and both Grimes and Trumbull supported Foster, the

18. *CG*, 38 Cong., 1 sess., 644–46, 694–99.

latter arguing that the nature of the pleading in the Court of Claims was much more efficient than the procedures of congressional committees, and the senator from Iowa emphasizing the importance of sound construction in army wagons.

Foster's motion failed by a vote of 18 yeas and 21 nays. The moderate Republicans split seven to three in support and the radicals thirteen to four in opposition to referral (I.D.: 46). Again, the radicals preferred their own brand of justice to that dispensed in the Court of Claims.

On June 2, 1864, Hale brought before his colleagues Senate Joint Resolution 50, which was a proposal to instruct the Secretary of the Navy to select a board of competent persons to investigate the contentions of some twenty contractors who claimed that they had suffered losses while manufacturing engines for the type of gunboat known as a "double-ender," and to recommend appropriate compensation. Officers of the Navy Department were reported to have advertised for bids and explained the design of the gunboat engines to the manufacturers and obtained oral commitments from them to undertake construction. The builders went to work but when they later received the contracts and written specifications, they discovered that the engines would require greater outlays than they had expected. In a letter transmitted to Congress, Gideon Welles explained that the contractors assumed their obligations voluntarily and in full knowledge of the requirements. The agreed price had been the lowest bid, after advertisement, from an experienced firm. The manufacturers, he noted, had failed by a good deal to meet the agreed date of completion. Losses sustained were not attributable to the Navy Department, argued Welles, and he left it for Congress "to exercise such liberality as . . . it may see proper."[19] Grimes focused the debate by moving an amendment that referred the claims to the Court of Claims for examination and adjudication.

The senators argued the matter on June 22, and Anthony strongly supported the cause of the contractors, explaining "they ask that if they have built engines more costly than those they were expected to build when they commenced their preparations for building, there may be a board of investigation to decide how much they are entitled to, or rather that is the resolution that the [Naval Affairs] committee report." He concluded, "To send them to the Court of Claims is to send them nowhere, because the Court of Claims can only pay them what is due under a contract. They do not profess to be entitled to anything under a contract." In response, Grimes maintained that the price agreed upon, $82,000, was so far in excess of the amount paid for the original prototype that the contractors must have been aware that the specifications

19. Ibid., 2653.

were different. He attacked the looseness of the resolution and particularly regretted the precedent that would be set if Congress decided to adjudicate on the basis of the problems involved in filling a valid contract. It would open up Congress, he suggested, to "every man who has done anything for the public service ... during ... this war."[20]

Grimes modified his amendment ultimately to meet the contention that the Court of Claims would not look beyond the terms of the contracts, as follows, "and said court is hereby authorized to examine and report to Congress what amount of work said contractors have done, and what amount of materials they have furnished in addition to their contract, and what is the fair value of the same." Eighteen senators supported the Grimes amendment and fifteen opposed it (I.D.: 43). Nine radicals were in the latter group but eight of the nine moderates voting supported the Grimes amendment as modified. Once again the moderates cast a vote of confidence for the Court of Claims, while a majority of radicals preferred to qualify their endorsement.[21]

One does not study the Congress during the Civil War for long before concluding that its legislative history would have been much simpler if the border region had been part of the Confederacy or, conversely, if slavery had not existed there. The loyal residents of the border states provided a base of operations for the Union and men and materials for its cause, but at the same time maintained the domestic institution that most Republicans believed to be the overriding reason why secession and war had occurred. This anomalous situation underlay much disagreement among the Republican senators. Some of the results have appeared in the discussion of legislative proposals concerning slavery, the status of blacks, and southern government. Similar disagreement seems to have run through the discussion of a number of relatively minor matters concerning loyal residents of border areas.

Two votes, for instance, relating to the city of Washington in 1862, produced sufficient disagreement between moderates and radicals to bring them to our consideration. The first took place on April 4, when Grimes, who was "so unfortunate as to be a member of the Committee on the District of Columbia," brought S. 231 before his colleagues, bestowing upon the city of Washington the power to levy a water tax on the real property in the city adjacent to thoroughfares, where water mains had been or would be laid by the federal government or by the city. Under the law then prevailing, the corporation was able to levy only upon actual users of city water, although the value of property owned by

20. Ibid., 3170-71.
21. Ibid., 3175. Private claims also produced factional division during this Congress in relation to the College Rancho and Miranda claims.

nonusers was greatly enhanced when water mains were laid adjacent to it. Presenting the position of various property owners, Ten Eyck proposed to strike the taxing provision from the bill and, when that destructive motion was lost, he moved that unimproved lots be exempted from tax. The effect of the provision, he argued, would be to allow "one or two persons who live half a mile from any other resident" to obtain water "at the expense of the owners of the intermediate ground, vacant, unimproved, and subject to heavy taxation now . . . with a view of raising a fund to discharge" debt that the city had incurred in developing its water facilities up to that time.[22] Six moderates supported Ten Eyck's second motion and five opposed it, while twelve radicals were opposed to it and only one supported it (I.D.: 47).

On June 10, 1862, Grimes proposed to amend a supplementary appropriations bill for civil expenses by adding a provision limiting the rates of the Washington Gas Light Company after July 1 to a maximum of twenty-five cents per hundred cubic feet on gas sold to the government and twenty-eight cents to other customers, subject to a discount of 10 percent for prompt payment, thereby providing a substantial reduction in the government's gas bills in the future.[23] Debate centered on the unsatisfactory quality of the company's service and the size of its profits. Twelve radicals supported this proposal and nine moderates opposed it (I.D.: 62).

During the second session of the Thirty-seventh Congress, the United States government authorized, or recognized, state forces in Missouri and Maryland. The Congress, however, did not act on a bill to raise a volunteer state force for service within Kentucky. During the next session that proposal, as developed in H.R. 137, emerged from the Senate Committee on Military Affairs and was defended by Davis in early January 1863. The little senator outlined the unique defensive problems of the Unionists in Kentucky, where proximity to the rebel states and the presence of the Knights of the Golden Circle made life dangerous despite the fact that "upward of one half of the loyal military population" was in Union service.[24] Davis visualized a volunteer force, not exceeding 20,000 men, composed of youths between sixteen and eighteen years of age and able-bodied men above the age of forty-five, who wished to stay within the boundaries of their state.

In the proposal Trumbull saw the possibility of a variety of separate state commands governed by different regulations, and he attacked H.R.

22. CG, 37 Cong., 2 sess., 1540; Bryan, *History of the National Capital*, 2:305–8, and Constance M. Green, *Washington: Village and Capital, 1800–1878* (Princeton: Princeton University Press, 1962), pp. 202–3, 255–56, 260.

23. Bryan, *History of the National Capital*, 2:295–302, gives background detail.

24. CG, 37 Cong., 3 sess., 186.

137 vigorously. On the other hand, Howe and Wilson defended the bill, expressing their willingness to recognize Kentucky's unique problems, provided that various ameliorative amendments were made. Howe was apparently impressed that Davis did not object to Collamer's amendment, specifying that the governor of Kentucky should act "by the consent and under the direction of the President of the United States" in raising this force and providing that it might be used outside in an emergency. Wilson supported the measure, stipulating only that these one-year volunteers should not exceed 10,000 in number nor receive bounty. The bill's opponents tried to generalize its provisions so that such a force might be raised in any state at the discretion of the President of the United States. The first of a series of amendments in that direction offered by Harlan deleted the phrasing, "The Governor of the State of Kentucky, by the consent and under the direction of," and carried by a vote of 19 yeas and 16 nays (I.D.: 43). Seven moderates joined Davis in the minority along with the radicals Hale and Wilson. Although he remarked that the bill would be "an absurdity" if amended as proposed, Fessenden was one of five moderates voting for the Harlan amendment. Shortly after this division, Wilson managed to move the chamber into executive session with a final admonition to "reflect on this bill."[25]

When the senators resumed work on H.R. 137 on January 12, they took up H. S. Lane's motion to reconsider Harlan's amendment. This time the Republicans were more strongly polarized in a vote of 21 yeas and 14 nays (I.D.: 76). Harlan's amendment was then lost. Citing recent evidence of opposition to the administration in Kentucky, Clark requested a week's postponement but was denied (I.D.: 69). After supporting statements by Sherman and Davis, H.R. 137, now in form satisfactory to the latter and Wilson, passed the chamber by a margin of 23 to 13. Twelve moderates and two radicals supported the bill while eleven radicals and two moderates opposed it (I.D.: 70). Did the radicals believe that this bill eroded federal power or was a concession to state sovereignty? Were they reluctant to assist border states? Were they suspicious of the loyalty of Kentuckians? Were they punishing them for their slowness in moving toward emancipation? Whatever the definitive answers to such questions, the President signed H.R. 137 on February 7, 1863, and Kentucky tried rather unsuccessfully to implement it.[26]

Less sweeping in its implications was S. 427, a bill for the relief of a

25. Ibid., 187, 189, 251–54. Field of New Jersey voted in this roll call but did not participate in enough divisions to be typed.

26. 37 Cong., 3 sess., Laws, Chap. XXIII in CG, App., 182. For the general background in Kentucky, see E. Merton Coulter, The Civil War and Readjustment in Kentucky (Chapel Hill: University of North Carolina Press, 1926). The efforts to implement the law are discussed on pp. 193–96.

loyal southerner, Charles Anderson, which the senators considered during the same session after Sherman brought it before his colleagues on December 19, 1862. By this time Anderson was a colonel in the Union forces, but he had fled Texas in September, 1861, after selling his property to a friend, John James, who paid him by assigning a claim for some $1000 against the United States government. Although the Quartermaster General recognized the debt as legitimate, Congress did not appropriate funds to settle this account. The members of the Committee on Military Affairs recommended that the claim be paid, but Grimes and Hale feared the precedent involved. By approving S. 427, the senators would provide a procedure by which disloyal individuals like James could collect claims against the United States government. The senators voted to disallow the claim by a margin of 22 to 17, but Davis and Sherman persuaded their colleagues to reconsider without a roll call. In the final vote on the bill, twenty-six senators voted in favor and only nine opposed (I.D.: 42), with a pronounced majority of moderates acceding to Anderson's plea and a smaller majority of radicals opposing.[27]

On April 12, 1864, Grimes moved an amendment to the Naval Appropriations Bill as follows: "*And be it further enacted,* That the United States Naval Academy shall be returned and established at the Naval Academy grounds in Annapolis . . . before the commencement of the academic year 1865."[28] At the time of the Baltimore riots in 1861, the officers of the academy had evacuated it; the buildings had since become part of an army base. Meanwhile, the Secretary of the Navy reestablished the academy at Newport, Rhode Island, where two of the classes of midshipmen were quartered in a hotel building in the city and the other two lived on barrack ships. The misfortunes of Annapolis and Maryland spelled opportunity to residents in other states. Newport offered municipal land to the federal government for a permanent establishment, and residents of New Jersey sang the praises of Perth Amboy. Now Grimes proposed to settle the matter by having Congress instruct the administration to move the academy back to Annapolis. Newport's character as a manufacturing town and watering place, combined with the unsatisfactory living arrangements at the academy there, maintained Grimes, tempted the midshipmen into breaches of discipline. The Newport location had also proved to be unhealthier than that at Annapolis and allowed less time for efficient outdoor training each year. None could now argue that the residents of Maryland were disloyal. The senator

27. *CG,* 37 Cong., 3 sess., 118, 139, 185, 205-6.
28. *CG,* 38 Cong., 1 sess., 1562. This incident has been of little interest to naval historians: Charles O. Paullin, *Paullin's History of Naval Administration, 1775-1911* (Annapolis: U.S. Naval Institute, 1968), p. 303; but see Frank Blake, *Memoir of George Smith Blake: Commodore U.S.N.* (Cambridge, Mass.: Welch, Bigelow, 1871), pp. 14-18.

from Iowa read letters from various naval officers favoring the return of the academy to its original location.

Anthony of Rhode Island opposed the Grimes amendment, arguing that the Navy Department had not requested removal and that there was no evidence that it favored the proposal. The Secretary of the Navy had authority to move the academy from Newport whenever he saw fit. Since enrollment had more than doubled, the buildings at Annapolis were no longer suitable. Should new buildings be erected there? He doubted that the current academy officers wished the school returned to Annapolis, and extolled the healthfulness and other advantages of the site which Newport had offered as a permanent location. Speaking as chairman of the Committee on Military Affairs, Wilson acknowledged the temptations of Newport, but believed it against the interests of the government to force the academy back to Annapolis. He favored deferring the matter until the next session.

Grimes responded that the needs of the army would not be jeopardized by surrendering the academy and maintained:

> What I want the amendment adopted for is, to give notice to all persons that it is not to be our policy to keep the Academy where it now is, and that we are not going to tempt, to allure into the public service the finest young men in the country and send them where they are to be tempted from the path of rectitude, and then ignominiously dismissed from the public service, and bear reproach the rest of their lives.[29]

Ten Eyck and Sumner joined the opposition to the amendment, Ten Eyck arguing for the appointment of a commission of experts, as in the selection of sites for arsenals and navy yards. Not unexpectedly, Johnson of Maryland favored the amendment, but Trumbull opposed it, because it left the school in an unsatisfactory state for the next year and a half.

Summing up, Fessenden noted that the residents of Rhode Island hoped that by retaining the academy for a time, they would ultimately acquire permanent possession. The question should be answered and the "game of grab" terminated; Annapolis was an excellent place and Newport "one of the worst places for a school of boys situated as these are, owing to the very nature of its society and its temptations." Grimes's amendment placed the date far enough in advance so that the War Department could make suitable arrangements, and it was unreasonable to continue to sacrifice the needs of the navy by refusing it use of the academy installation. Doolittle had "this sort of feeling that I am bound to restore the institutions of this country so far as the good institutions are concerned, and I will put them back to the place where they belong in spite of rebellion, in spite of this war." In the Committee of the Whole,

29. *CG*, 38 Cong., 1 sess., 1567.

the amendment carried by a vote of 20 yeas and 17 nays. Eight moderate Republicans, four radicals, and a collection of Democrats and Unionists supported the proposition (I.D.: 56). When the bill was before the Senate two days later, Anthony moved to strike all after the introductory "That" and insert, "the Secretary of the Navy shall appoint a board of five naval officers to examine and report upon the most suitable place for the Naval Academy." In brief debate, the senators added little to the earlier arguments, although Clark mimicked Sumner's dramatic device, "I hold in my hand . . ." to the great amusement of colleagues. Grimes announced that his amendment was satisfactory to the Secretary of War, and his colleagues rejected Anthony's substitute by a vote of 12 yeas and 28 nays (I.D.: 52).[30] Ten Eyck was the only moderate to support Anthony's amendment, while six radicals joined eleven moderates in successfully opposing it.

Although they considered at some length legislation that might have had far-reaching consequences upon the relations between the legislative branch and the executive or judicial, as well as those between the federal and state governments, the senators spent relatively little time in questioning their own procedures and obligations. We have in earlier chapters discussed efforts to change the rules of the Senate and the joint rules of Congress and to avoid conflicts of interest. The Senate's customary procedures proved sufficient to the task of expelling errant brethren who had cast their lot with the Confederacy and Senator Bright, who was too quick to accept the pretensions to national independence of such men. Such actions usually revealed no striking differences of opinion in voting between radical or moderate, although the ultras took the lead in these matters. But on some issues of practice or procedure, *entente* did erode and radicals aligned themselves against their party's moderates.

To fill the senatorial seat left empty by the shocking death of Edward D. Baker, the Democratic governor of Oregon appointed Benjamin Stark in October, 1861. After mercantile experience in New York until 1848, Stark rounded the Horn as a supercargo and was a merchant in San Francisco during the boom days of 1849 and 1850. Settling down in Portland in 1850, he became a lawyer by profession and a land speculator as well, a colonel during the Indian hostilities of 1853, and a member of the territorial and state legislatures. "Red-headed, dapper, shrewd and loquacious," he was a leader of the Breckinridge Democracy in Oregon. Stark achieved a brief notoriety denied to most interim senators and Republicans disagreed more sharply about seating him

30. Ibid., 1569, 1570, 1609, 1611; Grimes's amendment appears as 38 Cong., 1 sess., *Laws,* Chap. XCV, sec. 4 in *CG,* App. 165.

during the second session of the Thirty-seventh Senate than about issues which historians have treated in far more detail. (Indeed, most historians of the Civil War have ignored Benjamin Stark entirely.)[31]

On January 6, 1862, Nesmith of Oregon rose, after the approval of the previous day's *Journal,* to present Stark's credentials to the Vice President and to ask that the oath of office be administered. After the clerk had read the governor's letter of appointment, Fessenden moved that the oath should not be administered and that Stark's credentials should be referred, along with other documents in the Maine senator's possession, to the Committee on the Judiciary. These latter papers came from Secretary Seward and were, for the most part, sworn affidavits attesting that Stark was "understood by everybody" in the Portland region "to be an open and avowed supporter of secession," and that he had made various extreme statements in sympathy with the southern cause. Bright, soon to be expelled himself, immediately challenged Fessenden; when his right to be sworn in had been challenged, the Senate had decided that "a Senator presenting a *prima facie* case had a right to be sworn in, and that the Senate would, after the administration of the oath, take cognizance of any papers that might be presented questioning his right to a seat." Fessenden replied:

> The times are those when we are compelled to make precedents—not to be bound by mere forms of proceeding, precedents in the body which go only to ordinary transactions, but, if necessary, to make them. . . . I see no reason why this gentleman, under these circumstances, merely on account of a precedent, with such proof, should be permitted to take his seat, and to take a large sum out of our already wasted Treasury, which he would be entitled to, and then take the consequences of these declarations that are made here.[32]

Fessenden's motion precipitated debate as to whether there were indeed precedents for or against the recommended action. On January 10, Bayard gave a closely reasoned address in which he argued that when a senator-elect's credentials were in order and when he unquestionably fulfilled the constitutional requirements as to age, citizenship, and residency, he should be given the oath. The senators had the power under the Constitution to expel a member after a two-thirds vote and here lay the remedy in Stark's case if such was needed. "You are not deciding now a precedent only for the day . . ." he maintained. "In the fierce and close struggles of party that may at any time take place, just think how

---

31. See, however, G. Thomas Edwards, "Benjamin Stark, The U.S. Senate, and 1862 Membership Issues," Pts. 1 and 2, *Oregon Historical Quarterly,* 72 (December 1971), 315-38, and 73 (March 1972), 31-59. The quoted description appears in Pt. 1, p. 317. See also *Hinds' Precedents of the House of Representatives,* 59 Cong., 2 sess., 1:433-40.

32. *CG,* 37 Cong., 2 sess., 183.

many causes there are for which a bare majority of the body might refuse a political opponent the right to come in." He continued, "this idea of loyalty, founded on mere opinion [as contrasted with acts], would be subjecting a man to rejection by a mere majority of the Senate." In the past "the party was always admitted," Bayard argued, "unless the objection went to the authority to appoint or the credentials." He tried to amend Fessenden's motion by striking the word "not" from the phrase "be not administered," but in straight party votes the Republican senators defeated the amendment and referred Stark's credentials to the Judiciary Committee. "What will be the result," confessed Stark, "God only knows. (if he does)."[33]

On February 7, Senator Harris reported a resolution from the committee to the effect "that Benjamin Stark, of Oregon . . . is entitled to take the constitutional oath of office." The senator from New York noted that the committee majority had taken this action "without expressing any opinion as to the effect of the papers before them upon any subsequent proceeding." Trumbull, the chairman of the committee, filed a minority report on the ground that he believed it "the duty of the committee to pass upon the testimony before it."[34]

Debate on the committee resolution began on February 18. A distinguished jurist and lecturer in law both before and during his service in the Senate, Harris noted dispassionately: "I understand the Senate is the judge of the election of a Senator, of the sufficiency and genuineness of the returns furnished, and the evidence of that election; and also of the constitutional qualifications of the individual to hold a seat in the Senate. Beyond that I apprehend the Senate have no power at all." But what was to be Senate policy when an individual who had committed a "crime or infamous act" sought admission? The "appropriate remedy," contended Trumbull in his minority report, "would seem to be to refuse to allow him to qualify . . . not by way of adding to the qualifications imposed by the Constitution, but as a punishment due to his crime or the infamy of his character." The Senate was not "competent," maintained Harris, "to attempt to punish a man for . . . crime or misbehavior antecedent to his election."[35]

Sumner had argued for referral on the grounds of "reason and . . . precedent"; now he developed a full-scale attack upon the committee resolution. He spoke of the custom of flying the flag over the houses of Congress while they were in session; he touched upon the manifold

33. Ibid., 265, 267–69; Benjamin Stark to Samuel F. Butterworth, January 4, 1862. S. L. M. Barlow Papers, Henry E. Huntington Library, San Marino, Cal.

34. *CG*, 37 Cong., 2 sess., 696.

35. Ibid., 861–62.

legislative duties that the fluttering flag symbolized; the question was whether the "body . . . sitting beneath the flag" was "so utterly powerless and abject that, before admitting a person to participation in these trusts, it can make no inquiry with regard to his loyalty," and "consider evidence tending to show that he is false to that flag." If so, and "if its doors must necessarily swing open to any traitor, even, who presents himself with a certificate in his pocket, let the flag drop." Should that be the case, he stormed, the report of the committee was "in simple English . . . 'Free admission to traitors here and no questions asked.'" To allow admission to a man charged with disloyalty, in the hope that he could be expelled later, was voluntarily to surrender "the right of self-defense" which belonged to the Senate as much as to individuals. He repeated the verse once quoted by Daniel Webster:

> I hear a lion in the lobby roar!
> Say Mr. Speaker, shall we shut the door
> And keep him out, or shall we let him in
> And see if we can get him out again?

Loyalty, Sumner maintained, was an additional qualification for the admission of senators under the Constitution, established by the words, "The Senators and Representatives before mentioned . . . shall be bound by oath or affirmation to support this Constitution." That oath, maintained Sumner, was "evidence and pledge of loyalty" constituting a "condition precedent to admission as a member of the Senate."[36] With loyalty established as a qualification, Sumner considered the question of when the Senate should consider evidence concerning it. Since the Senate was exclusive judge of the qualifications of its members under the Constitution, that matter rested at the discretion of the senators. In the Stark case, he was certain that the qualification as to loyalty should be considered prior to the administration of the oath.

Trumbull cited the federal law disbarring judges guilty of accepting bribes from ever holding positions of trust or profit under the government, and the law forbidding members of Congress to hold government office, if shown to have taken a bribe tendered to influence their votes. The state laws to control dueling illustrated the government's right to set additional requirements for office holding beyond constitutional specifications. Other senators speculated upon the chamber's plight should the committee position be accepted and a horse thief, or a Negro slave, or—save the mark—a woman present him- or herself to the Senate with appropriate documents. In the constitutional clause, "but no religious test shall ever be required as a qualification" for public office, Clark

---

36. Ibid., 266, 862. The doggerel traces back to Restoration England; the "lion" then was the Duke of York, the future James II.

found the implication that some additional form of qualification might indeed be added in the case of senators.[37] Others found the letter which Stark wrote to the committee concerning the charges against him to be much less than a complete denial of their substance or an unqualified affirmation of loyalty.

Fessenden's motion in early January, 1862, initiated the Stark case. On February 18, the senator from Maine rose once more to discuss the matter. The language which the gentleman from Oregon had apparently used was very strong—so strong, he had believed in January, that to use it would demonstrate disloyalty if an individual was a senator at the time. He had wanted a committee of the Senate to consider the matter and this was done. He was disposed "to sustain" their position:

> Where the case depends entirely upon language such as this, used at a time anterior and, mostly, long anterior to the period when the party was elected a Senator, it being mere language, mere declarations, the committee might well be justified in the conclusion that it was not sufficient ground to say that he was so disloyal, and remained so disloyal up to the time of his appointment, that we, assuming the office of judges, in view of all the circumstances which we could not know, in view of all the incidents and accompaniments which we could not understand, are therefore justified in taking this high prerogative into our hands, and saying that the person being qualified so far as all the particular constitutional provisions are concerned to become a Senator, must yet be excluded.

Fessenden had concluded, he said, "to vote that the gentleman who presents his credentials be permitted to take the oath, and become a member of the Senate."[38]

Fessenden's speech by no means ended the matter; others spoke at length. Howard discussed the affidavits from Oregon in detail, drawing from them the conclusion that Stark had held "sentiments emphatically disloyal and untrue to the Government." Howe suggested that Sumner heard not a lion in the lobby but a disconsolate Oregon knocking for admission; he emphasized the disservice done by depriving that state of representation, argued that expulsion was the prerogative of two thirds rather than a simple majority, maintained that the oath bore on the future and did not "declare or import" that an individual had always supported the Constitution, and pointed out the difficulties of defining disloyalty. "When," he concluded, "we begin to fortify ourselves against the authority of the States we represent, either the American Senate will cease to exist or the American States will be despoiled of their choicest prerogative—the sacred right of representation." Finally Harris summed up his opinion of the affidavits. He doubted, he said, that some of

37. Ibid., 867.
38. Ibid., 870.

the distinguished lawyers among his colleagues who had detected disloyalty in the affidavits "would convict the most miserable vagrant that
walks our streets of the crime of petty larceny upon these affidavits."[39]
And he noted that Stark planned to request further investigation by the
Judiciary Committee, if he was allowed to take the oath.

The crucial votes in the Stark case occurred on February 27. Sumner
had proposed to reshape the Judiciary resolution into a short statement of facts ending with the pronouncement that Stark was "not entitled to take the constitutional oath of office without a previous investigation into the truth of the charge." Dixon, Doolittle, and H. S. Lane joined
fifteen radicals in support of the amendment. But the remaining moderates, plus the Democrats and Unionists, rallied twenty-six votes in
opposition (I.D.: 79), and Trumbull remarked bitterly: "A majority of
the Senate have . . . decided that no matter though a man comes here
covered all over with infamy, they will not look at a charge of treason or
anything else against him, but they will admit him to his seat, though the
testimony against him comes sworn to by, I believe, some fifty witnesses."
Next came the vote on the committee resolution as amended by Doolittle, who added the words "without prejudice to any further proceedings
in the case."[40] In this roll call, Foot swelled the radical ranks to raise the
total of opponents of the committee resolution to nineteen, but the moderates and their allies from the other side of the chamber again mustered
twenty-six votes and approved the committee resolution (I.D.: 79).

On the following day Stark moved that the papers relating to his
loyalty should be referred to the Judiciary Committee "with instructions
to investigate the charges . . . on all evidence which has been or may be
presented, and with power to send for persons and papers." The motion
provoked an amazing passage of recrimination. Sumner could not "express too strong a regret at the vote of the Senate yesterday," and was
"not astonished that other Senators . . . should seek, perhaps, also to remove from themselves the responsibility of the act." This brought Fessenden to his feet, irate and coldly devastating. The senator from Massachusetts, he said, "made some half dozen harangues to the Senate
upon this case which failed to convince a majority . . . and although he
undertook to say that the Senate would stultify itself by not following his
lead . . . I do not feel that I have stultified myself. . . . What right has he
to assume to lecture me . . . and the majority of the Senate, for the decision they have made?" Dixon described the vote of February 27 as "disastrous." In further discussion of Stark's resolution, Browning locked
horns with Hale, remarking that the gentleman from New Hampshire

39. Ibid., 872–73, 928–29, 974.
40. Ibid., 992–94, 1011.

"often permits his zeal to outrun his knowledge." Hale deplored those who, like Browning, charged senators of different view with "voting in violation of the Constitution of the United States." Trumbull called the admission of Stark a "fearful" and a "dangerous precedent" and Howe charged him with making "home-brewed thunder" and of speaking "somewhat sneeringly." On March 18, the senators approved Stark's resolution, amended so as to refer the matter to a select committee of five; only Bayard, Hale, and Saulsbury dissented.[41]

The select committee on the Stark case consisted of Clark and Howard, radicals who had earlier voted with the minority, Howe (soon replaced by Sherman), Wright, the Indiana Unionist, and Willey of Virginia. The members of the committee agreed that they would not take additional testimony, since most witnesses were in Oregon, unless Stark himself wished to present new evidence. Thus they placed the onus of bringing in additional evidence upon the Oregon senator. Stark appeared before the committee and requested them to prepare specific charges. This they declined to do, and Stark decided to submit only an additional personal statement for their consideration. "Accepting all the statements . . . to be true," he maintained, "and there is merely attributed to me *opinions* which, in the field of politics, might be regarded as heresies, and *expressions* charged upon me which might be characterized as idle, mischievous, and unwise." In his opinion, they were not sufficient grounds for expulsion. Stark did not deny the charge of disloyalty categorically, but he argued that he was as loyal as other senators, that the declarations were false in many particulars, that his "expressions" had been "wickedly and maliciously perverted," and that the allegations misrepresented his "real sentiments," and were "at variance with the whole tenor" of his life.[42]

In their report of April 22, the members of the committee reviewed the charges. Prior to the outbreak of actual hostilities, Stark had said that the Palmetto flag was the standard for him, that, if war broke out, he would sell his property and go south, and that peace could be achieved only if the free states joined the Confederacy under its constitution. He had mocked Lincoln's call for volunteers and toasted Beauregard with "a well-known secessionist" after Bull Run, although Stark suggested that the informant had misunderstood his conventional "my regards to you, sir." Stark had admitted at a committee hearing that he would be willing to see the loyal states absorbed under the Confederate constitution for the sake of peace. Its members emphasized that he had not called witnesses before them, nor presented additional evidence beyond his own

41. Ibid., 1011-12, 1263-64.
42. 37 Cong., 2 sess., United States Senate *Committee Report 38* (Select Committee on Charges of Disloyalty against Benjamin Stark), 3-4.

statement, and in this they argued, "There is not . . . a paragraph, nor a sentence, nor a line such as must spontaneously have burst out from a loyal heart under such an accusation."[43]

The committee members accepted the truth of the major allegations and concluded that Stark was "disloyal to the Government of the United States." Willey dissented from the last of these conclusions. Basing his action upon the committee report, Sumner asked on June 5 for consideration of his resolution that Stark be expelled from the Senate. Only thirteen senators voted in support of Sumner's motion, and of the group only Howe was a moderate (I.D.: 68). On the following day Sumner again presented a motion for consideration and again it failed by a vote of 16 to 21, with Lane and Wright of Indiana joining Howe among the radicals (I.D.: 83). After this vote, consideration of the Stark case ended. A few months later the Oregon legislature, now dominated by former Douglas Democrats and Republicans, replaced Benjamin Stark.

"Stark," wrote a shrewd Oregon observer at the time, "was not satisfied to let well enough alone." But, continued Matthew P. Deady, he "would not have missed the celebrity that the fight has given him for six quiet and obscure years in the Senate. In after years the great case of Sumner and Stark of Oregon, will be referred to as a precedent, and claim a page in the chapter of history." However perceptive this judgment may have been, the Stark case was only one element in the larger problem of insuring that the members of the Senate were indeed loyal Union men. Whether one considered that issue to be genuine, or an imaginary or political matter, depended in part on party allegiance and, among the Republicans, on whether the senator approached the issue as a moderate or a radical. Senator Stark does present a problem to Sumner's biographers. If they explain the Bay State senator's later pursuit of Bayard in 1863 and 1864 as an effort to forestall the return of disloyal southerners at the war's end, is not the argument weakened by evidence that he also played a leading role in questioning the loyalty of the chamber's Democrats and border-state men at a considerably earlier time?[44]

43. Ibid., 8, 11. Writing to Barlow on March 27, Stark asserted that he would never consent to a recognition of the independence of any portion of "the rebel confederacy" (Benjamin Stark to S. L. M. Barlow, March 27, 1862, S. L. M. Barlow Papers, Henry E. Huntington Library, San Marino, Cal.).

44. Matthew P. Deady, Portland, Ore., to James W. Nesmith, June 4, 1862, James W. Nesmith Papers, Oregon Historical Society. 37 Cong., 2 sess., *Committee Report 38*, p. 5. The vote of June 5 is not discussed in Edwards, "Benjamin Stark." According to Browning's biographer, that senator believed that Sumner's opposition to the admission of Stark reflected the desire to consolidate Republican control of the Congress rather than concern about the loyalty of its members: Maurice G. Baxter, *Orville H. Browning: Lincoln's Friend and Critic* (Bloomington: University of Indiana Press, 1957), p. 135. Stark does not appear in the index of David Donald, *Charles Sumner and the Rights of Man* (New York: Knopf,

The senators of the Thirty-seventh Congress again considered the question of loyalty when Trumbull began discussion of H.R. 371 on June 13, 1862. This bill provided an oath to be taken thereafter by every person who was elected or appointed to any office of honor or profit under the government of the United States, "either in the civil, military, or naval departments of the public service." Such individuals were to be required to swear or affirm that, as citizens, they had never voluntarily borne arms against the government of the United States, nor aided individuals doing so, that they had never sought nor held office under an authority hostile to the United States government, that they had never renounced their allegiance to the United States nor given voluntary support to "any pretended government, authority, power, or constitution hostile or inimical thereto." A concluding statement, pledging the office holder to continued support of the government, included the passage, "to the best of my knowledge and ability, I will support and defend the Constitution and Government of the United States, and all laws made in pursuance thereof, against all enemies, foreign and domestic." False swearing was to be deemed perjury, and the guilty party was subject not only to the legal penalties for that offense but was to be deprived of his office and forever barred from holding "office or place" under the United States government.[45]

The oath of office bill did not embroil the senators in protracted debate, but Saulsbury argued that "for many officers, the Constitution prescribes the oath, and says what the oath shall be." Was it proper therefore, he asked, to require such individuals to take an additional oath? Actually the Constitution prescribes the exact wording of the President's oath alone (Art. 2, sec. 7) and merely requires various other categories of public officials, including members of Congress, to make oath or affirmation (Art. 6, sec. 3). Carlile and Davis, however, carried that general line of argument further. Confessing that it was "becoming odious, and . . . stale, and almost disgusting, to make constitutional objections to a proposed law here," Davis maintained:

> The qualifications for a candidate for the Presidency and Vice Presidency are prescribed and established by the Constitution. . . . There are certain qualifications which are necessary to make a man eligible to a seat in the

1970), nor in that of Edward L. Pierce, *Memoir and Letters of Charles Sumner* (Boston: Roberts Brothers, 1893). Pierce does mention that Sumner participated in the debate on the Oregonian's admission (4:79), but without describing his prominent role or his tactics. Charles B. Going, *David Wilmot, Free-Soiler: A Biography of the Great Advocate of the Wilmot Proviso* (New York: Appleton, 1924), pp. 584–94, summarizes the course of expulsion efforts during the second session of the Thirty-seventh Congress.

45. *CG*, 37 Cong., 2 sess., 2693. See Harold M. Hyman, *Era of the Oath: Northern Loyalty Tests During the Civil War and Reconstruction* (Philadelphia: University of Pennsylvania Press, 1954), pp. 21–32, for a general account.

Senate or House of Representatives. These qualifications cannot be enlarged by an act of Congress; they cannot be diminished by an act of Congress. . . . This bill. . . . Lays down as a rule, though a man may have all these qualifications, unless he takes the oath prescribed by this bill he shall not be eligible to his seat and shall not be admitted.[46]

Trumbull proposed to meet Saulsbury's objection by inserting the words, "and for whom the form of the oath of office is not prescribed by the Constitution," thereby eliminating the President from the requirements of the bill. Unsatisfied, Davis promptly moved to alter Trumbull's amendment by adding "except the Vice President and Senators and Representatives in Congress." Although Trumbull maintained that precedent for the bill was provided by federal and state laws forbidding individuals convicted of certain crimes from holding public office thereafter, Davis held that it was an effort by Congress to add to officeholding qualifications "defined and enumerated" in the Constitution. This differed from denial of office as part of the punishment for criminal acts. When Trumbull read the federal law of 1790, disqualifying judges who had accepted a bribe from holding federal office, Carlile noted that the statute was designed "to protect the Government . . . from having its offices filled by men who are unworthy . . . but this is a proposition to administer an oath to one who claims a right to office."[47]

Doolittle declared that he would support the Davis amendment to Trumbull's amendment, arguing that the Vice President and the President ought to take the same oath of office and explaining that he had "some doubts of the propriety of the two Houses of Congress prescribing what each House shall do with its own members, when the Constitution says expressly that each House shall judge for itself." The federal law of 1790 was inadequate as precedent. It contained, Doolittle said, "these six very important words, 'and he shall be thereof convicted.'"[48] Browning, Cowan, Dixon, Doolittle, Harris, and Sherman joined the Democrats and border-state senators in support of the Davis amendment, as did one radical, Wilson of Massachusetts (I.D.: 53).

Trumbull accepted minor amendments from Henderson relating to the phrasing of the oath of office bill, but he opposed Henderson's recommendation that the phrase "levied war" be inserted in place of "borne arms." Henderson explained, "I suppose the object of the bill is to reach those parties who have been guilty of treason. The Senator will see that an individual may very easily be guilty of the offense of treason without having actually borne arms." Trumbull maintained that the bill's wording in this respect was more easily understood than Henderson's

46. *CG*, 37 Cong., 2 sess., 2693–94.
47. Ibid., 2861–62, 2872.
48. Ibid., 2871–72.

alternative, and that definition of treason was not at issue, but eight moderates supported the Missouri senator's wording in contrast to one radical. However, the radicals found Davis in their camp on this division, plus a few moderates, and the amendment was lost, 19 to 19 (I.D.: 60). In offering this particular amendment, Henderson was of course trying to insert the phrase found in Article 3, section 3 of the Constitution. And when he tried to insert the constitutional phrasing "not during said period adhered to their enemies, giving them aid and comfort," in place of "voluntarily given no aid, countenance, counsel, or encouragement to persons engaged in armed hostility thereto" as found in the bill, Collamer noted that the courts had ruled that the terminology of the Constitution applied to "public enemies of the nation" and would not reach "the case of a man engaged in this rebellion."[49]

The moderates were not able to savor their victory in exempting congressmen from the oath for long. The members of the House disagreed as to all of the Senate amendments and the bill passed into the hands of a committee of conference in which the senators were Lyman Trumbull, Preston King, and Garrett Davis—two radicals and a Kentucky Unionist. With Davis dissenting, the committee recommended that the House of Representatives accept all the Senate amendments except the Davis amendment, and that the Senate should accept the substance of Trumbull's original corrective amendment, "excepting the President of the United States."

Howe and Foster greeted the report with a bitter attack on the procedures for dealing with recommendations from conference committees. It was contrary to the precedents of parliamentary procedure, Howe argued, to force the members of a chamber to vote simply yea or nay on conference reports; he maintained rather that each constituent part of the agreement between the House and Senate managers should be voted upon. Although incensed by this particular instance, he felt that the effect of the system on the internal revenue bill was even more regrettable. Foster argued that the organization of the conference committee on the oath of office bill was "not in accordance with parliamentary law" because "persons should be appointed upon the committee who represent the views of their respective Houses." Trumbull, he pointed out, had not agreed with the vote of the Senate. Trumbull blandly noted that Howe and Foster were apparently "very sore" concerning past events and that it would be very difficult to find managers who had voted for all the amendments on any particular bill.[50] When the president *pro tempore*

49. Ibid., 2872–73.
50. Ibid., 3013–14.

called for the vote on the committee report, party discipline ruled and the Republicans voted solidly for it.

As we have seen, Trumbull and Sumner forced newly elected senators to subscribe to the "ironclad" test oath in March, 1863, and, in the face of Bayard's recalcitrance, Sumner brought his motion making such action mandatory to a vote in late January, 1864. Republican strategy apparently then called for objection should Bayard try to vote and for a request that he take the oath. Refusal would bring a resolution of expulsion but Bayard took the oath and then resigned. In the vote on Sumner's resolution, four Republicans stood with the minority: the moderates Doolittle, Howe, Cowan, and Harris.[51]

As the late spring of 1862 passed, some radicals came to believe that Congress should ignore the customary time of dissolution and sit on, perfecting unfinished legislation, and keeping the Executive and the army under surveillance. Various moderates refused to admit that such self-sacrifice was either wise or necessary, and this disagreement over legislative strategy and practice was revealed in the voting of the senators. In mid-June, Senator Latham proposed that the Senate meet thereafter at 11 A.M. rather than at noon. This practice was commonly approved during the concluding weeks of a long session. By that time the committees had wound up most of the legislative business which they conducted during the morning hours, and the additional hour of debate assisted the legislators in completing the business on the floor. On June 16, Hale moved that Latham's resolution "fixing the daily hour of meeting" be taken up. Remarking that he was "quite anxious that we should bring the session to a close within a reasonable time," Fessenden endorsed the action. In the vote, eight radicals opposed the motion and Browning joined them (I.D.: 46). As with most divisive issues, there was disagreement, even within the "faction" most opposed to adjournment. Hale later confided to his wife that there were "a number of wretches in the Senate who are opposing not only our adjournment, but even the considering of a day for adjournment."[52]

When the question became that of agreeing to the resolution, "That on and after the 19th of June, the daily hour of meeting of the Senate

51. New York *Daily Tribune,* December 15, 1863, January 26, 1864; Washington *National Intelligencer,* January 27, 1864; Chicago *Tribune,* January 29, 1864.

52. *CG,* 37 Cong., 2 sess., 2732. John P. Hale to Lucy Hale, June 18, 1862, John P. Hale Papers, New Hampshire Historical Society, Concord, N.H. See Pierce, *Sumner,* 4:86, n. 5, for comment on that senator's reluctance to adjourn. The New York *Herald,* July 3, 1862, noted, "The Senate until now has been strongly opposed to an early adjournment," but mentioned that sickness and absences had made it difficult to make a quorum. The paper did not distinguish differing attitudes on adjournment among radicals and moderates.

shall be eleven o'clock, a.m., instead of twelve m," Trumbull derided the proposal:

> Now it is proposed to commence the daily sittings an hour earlier, with a view of hurrying the session to a close. I expected this. I think it is the policy of some persons to hurry through the business of appropriation and revenue bills and get the Congress of the United States out of the way. . . . I am opposed to an adjournment of the Congress of the United States in the present condition of the country. I believe it due to our constituents, due to the people of this nation, that we should remain here while the country is in its present condition, unless it is the intention of Congress to abdicate its powers, to give up its authority, to do nothing more than to raise men and money, and not attempt to indicate the policy of the Government, but to leave the Executive of the nation, without any expression of opinion, to assume responsibility, and to compel him to assume responsibilities because Congress has refused to discharge its duty. . . . We ought to stay here until we can see a different condition of things in the country.

Trumbull referred specifically to the need for a "law to regulate the condition of things in the South as our armies march South" and briefly reiterated his position that the "war power" rested in Congress "and nowhere else."[53]

Fessenden argued that the senators owed it to themselves to take some respite. Nor could he see what Congress could accomplish by staying in session indefinitely. The bill to establish provisional governments in the South, to which Trumbull referred, had been in the hands of Trumbull's Judiciary Committee since mid-February and had not been reported until June 11, being but a bill of seven sections. The senator from Maine thought the circumstances "remarkable." He agreed with Trumbull's position concerning the powers of Congress, but if much remained to be done, all the more reason for meeting at 11 A.M. There was no reason to remain in session longer than necessary to attend to any essential business. "We have a perfect right," he said, "after the severe labors to which we have all been subjected . . . to do up as we can, and as best we can, the essential business of Congress, and go home to our families for a time, and not stay here to watch the President, or to watch the Army, unless we see some particular occasion for it."[54] Senators pointed out that members of the House of Representatives were anxious to adjourn around July 1, and there was discussion of the problem of changing breakfast arrangements, of the need to spend mornings in the departments, and of the number of times that Sumner's committee met each week (sometimes as often as twice), of essential legislation still unconsidered, of the unproductiveness of late sessions and the reluctance of some senators to endure them, and of the opportunity to demonstrate senatorial patrio-

53. *CG*, 37 Cong., 2 sess., 2732–33.
54. Ibid., 2733–34.

tism by meeting not at 11 A.M. or noon, but at 9 A.M., as was the practice in some state legislatures.

Perhaps with several of the horrible grimaces for which he was famous, Chandler expressed his desire to make a "prolonged speech" on this "very interesting" and "important subject," but contented himself instead with moving adjournment.[55] Eight radicals were joined by Davis and Lane of Indiana in sustaining the motion (I.D.: 42). After Trumbull had accused Fessenden of choking the Senate with appropriation bills so that there was no opportunity to discuss the southern governments bill, he described the problems faced in representing constituents in time of war; then the question came to a vote (I.D.: 42). Browning and Davis joined eight radicals in opposition to Latham's motion. The radical phalanx was very much the same in all three votes. Harlan, Howard, King, Sumner, Trumbull, and Wilmot voted against the Latham motion in all three divisions; Chandler and Pomeroy each joined them in two divisions, and Morrill and Grimes both voted against the initial effort to bring up the resolution.

The reluctance of a majority of radicals to close the business of the session was also reflected in votes of Friday, June 20, and Thursday, July 3. On the first occasion Grimes moved that adjournment should be to the following Monday, and in the second instance he moved to adjourn through July 4. In both cases a majority of moderates and non-Republicans in the chamber rejected the motion, but ten and eleven radicals supported the suggestion that the Senate suspend work temporarily (I.D.: 54; 63). As in the earlier debate on the hour of meeting, Clark, Hale, and Lane of Kansas proved to be the radicals who desired to push the Senate's business to a rapid conclusion.

Following the practice which was usual in the last days of a session, Sherman on July 11 asked consideration of the resolution that the sixteenth and seventeenth joint rules be suspended with the concurrence of the House of Representatives. These provided that:

> 16. No bill that shall have passed one House shall be sent for concurrence to the other on either of the last three days of the session.

> 17. No bill or resolution that shall have passed the House of Representatives and the Senate shall be presented to the President of the United States for his approbation on the last day of the session.[56]

On the next day Sherman asked that the resolution be considered, noting that it must be disposed of without debate under the twenty-sixth rule of the Senate. Despite such constraints, King, Sumner, and Trum-

55. Ibid., 2736.
56. Ibid., 3271–72.

bull all managed to record brief protests before submitting to the roll call. All Republican moderates recorded in the division supported Sherman's motion; eight radicals opposed it (I.D.: 53).

On July 12 also, Sherman reported a resolution from the Committee on Finance setting July 14 as the day of adjournment, with the committee's amendment that it read July 16. King, Sumner, Trumbull, Wade, and Wilkinson voted against the recommendation, as did Willey, fearful that the West Virginia bill might be lost. They were overwhelmed by the votes of thirty-three other senators. Fessenden spoke briefly in behalf of the amended resolution, stressing the difficulty of maintaining a quorum in either chamber if the Senate failed to accept an early adjournment; Clark and Sherman later supported him. Trumbull disavowed interest in having Congress sit permanently but discounted the quorum problem. Perhaps as many as fifty bills remained on the calendar, some of importance, especially the bill to establish provisional governments in the South. Wade and Willey made special pleas for the West Virginia bill. Sumner, King, and Grimes all opposed the resolution, and the senator from Massachusetts listed important matters which might occupy the Senate for weeks to come. Three major bills deserved careful and deliberate discussion. These were the West Virginia admission bill, the bill to establish provisional governments, and the army bill, so important because it included a revolutionary system of conscription. In addition, there was much executive business and the "whole Calendar" demanded attention. "Yet, sir," he declaimed: "Senators propose to go home; Senators are weary; Senators would like to find a retreat, away from these legislative cares. I can enter into that feeling. Sir, I should be glad to be at home. I suppose the gallant soldiers on the James river, on the Chickahominy, would also be glad to be at home. They are not excused; they have not a furlough; and yet we Senators propose to take our furlough."[57] This sarcastic homily aroused Clark, who pointed out that the President had requested him and others to aid in the task of recruitment. He invited Sumner to accompany him to the banks of the James, where they could both bare their bosoms to the bullets of the enemy. But Grimes returned to the subject of business still pending. None knew what the chief executive's reaction to the confiscation bill might be; his action might in turn require additional response from Congress. He could think of other measures which needed the attention of the Senate. He was not impressed by the argument that the House of Representatives planned to adjourn. The last-minute oratory was futile. Twenty-nine senators defeated the nine radicals and Willey, who opposed adjournment on the 16th (I.D.: 56).

57. Ibid., 3286.

A less protracted disagreement over final adjournment occurred at the end of the first session of the Thirty-eighth Congress, producing five roll calls that reflected substantial differences between radicals and moderates, as well as others that fell somewhat short of our disagreement threshold, in a marathon sitting of the Senate that ran deep into the morning hours of Sunday, July 3, 1864. Some Republicans, particularly moderates, as well as the senators of the opposition, wished to approve a joint resolution of adjournment received earlier from the House, as amended to set final adjournment at noon on July 4. But other Republicans, mainly radicals, opposed fixing a specific time of adjournment before the Senate approved H.R. 120, imposing a special income tax, that was expected shortly from the House and which most Republicans believed was essential if the cost of bounties authorized in the Enrollment Act passed on July 2 was to be met.

Suspicion abounded on both sides of the argument. Senators advocating adjournment apparently feared that their opponents would continue to oppose final adjournment whether the tax measure from the House was approved or not; they wished to approve the adjournment resolution before the revenue bill arrived. But the recalcitrants suspected—so they said—that if the time of adjournment was fixed, opposition senators or renegade Republicans might refuse to concur in the unanimous consent necessary to carry a bill through successive readings in less than the three days prescribed in the normal procedures of the Senate. Some went further, opposing final adjournment *per se*. To some degree, the battle lines followed the patterns visible at the end of the second session of the Thirty-seventh Congress, but now Trumbull argued vigorously for adjournment. The major spokesmen of business as usual were Chandler, Sumner, and Conness. Said Chandler:

> Our armies are facing the enemy; our armies are prepared, in my judgment, to crush that enemy, to grind him to powder. If they fail, what then? If they fail the Congress of the United States should be in session, and, if necessary to put down this accursed rebellion, order out the number of men required to do it, and, if it be necessary, order a levy *en masse* to accomplish it, and let Senators and Representatives lead the van; and I am prepared to shoulder my musket and march into the front ranks.[58]

Sumner argued that the supplementary revenue bill of the House of Representatives was inadequate, and he wished the Senate to amend it and force the House to meet the real needs of the country. Iowa's eminent Methodist, Harlan, complained that there was no need to sit on the Sabbath; they could not expect God's blessing on measures approved on His Holy Day. But motions to adjourn without setting the time of final

58. *CG*, 38 Cong., 1 sess., 3508.

adjournment prior to the arrival of the tax bill from the other House were rejected.

After H.R. 120 arrived, the senators voted on Wilson's amendment to the motion for final adjournment, changing the time to noon on Tuesday, July 5, rather than on Monday, as in the original motion. Nine radicals and only one moderate voted for the amendment. Five radicals and six moderates joined the opposition to defeat the motion, 22 nays and 11 yeas (I.D.: 50). Chandler then called for a simple adjournment and failed, finding one supporter less than had Wilson (I.D.: 71). Powell assured the chamber that he and his colleagues of the opposition would not defeat the tax bill by refusing to allow suspension of the rules, although they planned to vote against it. After this, the senators voted on James Lane's amendment to the House resolution, specifying July 4 at 12 noon as the time of final adjournment, and approved it by a vote of 22 to 9 (I.D.: 44). Next, Sumner tried to carry adjournment but could only muster support from Chandler, Conness, Harlan, McDougall, Morgan, and Wilkinson (I.D.: 50). After considerable discussion in which Sherman defended the Monday adjournment on the grounds that the House would not provide any better revenue measure than H.R. 120, the senators finally voted on the adjournment resolution and passed it by a vote of 20 to 11 (I.D.: 53). Although this series of votes does appear to reveal substantial disagreement between radicals and moderates, only nineteen Republicans were voting in a thin chamber and only seven of them were moderates.

After the first reading of H.R. 120, "imposing a special income duty," Chandler vindictively objected to the second reading as he had threatened to do. Pomeroy introduced a resolution calling for amendment of the twenty-sixth rule of the Senate to allow several readings of bills or joint resolutions on the final day of the session and Chandler, fortified by liquid lightning, objected to consideration of that. After a little more business, the Senate adjourned until Monday morning; the time was ten minutes past three o'clock on Sunday morning, July 3. The skirmish over final adjournment had been much less prolonged than in the Thirty-seventh Congress, but so marked by sarcasm, impugned motives, outraged sensitivities, senatorial stubbornness, and incongruous piety that Sherman was very restrained when he described it as an "extraordinary . . . scene," and Sumner, as a leading participant, perhaps missed the full implications of his charge that Sunday morning was turned into Walpurgis night.[59]

In Chapter 8 the reader has examined disagreement among the Re-

---

59. Ibid., 3512–3511.

publican senators relating to the court system, to various concerns of interest to southerners of the border region and, finally, to matters of self-governance within the Senate. Only in discussion of the suspension of habeas corpus and executive indemnity were major constitutional issues revealed in Republican disagreement on those matters relating to the courts discussed in this chapter. And in that instance discord actually centered on the mechanics of jail delivery. Other differences relating to the courts seemed to reflect party and punitive considerations and differences of opinion concerning the wisdom of surrendering congressional prerogatives to the Court of Claims. In matters relating to the loyal southern-border community or its members, the senators appeared to differ on matters of equity and political expediency. Problems of self-governance opened up interesting constitutional dimensions of debate in the senators' discussion of the Stark case and the oath of office. Their adjournment problems focused on the question of the relative degree of direct control or surveillance that the Congress should exercise over the executive branch and its concerns.

# 9

# Designs and Perspectives

The preceding chapters have sketched in detail some of the legislative positions of radicals and moderates. When selecting issues for discussion I did not use intuition, but looked rather to the range of attitudes revealed by scaling analysis and examined roll calls that showed substantial disagreement between the two ends of the Republican voting spectrum, as it was revealed in those on southern issues and related matters. In trying to explain the reasons for the differences in voting behavior among the Republican senators, I have reviewed their statements of explanation and justification in the columns of the *Congressional Globe*.

No one can read this source at length and argue that the senators took their tasks and obligations lightly. Obviously, too, they attached considerable importance to showing themselves to be consistent in their approach to specific issues, and scaling analysis demonstrates that in great degree they did demonstrate this characteristic. They were aware that their votes and utterances appeared in dozens of papers across the land and many of them were at great pains to explain their positions in detail, not only, we can assume, to influence their colleagues but more important, perhaps, to keep the approval of their constituents. In making such statements, some senators perhaps fooled themselves or tried to mislead their fellow senators or the voters. But it was a period of frenetic politics in which constituency interest in national affairs was at fever pitch, when evidence of erratic behavior or opportunism was publicized immediately, and when playing fast and loose with the truth or misrepresenting one's position was hardly worth the risk. Although the political tides of the 1850s and early 1860s bore some unusual flotsam into the chambers of the Congress, most senators of the Civil War congresses were extremely able politicians who well understood the political demands and dangers of the time. While maintaining a certain skepticism, we can therefore put some dependence on analysis of the substantive import and the rhetorical content of those roll calls that reveal disagreement on war matters within the Republican senatorial contingent.

On the basis of the materials in the last several chapters, let us consider some of the patterns of difference in the behavior of radicals and moderates and speculate upon their meaning, remembering of course that motivation and the justifications of position are apt to be highly complex and puzzling phenomena. We are dealing, let us remember also, with tendencies and not certainties; the various pieces will not bear the same relation to others in our various puzzles each time we try to assemble one but if they tend to do so, we shall have learned much.

### A Punitive Temper

James G. Randall was perhaps the most eminent historian of the Civil War to emerge between 1930 and 1960, and to him the Republican radicals were the "vindictives," men who sought not only victory but revenge against southerners who defended slavery, against generals who seemed to condone or sustain the institution or who lacked vigor, and, at times, even against Lincoln, whose judicious temper and political pragmatism seemed to threaten or defer the attainment of radical objectives.[1] Randall wrote in a different era; more recent historians have found him unduly critical of the radicals and too tolerant of the willingness to accept the fact of slavery and arguments positing the inferiority of blacks that moderate and conservative Republicans displayed. But although "vindictive" is perhaps too harsh a word, there is evidence in the voting alignments and the supporting debates that suggests a willingness—even a desire—among the radicals to subject loyal southerners to special disabilities. This punitive temper was most evident in legislative proceedings bearing on matters of interest to the residents of the loyal slave areas. Conversely, it was the moderates who displayed the greater willingness to provide sympathetic support for the people of the border regions.

During the second session of the Thirty-seventh Congress, Senate radicals supported the idea of taxing slaves at relatively high levels, a policy designed in part "to gratify ... resentment ... against ... persons ... who are not here," thought one moderate, and one which, incidentally, struck particularly at the loyal slaveholders.[2] Radicals, moderates believed, manifested similar hostility toward this class of citizens when they

---

1. James G. Randall, *The Civil War and Reconstruction* (Boston: Heath, 1937), pp. 362, 957; *Lincoln the President, 2: Bull Run to Gettysburg* (New York: Dodd, Mead, 1945), pp. 204–5; and "Radical Republicans," in James T. Adams, ed., *Dictionary of American History* (New York: Scribner, 1940), 4: 395.
2. *CG*, 37 Cong., 2 sess., 2403.

tried, under plea of military necessity and the desirability of human-itarian reform, to use the Militia Act of 1862 to free the slaves of loyal masters in the border states. The ultras were arrayed once more in al-most solid phalanx in an effort to force immediate rather than gradual emancipation upon the West Virginians. As for the southerners who lived beneath the Stars and Bars, the radicals were reluctant to distin-guish between the notorious secessionist and his "humble dupe" when shaping the Confiscation Act during the same session. Radicals, in other words, desired in these matters to extract financial sacrifices from loyal slaveholders beyond what a majority of their colleagues believed was fair and to refuse to recognize different degrees of responsibility in precipitating and waging the war.

When the Missouri Emancipation Act came before the Senate during the third session of the Thirty-seventh Congress, the radicals were less generous, for the most part, in proferring financial assistance to reim-burse slaveholders in that state for their slaves and more concerned with insuring that the emancipation process was carried through rapidly than were the moderates. Although the federal government had approved the mustering of state forces in Missouri and Maryland at an earlier time, the radicals opposed efforts to provide a volunteer state force in Kentucky to a relatively greater degree than did moderates during the early months of 1863. We exaggerate, perhaps, if we consider this course of action to be punitive, but certainly the incident did reveal a greater willingness among moderates to trust the Kentucky Unionists and to meet their needs, than was the case among the radicals.

At pettier levels during the same session, radicals proposed to remove jurisdiction of the Washington jail from the hands of Ward H. Lamon, who, in their eyes, had allowed that institution to serve the interests of the slaveholders of the District and who had been uncooperative with radical members of the Senate Committee on the District of Columbia. A few moderates apparently believed that the proposal to codify the laws of the District also carried punitive overtones, although this interpreta-tion of the vote is conjectural. Some local residents regarded senatorial action on water taxes in the District and the cost of illuminating gas provided to the federal government by a local supplier to be unfriendly revisions of existing arrangements, and radicals favored the changes to a greater extent than did the moderates. And we find the latter more sympathetic to the pleas of a union officer and former resident of Texas who asked Congress to appropriate funds to extinguish a legitimate claim, owed by the government to a Confederate sympathizer, that he had acquired during the secession process as a means of converting his property into movable assets, before fleeing to Union territory.

Recalling the aggressively offensive tactics of slave-state senators during the 1850s, Trumbull suggested that Sumner's war upon the rail carriers of the District might also be designed to be "offensive to somebody."[3] Undoubtedly, he viewed Sumner's efforts to give the vote to Washington blacks during the Thirty-eighth Congress in much the same light. In 1864, Grimes discoursed upon the corrupting influence that wicked Newport was exercising upon impressionable naval cadets and the senators representing the state which carries the word "Hope" upon its seal quite obviously yearned for another permanent naval installation. But the voting on the Iowa senator's motion to return the Naval Academy to Annapolis apparently also identified radicals who were reluctant to forgive another state whose residents had been so recusant as to divide their loyalties. In moderate eyes also, the framers of the Wade-Davis bill were so intent on wringing obeisance from residents of the rebellious states that they ignored the civil rights of loyal minorities; and the controversy over counting Louisiana's electoral votes and seating the congressional delegation from that presumptive state during the second session of the Thirty-eighth Congress was in part a logical extension of disagreement on such matters.

## Racial Prejudice

If the zeal displayed by the radicals in prosecuting the war on slavery seemed in the eyes of moderates to extend at times to the persecution of loyal slaveholders, the voting of the moderates and their attendant objections, doubts, and hesitancies suggest that these senators were more deeply committed to the racist prejudices that were so prevalent in the northern states during these years than were their radical colleagues. This is not to say that all, or even most, of the radicals envisioned a fully integrated society in which blacks would encounter no more, and no less, in the way of personal prejudice and institutional restraints than did whites and would display a capacity to support themselves and participate in the institutions of American society in every way equal to that found among white Americans. But even though some of them seem to have said little or nothing on the subject, and others went no further than to maintain that, given their full civil liberties, blacks would get by, the radicals, in general and particularly in their voting, displayed more confidence in the intellectual and civil potential of the Negroes than did the moderates, and more concern about insuring their civil liberties.

In voting during the second session of the Thirty-seventh Senate, the moderates particularly betrayed their biases by supporting the colonization amendment to the Emancipation Act for the District of Columbia. And the colonization clause in the Confiscation Act of 1862 was also a

3. *CG*, 38 Cong., 1 sess., 3132.

concession to such sentiment within the Republican party. The moderates opposed Sumner's efforts to open the door to black witnesses in judicial proceedings under that statute. During the third session of the Thirty-seventh Congress some moderates formally opposed bestowing commissions upon black soldiers. Although other considerations were perhaps also involved, notably Sumner's legislative style, the proposals of the senator from Massachusetts to insure the rights of blacks to participate as witnesses in all legal processes, to ride freely upon the rail carriers within the District of Columbia, and to vote in Washington elections may have tapped a strain of racial prejudice in the broader spectrum of radical-moderate disagreement, similar to that revealed by the colonization proposals of 1862. We may view the moderate opposition to Wilkinson's attempt to strike the word "white" from the suffrage provision of the Montana Organic Act in the same light, although other considerations were involved as well.

Opposition to allowing eastern state recruiters unrestricted access to the conquered South seems to have flowed in part from anti-Negro prejudices as well as from sectional jealousies. True, Brown of Missouri maintained that western states would not "stand to" an arrangement in which eastern states used their capital to enlist Negroes while "the people of the West" sent their sons and brothers to fight and die in the field.[4] The disagreement coefficients reveal a sectional dimension in the voting on state recruitment of southern blacks, but the radical-moderate coefficients were stronger than the East-West coefficients and apparently, therefore, the racial views of Republicans were also important in shaping the voting on this issue, more so perhaps than were sectional jealousies.

The moderates, of course, did not blatantly proclaim their racial prejudice. Republicans, for example, who opposed the Sumner and Wilkinson proposals concerning black civil rights challenged these amendments on the grounds that they needlessly exacerbated feelings. So, in assessing the evidence in such matters in the Thirty-eighth Congress, must the reader view the moderates as standing righteously arrayed against what they considered to be vain self-advertising and posturing on the part of Sumner or other radicals? Or were they men who were reluctant to proclaim, or enforce, the rights of blacks to equal treatment under the law, because of ingrained prejudices or their unsuppressed convictions that the Negroes did not deserve equal treatment because they were indeed inferior to whites? Actually, there is no reason for us to accept either of these explanations at the expense of the other. No doubt both considerations were involved in the thought and behavior of the moderates, as well as other motivations.

4. Ibid., 3382.

### National Power and State Rights

Taking another point of departure, we may perhaps argue that differences between radical and moderate appear in their attitudes on the relations between the federal and state governments. The radical wished to exercise the federal powers vigorously and found excuses in the crises of war for policy or action that in the minds of moderates needlessly disregarded the domestic prerogatives of the states. As we have seen, the moderates were more solicitous of the rights of the states and of the needs or wishes of loyal elements within the border region. During 1862 they opposed the efforts of the radicals to free the relatives of black soldiers in the loyal South and voiced similar reservations when the same subject came before the Senate two years later. And a number of moderates believed it proper in 1862 that state rules of evidence should be applied in certain categories of cases in the appropriate federal courts, thereby implicitly placing an additional restriction on blacks in those states where the codes denied them the witness stand; Sumner and a phalanx of radicals disagreed. Moderates believed that the federal government was obligated to maintain a fugitive slave law until the peculiar institution was eliminated by constitutional amendment; radicals, on the other hand, tended to support Sumner in his efforts to wipe all such legislation from the federal statute books.

Obviously, the agencies of the federal government could move more freely in the processes of reconstruction if it was agreed that the southern states were indeed out of the Union in all respects. Some legislation reflected the judgment of many senators that this was not in fact the case. But the moderate Doolittle argued that the radicals accepted that assumption in approaching reconstruction and branded it "one huge, infernal, constitutional lie." State suicide or, more appropriately, severance theory was emphasized in Sumner's pronouncements, and Howard developed the position that southern states were out of the Union *de facto* at some length. The guarantee clause, however, held out greater promise of providing justification for elaborate reconstruction procedures specified by the Congress that would be acceptable to some moderates as well as to radicals, than did theories stemming from the premise that the act of secession had destroyed the relationships between the federal government and the southern states as these had prevailed in 1860. Such moderate men as Harris and Collamer embraced the guarantee clause, and the latter's statement in 1864 was particularly elaborate and lucid. But other moderates remained willing that the rebellious states should return to "their old orbits" with a minimum of institutional readjustment.[5]

5. *CG*, 38 Cong., 2 sess., 578, 535.

The interrelations between the New Jersey railroad bill and the Louisiana seating resolution are highly suggestive. The advocates of the first measure proposed a forthright enunciation of federal power in a legal area where the impact of previous judicial action on state powers was unclear. In the latter case much the same group of Republicans rationalized an action—which, in terms of accepted precedents concerning the seating of members, the Senate had every right to take—on the grounds of national and congressional powers that profoundly shocked moderate Republicans, who cherished different views of the balance between state and federal powers.

In discussing state bank notes, Sumner fulminated, "The rebellion began in State rights, and all the opposition to those measures which have been conceived in order to crush it has been made in the name of State rights. It is hard that we should be obliged to meet State rights not only on the battle-field, but also in this Chamber." In full cry against the transportation monopoly in New Jersey, he thundered, "Sir, the Senator flings into one scale the pretensions of State rights. Into the other scale I fling the Union itself."[6] Historians may argue as to whether Sumnerian rhetoric should sell at a discount in their market place, but surely he identified a basic element in the disagreement between radical and moderate Republicans.

### Separation of Federal Powers

If radical and nonradical differed in their approach to state and federal powers, they differed as well in their attitude toward the other branches of the federal government. Thus, in 1862 the radicals favored a confiscation bill which would have denied discretionary powers to the President and denied full judicial process to southerners touched by the provisions of the legislation. When moderate Republicans, Democrats, and border-state senators demanded adjournment in 1862, more radical Republicans were reluctant to set the date, and various radicals were of similar mind in the summer of 1864. Although they did not put the matter so bluntly, preferring to emphasize unfinished business, they were clearly unwilling to suspend active supervision of the President and cabinet for any longer period than was absolutely necessary. When Sumner tried to raise the rank of the minister resident in Brussels, the eminent Boston intellectual, John G. Palfrey, to that of a minister plenipotentiary, Fessenden balked. Such action, he argued, departed from the general practice of maintaining ministers of the latter rank only at

6. *CG*, 38 Cong., 1 sess., 1893; 2 sess., 792; also quoted in David F. Trask, "Charles Sumner and the New Jersey Railroad Monopoly during the Civil War," *Proceedings of the New Jersey Historical Society*, 75 (October 1957), 272, citing Charles Sumner, *Works* (Boston: Lee & Shepard, 1875), 9: 257.

the courts of first-class powers and pointed out that it was the President's prerogative, not that of the Congress, to regulate the rank of American diplomats.

When the President and western governors agreed in 1864 upon the expediency of raising a force of volunteers in the West for one-hundred day service, Hale snorted that to approve the bill authorizing the force was to prove that Congress, in the words of the younger Pitt, remained "stupid in spite of experience," and radical senators led the effort to eviscerate it by amendment. The Wade-Davis bill, a radical measure, clearly represented an effort to replace announced executive policy with a harsher program and was, therefore, in a sense, a disavowal of the President. Although B. Gratz Brown, in effect, defended his amendment which almost displaced the Wade-Davis bill as a stopgap measure, a holding action, Sumner described it as a measure that would bring "all the activities tending toward reconstruction . . . under the rule of Congress."[7] And Sumner himself proposed to add to it a clause that would have written the Emancipation Proclamation into the federal statutes. In the debate on counting Louisiana's electoral votes, Wade digressed into a wrathful denunciation of Lincoln's pretensions to manage the reconstruction process. But in developing the moderate position in this debate, Doolittle argued that congressional action in this instance would constitute an invasion of executive prerogatives, more precisely, in this instance, the obligation of the Vice President to open the state certificates, although the senator from Wisconsin specifically admitted the right of the members of the two houses to regulate their own membership.

In general, the radicals viewed the judiciary in its various branches with less respect than did the moderates, and when Sherman, in early 1863, implicitly criticized the policy of arbitrary arrests and use of military tribunals, by proposing that individuals arrested as threats to the war effort must be charged within a prescribed period of time in areas where the federal courts were in normal operation, a preponderance of moderates rallied in support of his amendment. Some two years later the senators locked horns once more on the subject of military courts when the moderates balked at allowing offending civilian recruiters to be tried in military tribunals. And both in debating matters relating to the Court of Claims and in handling specific claims cases, radical senators usually showed themselves more reluctant to surrender their right to review claims against the United States government than were the moderates. It was the radicals, too, as we have already seen, who were the more eager to modify the court system in the District of Columbia.

7. *CG*, 38 Cong., 1 sess., 2022, 3461.

*Congressional Precedents and Procedures*

The evidence suggests a tendency among radicals to be impatient of procedural and administrative precedents in the Senate. Thus, they, in general, opposed seating Benjamin Stark before charges of disloyalty were weighed during the Thirty-seventh Congress. More moderate Republicans argued that this was a breach of precedent, as well as an act of dubious constitutionality, an act which deprived a loyal state of representation, and one which might delay the seating of deserving candidates in the future on trivial grounds. No doubt moderates viewed the oath of office bill in somewhat the same light, and radical proposals to prolong the session shocked and annoyed them at the conclusion of the long sessions of both the Thirty-seventh and the Thirty-eighth Congresses.

The appeal of moderates to precedent and established procedures was strongly evident in 1864. When radicals supported Sumner's efforts to defend the black man's right to testify in court proceedings by attaching an amendment to the civil appropriations bill, their moderate colleagues maintained that the Massachusetts senator was encumbering an appropriations bill with extraneous matter. They took a similar position when he tried to smuggle a rider aboard this "through train," repealing the clauses of the slave exclusion law of 1807, which regulated the coastal slave trade. They reiterated their objections when Sumner tried to stipulate that witnesses should not be barred from United States courts on account of color in a section of the civil appropriations bill providing funds for the apprehension of counterfeiters. Moderates reacted in much the same way when he tried to provide retroactive pay for Massachusetts black regiments in a general bill, equalizing the pay and perquisites of white and black soldiers. When Sumner and his fellow managers brought the freedmen's bureau bill back from the meeting of a committee of conference in a form that included matter absent in the two bills sent to the committee for reconciliation, moderates protested that they had abrogated the rules governing the actions of conference committees. Yet the moderates occasionally jettisoned precedent also, as when several proposed in exasperation to ignore senatorial courtesy and force a vote on the emancipation amendment despite Wilson's appeal that his colleague Sumner wished to speak on that subject on the morrow.

Sumner dominates the narrative of the last several paragraphs. Have we perhaps little more here than discussion of his efforts to bend his fellow senators to his imperious will? Some may prefer this interpretation, and I shall say more about individual cue-givers in the final section of this chapter. But for the moment we must remember that our analysis is based not on the statements or idiosyncratic behavior of any one senator but rather upon voting patterns. If Sumner fiddled, other radicals certainly danced; although his actions and utterances may have crystallized sentiment or shaped the structure of the debate and roll calls, colleagues voted with him, or against him, in ways that were surely neither random nor capricious. But do not conservatives usually appeal to precedent and innovators always argue that the circumstances are extraordinary? True enough, to some degree, and surely the tactic in this instance overlay other concerns of the moderates. But the appeal to precedent was part of the moderate style, and the forms that these appeals took are part of the genuine contrast between senators of the two persuasions.

### Constitutional Interpretation

The distinctions drawn in the preceding sections are almost solely behavioral in nature. Quite clearly, the Republican moderate often reacted differently from the radical in matters involving the distinction between state and federal powers, and the same was true concerning presidential powers, issues related to race, and other subjects discussed above. But did one or more common denominators of belief or attitude seem to run through a considerable number of the debates that produced disagreement between moderate and radical Republicans? In an earlier chapter we explored the possibility that common experiences in the life histories of the senators were involved, but here we shall merely consider the rhetorical evidence. And this evidence indeed suggests that radicals and moderates regarded the Constitution somewhat differently. The radical either found no constitutional impediment in his path or adeptly discovered constitutional means to sanction his ends, while the moderate was more apt to recognize constitutional restraints upon congressional action. Of course, the constitutional basis of radical and moderate positions was not always spelled out; it would have been difficult to develop such rationale in the case of some votes, and explanations for this fact are offered elsewhere. But in the debates on many important wartime issues, the contrast between radical dash and ingenuity and moderate hesitancy and scruple is marked indeed.

The opponents of Trumbull's confiscation bill in 1862 believed that confiscation procedures should be reconciled with the clause in the Constitution relating to treason. They preferred also to approach the subject through the military powers of the President as commander-in-chief, in contrast to radicals who wished to limit presidential discretion in the confiscation process and to prescribe procedures for confiscation that were unacceptably novel and harsh in the eyes of doubting colleagues. In this instance, as in many others, both groups stood in relatively uncharted territory. Sumner's efforts to place a tax upon slaves or, more delicately, a tax upon the slaveholder's right to hold slaves, roused Sherman to attack the proposal as an unconstitutional capitation tax. When the radical hounds were bugling in pursuit of Stark of Oregon, Howe maintained that their efforts would frustrate the constitutional clause guaranteeing representation to the states in the chamber. Others charged that the oath of office bill imposed a qualification upon the members of Congress beyond that specified by the Constitution and supported Henderson in trying to introduce constitutional phrasing into the oath.

Although the Republicans hoped that ways could be found to obliterate slavery, the less radical among them found it difficult to ignore the hoary constitutional maxim that it was a domestic state institution, which federal powers could not touch directly. The suggestion that the revision to the Militia Act, passed in July, 1862, should free the immediate families of black recruits, even those owned by loyal men of the border states, horrified the moderate Republican.

The senators did not raise constitutional issues so vehemently in the third session of the Thirty-seventh Congress as they had during the preceding session, but such matters were certainly in their minds to some degree when they discussed the Missouri emancipation aid bill and the habeas corpus indemnity bill. Fessenden noted somewhat dubiously that the constitutionality of the Missouri aid bill must rest upon the war power—in other words, it was a measure unthinkable in times of peace but now permissible because it would, if implemented, help bring the war to a speedier conclusion than otherwise would be the case. Illness prevented Sumner from participating in the early stages of the debate on this bill, and we cannot know how generally his views were known or shared by his colleagues prior to his statements on the floor. But when he did join the discussion, he picked up the war-powers argument and used it as the basis for maintaining that it would not sustain anything in this case but immediate emancipation. The constitutional issues involved in the act to indemnify the President and other executive officers against their actions in suspending the right of habeas corpus were even less clearly expressed in the process of debate. But moderates supported Sherman's amendment, implicitly criticizing the use of military tribunals when the federal civil courts of the locality were in normal operation, suggesting moderate concern about the denial of the guarantees to speedy and impartial trial found in the Sixth Amendment. Their concern about the abuse of military courts spilled forth again in the Thirty-eighth Congress, when it was proposed to try delinquent civilian recruiters and substitute brokers in such bodies rather than in the civil courts. And the major thrust of the argument focused on the interpretation of the Fifth and Sixth Amendments.

In 1864, Sumner argued ingeniously that the Founding Fathers had actually failed to reach the slave in the so-called slave clauses of the Constitution and that the real meaning of these passages was in doubt. He championed a flat-out proposal to repeal the fugitive slave laws, a proposal that he described as "perfectly plain. . . . Like a diagram . . . like the multiplication table . . . like the ten commandments," but the moderates balked on constitutional grounds.[8] Renewed efforts to free the families of black soldiers in the border states during 1864 once more brought the moderate Republican up against his conviction that it was unconstitutional to interfere in this way with the domestic institutions of loyal states. Such men could accept emancipation by executive action on the clear grounds of military necessity, or by constitutional amendment, but at that point they stuck. And when Sumner, during the same session, proposed to convert the commutation fee prescribed by the Conscription Law to a tax based on the income of the draftee, Sherman was quick to respond that this was differential taxation and therefore unconstitutional. Other moderates agreed.

Brought before the senators in the closing days of the first session of the Thirty-eighth Congress as it was, the Wade-Davis bill produced surprisingly little floor debate within the Republican ranks. But the justification that Wade advanced in its behalf was essentially constitutional in nature. The votes that some moderates cast, or failed to cast, during the course of the discussion on the Wade-Davis bill showed that the senator from Ohio had not convinced them. In the next session, moderates articulated these doubts during the course of the discussions about counting the Louisiana electoral returns and admitting the congressional delegation from the Pelican State.

More than one hundred years have caused the ink to fade and the paper to brown in the *Congressional Globe* of the Civil War years, but the passion with which moderate senators of that time invoked the Constitution still arrests the reader: "Men cannot be compelled to yield their views of the Constitution," said Fessenden. The war, proclaimed Cowan, most conservative of the Republican senators, was being fought "solely for the Constitution, and for the ends, aims, and purposes sanctioned by it, and for no others." Responding to Sumner, the soft-spoken senator from Connecticut, Lafayette Foster, said, "If the honorable Senator cannot find anything in the Constitution . . . which are any impediments or restraints upon him, I trust that he will realize that others may," and again, he insisted, "Let men think or say what they will; let them imagine that exigencies or so-called necessities may arise where we had better step aside from the Constitution, we delude ourselves if we think we can

8. Ibid., 1709.

abandon that instrument and go on to victory." Doolittle raised his sonorous voice to maintain that there were "a great many gentlemen on this side of the Chamber who believe that under the Constitution as it now stands, and by the decisions of the courts as they are made, they are under obligations and the obligations of their oaths, that there should be some kind of law to enforce that provision of the Constitution of the United States," and at a later time he pledged his desire to give the "Government all the power . . . conferred upon it by the Constitution, and not . . . more." Trumbull told his colleagues in 1864:

> We want to get up no divisions about . . . establishing for a temporary purpose in some far-off Territory a principle that is to alienate and divide loyal men and friends of the Government . . . it is of a piece with another declaration that I have heard sometimes in this Chamber . . . and that was that it mattered not whether a thing was constitutional or not. Sir, the Government cannot be saved, constitutional liberty cannot be saved, unless we save it under the Constitution.

On occasion even radical centrists resorted to similar rhetoric in protest against the extremists within the Republican ranks. Baited to exasperation by Sumner, the former Democrat from Maine, Lot Morrill, flashed out that in the future he would be found standing "on the line . . . broad and deep, between the reserved rights of the American people . . . reserved to them expressly in the Constitution of the United States and those granted to the General Government, to say, 'Thus far, but no farther.'"[9]

And what does the historian say in response to such declamation? Is it all to be dismissed as posturing, a farcical recourse to the tactics of the debating class, mere rhetorical rationalization of positions better explained in terms of political exigency, or the needs of the economic interests for whom the senators spoke? On one occasion, in the course of the Louisiana debates, Wade tried to bring his Republican colleagues back to political realities. He challenged any to declare themselves who would have been willing to count southern votes if that action meant the election of McClellan. The incident, of course, reveals Wade's conviction that the needs of party must prevail in the crunch, but also suggests conversely that some of his colleagues were allowing other considerations to influence their behavior. And the further context of the debate suggests that these considerations were mainly constitutional in nature. Indeed, Wade made this fact amply clear on an earlier occasion, remarking in the confiscation debate, "with some gentlemen the Constitution of the United States is a stumbling-block." In 1864, his radical colleague,

---

9. *CG*, 37 Cong., 2 sess., 3003, 1050; *CG*, 38 Cong., 1 sess., 1749, 3128, 1706; *CG*, 38 Cong., 2 sess., 550, 1340.

Chandler, was more pungent; various of his colleagues, he snorted, had "constitution on the brain."[10]

Sumner's behavior was more equivocal than that of Wade and Chandler, for none played the game of constitutional justification with more élan than he. In the debates central to our narrative, Sumner was the only radical to develop the abolitionist "freedom national" line of constitutional exegesis in full-blown form, maintaining that the natural rights principles of the Declaration of Independence must govern interpretation of the Constitution and that the latter was essentially a document of freedom. In contrast, other radicals often seemed to prefer invoking the "war powers" of the government. But "freedom national" theory had evolved in the long struggle against slavery; although perhaps suggestive, its precepts did not apply directly to many issues of the war congresses. Despite many years of effort, antislavery lawyers had not been successful in winning the kind of judicial validation of natural rights theory from the courts that would have impressed jurist-senators like Collamer or Harris, or lawyer-senators like Fessenden and Foster. The greatest judicial triumph of the abolitionist forces, the Booth cases, was ultimately reversed. None of this deterred the senator from Massachusetts from developing audacious constitutional arguments to meet the needs of debate while more conservative colleagues pulsed with derision, contempt, or frustrated fury because they believed that his positions were too extreme and his authorities unduly strained. The Democrat Reverdy Johnson doubtless spoke for a good many of Sumner's party colleagues, when he suggested acidly that the Massachusetts senator's "view" was "always the constitutional view." On the other hand, Sumner derided those who opposed his legislation on the grounds that it was unconstitutional. That objection, he once remarked, "is a commonplace of opposition. When all other reasons fail, then is the Constitution invoked."[11]

The evidence summarized here is by no means conclusive, but surely it provides grounds for arguing that some, perhaps much, of the contrast in behavior between radical and moderate Republicans may rest in different readings of the mandates and restrictions found in that great document. The senators were almost all lawyers, and those who were not had worked in close contact with attorneys for considerable periods of time. They scattered complimentary references to their colleagues' knowledge of the Constitution throughout their speeches and remarked

10. *CG,* 37 Cong., 2 sess., 1957; *CG,* 38 Cong., 1 sess., 1892.
11. *CG,* 38 Cong., 2 sess., 1105, 790. Robert M. Cover, *Justice Accused: Antislavery and the Judicial Process* (New Haven: Yale University Press, 1975), is a fascinating account of antislavery activity in the courts and of the failure of judges who were antislavery in sentiment to accept the natural rights line of argument.

on their preeminence as constitutional lawyers. In seeking election in 1854, Harlan distinguished between constitutional questions and questions of legislative expediency or of conscience. His guide in matters of the first type, he affirmed, would be "the decisions of the Supreme Court and the well settled principles of Constitutional Law."[12] And although *Dred Scott* v. *Sanford* later gave Republicans ample grounds for meditating upon the fallibility of judges, it is clear that the senatorial moderates at least did not consider interpretation of the Constitution to be merely an exhilarating game played to achieve legislative goals that were dictated solely by practical considerations or by party needs. They believed that there was a right way as well as a wrong way to read the clauses of the Constitution and its amendments. When colleagues proposed legislation that ran counter to a "right" reading or proposed to justify it by a constitutional reading that was "wrong," moderates dug in their heels. They had, as we have already heard Chandler say, "constitution on the brain." They would not have denied that the Constitution was a "living instrument," nor that the circumstances of the war opened the possibility of interpretation and acts unthought of in times of peace or in straightforward war with foreign nations. Indeed, in some respects, some moderates welcomed the additional range of options that the war provided as the better side of a bad business; troublesome constitutional dilemmas might now be avoided. But in general they would have held that the "instrument" must change and grow through the amendment process, and not because legislators disregarded inconvenient precedents, or developed interpretations for which seventy years of federal judicial precedent provided little support.

Are these contrasts between radical and moderate style and position perhaps subsumed by some other structure of contemporary disagreement? Were they, perhaps, mere permutations of continuing disagreement between the factions over the appropriate policies on slavery and race? Were these related issues the real foci of the war and all else subsidiary? Unquestionably the dilemmas presented by the presence of involuntary labor and caste distinctions were part of the wartime agenda, both explicitly and implicitly. In retrospect, the war-born solutions to these matters were fateful and to some observers, then and later, the most important results of the conflict. But at the time, surely, others would have objected to this view—others who saw the task of preserving the Union, or punishing white southerners, defeating the armies of the Confederacy, or reestablishing the structure of federal government as

12. Johnson Brigham, *James Harlan* (Iowa City: Iowa State Historical Society, 1913), p. 87.

being equally, or even more, important objectives. Almost all, if not all, of the Republican senators wished to see an end to slavery and subscribed in principle to equality before the law. They differed considerably about the most appropriate legal and constitutional principles and institutional mechanisms to achieve these ends. Such disagreements set moderate against radical but did not provide the only substance of dissension if our description of confiscation, Stark of Oregon, loyalty oaths, military courts, reconstruction, state bank issues (see below) and other matters is to be given any weight.

But there is at least one other way in which the divisions between radicals and moderates may be viewed as part of a larger whole. In recent years, constitutional and legal scholars have tried to identify and characterize various eras of judicial interpretation in America. According to one authority, many appellate judicial decisions prior to 1860 bore the stamp of a "grand style"; in those days judges were bold, imaginative, and creatively innovative. Subsequent to the Civil War, the great figures of the bench usually wrote their opinions in a spirit of formalism, binding themselves with narrow rules or precedents, construing the law conservatively and acting with reluctance in areas of interpretation. But the formalists ultimately gave way to the legal realists and so on. One legal historian has argued recently, however, that judges before the Civil War tended to approach one policy issue—slavery—in a formal and conservative manner. Still another sees the prewar years as a time of innovation in personal law and formalism in public law.[13]

The specialists in legal and constitutional history must decide whether such scholars have as yet built a foundation of research adequate to support their assertions. We can speculate that the scholar who has analyzed the jurisprudence of slavery may actually have detected only part of the more conservative end of a behavioral continuum. Although some of the senators of the Civil War congresses had been judges, and others would be, our study is one of legislators and not of jurists. But the preceding chapters show that among the senators, neither radical nor moderate, as a general rule, ceased to be either radical or moderate when he passed beyond slavery in discussing war issues. May I suggest that perhaps there was a broader continuum of attitude among national legislators during, and before, the Civil War, of which the poles may be termed modernizing-instrumental on the one hand and traditional-formal on the other, and that it is this structure of attitude that we detect—imperfectly because it was, after all, imperfect—when we make

13. Karl N. Llewellyn, *The Common Law Tradition: Deciding Appeals* (Boston: Little, Brown, 1960); Cover, *Justice Accused;* Morton J. Horwitz, *The Transformation of American Law, 1780–1860* (Cambridge: Harvard University Press, 1977); Grant Gilmore, *The Ages of American Law* (New Haven: Yale University Press, 1977).

distinctions between radicals and nonradicals? And what of racism and manifestations of it such as colonization? Cannot these too be regarded as evidences of traditionalism in the United States of the 1860s? At this writing the advocates of modernization theory are in disarray, but it does hold out some promise that we can place the social processes of the industrializing nation in better perspective.

This twist of the argument leads me to a caveat and a disclaimer. We have been warned recently (see Appendix A) that the individuals who appear in the same position in a Guttman scale may not have voted in the same way for the same reasons. Too much can be made of this assertion, but it is reasonable to suggest that a different melding of social and political conditioning and personality may have brought different senators into rather similar positions concerning the Constitution. Who is to say what combination of moral commitment, interpretation of his own and the country's needs, and sour vindictiveness, made an extreme modernizing-instrumental approach to constitutional matters most congenial to a particular senator, or what elements of personal history placed senators among the traditional-formalists? Emerson believed that he in part knew, as we have seen, and other clues have passed before us as well.

The scales fundamental to this work were derived from those numerous roll calls in each session that were particularly related to the struggle with the South. Using these scales I was able to rank the senators in terms of their tendencies to vote either more or less radically or more or less conservatively on the great war issues. Within the Senate generally and among the Republicans as well, the voting usually revealed a range of positions from radical to conservative. Fascinating and important as individual positions are, the historian also finds generalization useful, and certainly the writers of that time and historians since have frequently talked in terms of radicals and conservatives, or some such descriptive terms. I found it useful, therefore, to break the Republican part of the generalized scale ranking into two in order to make comparisons between those who tended toward the radical end of the scales and those whose voting ranked them toward the moderate or conservative pole. With this done, I was able to examine votes that most obviously produced markedly different reactions among the more radical and moderate senators and the issues and attitudes underlying such divisions.

But having divided the Republicans into radicals and moderates in this way, I also examined *all other* votes to discover whether the same alignments appeared in voting on issues which at first glance appeared unrelated to the major civil issues involved in the war, or at least seemed more appropriately grouped with other types of roll calls. Some of these roll calls did indeed reveal voting alignments in which numbers of radicals and moderates were opposed, and it appeared reasonable to discuss such votes in conjunction with those considered in the initial scaling analysis. Others remained puzzling, and such roll calls deserve some attention, both because they may provide clues to the broader meaning of radicalism in the Civil War and because they raise questions concerning the methods used in this book.

Why should radical and moderate alignments have appeared in votes on the tariff, on internal revenue, on the national banking system, on mundane aspects of army and naval organization or remuneration, and on a variety of other issues including California land claims and the establishment of a branch of the United States mint in Oregon? One possible response to this question is to argue that such roll calls were mere accidents and should be ignored. Some social scientists interested in dimensional analysis discount the occasional appearance of highly similar alignments on isolated votes in scales summarizing voting on different issues, when the scales in sum are not strongly correlated. It is true that the anomalous roll calls appearing in this research typically produced disagreement indices on the magnitude of 40 to 50 percent, scores at the lower edge of the range that we have found interesting and which could be produced by deviance on the part of some six to eight united radicals or moderates from the positions held by the remainder of their Republican colleagues. By reducing the number of senators required to produce disagreement in the 40 to 50 percent level, absenteeism might also at times have enhanced the possibility that anomalous votes merely reflected accident, rather than senators acting in accord with radical or moderate sentiments. This might particularly have been the case in the Thirty-eighth Congress after the senators relaxed their quorum rule in May, 1864, and certainly such votes were more frequent in the Thirty-eighth than in the Thirty-seventh Senate.

Despite such considerations, the votes in a full Senate chamber of the Thirty-seventh Congress that produce disagreement indices in the 40 to 50 percent range also generate probability scores which show that the possibility of such alignments occurring by chance is less than one in a hundred. Although some of the anomalous roll calls perhaps do represent chance groupings, I think it most unlikely that all, or even the greater share of them do. Influences other than mere chance may have been at work, and, of these, two seem most plausible: (1) Radical and moderate alignments resulted in areas of legislative voting peripheral to southern issues broadly defined, when the subjects under debate involved constitutional attitudes and positions that were the same as, or similar to, those involved in the discussion of the great civil problems of the war; (2) Radical and moderate alignments sometimes appeared in unexpected areas of debate because the action or position of prominent radicals or moderates rallied to their support colleagues who were accustomed to accepting them as cue-givers in the areas of debate that normally produced radical-moderate alignments. We shall not discuss all of the anomalous votes here, but merely use illustrative issues to demonstrate the possible utility of these hypotheses.

Following the lead of Charles A. and Mary Beard and Howard K. Beale, a generation of American historians believed that the radicals of the Republican party were the advance agents of American industrialism and that there was, in other words, a discernible economic dimension in Republican radicalism. Since the 1950s that view has been severely qualified, as more detailed analysis of the reconstruction era identified conflicts of economic interest among business groups and within the Republican party that were not emphasized in the earlier writing. Although Robert P. Sharkey's work was, in part, an exception to the rule, most of the revisionary writing treats the reconstruction years rather than the wartime period of policy development. In his introduction to the third edition of *Lincoln and the Radicals*, T. Harry Williams confessed that his "statement . . . concerning the economic cohesiveness of Republicans and Radicals is exaggerated and needs modification." But he also emphasized correctly that much more research is in order on these matters. More recent scholars, notably Glenn M. Linden and Michael L. Benedict have presented quantitative analyses of roll calls from the congresses of the Civil War and reconstruction era that further contradict the Beale thesis. But, with the exception of Linden, scholars have emphasized evidence from the reconstruction years rather than from those of the Civil War. And the more recent research on the period 1860–77 may be vulnerable because of the failure to distinguish the relative importance of particular interest groups or specific roll calls, the tendency of scholars to define legislative groups impressionistically or unrealistically, and the difficulty of identifying the links between constituency groups and legislative actors.[14]

14. Charles A. and Mary R. Beard, *The Rise of American Civilization* (New York: Macmillan, 1927); Howard K. Beale, *The Critical Year: A Study of Andrew Johnson and Reconstruction* (New York: Harcourt, Brace, 1930); Robert P. Sharkey, *Money, Class, and Party: An Economic Study of Civil War and Reconstruction* (Baltimore: The Johns Hopkins Press, 1959); Irwin Unger, *The Greenback Era: A Social and Political History of American Finance, 1865–1879* (Princeton: Princeton University Press, 1964). Unger's work contains an interesting introductory chapter dealing with developments prior to the conclusion of the Civil War, pp. 13–40, and it is important to remember that his first formulation of position appeared in the periodical press in 1959, as did Stanley Coben's "Northeastern Business and Radical Reconstruction: A Re-examination," *Mississippi Valley Historical Review*, 46 (June 1959), 67–90. (Both Sharkey and Unger provide listings of other relevant literature.) T. Harry Williams, *Lincoln and the Radicals* (Madison: University of Wisconsin Press, 1965, 3d edition), pp. x–xi. Glenn M. Linden, "'Radicals' and Economic Policies: The House of Repre-

# Designs and Perspectives

My initial research in the history of the Thirty-seventh Senate show.
that during the second session the Republican senators often divideú
along East-West lines in their voting on major economic issues, and this
was found to be the most important subsidiary alignment among the
Republicans on economic matters in other sessions as well. But as work
progressed on this and later sessions, various votes on economic matters
were identified in which there was some alignment of moderate against
radical Republicans. This was illustrated particularly by some (by no
means all) votes on national banking policy, which seemed to reflect a
category of voting behavior that is explained by hypothesis (1) above.

During the third session of the Thirty-seventh Congress, the senators
and representatives passed the National Banking Act, S. 486, "to provide
a national currency." Although he eventually voted for it, Howard opposed the bill during debate on the grounds that any scheme of paper
currency should allow conversion to specie at will, that the national
banks would injure the state-chartered institutions, and that the new
system would precipitate conflict in local politics.[15] At one point he offered an amendment requiring that the certificates of the Comptroller
of the Currency, certifying that national banking associations had met all
legal requirements, should be published in the laws of the United States.
As rationale for this procedure, Howard pointed out that there was no
provision in S. 486 specifying that the articles of association of such
institutions be printed or published. He succeeded in attaching his
amendment to section 6 of the bill without a recorded vote, but when he
tried to add it to section 10 as well, Sherman balked, arguing that such
material would clutter up the statute books and that the procedures
outlined in the bill would provide ample information to the public concerning the stockholders and the ongoing business of the new banking
associations. At his behest the senators rejected Howard's amendment to

sentatives, 1861–1873," *Civil War History*, 13 (March 1967), 51–65, and *Politics or Principle: Congressional Voting on the Civil War Amendments and Pro-Negro Measures, 1838–69* (Seattle: University of Washington Press, 1976). Michael L. Benedict, *A Compromise of Principle: Congressional Republicans and Reconstruction, 1863–1869* (New York: Norton, 1974).

15. *CG*, 37 Cong., 3 sess., 848–49, 878–79. For general background concerning John Sherman's role in these matters see John Sherman, *Recollections of Forty Years in the House, Senate and Cabinet: An Autobiography* (Chicago: Werner, 1895), 1: 268–309 and 329–50; Winfield S. Kerr, *John Sherman: His Life and Public Services* (Boston: Sherman, French, 1908), 1: 148–63. Jeannette P. Nichols, "John Sherman," in Kenneth W. Wheeler, ed., *For the Union: Ohio Leaders in the Civil War* (Columbus: Ohio State University Press, 1968), 377–438, is excellent but all too brief. See particularly pp. 402–12, 423–27. See also: John J. Knox, *A History of Banking in the United States* (New York: Bradford Rhodes, 1903), pp. 221–86; Davis R. Dewey, *Financial History of the United States* (New York: Longmans, Green, 1920), pp. 305–30; Paul Studenski and Herman E. Kroos, *Financial History of the United States: Fiscal, Monetary, Banking, and Tariff, Including Financial Administration and State and Local Finance* (New York: McGraw-Hill, 1963), pp. 137–60.

section 10, and Sherman requested reconsideration of the amendment to section 6. Most moderates supported Sherman, as did a majority of the Senate, but an index of disagreement between radicals and moderates of 40 is found, whereas the difference between eastern and western senators is less than 10 points. It is hard to read anything of consequence into this vote, but in the first session of the Thirty-eighth Congress votes relating to the national banking system are more intriguing.

During late April and early May, 1864, the senators debated the provisions of H.R. 395, designed to "provide a national currency, secured by a pledge of United States bonds, and to provide for the circulation and redemption thereof."[16] This was a bill amending and amplifying the legislation of 1863 that established the national banking system; the debate on it produced five votes in which the disagreement between radicals and moderates rose to 40 percent or more.

To what degree were the states to be allowed to tax the national banks and their stockholders? Under the most generous interpretation of the act of 1863, state and municipal governments had limited rights of taxation; some believed they had none. H.R. 395 definitely opened the door to the states and municipalities, but exempted that part of the capital stock of associations that was invested in bonds of the United States. Amendments of the Senate Finance Committee deleted this exemption and also made stockholders liable on their stock, providing:

> That nothing in this act shall be construed to prevent the market value of the shares in any of the said associations, held by any person or body-corporate, from being included in the valuation of the personal property of such person or corporation in the assessment of all taxes imposed by or under State authority for State, county, or municipal purposes, but not at a greater rate than is assessed upon other moneyed capital in the hands of individual citizens of each State . . . [and that] nothing in this act [shall] exempt the real estate of associations from either State, county, or municipal taxes to the same extent, according to its value, as other real estate is taxed.[17]

Since the bonds of the federal government were exempt from taxation beyond the level of 1.5 percent provided in the income tax law, argued Chandler, speaking as a "practical banker," the committee provision indirectly laid all those bonds subscribed as capital stock under the national banking law open to higher rates of taxation. This would be a great burden to western bankers and prevent the establishment of additional national banks in the West. He predicted that the committee amendment would "kill the bill" if adopted.[18]

16. *CG*, 38 Cong., 1 sess., 1865.
17. Ibid., 1871.
18. Ibid., 1872.

In defending the committee amendment, Fessenden engaged in a passage of arms with the senator from Michigan. To Fessenden, "The question simply is, and it has no very great scope, whether the power of taxing the stock of the banks and of taxing the persons holding the shares shall exist and shall be exercised by the States or by the General government." He pointed out that the states were limited in the amount of tax which they could lay upon the banks. Rather than killing the bill, the committee amendment would make it more acceptable to many. The tax fell on those most able to pay, whereas exemption would withdraw a large amount of capital from the reach of state taxation. He derided Chandler's claim to be a "practical banker," pointing out that there were wide differences of opinion among "practical bankers" on these matters. Chandler responded that the Finance Committee needed more practical business knowledge upon it, and Fessenden admitted that a great mistake had been made in not putting Chandler on the committee, although "we get along very well notwithstanding." Finally the senator from Michigan thundered: "The Senator from Maine has lectured this body about enough, not only on practical knowledge, but about its business and general conduct. For my part I have got about enough of his lecturing, and I will thank him to lecture somebody else next time."[19] He wanted the committee amendment altered by striking out the proviso concerning the taxation of bank shares and substituting the phrasing of the original bill, denying states the right to tax that part of the capital stock of national banks invested in United States bonds.

On April 28, Pomeroy proposed to amend the committee amendment in conformity with Chandler's ideas, striking the committee stipulation concerning state taxation and substituting

> *Provided*, That nothing in this act shall be construed as exempting the capital stock of an association, beyond the amount invested in United States bonds and deposited with the Treasurer of the United States as part of its capital or as security for its circulating notes, from being subject to the same rate of State and municipal taxation as is imposed upon other personal property in the State or city or town in which the association is located.

Among Republicans, Howe and Collamer opposed this amendment and Sumner, who had endorsed Chandler's position as patriotic, returned to the floor to link the committee position with state rights.

> No single proposition has been brought forward on this floor, having for its object the salvation of the Republic, by infusing into it new energy and new vitality, which has not been encountered in the name of State rights. And now, sir, while considering how to secure the financial stability of the Republic, we are doomed again to encounter the oft-repeated objection.

19. Ibid., 1872–73.

He drew upon Milton to point out that "iron and gold" were the "two main nerves" in the "equipage" of war and launched a long disquisition on *McCulloch* v. *Maryland.* Either direct *or indirect* taxation of national banking agencies was unconstitutional, he concluded, and demanded finally: "Are you in earnest to place the national credit on a sure foundation? Are you in earnest for the national banks as a proper agency to this end? If you are in earnest for these two objects, then I entreat you not to allow them to be sacrificed in subserviency to State rights."[20]

Fessenden riposted, paying due respect to Sumner's poetical bent, suggesting indeed that his whole position was "poetical," based upon "his imagination" and having "no earthly application as a matter of law to the question now before" the Senate.[21] He was unimpressed by the argument of opponents of the committee amendment that state taxation would place the national banks in various states on an uneven footing one to the other because state taxation varied. Conditions in the states were uneven in other respects as well. As for Chandler's contention that government bonds should not be taxed at a rate beyond 1.5 percent, he noted that this restriction was not part of a contract with bondholders but merely a provision of the internal revenue law, subject to change at the will of Congress. He attacked the rendering Sumner had given *McCulloch* v. *Maryland,* pointing out that the Maryland law at issue was declared unconstitutional because it was directed against the operations of the Bank of the United States; the decision did not forbid the taxation of other bank assets.

> After all it comes back to the simple question of expediency, and there it must rest; it is a mere matter of money. Shall the Government of the United States be permitted to do what they did not attempt to do when they established the Bank of the United States, to deprive the people of the States of the right and the power to make their citizens pay a tax upon their own property which they held in these institutions; or shall the income, the revenue to be derived from that source, belong entirely to the United States, and the States have no part in it?[22]

When the senators voted on Pomeroy's amendment on April 29, eleven voted for it and twenty-eight opposed it (R-M I.D.: 25; E-W I.D.: 61). Eight radicals, two moderates, and Harding of Oregon supported the Kansan's proposal. Both moderates and six of the radicals were westerners, who were joined by Sprague and Sumner. Somewhat modified, the committee amendment would become part of section 41 of the act of June 3, 1864.

20. Ibid., 1889, 1893–94.
21. Ibid., 1894.
22. Ibid., 1895.

On the next day, Howard proposed that the holders of stock in national banking associations should be taxed on that stock in the state where the bank was situated. This, of course, ran counter to the usual practice of taxing personal property at the place of residence. In defense of his motion, Howard argued that it was very doubtful whether Congress could constitutionally distinguish between taxation which was unconstitutional in the sense of *McCulloch* v. *Maryland* and state taxation of the sort envisaged in the bill on the shares of capital stock in the bank, when such taxation might also impede the operation of "a lawful instrument of the United States in carrying out its powers." Where was the line to be drawn on state taxation? Howard believed that the power to tax the associations lay in the federal government and was "an exclusive power." Specifically, Howard justified his amendment on the grounds that it would make the law more acceptable to residents in those states where stock was "not subscribed as readily as in other States."[23] The amendment failed, 11 yeas and 27 nays, with much the same lineup of Republicans in the minority: Chandler, Conness, Howard, Pomeroy, Ramsey, Sherman, Sumner, and Wilkinson, united as before, were joined by Harlan and Morrill, while Lane of Indiana and Sprague dropped from the ranks of the dissidents (R-M I.D.: 40; E-W I.D.: 47). The processes of legislative reconciliation ultimately brought this provision into the act.

When the committee amendment on bank taxation came before the Senate, Sumner moved a substitute amendment. He proposed to double the rate of federal taxation on the average amount of notes circulating (i.e., from .5 to 1 percent each half year), with similar rates of increase on deposits and on capital stock beyond the amount invested in United States bonds; limit state and municipal taxes to bank real estate; and provide that all national taxation raised in this manner should be used exclusively in paying the interest and principal of the national debt. Sumner made a rather long statement in support of his amendment, beginning: "At last in this discussion it is clear that we have come to the place where the road branches in two opposite directions—one way toward the support of the whole country, and of that *improved currency* which is essential not only to the general welfare but also to the common defense, and the other toward State rights, State taxation, and State banks. Which road will you take, Sir?" He extolled the virtues of a sound currency at length and compared the advocates of state taxation to wretched John Hook, who had harassed the beleaguered patriot forces in their time of greatest crisis during the American Revolution because they had not paid him for beef. "The State banks," he declaimed, "have

23. Ibid., 1958.

performed their tasks as agents of currency, and the time has come for them to abdicate . . . at least to conform to the new system."[24]

Following Sumner, Chandler attacked state bank issues and quoted a banker correspondent in the West who assured him that the state taxation amendment of the Finance Committee would ruin his bank and force him to reorganize under state law. This, he told his colleagues, was his opinion also. He continued:

> I am glad, however, to find that the Finance Committee is not a unit on this point. I am glad to find that there is some practical business knowledge even in that Finance Committee. I have the most profound respect for the members of that committee as lawyers and as statesmen, but for their practical business knowledge I have about the same respect that they have for my legal attainments, and if they have the slightest for those they have more than I have. [Laughter] I hope that the Senate will disregard the recommendation of that committee. I hope the Senate will adopt the broad view of the Senator from Massachusetts. I hope they will look above these little local interests, and adopt a national system of banking which will do credit to the country, save the Treasury, and fill your coffers.[25]

Fessenden lashed back, chiding Sumner for his attack on the wisdom and patriotism of the twenty-eight senators who voted for the committee amendment in Committee of the Whole, "in his written speech which he has read to the Senate, which he has carefully elaborated in his closet." He described the attitudes in the House and in the Treasury concerning state taxation of national banks—favorable in the one and not really opposed in the other—and he wished to know what "the question of state taxation or of United States taxation . . . has to do with the question of currency?" He pointed out that the increased rates of federal taxation prescribed in the Sumner amendment would more than cover the amounts taken by state taxes under the committee proposal. He denied Sumner's charge that he was willing to give General Grant everything necessary but refuse the Secretary of the Treasury his needs. As for Chandler's innuendos, Fessenden noted that many men possessed of "practical business knowledge" in the House supported the Finance Committee's position. "The Committee," he said, was "endeavoring to approach the high standard of the honorable Senator from Michigan and the honorable Senator from Massachusetts in practical business knowledge."[26]

In response, Chandler cited the number of practical businessmen on the House Committee of Ways and Means who disagreed with the position of Fessenden's committee. He denied that the states needed the

24. Ibid., 2128–29.
25. Ibid., 2130.
26. Ibid., 2130–31.

revenues reserved by its amendment to sustain their credit. Had the senators who stressed the importance of maintaining the credit of the states considered what would happen if the nation's credit failed? The states were little burdened with debt. The proper course was to: "simply come in and say, what you have the power to do, as I believe, under the Constitution, that the financial issues of this Government shall be simply subject to national taxation. I believe you have a right to say it. I believe you have a right to insist upon it. I believe it to be the duty of the Senate to insist upon it in this hour of peril." Supporting Sumner, although a member of the Finance Committee, Sherman pointed out that the rates of tax in Sumner's amendment showed "that the friends of exclusive national taxation do not wish to relieve these banks from their fair share of taxes."[27] When the senators voted on Sumner's amendment on May 6, Chandler, Conness, Howard, Lane of Indiana, Pomeroy, Ramsey, Sherman, Sprague, Wilkinson, and Wilson supported Sumner, and the tally was 11 yeas and 24 nays (R-M I.D.: 42; E-W I.D.: 54).

Also on May 6, Chandler moved to withdraw the national banks of twelve cities from a list of fifteen cities designated as redemption centers for member banks, leaving only those of New York, Philadelphia, and Boston serving in this capacity. This amendment squeaked through by a margin of one vote, 15 yeas and 14 nays (R-M I.D.: 47.5; E-W I.D.: 2) but did not survive to shape section 31 of the statute.

On May 10, Collamer introduced two motions, both destined to fail, but also illustrating disagreement between radicals and moderates. In the first of these, he proposed to require national banks to retain one quarter of the bond interest, which they received in coin as part of their required cash reserves, until they had converted the full amount of that reserve to that form. This, he suggested, would be a step toward the resumption of specie payments, which authorities considered desirable. But twenty of his colleagues considered his amendment undesirable and only fourteen supported him. (R-M I.D.: 44; E-W I.D.: 10). Later Collamer proposed that the amount of Treasury notes currently authorized but unissued should be reduced by the amount of national bank currency issued by the associations. This too perished, although by a slightly smaller overall margin, yeas 14 and nays 17 (R-M I.D.: 49; E-W I.D.: 23.5). In a sense, Collamer's motions represent the moderate dissent from the majority position, as the Pomeroy, Howard, and Sumner motions illustrated radical departures from majority positions. But the radical senators based their case unabashedly on the grounds that national power should prevail.

During the Thirty-seventh Congress Sherman had proposed that state

27. Ibid., 2132, 2142.

bank users should be taxed at rates above those placed on national bank notes, a policy designed both to encourage the development of the new system and to discourage weak state banks from issuing unsound currency. His colleagues failed to support his measures at that time, but when the senators were debating the internal revenue bill of 1864 (H.R. 405), he tried once more to attack the note issues of state banks. As desired by a majority of the Finance Committee, section 109 provided that state and national banks should pay the same level of tax on their circulating notes, one percent per annum. On May 30, Sherman presented an amendment to replace this section, providing that state banks pay an aggregate tax of 2.4 percent per annum, payable on a monthly basis on that amount of their circulation equivalent to 90 percent of their capital, whereas the national banks must pay a duty or tax every six months to a cumulative total of one percent. During the course of the debate, Sherman revised the proposed tax on state note issues downward to one sixth of a percent per month, totaling 2 percent. In these maneuvers he did not equivocate: "I frankly admit," he said, "that my purpose in this amendment is to make a discrimination against the State banks, and to compel them to withdraw their circulation." Other Republicans said little on the floor concerning the Sherman amendment, but McDougall flailed away for some time, seeing it as illustrative of the "strong disposition" on the "part of many Senators to extinguish all the boundaries of the States and to establish here a central Government."[28] Sherman's effort to replace section 109, as approved by the Finance Committee, failed: yeas 11 and nays 25. Ten radicals supported him but five radicals, nine moderates, and various Democrats and border-state senators united in opposition (R-M I.D.: 57; E-W I.D.: 44). The radical cohort supporting Sherman's proposition included Sumner, Wilson, Anthony, and seven westerners.

In early June, Sherman tried to save part of his proposal by moving the first of a series of amendments that would require the state banks to report on their circulation and pay taxes to the federal government on a monthly basis, a proposal found in the original House bill. Henderson implored Fessenden to oppose the proposal, which was a "discrimination against the local banks," explaining "if the Senator does consent the Senate will adopt it. . . . I am controlled ordinarily by his views, and by his opinions on this subject; and though I have desired to offer some amendments to this bill I have refrained from doing so simply because they were against his wishes in regard to the matter." Johnson inveighed

28. Ibid., 2563, 2590. In 1863, Sherman put forward his ideas on differential taxation both in the form of an amendment to the revenue bill of 1862 and as a bill (S. 445) introduced in the next session of Congress. S. 445 unfortunately does not appear in its proper place in the congressional bill file.

against Sherman's amendment also and Davis predictably damned the "whole scheme of national banks" as "unconstitutional, impolitic, and in many of its features a direct and flagitious infringement upon the rights of the State banks."[29] This time the vote was close, and Sherman carried eleven radicals and three other moderates with him, but Fessenden and four other moderates, as well as Clark, a radical member of the Finance Committee, found ten Democrats and Border Unionists willing to join them, producing a result of 15 yeas and 16 nays (R-M I.D.: 47; E-W I.D.: 31).

His colleagues confirmed Lincoln's nomination of Fessenden to become Secretary of the Treasury on July 1, 1864, and the ambitious Sherman replaced him as chairman of the Senate Finance Committee. As far as the friends of state banks were concerned, the fox was now in charge of the hen house. As the internal revenue bill (H.R. 744) emerged from the committee during the second session of the Thirty-eighth Congress, section 5 provided, "That every national banking association, State bank, or State banking association, shall pay a tax of ten per cent on the amount of notes of any State bank or State banking association, paid out by them after the 1st day of January, 1866," and the committee majority recommended that it be struck out. In his general remarks upon the bill, Sherman referred to this clause as an "important feature," and briefly explained the reasons for it:

> The refusal of Congress, at the last session, to pass restrictive measures to compel . . . redemption [of State bank notes] has seriously affected the value of our currency. The national banks were intended to supersede the State banks. Both cannot exist together; yet, while the national system is extending, the issues of State banks have not materially decreased. Indeed, many local banks have been converted into national banks, and yet carefully keep out their State circulation. . . . They issue two circulations upon the same capital. . . . If the State banks have power enough in Congress to prolong their existence beyond the present year, we had better suspend the organization of national banks.

Later he admitted that the circulation of state banks had actually declined by something in excess of $3 million since passage of the National Banking Act but noted that this decline was attributable solely to withdrawals in the border states plus Indiana, while eastern state banks had actually increased their circulation by some $10 million. He reported that committee members had disagreed about the clause and suggested that, although a majority of the committee had recommended striking the section, their action was "for the purpose of bringing it to the attention of the Senate, as much as anything else."[30] He himself was willing to

29. Ibid., 2734, 2736.
30. *CG*, 38 Cong., 2 sess., 1194, 1139, 1195.

let the section be struck, trusting that the committee of conference would restore it.

Howe favored eliminating the section. He had supported the National Banking Act, believing it to be a better system of banking that would replace the state systems in time. He thought that the effort to bring this about with the speed envisioned here was destructive, "full of peril to the people of" Wisconsin as well as "pernicious" with "an amount of viciousness in it which overbalances all the virtue that the extremest friends of this bill can claim for it." Ramsey introduced an amendment exempting state banks from the operation of section 5 if their circulating note issue was backed by government bonds to the amount of 10 percent more than the total amount of such issues. He argued that the section, as originally drafted, was designed to drive state banks into the national system and was "manifestly unjust" to such institutions with a capital of less than $50,000 since they could not become national banks under the federal law. He pledged to vote for section 5 if his amendment was adopted but would "do so with great hesitation, if at all," were it not accepted.[31] Ramsey and Howe were the only Republicans to complain about section 5 on the floor, although Collamer eventually demanded that a separate vote be taken on it in the Senate after the bill had been perfected in the Committee of the Whole.

Opposition senators were less restrained. McDougall, particularly concerned as to the effect of the clause in California, read the legislation as an effort "to deny to the States the right to control their own financial affairs in their own way," and believed that it meant "the upturning of our institutions, the affirmation that the States have no rights, and that the men who established this Republic . . . were ignorant of what they were about." It was, he believed, "a proposition to usurp the powers of the States." Hendricks saw in *McCulloch* v. *Maryland* the affirmation of his position that Congress had not "the power to defeat" a State "by indirect legislation in an effort to exercise the power which it is conceded she possesses." He rehearsed the banking situation in Indiana and the various business advantages enjoyed by national banks at some length before ending with the hope that the senators would "decide, as we did at the last session, that equality is justice and right." Subsequently, Johnson took the floor; he had understood Sherman to say that the supporters of section 5 sought "to drive out of existence State bank notes." This, he said, was "to deny to the State banks the authority to issue notes by imposing upon them a tax which will render that authority absolutely futile. . . . Precisely the question upon which the Supreme Court . . . unanimously declared that the tax proposed by Maryland

31. Ibid., 1196, 1238.

upon the Bank of the United States could not be maintained."[32] Powell and Henderson followed, reiterating the constitutional issues involved and seeking to demonstrate that western states were indeed behaving responsibly and reducing their note issues. The measure would not assist the government in its fiscal policies, maintained the senator from Missouri.

The senators refused to strike section 5 by a vote of 20 yeas to 22 nays (I.D. 1–38: 45; 2–38: 25). Those moderate Republicans voting to strike the section were Collamer, Doolittle, Foster, Harris, Howe, and Ten Eyck. They were joined also by Anthony, Dixon, and Foot, of whom only Foot was consistently radical in his voting throughout the war and, actually, his voting usually placed him near the center of the party. After the senators perfected the bill in Committee of the Whole, Collamer insisted that a separate vote be taken on section 5, still standing untouched in the measure and, after a flurry of technicalities, this was done. Now Harris moved to support the section under attack and the result was more decisive than the earlier roll call, yeas 17 and nays 21 (I.D. 1–38: 37.5; 2–38: 24). The matching indices of East-West disagreement were 38 and 24.

The debates that produced these divisive votes concerning the national banking system suggest that the issues of constitutional interpretation, economic development, sectional differences, and party were complexly intertwined. But, although the moderate Sherman provided leadership in this instance, the radicals were prepared to expand the role of the national banks and circumscribe the activities of state-chartered banks to a greater degree than were the moderates, who wished to treat local interests more generously in prescribing the boundaries of state and federal powers. A similar situation prevailed when the senators were considering slavery and the southern situation generally. We need not be surprised, therefore, that the alignment of Republicans on some economic matters was sometimes similar to the radical-moderate division. The senators brought the same general constitutional perspectives to bear on issues that at first glance might appear extremely disparate. The national banking legislation provides the greatest number of votes on economic matters of this type, but there were other illustrations as well, as in debate upon the desirability of intervening in the adjustment of land titles in California.

Cue-giving may also explain some of the anomalous votes that aligned radicals against moderates when the subject under debate seemed to bear little apparent relation to the central issues of the war.[33] Cue-giving,

32. Ibid., 1238–41.
33. Donald R. Matthews and James A. Stimson, "Cue-Taking by Congressmen: A Model and Computer Simulation," in William O. Aydelotte, ed., *The History of Parliamentary Be-*

of course, may be either positive or negative in nature. In the first instance, members of legislative bodies follow the lead of individuals, such as committee chairmen, whom they believe to be particularly knowledgeable about the merits of particular legislation. On the other hand, some members may differ so strongly from other members of their own party on ideological or personal grounds that they are prejudiced against proposals that the latter champion.

Among the radicals, Sumner particularly, and perhaps Hale as well, may have inspired instances of knee-jerk hostility among moderates, whatever the subject under consideration. On the other hand, Fessenden appears to have aroused the animosity of some radicals during the Thirty-eighth Congress to the point where they were prepared to forget their common party affiliation in order to humble the touchy chairman of the Finance Committee. He, in turn, wrote of his disenchantment with Sumner and of "the two or three drunken rowdies, and small fry" who were his "followers."[34] Thus, when Sumner opposed placing duties upon the raw materials of book making and upon philosophical instruments destined for college use, alleging that they constituted a tax on knowledge, men like Wilkinson and Chandler who had smarted under the lash of Fessenden's sarcasm fell into line behind Sumner, and moderates, infuriated by Sumner's animadversions, rallied to the support of Fessenden, who had the revenue bills in hand and who opposed the exemption of special interests from taxation. No senator's motions produced as many cases of factional division within the Republican party as did those put by Sumner. This is attributable in part to the fact that he specialized, so to speak, in legislation on a very sensitive subject and brought to his advocacy a constitutional exegisis abhorrent to more moderate Republicans. But they also saw in him a bull-like single-mindedness, and a cavalier disregard of practicalities, subtlety, and the feelings of fellow senators, qualities that undoubtedly added to his potency as a negative cue-giver.

The strange case of the Oregon mint illustrates some of the complexities in understanding cue-giving across a chasm of more than a century. On April 1, 1864, Nesmith of Oregon succeeded in persuading his colleagues to consider S. 185, a bill to establish assay offices at Carson City, in the Territory of Nevada, and Dalles City, in the state of Oregon, and for other purposes. Initially Nesmith had submitted a bill authorizing creation of a branch of the United States mint at Portland, Oregon.

---

*havior* (Princeton: Princeton University Press, 1977), pp. 247–73, is a good introduction to the concepts of cue-giving and cue-taking.

34. William Pitt Fessenden to Francis Fessenden, May 7, 1864, Fessenden Papers, Bowdoin College Library.

But the director of the mint at Philadelphia, James Pollock, a former governor of Pennsylvania, recommended against establishing additional minting facilities on the northwest coast, maintaining that the branch mint at San Francisco had sufficient coining capacity for western needs. Pollock cited the lack of skilled personnel in the West, the difficulties of transporting supplies for minting operations there, and the high costs of construction and materials, as well as the need for governmental economy. He suggested that the creation of additional mints might "tend toward national disintegration," and he concluded that the needs of the Northwest would be met adequately by establishing a government assay office with "proper facilities for melting, assaying, and stamping of bullion."[35] On these grounds, the Finance Committee altered Nesmith's original bill to provide for the development of a government assay office at Dalles City.

A man of formidable, although somewhat uncultivated wit, Nesmith slashed at the revised bill, bemoaning the fact that it had "returned from its peregrinations hawked at, torn, and dilapidated by the stupidity and ignorance of the company it" had "kept." He ridiculed "Disintegration Pollock.... The little old man who so complacently sits in the little old Government workshop in Philadelphia," described the riches and progress of the Pacific Northwest, and observed that it seemed to him "that the Government, instead of pursuing a niggardly policy toward the hardy pioneers engaged in developing the region ... should extend toward them all reasonable facilities for the successful promotion of an enterprise so fraught with the present and prospective interests of the nation." The cost of sending bullion to San Francisco for minting amounted, he charged, to a tax of about 10 percent. He asked his colleagues to support an amendment striking section 9 of the bill, authorizing the establishment of an assay office at Dalles City, and replacing it with a provision authorizing a branch mint. Howe tried to refute Nesmith's argument, arguing that the interests of both the miner and the United States were best served by the committee bill. He suggested that Nesmith's use of wit might not be "legitimate" in considering the issue as well as giving "rather a partial and incomplete view of the subject," and this sally recharged the senator from Oregon. Howe brought to his subject, Nesmith responded, "all that profound wisdom, all that dignity of character, all that quiet demeanor which I have sometimes thought characterized a women's sewing society." He quoted Byron on the bard who elegized the ass.[36] The senators voted to accept the Nesmith amendment in a vote which did not show substantial disagreement be-

35. *CG*, 38 Cong., 1 sess., 1773.
36. Ibid., 1383, 1385, 1384, 1774.

tween radical and moderate (I.D.: 24). Fessenden changed his vote to yea so that he could move a reconsideration, but when he discovered that the bill was still in Committee of the Whole he withdrew his motion to that effect, suggesting that he would return to the subject when the bill came before the Senate.

The amended bill came before the Senate on April 29, and Fessenden argued that it would be better to enlarge the San Francisco mint than to accept Nesmith's proposal, which would establish the precedent of creating a branch mint in every new mineral area, a costly and unnecessary policy, although one for which the Denver mint already served as precedent.

At this point Sumner came to Nesmith's assistance, despite the fact that he had voted the committee position in the earlier division. He gave a considerable discourse on European minting practices and then, in a metaphor belying his usual style, he summed the case in a "nutshell": the gold in Oregon "ought to have every advantage as merchandise which it can derive from the inspection of the Government. Call it protection if you will; but I beg to submit that an interest so important, so peculiar, and so delicate deserves this protection." There were yet passages of argument between Fessenden and Nesmith, as to the latter's charge that Fessenden always discriminated against Oregon and its senior senator, and the comparability of Maine codfish and the circulating medium of Oregon, and Cowan came to the injured Pollock's defense only to learn that he and Howe reminded Oregon's senior senator of the verse that ran:

> The bull-frog cocked his tail on high
> And went bounding o'er the plain,
> The bumble-bee went thundering by,
> And then came down the rain. [Great laughter][37]

The vote on accepting the Nesmith amendment was a defeat for Fessenden and the committee position; there were twenty-three senators voting yea and fifteen nay (I.D.: 53).

In that vote, a majority of the senators rejected the recommendation of the Committee on Finance and its powerful chairman. We cannot say in this instance that Sumner inspired his "followers" to revolt, since (if we have identified some of them correctly) they supported Nesmith in the first vote on the Oregonian's amendment, while the senator from Massachusetts voted the committee position. But the opportunity to add to Fessenden's frustration was apparently too tempting to ignore. Sumner brought his oratory to bear and the minor reshuffling in the vote in the Senate that followed produced a disagreement score of some mag-

37. Ibid., 1948, 1951.

nitude. In rallying to a Democrat such as Nesmith, the radicals were consorting with the political enemy. On the other hand, none could argue that the fate of the Union was trembling in the balance in this roll call, and the issue was not one in which hard-and-fast party lines had been drawn in long-extended debate. The satisfaction of thwarting Fessenden and so consistent a supporter of his position on financial matters as Howe could be enjoyed without endangering the party or its major policies. Self-restraint was not a virtue of the radicals—a coterie of them willingly accepted Fessenden as a negative cue-giver in this instance and doubtless enjoyed their victory.

# 10

# Afterword

The second session of the Thirty-eighth Senate ended with the Louisiana issues and the broader problems of reconstruction unresolved. A little more than a month later Lee surrendered his tattered veterans, beginning the sequence of capitulations that returned the South's surviving defenders to the farms, plantations, workshops, and offices of the nation that was not to be. A few days more and the presidential carriage made its sad trip to bring the wife of Senator Dixon to comfort the distraught Mary Todd Lincoln. Thus was the ending of the President's war and the Senate's war interwined. The nation was still far from formally restored, the legislative tasks ahead were still formidable, but the great war machine that the Congress had financed and helped to shape had done its job, and the statute books stood witness to the wide-ranging concerns of the members of the Thirty-seventh and Thirty-eighth Congresses. Indeed, when the southerners left their congressional desks in the prelude to war, they offered the Republicans an unparalleled opportunity to write the free-soil agenda of the 1850s into law. Free homesteads, subsidized transcontinental railroads, land-grant colleges, the Department of Agriculture, tariffs, national banks, emancipation—potentially if not completely realized at the war's end—as well as many less spectacular but significant changes or additions to federal law, attest to the success with which the members of the party of Lincoln capitalized on their opportunities, while smothering the great rebellion. Never before or after in American history was such massive progress made in realizing political prescriptions for reform during the processes of electoral realignment. And never before or after were so many Americans asked to pay the ultimate price; the Free-Soil agenda was, sadly enough, achieved at the cost of turning a region of the country into a vast charnel house, an outcome hardly less unhappy because southerners themselves insured that the drama would be played out on those terms.

Some contextual or background factors do provide clues to voting behavior in the Senate during the war years, although their predictive power is hardly overpowering. Episcopalians, for instance, were less willing to espouse ultra measures than were Congregationalists or Presbyterians. Former Democrats among the Republican senators appear to have reacted somewhat differently under certain conditions than did former Whigs. But party was an omnipresent influence, though often honored in the breach and occasionally—as by Joe Wright—denounced as a malign power to be ignored in such times of national distress. And within the fabric of party, the disagreement between radicals and the more moderate or conservative party members helped shape the Republican response to the challenge of both the era and the hour. The correlation coefficients displayed in Chapter 3 show that this voting alignment accounted for as much as 37 percent of the variance in scale ranking across sessions when a very important part of the congressional agenda is examined, and some 67 percent on occasion from bill scale to bill scale, when we focus upon major pieces of legislation. Had there been no turnover of personnel, the percentage might have been higher or lower in some cases. But all things considered, the radical-moderate continuum was an impressive predictor of intraparty alignments in certain categories of voting.

As we have seen, disagreements between radicals and moderates did not affect all the voting in the Senate. Nor was that structural division the only one that disturbed the harmony of the Republicans' councils or the cohesion of their voting alignments; it is also relatively easy to document the presence of differences between eastern and western members of the party. Basically, Republicans honored the bonds of party, although to varying extents and with varying degrees of satisfaction. Still, the difference between radicals and moderates was very important because it appeared in the discussion of a wide range of crucial issues faced by the members of the Civil War congresses. And traces of this alignment are to be found in many votes that did not meet the screening criterion used in selecting divisive roll calls along the radical-moderate dimension of disagreement.

Within the Senate there was much play of personality, and senatorial style may indeed have affected voting alignments on occasion. The acrimonious exchanges were probably more indicative of the depth of conviction and the tensions of overburdened lawmakers than direct clues to voting outcomes. Still, the outbursts of temperment do run counter to the arguments of those who place extreme stress on the unity of the Republicans during the war. More fundamentally damaging to the thesis that the Republicans were united on basic matters were the disagreements over policy preferences and justifications, as well as concerning political strategy, that were revealed in the discussion and voting on southern issues and racial matters. As to desired end results, there was, of course, little disagreement; to read that consensus into the actual processes of winning the war and shaping the peace is to carry reductionism to extremes and practice a consensual history that has been long discredited.

The radical dimension is not easily defined, nor is its specific substance easily revealed. In the operational definition in this book, the Senate radicals were those who most consistently appeared in the voting scales on southern and racial issues at the end farthest removed from the position of the opposition members from the loyal slave states. Sometimes, however, such senators voted with senators from the border states in an ends-against-the-middle pattern. And reality is almost invariably more complex than operational definitions. Preserving the Union by winning the war, punishing rebels, emancipating their slaves, freeing the bondsmen of Unionists, establishing and guaranteeing the civil rights of free blacks in both North and South, and reestablishing the southern states within the federal Union were all major tasks addressed by the Civil War senators with varying degrees of enthusiasm, imagination, and confidence in the means at hand. Of course these great labors were interrelated, but is it reasonable to assume that the politician who took a "radical" approach to achieving one must take a correspondingly "radical" position on all of them? As we have shown, the number of Republican senators who did so was relatively small, and the number who took consistently conservative positions perhaps even smaller. However, such men provide basic reference points in senatorial voting patterns which allow us to place the responses of newcomers, centrists, and more volatile colleagues in perspective. The terms "radical" and "conservative" were of the age, the historian should not abandon them, but, when applying such labels to Civil War senators or representatives, those interested in precise and accurate historical analysis must explain the degree to which they are appropriate in various contexts, if our understanding of Civil War legislative behavior is to advance.

I have suggested that the approach of Republican senators, in voting as radicals or as moderates, was tempered by a relatively small and closely interrelated set of attitudes, of which those concerned with constitutional interpretation and race were the most important, and I have speculated on the possibility that these were really manifestations of broader attitudes toward societal change. Changes in the scale positions of some senators through time may have reflected nothing more than the fact that the salience of particular war issues was increasing or diminishing. The result of such modifications in the congressional agenda was to alter the voting positions of particular senators relative to those of colleagues. Thus, on June 27, 1864, Trumbull, seemingly moderate in voting in the Thirty-eighth Congress, first session, sought to repeal the last clause of the resolution explanatory of the Confiscation Act of 1862 by amendment to the freedmen's bureau bill, a tactic fully consistent with his radicalism in the Thirty-seventh Congress. But such continuity in attitude suggests that to some extent we may trace behavioral patterns back to the state electoral processes that sent individuals of particular views to the Senate and underlines the importance of reexamining the political processes and public opinion in the constituent states. That must be a task for another time or other scholars.

A recent generation of historians has scorned the suggestions of an earlier generation that radicals were the advance agents of American industrialism and that there was, in other words, a consistent economic dimension of radicalism. Both groups were sufficiently imprecise in their definitions and analysis to suggest that further research may be in order. Here we have noted that the attitude of various radicals upon the proper relationship between the states and the federal government was certainly such as to gratify the industrialist interested in untrammeled development of the nation's economic potential. Various votes concerning national and state banking show definite traces of the radical-moderate division, as did the New Jersey railroad imbroglio.

"The one thing that did unite" the radicals, wrote an eminent historian, "was their implacable insistence that the war be prosecuted with ever more vigor."[1] As the historian painfully scans the sepia-hued columns of the *Congressional Globe,* reads the uncertain chirography in the surviving letters of the senators and informed observers, or follows the day-by-day unfolding of wartime events in leading newspapers of the period, it becomes clear that an important code word indicating attitude was "earnest."[2] Once attuned to its significance, a reader is struck by the

1. Eric L. McKitrick, "Party Politics and the Union and Confederate War Efforts," in William N. Chambers and Walter D. Burnham, eds., *The American Party Systems: Stages of Political Development* (New York: Oxford University Press, 1967), p. 145.

2. I pointed out the curious emphasis (in our eyes) of Civil War lawmakers upon the word "earnest," as well as their concerns over constitutional matters, in a paper, "The Substantive Meaning of Radicalism in the United States Senate during the Civil War," delivered at the Annual Meeting of the Organization of American Historians, April 1972. In *Emancipation and Equal Rights: Politics and Constitutionalism in the Civil War Era* (New York: Norton, 1978), Herman Belz, a commentator at the 1972 session wrote "According to Bogue, radicals saw themselves as 'in earnest,' while moderates preferred to express their attitude in the phrase 'men, money, and the Constitution'" (p. 30). In thus drawing on my 1972 paper, Belz ignored the fact that it was I, rather than the moderates, who stated this distinction. In this and other works, Belz minimizes the importance of the distinction between radicals and moderates.

constant reiteration of this rather prim word in the discourse of the day. On May 19, 1862, Sumner made it the text of a speech on confiscation, demanding, as he faced his colleagues, "Are you in earnest to strike this rebellion with all the force sanctioned by the rights of war, or do you refuse to use anything beyond the peaceful process of municipal law?" Thus, with magnificent intolerance, he denied the right to consider themselves in earnest to those senators who disagreed with him about the means that the Union government might use in waging war. "Two transcendent powers," he said, "have already been exercised without a murmur: first, to raise armies, and secondly, to raise money.... But there is another power without which, I fear, the end will escape us. It is that of confiscation and liberation, and this power is just as constitutional as the other two."[3] It was not enough, in other words, to raise money and armies; confiscation and emancipation must be part of an earnest or vigorous war effort.

A moderate such as Doolittle refused to accept the radical definition of what constituted a vigorous war effort. But though he disagreed with Sumner and other leading radicals, Doolittle too proclaimed his earnestness, as we have seen. If challenged, the more moderate Republicans might have expressed their formula for victory as "Men, money, and the Constitution," which to the radicals would have seemed no less irritating and misleading than the moderates found the presumption that only radical prescriptions reflected earnestness. By their own tests, all Republicans were in earnest and all revered the Constitution.

I have made the point that issues changed materially during the course of the war congresses. Does this conflict with the suggestions that reconstruction was much in the minds of the members of Congress from early in the war and that the actual process of reconstruction should be viewed as beginning during the early stages of the war as well? Here the issue is in part semantic. Certainly, in emancipating the slaves of the District of Columbia and in linking emancipation to service in the armies of the Union, the Congress was setting *de facto* terms of readmission. Whatever might happen to the institutions of the rebellious states, the Union they rejoined was going to be different because of the institutional changes that had occurred in the northern and border states during the course of the war. And to use emancipation as our example is merely to select one of many illustrations of fundamental change within the Union which would inevitably have its effect upon the returning states. But the specific arrangements under which the southern states were once more to take their places in the Union are another matter. As a legislative issue, these arrangements became increasingly salient dur-

3. *CG*, 37 Cong., 2 sess., 2195.

ing the course of the conflict, although they were in the minds of the senators from the beginning of mobilization, and some senators endeavored to lay out governing principles and specific legislative procedures for reconstruction during the Thirty-seventh Congress. But some historians to the contrary, it is amazing how little floor time the senators gave to reconstruction even during 1864.

There is currently some tendency to suggest that, radicals or no, the Republican party's solution to the dilemmas of reconstruction was essentially conservative in nature. After all, the argument runs, the Republicans avoided making any permanent redistribution of federal and state powers. We are not concerned with the reconstruction era proper in this book, but since much is also made of the wartime aspects of reconstruction and the same contention can be made about other wartime policies, we should consider this line of argument. But to examine this contention is also to reject it. In the first place, the three constitutional amendments stemming from the war did implicitly effect a redistribution of government power. And perhaps more important, the historian must take an era on its own terms. The Civil War generation discerned radical Republicans and more moderate members of the party. Radical positions were those positions enunciated and supported by radicals when considering certain areas of public policy, and moderate positions must be defined similarly. In the give and take of legislative strategy and debate, much legislation during the Civil War was tempered by the interplay of radical and moderate Republicans and also, as is often forgotten, by the actions of the members of the opposition bloc which could be very important when Republican senators disagreed. To argue that a legislative solution was not radical because more radical solutions were rejected may be to ignore the moderate or conservative alternatives that were also rejected. The degree to which a specific law incorporated radical or moderate proposals is surely the best measure of whether it was a radical or conservative solution to the issue at hand. The lawmaking process in the war senates was much more a process of interaction between radical, moderate, and opposition senators than one in which radicals or moderates invariably carried the day.

Some of the broader implications of the patterns of behavior discerned in the Senate during the Civil War years can become clear only as scholars pursue similar research in the contemporary House of Representatives and in the other wartime or realignment congresses of our history. If we hypothesize that the voting cohesion of the dominant party decreases progressively in proportion to the length of time that has elapsed since the preceding realignment, we find some support for that position in the history of the Civil War senates. There may also be support here for the suggestion that party efficiency, as reflected in strong

# The Substance of Disagreement

is maximized when the party majority is a small one. It
the commanding majority that the Republicans enjoyed
ouraged the growth of factionalism, as individual
owing the preponderance of their party, argued more per-
ently for their own solutions than they would have if the party had
possessed a slimmer margin of control. Informal cue-giving and reference group activity, as in the case of the Oregon branch mint, probably
frustrated caucus discipline on occasion; yet on the other hand, the
amount of legislation discussed and passed during the Civil War congresses was staggering by all nineteenth-century standards. The Free-
Soil agenda was attained to a phenomenal degree, encouraging one to
suggest that the degree of agenda realization is directly related both to
the seriousness of the crisis and to the degree of disorganization found
in the opposition party.

Few of the forty-three men who entered the legislative sessions of the
Civil War Senate as Republicans were political novices. But only Hale
and Simmons had known the chamber during the 1840s and their service was not continuous. Although twenty-two of them were in place by
the end of 1860, the largest single annual increment of ten took their
oaths in 1861 (see Table 10-1). Thereafter, only eleven new Republican
senators entered the Senate during the conflict, if we ignore men of the
border states like Henderson, Willey, and Van Winkle, who moved to
full-scale support of the Republicans only during the last years of the
war. Vacancies were created when Bingham of Michigan died suddenly

TABLE 10-1.
The Republican war senators: arrivals*

|      | Number | Cumulative percent |
| ---- | ------ | ------------------ |
| 1851 | 3      | 7                  |
| 1854 | 1      | 9                  |
| 1855 | 5      | 21                 |
| 1857 | 7      | 37                 |
| 1859 | 5      | 49                 |
| 1860 | 1      | 51                 |
| 1861 | 10     | 74                 |
| 1862 | 3      | 81                 |
| 1863 | 5      | 93                 |
| 1864 | 3      | 100                |

*Simmons served 1841–47 and 1857–62.
Hale served 1847–53 and 1855–65. The increment of 1861 was swelled by the departure of
Cameron (elected 1857), Chase (elected 1857),
and Seward (elected 1849) to serve in the cabinet.

in early October, 1861, and Baker fell at Ball's Bluff some two weeks later. Simmons resigned under fire at the conclusion of the second session of the Thirty-seventh Congress, and state legislators replaced five senators at the conclusion of the third session; of the group, only King had served a full six-year term. The only major Republican leader to leave the Senate during the course of the conflict was Fessenden, who resigned in early July, 1864, to become Secretary of the Treasury.

Fessenden returned to the chamber in 1865; four of his colleagues also interrupted their service subsequently and held a cabinet position in the interim. William Stewart of Nevada was the only other wartime senator to serve in the Senate twice. Adding the six repeaters to the original number of Republican senators yields 49 departures in all (see Table 10-2). Although the turnover during the war was not great, the ranks of the war senators dwindled rapidly during the latter half of the 1860s. By the end of 1871, 66 percent of them were no longer in the Senate. At the conclusion of 1875, only Morrill, Sherman, Howe, and Anthony remained, although Chandler was reelected a few months before his death in 1879. After serving from 1864 to 1875, Stewart returned to the Senate in 1887 and continued in the chamber until 1905. Although the leading citizen of Bullfrog, Nevada, then elected to spend most of his time in the capital city until his death in 1909, an era of senatorial history had ended.

Nine of the forty-three Republican senators died in office. Of those who survived their service in the Senate, ten ran again for elective federal or state office, quite apart from allowing their names to stand in senatorial balloting by state party caucus or legislative assembly. Only three of this group were successful; Henry Wilson won the vice presidency, B. Gratz Brown became governor of Missouri, and Morton Wilkinson won election to the House of Representatives and also served four terms in the Minnesota state senate. These successes all occurred during the 1870s. Doolittle emerged as the most tireless unsuccessful campaigner, running for governor and the state judiciary of Wisconsin once, and twice for the United States House of Representatives. Discredited by accusations of bribery when seeking reelection in 1873, Pomeroy launched the most futile candidacy of all eleven years later, when he allowed his name to stand as the presidential nominee on a national prohibition ticket. Three other former senators served as members of state constitutional conventions.

In their continuing political activities, at least seven of the war senators reconsidered their party affiliations. Brown, Browning, Doolittle, and Trumbull ultimately made unabashed commitment to the Democrats, after embracing the liberal Republican cause in 1872. Foster ran for Congress on a fusion ticket in that same decade. Sprague was the Demo-

TABLE 10-2.
The Republican war senators: departures*

|      | Number | Cumulative percent |      | Number | Cumulative percent |
| ---- | ------ | ------------------ | ---- | ------ | ------------------ |
| 1861 | 2      | 4                  | 1873 | 5      | 76                 |
| 1862 | 1      | 6                  | 1874 | 1      | 78                 |
| 1863 | 5      | 16                 | 1875 | 4      | 86                 |
| 1864 | 1      | 18                 | 1876 | 1      | 88                 |
| 1865 | 6      | 31                 | 1877 | 1      | 90                 |
| 1866 | 3      | 37                 | 1879 | 2      | 94                 |
| 1867 | 5      | 47                 | 1884 | 1      | 96                 |
| 1869 | 8      | 64                 | 1897 | 1      | 98                 |
| 1871 | 1      | 66                 | 1905 | 1      | 100                |

*Through death or other form of withdrawal. Six senators interrupted their service during the war or thereafter: Fessenden, Harlan, Morrill, Chandler, Stewart, Sherman.

cratic candidate for governor of Rhode Island in 1883 and Wilkinson switched his allegiance during the mid-1880s. Trumbull went to the point of drafting a Populist platform which Illinois delegates carried with them to a convention of the People's party. We cannot generalize confidently on the basis of the behavior of seven men; the antecedents of three of them were Whig and the other four had come to the Republican party from the Democracy. Since there were more old Whigs than former Democrats among the forty-three Republican senators, there was in proportional terms a greater tendency among the old Democrats to become Democrats after 1870 than among those of Whig antecedents. Although he did not run for popularly elected office, the conservative Cowan received Democratic rather than Republican support in his unsuccessful efforts to win reelection in Pennsylvania in 1867. Browning, Doolittle, and Foster had been consistently moderate or conservative during the war years. Trumbull and Brown, on the other hand, were considered to be radicals during part of their wartime service but were not consistently ultra. Sprague was radical but somewhat centrist in voting. Thus, of those who made common cause with the Democrats at some point after the war, only Wilkinson had been markedly and consistently radical in his voting behavior during all of his wartime service in the Senate.

Eight of the forty-three Republican senators served in the cabinet; Fessenden, Chandler, Harlan, Morrill, and Sherman regained their seats after a tour of service in the executive branch. Only Sherman had two terms of such service, which were separated by a broad interval of time; he performed both as Secretary of the Treasury for President Hayes and as Secretary of State in the first McKinley administration. In effect, he, Browning, Howe, and Ramsey ended their national political careers in the cabinet.

Only four of the Republican senators served in the judiciary subsequent to their Senate service: Clark, Field, and Wilmot remained in the federal judiciary until their deaths and Foster sat for six years on the superior court of Connecticut. The old senators shook various other plums from the tree of patronage, however. Hale, for example, spent a contentious but relatively brief period as minister to Spain. But his former colleagues paid the ultimate senatorial discourtesy to Cowan, when Johnson tried to send him in the same capacity to Austria; they rejected the Pennsylvanian as a traitor to the party. King of New York accepted the position of collector of the Port of New York, and Lot Morrill ultimately took the same post in Portland. Harlan graced the Alabama Claims Commission with his presence; Henry S. Lane was both a special Indian commissioner and member of a commission for the improvement of the Mississippi River. Wade served both as a member of the celebrated Santo Domingo Commission and as a government director of the Union Pacific Railroad. After failing to obtain reelection, Howe was an Indian commissioner, charged with the purchase of the Black Hills, and an American representative to the International Monetary Conference in Paris before joining President Arthur's cabinet. Alexander Ramsey's reward for faithful party service was the chairmanship of the commission designed to purify the land of the Mormon Saints according to the gospel of the Edmunds Act.

Although it reveals the relatively minor role of the war senators after 1870, and illuminates various features of the American political and party system, such recital of the bare bones of individual political biographies hardly hints at the variety of experience that one finds in their later lives. Grimes and Dixon ministered to their delicate health, the latter spending his time in "literary pursuits," as befitted the only poet in the war senate, and in travel. Some returned to their old occupations and lived on placidly for years. Harris resumed his law practice and his lectures at the Albany Law School and served as a trustee of other institutions of higher learning. Despite his continuing interest in politics and its rewards, Doolittle lectured at the law school of the University of Chicago and even held the presidency of that institution for a year. Trumbull too was a leading figure in the law community in Chicago and, indeed, the two old senatorial colleagues formed a partnership.

Clark died peacefully in 1891, his head cradled on his arm in a habitual pose, after twenty-four years on the federal bench; but Howard's heart failed him only a month after leaving the Senate in 1871. The ponderous and good-hearted radical from New York, King, broke under the strain of administering the New York custom house and leaped from a ferry in New York harbor, well weighted with lead shot. In disfavor among his constituents for supporting Johnson and charged with corrupt acts, the violent Jim Lane put a bullet in his brain. But it was not until 1915, when they brought Rhode Island's boy governor and colonel back from Paris for burial with military honors that the name of the last war senator was scratched from the roll of the living. Long since divested of most of his fortune and divorced from Kate Chase, his son a suicide, William Sprague spent his later years quietly in Paris with his protective second wife. Although old and frail, he had not been too feeble to drape the American flag over the top of the car that carried them to safety when the German troops threatened to reach Paris in their first great surge toward that city.

A few of the war senators are today represented in the statuary collections of the Capitol. Sumner's betogaed bust commands a stairway and Baker, also in toga, towers in the rotunda, while at his feet sits the battered old hat that held his papers while he was on circuit. Harlan is here, but not his much more forceful and constructive colleague, Grimes. Maine's wartime delegation is represented by Hannibal Hamlin rather than by the hard-working Fessenden. Chandler's arrogant countenance scowls at throngs who have never heard of the Joint Committee on the Conduct of the War, nor seen a general cringe. One historian has inquired, "Why Jacob Collamer?" in latter-day response to Vermont's choice of that gentleman to stand with the colorful Ethan Allen in the National Statuary Hall Collection. But the wartime contributions of the sage old judge certainly outweigh the national contributions of many others enshrined here. At any rate, his statue stands in the Hall of Columns, the face square and benevolent, the hands clasped behind his back and, on a recent day, they held a penny delicately between thumb and finger, the work of schoolboy pranksters but rather appropriate, given the Vermonter's continuing interest in banking and monetary matters. Of the opposition, only Rice may be found among the capital statuary, a selection attributable to his contribution in the making of Minnesota. Clearly the wartime activities of the senators remembered here were important, but only Sumner, and perhaps Collamer, are truly entitled to be considered among the lawmakers who had the greatest influence on legislative outcomes in the Senate during the years of the Civil War.

The Civil War senators wrote surprisingly little of their experience during the war, either to defend or to glorify their actions. The generals proved far more eager to take pen in hand than these politicians. The funerary monuments of some contributed to the war of words and symbols that followed the war in the field. Wilmot was laid to rest beneath a marble spike that bore simply the words of the famous proviso. The mourners of Waldo Johnson, who had served in the first session of the Thirty-seventh Congress before espousing the Confederacy, etched the flag of the Confederate States upon his tombstone of Missouri granite. But in addition to the few memoirs and fragments of reminiscence and collections of personal papers that they bequeathed to posterity, the war senators left a public monument in the volumes of the *Congressional Globe* and one-and-a-half volumes of the *Statutes at Large*. The effects of some of their legislation was negligible, that of other statutes transient, some the senators themselves scorned for the compromises that they represented, but others were the foundation of victory and of a world that was to be different in its economic organization, its polity, its very society. As the astute Garfield argued, the war helped produce major changes in American legislative processes.[4] Although that able soldier and politician did not know the word, he identified what today we call institutionalization or modernization. Surely the men whose work this was can have no better epitaph than a simple "They served in the Civil War Senate."

4. James A. Garfield, "A Century of Congress," *Atlantic Monthly*, 40 (July 1877), 62.

# Roll-Call Analysis Procedures

A student of Civil War history who determines to investigate the degree to which individual senators were radical or nonradical learns immediately that the sources leave something to be desired. Excellent biographies portray the political careers of some Civil War senators but of only a minority. The *Dictionary of American Biography* provides useful short sketches of many but not all. And in preparing these essays, the authors had space at best to discuss the legislative position of their subjects on only a few pieces of legislation. All of the senators of the Civil War era appear in the *Biographical Directory of Congress,* but the sketches there give little clue to specific legislative attitudes. Other biographical compendia have similar shortcomings. The activities of some senators received considerable coverage in newspapers; the names of others seldom appeared in the press. The manuscript papers of only a minority of senators survive, and even so massive a collection as that accumulated by John Sherman tells much more about the feelings of his constituents than about the behavior and attitudes of the junior senator from Ohio during the Civil War. When we turn to the pages of the *Congressional Globe,* we discover that some senators explained their legislative objectives in great detail while others seldom if ever spoke. In the roll-call responses, however, we find data that is uniform in nature, relevant to most of the great issues of the war, and elicited from almost all of the members of the chamber in a systematic form that can be used to build a rather formidable structure of quantitative analysis.

A few simple statistical tools can be of great assistance in the analysis of legislative behavior, providing standard measures that allow us to compare the reactions of one group of legislators in particular roll calls with those of another. An index number of cohesion shows the extent to which a political party or group is united in a particular roll call on a scale running from one to one hundred. The cohesion index used in this study is calculated by subtracting the proportion of a given party, or other designated group, represented by the minority from the percentage that the majority represents. Equal proportions, a tie (50-50), produce a cohesion score of 0. Similarly, an index number of agreement or likeness measures the degree to which the members of two parties or groups vote alike in a division, and the converse of such a number can be called an index of disagreement. Thus, if Democrats and Republicans agreed on a particular vote to the amount of 40 percent of the maximum agreement which would result when all Republicans and all Democrats voted alike, the index of likeness would be 40 and the index of disagreement would be 60. The index of likeness is calculated by subtracting the positive difference in the affirmative or negative votes of two parties, or groups from 100 (I.L. = 100 − (Republican percent yea − Democratic percent yea).

Cohesion and likeness scores are very useful measures when we are seeking to understand or contrast the behavior of nominal or categorical groups like Democrats and Republicans or Protestant and Roman Catholic legislators or western and eastern lawmakers. The differing political, religious, or regional affiliations identified in such groupings are usually well documented and, on occasion, have an institutional foundation. But some types of political groups are less easily isolated or defined for purposes of study. The farm bloc of the 1920s and the conservative alliance of northern Republicans and southern Democrats that allegedly emerged during Franklin Roosevelt's presidency both brought Republican and Democratic congressmen together in political groups that apparently exercised considerable control over various types of legislative outputs. The challenge in such cases is to devise methods of analyzing roll-call responses that will reveal the outlines of the *de facto* groups with the greatest possible accuracy, and such activity leads us into the land of "empirically ordered" groups, a treacherous region where mountains may have neither base nor summit and oasis becomes mirage in a twinkling.

Before I describe two other analytical tools used in this work, let us examine some of the implications of a common-sense method of grouping that has been used in some studies. Confronted with the necessity of dividing legislators into antagonistic groups such as radicals or conservatives, the authors selected a number of roll calls in which they believed the voting would distinguish conservative lambs from radical wolves. They then decided whether yea or nay constituted a radical response and grouped the legislators on the basis of the total number of radical responses made. At first glance this method appears to be neat, sanitary, and utilitarian. Unfortunately, corruption lurks below the cellophane.

The investigators have used their own subjective judgment in deciding the roll calls that provide a good test, and the smaller the number selected the greater the chance of selecting votes that inadequately reflect the legislative patterns and attitudes involved. In deciding what constitutes a radical or nonradical response such researchers again inject a subjective judgment. And finally, in grouping legislators with similar gross scores into the same categories, they make the fallacious inference that two legislators who in gross agree with the researchers' standard of radicalism at a particular level of intensity agree with each other in the same degree. Table A-1 shows the error that may occur when the votes of legislators A and B are compared to a radical standard of behavior devised by the investigators. In the research designs used by a number of scholars during the last decade, legislator A and legislator B would be grouped together since the responses of both coincided with the investigator's standard in 50 percent of the roll calls. As the illustration shows, however, legislators A and B disagreed with each other in every single roll call. Although characteristics of particular roll calls studied may alleviate this grouping problem, the method in general is obviously suspect.

Other techniques are basically more reliable than grouping to the investigator's standard, and of these I have relied heavily upon two in this study. One is the cluster-bloc technique used most notably by David B. Truman in his book *The Congressional Party*. If we record the number of times that each senator votes with every other lawmaker in a set of roll calls, we can find groups of like-minded individuals by fitting the pair-agreement scores into a matrix with the highest agreements in the upper left corner. Computers, of course, are delighted to construct the matrix in such analysis, and the legislative groups derived by this process are often called cluster blocs. Of course the investigator must decide on the selection of roll calls to be analyzed in this way, so the subjective element is by no means completely removed. The cluster-bloc technique may not reveal the shifting patterns of agreement among legislators over time and gives no hint of the relative extremeness in attitude of group members in comparison with the positions taken by the members of other groups. It requires the researcher to make arbitrary decisions concerning the outer limits of the groups or clusters.

On first acquaintance the Guttman scale appears somewhat more intimidating than the cluster-bloc technique. It has, however, been in use among historians for some twenty-five years and is a highly useful tool when gradations of attitude are involved. Those who have not given the method any serious consideration may find it helpful to consider the hypothetical situation depicted in Table A-2. Let us imagine that the United States congressmen of the 1850s decided to establish a new terri-

TABLE A–1.
TABLE A–1.
Grouping to prescribed standard

| Votes | Radical response defined by investigator | Legislator A | Legislator B |
|-------|------------------------------------------|--------------|--------------|
| 1 | Y | N | Y |
| 2 | Y | N | Y |
| 3 | Y | N | Y |
| 4 | Y | Y | N |
| 5 | Y | Y | N |
| 6 | Y | Y | N |

tory, the Territory of Kanneb, and that positions concerning the treatment of slavery and race in that region were well developed among the congressmen. As the discussion of the Kanneb organic act developed it became clear that seven propositions were to be introduced and voted on, it being recognized by the reader that in other than an imaginary situation the introduction of several of these propositions might not have been tolerated at the time. The reader will note too that, when arranged as in the upper half of Table A-2, these propositions seem to represent a progression in attitude from 1, in which the federal government actually reimburses the slaveholder for slaves lost through flight, to 7, in which the Negro is allowed to reside as a free man and enjoy the right of suffrage in the Territory. There seems, in other words, to be an attitudinal continuum and this is reflected in the voting patterns of eight illustrative congressmen as arranged in the bottom half of Table A-2.

If we examine the positions which Congressmen A through H took on the seven proposals, we note diminishing enthusiasm for the support of slavery, and restriction of the individual on racial grounds, and the reverse is true if one first examines the positions from H to A, since the former forthrightly supported the vote for free blacks and would not even support squatter sovereignty. In terms of attitude or opinion there seems, in other words, a cumulative progression in these propositions, of rising or diminishing intensity of "extremeness" or attitude on the race issue. Every one of A's seven responses can be regarded as proslavery or racist in varying degree, and we can therefore assign him a score of 7, while the liberalism of H earns a 0, and their colleagues range between these polar types in a scale that includes eight voting or scale types in all. If we had wished to interpret the scale in terms of antiracism we could equally well have scored H as 7 and A as 0. Although it may seem obvious to the point of truism, our example shows that the policy positions taken by the legislators become more extreme as one works out from the center of the scale toward the poles and suggests also that the more extreme the proposition the fewer will be its supporters. There has been some cautioning to the effect that such patterns need not necessarily reflect varying degrees of a particular stimulus, and this may well be true in certain instances. Certainly, however, such scales are useful means of summarizing group behavior, and the problem of underlying attitude is one upon which additional evidence may be brought to bear, particularly the substantive content of the propositions involved.

In constructing this illustration I have in effect turned the process of constructing scales back to front by progressing from the voting propositions to the voting matrix and scale scores. But once the general universe of real roll calls to be considered is decided, scale construction is actually governed by the degree to which the roll calls resemble each other. In practical terms, it is probably most easily visualized as a process in which the researcher selects from a set of roll calls the one that has the smallest group ($G_1$) of legislators voting together against the remainder of their colleagues. To this roll call is then added one in which the members of $G_1$ voted in bloc but also voted in company with a small number of additional legislators ($G_2$), and to this roll call is then added a third in which $G_1$ and $G_2$ were joined by the members of $G_3$ who voted

TABLE A-2.

Slavery and race in Kanneb Territory

Propositions relative to race in Kanneb Territory:

1 Slaveholders to be reimbursed for lost fugitives by federal government
2 Approval of federal constitutional amendment guaranteeing perpetual slavery
3 Slavery declared a legal institution in the territorial organic act
4 Slavery to be allowed by settler referendum
5 Slavery forbidden under the terms of the organic act
6 Free Negroes allowed to reside and own property in the territory
7 Free Negroes allowed the suffrage in the territory

Voting Matrix

| Propositions | 1 | 2 | 3 | 4 | 5 | 6 | 7 | 1 | 2 | 3 | 4 | 5 | 6 | 7 | Scale type |
|---|---|---|---|---|---|---|---|---|---|---|---|---|---|---|---|
| Congressmen | Y | Y | Y | Y | N | N | N | N | N | N | N | Y | Y | Y | |
| A | X | X | X | X | X | X | X | | | | | | | | 7 |
| B | | X | X | X | X | X | X | X | | | | | | | 6 |
| C | | | X | X | X | X | X | X | X | | | | | | 5 |
| D | | | | X | X | X | X | X | X | X | | | | | 4 |
| E | | | | | X | X | X | X | X | X | X | | | | 3 |
| F | | | | | | X | X | X | X | X | X | X | | | 2 |
| G | | | | | | | X | X | X | X | X | X | X | | 1 |
| H | | | | | | | | X | X | X | X | X | X | X | 0 |

with $G_1$ and $G_2$ in additional roll calls subsequently added to the scale matrix, and so on.

In practice the strength of the relationship between any two roll calls is usually determined by calculating the value of one of a number of appropriate contingency coefficients, of which Q has been used most frequently.

With absences ignored, a lawmaker's responses in two roll calls will assume one of four different patterns, Yea—Yea, Nay—Yea, Yea—Nay or Nay—Nay. The voting of legislators in two roll calls can be summarized, therefore, in a four-cell table as follows:

| YY | NY |
|----|----|
| YN | NN |

although some analysts prefer to summarize in terms of polar tendencies rather than in terms of yea or nay. Such four-cell values can be substituted in the formula of the Q coefficient. Q values may run from + 1 to −1 and high values, either plus or minus, denote strong scaling relationships.

$$Q = (ad - bc)/(ad + bc) \text{ where}$$

| a | b |
|---|---|
| c | d |

or, if roll calls 1 and 2 from Table 3-2 are used:

$$Q = (6 \times 18 - 1 \times 4)/(6 \times 18 + 1 \times 4)$$
$$= (108 - 4)/(108 + 4)$$
$$= (104)/(112)$$
$$= .928$$

Scales can be presented in various formats and summary formats. For illustrative purposes, I present a skeleton mirror scale based on the dominant scale on southern issues found in the Thirty-seventh Senate, second session, which in its original form ranked thirty-nine senators on the basis of their responses in fifty-two scaling roll calls. The six roll calls used here relate to emancipation, the use of black soldiers, and confiscation (see Table 3-2 for the full scale in its six vote form).

As presented here, a plus sign represents support for southern institutions and a minus sign represents opposition. Republican radicals therefore appear at the bottom. Had the order of the votes been re-

TABLE A-3.

Skeleton scale based on southern issues

| Senator | Party–State | Scale type | 1 Y | 2 Y | 3 Y | 4 N | 5 Y | 6 Y | 1 N | 2 N | 3 N | 4 Y | 5 N | 6 N |
|---------|-------------|------------|-----|-----|-----|-----|-----|-----|-----|-----|-----|-----|-----|-----|
| Powell | D–Ky. | 6 | + | + | + | + | + | + | | | | | | |
| Willey | U–Va. | 5 | | + | + | + | + | + | 0 | | | | | |
| Henderson | D–Mo. | 4 | | | + | + | + | + | − | − | | | | |
| Sherman | R–O. | 3 | | | | + | + | + | − | − | − | | | |
| Foot | R–Vt. | 2 | | | | | + | + | − | − | − | − | | |
| Sumner | R–Mass. | 1 | | | | | | + | − | − | − | − | − | |
| Chandler | R–Mich. | 0 | | | | | | | − | − | − | − | − | − |

versed and the Republicans moved to the top, (as in Table 3-2) the + would then have represented opposition to southern institutions and Chandler's scale type would have become 6, reflecting the fact that he had voted against southern institutions in all six voting tests. The 0 under vote 1/N shows that Willey was absent in vote 1 which, had this been a complete scale, would have raised the question of whether he should be considered to be in the same voting type as Powell.

Roll calls are assumed to enter the scale matrix in descending or ascending order according to the "extremeness" of the voting tests involved; the order in which lawmakers join the original group ranks them in terms of "extremeness" of their attitudes on the issue involved. However, a Guttman scale does not tell precisely how much more extreme in attitude the members of scale type 5 are in comparison to the members of scale type 4. It is therefore an ordinal rather than an interval scale.

Similarly, scales measure different voting continua, and it would be inappropriate to summarize legislator A's position in three scales by merely dividing the sum of his three scale positions by three. This latter dilemma can be solved by standardizing scales, that is, by adjusting the scale type units within them to a common base. To do this we may calculate for any scale the percentage of the whole group that the members of each scale type comprise and set them in order within a scaling metric of 0 to 100 by assigning the midpoint of that scale type's portion of the scale as the common score of all members of that group. Thus if the moderate pole is estimated at 0 and the five members in the most moderate scale type comprise 11 percent of the membership, the standardized scale score of each senator in that scale type would be 6. After this transformation the standardized scores of a lawmaker may be averaged across scales and a final value obtained that summarizes his or her tendency to take a moderate or radical position on all of the scales under study. The summary rankings of the senators relative to southern issues in the various sessions of the war congresses are shown in Table 3-6. The number of roll calls and scales involved insured that there would be little grouping on the same scores in the summary lists. The cross-session correlations between the listings displayed in Table 3-7 rose only by .08 when the numerical mean scores were used to calculate Pearson's r instead of using a rank-order coefficient.

The scalogram masks but does not completely destroy temporal relationships, and discards roll calls that will not scale. There is also involved in scaling the assumption that legislators will vote for measures which in their minds represent only half a loaf because half is, after all, better than none. Not all representatives and senators reason in this way at all times; some, in frustration, vote against bills because they deem them too weak. But in general the principle holds. Indeed, John Sherman stated it neatly on one occasion in the Thirty-seventh Congress, "It is always better, in a legislative body . . . to do the best you can. It is a principle by which I have always been governed."[1]

When the Guttman scale technique is applied to a large universe of roll calls, it may reveal that the roll calls under consideration break into several scales. The votes involving one issue form a scale, perhaps, and in another instance the roll calls relating to several other issues may all fit together, showing, most would argue, that in the minds of the legislators these issues were viewed in a common perspective, revealing what some would call a policy dimension. Scaling, as a result, may reveal unexpected relationships between issues. When the roll calls generated by a particular issue do not demonstrate a scaler relationship, we assume that the lawmakers voted idiosyncratically, saw little or no relationship among the various proposals at vote, or changed their minds several times during the course of voting. But if, as over a period of time, the members of a legislative chamber develop their ideas about an important issue systematically, the roll calls may produce Guttman scales of high quality. And in a case such as the Civil War congresses in which the terms "radical" and "conservative" emerge from the rhetoric of the debates, the Guttman scale appears to be an extremely useful tool. But no one measure of legislative behavior is perfect or all-revealing; the strategy of this study has been to use a combination of techniques.

After some experimentation with the Guttman-Lingoes program I constructed the scales used in this book by having Gerald Kreuser develop a computer program that calculated the numerical four-cell values and Q scores for all pairs of roll calls under examination. On the basis of these results I constructed the largest scales possible from the universe of votes on southern issues and racial matters. I always examined the Q

1. *CG*, 37 Cong., 2 sess., 2999.

scores but established, as the basic criterion, the rule that no vote would be placed in a scale if more than 10 percent errors were generated in comparing it with any other roll call in the scale set. The .90 score on the most commonly used measure of scale quality—the coefficient of reproducibility (1 − errors/responses)—is usually considered adequate and our criterion for inclusion produced coefficients well above that level. In assessing a paper developed at an intermediate stage of the research, a commentator questioned the wisdom of scaling within a sizable universe of roll calls and argued that the roll calls relating to the various issues should have been scaled separately. Actually, in a very broad sense I used a policy-dimension analysis approach, but this could not be applied with the confidence that analysts of the modern Congress justifiably display. I verified my assumption that the senators did more than deal with specific issues on an ad hoc basis by testing the correlations between the scales emerging from roll calls that appeared from the universe of southern roll calls. But to meet the argument that scales should have been prepared on an issue-by-issue basis, I also prepared individual scales for some of the major legislative issues, and these were discussed in Chapter 3. The results did not fundamentally change the broad conclusions to which the initial procedures had pointed.

We should, of course, avoid imposing unreasonable standards in evaluating the behavior of political groups or individual legislators. To expect voting blocs or factions to maintain the same membership over long periods of time is unrealistic. The erratic legislator is hardly unique to our harried age. It is similarly unrealistic to suppose that all legislators will maintain exactly the same ideological position relative to colleagues over a period of two or more sessions, or even during a session. It is unreasonable to assume that group feeling must be reflected by agreement across a number of different kinds of issues or that all members of a group should reflect the same intensity of attitude concerning even those issues on which they most strongly agree. The crucial defection or the betrayal of friends provides us with the high drama of political history, but such acts must be viewed in the general perspective of voting frequencies.

During the course of the research, several suggestions have been advanced in the social-science literature for improvement or alteration of scaling procedures. Some writers have suggested the coefficient phi as a proportion of the maximum value attainable by phi as an alternative to Q. Others have found the Guttman scale overly rigorous and suggested modification or alternative procedures. Still others have suggested that multidimensional scaling techniques are far superior to a unidimensional scaling procedure. Most of the suggestions relate to issues of fine tuning. They would not, if used, lead to a substantially different picture than that presented here. And in a recent paper Aage Clausen and Carl Van Horn have shrewdly noted the weaknesses in the arguments on behalf of multidimensional scaling. This is not to say, however, that Guttman scaling analysis allows us to give the last word concerning the behavioral dimensions and voting relationships of the Civil War Senate. But by using it we can lay the groundwork for the more sophisticated studies that may appear at a later time.[2]

A reference is made in Chapter 3, note 18, to factor analysis. In this technique, which has many variants, it is assumed that "a set of variables" may be expressed "in terms of a smaller number of hypothetical variables."[3] Matrices of agreement scores between variables are analyzed to obtain measures of the relationship between the variables and such hypothetical variables or "factors." The technique was used as an exploratory device on occasion and most specifically to obtain a more precise statement of the clustering effects that appeared in Table 3-11. The results did not, however, fundamentally change our understanding of the relationships revealed by other types of agreement analysis.

2. A good introduction to the methodology is provided by Samuel G. Patterson, *Notes on Legislative Behavior Research* (Iowa City: University of Iowa, 1965); Lee Anderson et al., *Legislative Roll-Call Analysis* (Evanston: Northwestern University Press, 1966); and Duncan MacRae, Jr., *Issues and Parties in Legislative Voting: Methods of Statistical Analysis* (New York: Harper, 1970). Pages 299–309 of MacRae's work contain an excellent bibliography of articles and books, including both studies that stress substantive findings and those concerned primarily with statistical methods and analysis. See also Charles M. Dollar and Richard J. Jensen, *Historian's Guide to Statistics: Quantitative Analysis and Historical Research* (New York: Holt, Rinehart, & Winston, 1971). The "proximity model," a related but in some cases more flexible scaling model than the Guttman scale, is described in Herbert F. Weisberg, "Scaling Models for Legislative Roll-Call Analysis," *American Political Science Review*, 66 (December 1972), 1306–15; see also his "Dimensionland: An Excursion into Spaces," *American Journal of Political Science*, 18 (November 1974), 743–45. David C. Leege and Wayne L. Frances, *Political Research: Design, Measurement and Analysis* (New York: Basic Books, 1974), pp. 134–69, briefly introduce some of the more troublesome problems about the validation of measures such as the Guttman scale. See also Murray G. Murphey, *Our Knowledge of the Historical Past* (Indianapolis: Bobbs-Merrill, 1973), pp. 181–90, and Aage Clausen and Carl E. Van Horn, "How to Analyze Too Many Roll Calls," *Political Methodology*, 4 (Autumn 1977), 313–31.

3. Jae-On Kim and Charles W. Mueller, *Introduction to Factor Analysis: What It Is and How to Do It* (Beverly Hills: Sage Publications, 1978), p. 9.

# The Screening Procedure for the
# Selection of "Divisive" Votes

Very early in my research, it became clear that the ranking of individual senators along a radical-moderate or radical-moderate-conservative continuum or continua was a useful exercise and cleared the way for a definitional clarity that was often lacking in earlier discussions of Republican radicals and moderates. It also became clear that the substantive legislative content and the ideological implications involved in the votes that ordered the scale rankings of senators deserved a good deal more scrutiny and analysis than was to be found in earlier scalogram analysis. The content of the matters which precipitated votes showed that the more radical differed from the less radical in their approach to the issues and might also suggest, when taken with the testimony of the debates and other supporting evidence, why these senators held different positions or at least how they explained such divergencies. But how to select those votes which would be most useful in this respect? The combined scale rankings based on southern issues ranked all senators according to their tendency to take polar positions in the voting. A matrix of percentage agreement scores on the same issues showed that there was some tendency for a break to appear in the middle ranges of the rankings in the Thirty-seventh Senate such that those senators on the side adjacent to the radical pole voted much more strongly in agreement with their fellows than with the senators on the moderate side of the break and such that the opposite was true on the moderate side of the division. That voting pattern also seemed basically congruent with the biographical information available, although the latter sources were incomplete and in some individual cases conflicting. Dealing with the second session of the Thirty-seventh Congress, I broke the scale-summary continuum so as to provide a radical group of seventeen and a moderate group of fourteen. The votes of major interest to me, I assumed, were those in which there was substantial disagreement between the members of the two groups.

But what should be considered as constituting "substantial disagreement"? If the radicals, given the distribution above, voted in concert and six of the moderates (43 percent) deserted their party fellows, both radicals and other moderates, cohesion in the radical camp would stand at 100 and that on the moderate side of the party at only 14 (57 percent − 43 percent), certainly a considerable contrast. Calculation of the coefficient of likeness in this same situation would produce a result of 57— [100 − (100 − 57)], or a coefficient of disagreement of 43, where we take the difference between the coefficient of likeness and 100 as our measure. The magnitude of these scores seemed sufficiently impressive to justify investigation, meaning, as they do, that almost 20 percent of the Republican senatorial party had deserted their colleagues. We know also that deviant votes of this sort frequently indicate unease within a congressional party beyond that specifically shown by the errant voters, party discipline or other considerations finally leading some waverers to conform to the party majority. Considerations of this sort led us to establish a coefficient of 40 as indicating the minimum level of disagreement which would be used in searching for divisive votes that particularly revealed those issues on which radicals and moderates differed.

In the final analysis the researcher must use judgment in deciding where boundaries are to be drawn; even when statistical tests of confidence or significance are used, the researcher will typically decide whether .10, .05, .01 or .001 is to provide the appropriate level. Strictly speaking, since we are studying a whole population (all Republican senators) such tests are not directly applicable here, but distributions of radical and moderate votes that produced disagreement coefficients in the 40 percent range revealed, where amendable to chi square analysis, that such patterns would have occurred by chance less than once in a hundred times. Another type of probability analysis tells us that the probability of obtaining by chance the division used for illustrative purposes in the preceding paragraph is .004. Since the groups were unequal in size, it took a slightly larger number of deviant radicals than of moderates to produce a disagreement coefficient of 40 or better; seven, in the case in which the moderates stood fully united.

It is important to remember that in this operation we are *not* trying to establish that senator A was a radical and that senator B was a moderate, or arguing that because A and B disagreed 40 percent of the time one should be considered a radical and one a moderate. The tendencies of the senators to vote on the radical or moderate end of the party voting spectrum were established in earlier chapters; those tendencies were summed up in one ranking, combining the standardized scale scores, and the groups used in screening for divisive votes are simply the summary scale ranking broken in two. So my screening groups had a very special structure; in each case they included individuals who, in my scales, showed a tendency to be very moderate or very radical but they also included centrists, and when I examine individual roll calls the centrists tended to be much more variable in their voting than the polar types: that is, a centrist inclined in sum to take moderate positions would still vote more frequently with the radicals than would a moderate whose scale positions placed him adjacent to the Northern Democrats, and a centrist inclined in sum toward the radical pole would be found voting with the moderate polar types more often than would a Sumner or a Chandler. If I had eliminated the middle third of the Republican voting spectrum for the purpose of calculating disagreement scores, those scores would have risen very sharply indeed, and if only the Republicans who voted in the radical half of the summary scale rankings in all sessions of the Civil War congresses and those similarly appearing always in the moderate half had been considered, the disagreement scores of votes that I found to be in the 40 percent range would usually have reached very high levels, and additional votes would have generated coefficients in the 40 percent range. Since there was some question as to the exact time when Henderson, Willey, and Van Winkle should be considered as becoming Republicans, they were left in the Border Unionist category in the analysis of the votes of the Thirty-eighth Senate. To have included them as moderate Republicans, and a case can be made for this procedure, would have materially raised the level of the disagreement coefficients. My scoring in this respect is therefore conservatively low.

By arbitrarily constructing two groups, I have masked the radical and moderate structures to some degree. Given the fact that minority voting within the party was shaped to a very considerable extent by those who tended more definitely toward the poles of the scales, a division of Republicans which merely broke the summary scale ranking in two equal parts would have identified many of the same roll calls as those revealed in the present research. And the technique identifies roll calls in which the radicals and moderates were arrayed in an "ends-against-the-middle" pattern, as well as in the more common polar spectrum.

As I have pointed out, individuals changed position in the scale rankings as they moved from session to session. Since the universe of substantive roll calls on issues other than appropriation measures was always much smaller in the short sessions, it seemed reasonable to use the rankings established in the long session when dealing with the Thirty-seventh Senate, third session, merely classifying the new senators as the scales of this short session indicated should be done. The Thirty-eighth Senate presented some problems. Clearly some carry-over senators, notably

Trumbull, were in very different positions in the overall scale rankings than had been true in the previous Senate. It would have been highly unrealistic to maintain the same screening groups, and so these were changed to accommodate the new positioning. This plus the entry of new senators suggested radical and moderate groups of nineteen and thirteen, a somewhat greater disproportion in group size than desirable. The relaxation of the quorum rule raised the number of absences, which also resulted sometimes in coefficients based on somewhat smaller groups than in the Thirty-seventh Congress. The possibility of discovering "accidental" alignments of radicals versus moderates was somewhat greater therefore in the analysis of the Thirty-eighth Senate. Since the central portion of the scale listing of the second session of the Thirty-eighth Congress showed positioning that was somewhat anomalous in view of earlier behavior (no doubt because of the new salience of reconstruction issues), I have analyzed the roll calls of that session using both the ranking of the first session and that of the second as well (see Table 3-6). Thus the first division broke the scale summary list above Fessenden, and in the second case I posited a transition zone between Morrill and Harlan and assigned the five Republicans involved on the basis of past behavior.

This is perhaps an unduly long discussion of a relatively simple procedure but it is important that the reader who wishes to confront the procedural issues involved may be able to do so. On the other hand for those who distrust such measures, and find discussion of techniques tedious, it may be enough merely to point out that the roll calls analyzed in Chapters 5–9 were basically those in which Republican cohesion was low and in which radical Republicans obviously tended to oppose moderate Republicans.

# Roll Calls Used Initially
# in Scaling Analysis

The letters a, b, c, d indicate the order in which the numerical summary of a particular roll call appears on the listed page.

1. Original scaling universe; southern and racial issues, 37 Cong., 2 sess.: *SJ*, 37 Cong., 2 sess.: pp. 109a; 110a; 334a; 334b; 337a; 340a; 342a; 355a; 356a; 358a; 363a; 365a; 365b; 367a; 368a; 368b; 389a; 465a; 621a; 621b; 767a; 767b; 88a; 176a; 196a; 239a; 284c; 285a; 423b; 424a; 716a; 754a; 754b; 833a; 834a; 834b; 835a; 835b; 852a; 853b; 284a; 284b; 150a; 150b; 150c; 151a; 151b; 422a; 423a; 437a; 437b; 450a; 450b; 468a; 469a; 501a; 501b; 502a; 502b; 506a; 507a; 507b; 508a; 508b; 508c; 509a; 509b; 723a; 726a; 726b; 727a; 794a; 794b; 795a; 795b; 796a; 810a; 817a; 817b; 843a; 844a; 844b; 844c; 845a; 860a; 861a; 277b.

2. Original scaling universe; southern and racial issues, 38 Cong., 1 sess.: *SJ*, 38 Cong., 1 sess.: pp. 259a; 348a; 348b; 349a; 349b; 349c; 560b; 600a; 606a; 614a; 614b; 614c; 615a; 615b; 615c; 621a; 621b; 621c; 645a; 646a; 647a; 646b; 601a; 602c; 362a; 363a; 363b; 364a; 180a; 230a; 143a; 488a; 488b; 255a; 536a; 536b; 533a; 562b; 562c; 656a; 657a; 663a; 663b; 664a; 664b; 664c; 669a; 669b; 257a; 484b; 685a; 704a; 704b; 714a; 714b; 714c; 714d; 726a; 134a; 294a; 292a; 297a; 300b; 301a; 301b; 303a; 303b; 304a; 313a; 552a; 677a; 677b; 5a; 38b; 106a; 109a; 143b; 143c; 660a; 90b; 449b; 438a.

# Divisive Roll Calls—
# Radical-Moderate Division

The letters a, b, c, d indicate the order in which the numerical summary of a particular vote appears on the listed page. The motion is occasionally attributed to the committee chairman or other spokesman. Motion 227a is found in the *Executive Journal*.

| Moved by | Date | Journal page | Moved by | Date | Journal page |
|---|---|---|---|---|---|
| | 37 Cong., 2 Sess. | | Trumbull | 5–20–62 | 513a |
| | | | Fessenden | 5–29–62 | 541b |
| Hale | 1–9–62 | 91a | Sumner | 5–29–62 | 542a |
| Fessenden | 1–9–62 | 95a | Sherman | 6–4–62 | 570a |
| Grimes | 1–24–62 | 139a | Sumner | 6–5–62 | 581a |
| Fessenden | 2–17–62 | 215a | Sumner | 6–5–62 | 588a |
| Sumner | 2–27–62 | 247a | Sumner | 6–5–62 | 612a |
| Harris | 2–27–62 | 247b | Sumner | 6–6–62 | 616a |
| Fessenden | 2–28–62 | 253b | Anthony | 6–6–62 | 617a |
| Hale | 3–12–62 | 295a | Howe | 6–6–62 | 618a |
| Doolittle | 3–24–62 | 334a | Grimes | 6–10–62 | 628b |
| Davis | 3–24–62 | 334b | Wilson | 6–16–62 | 653a |
| Ten Eyck | 4–4–62 | 372b | Hale | 6–16–62 | 656a |
| Trumbull | 4–9–62 | 227a | Chandler | 6–16–62 | 656b |
| Doolittle | 4–10–62 | 384a | Latham | 6–16–62 | 656c |
| King | 4–24–62 | 422a | Powell | 6–17–62 | 659a |
| Sherman | 4–24–62 | 423a | Grimes | 6–20–62 | 689b |
| Sumner | 4–24–62 | 420a | Davis | 6–23–62 | 694a |
| Cowan | 4–30–62 | 437b | Henderson | 6–23–62 | 694b |
| Anthony | 5–6–62 | 450a | Sumner | 6–28–62 | 723a |
| Wade | 5–19–62 | 508c | Clark | 6–28–62 | 726a |
| Clark | 6–28–62 | 726b | Hale | 2–15–64 | 157a |
| Hale | 7–2–62 | 743a | Foster | 2–17–64 | 164a |
| Grimes | 7–3–62 | 749a | Doolittle | 3–7–64 | 219a |

APPENDIX D—*continued*

| Moved by | Date | Journal page | Moved by | Date | Journal page |
|---|---|---|---|---|---|
| Sumner | 7-3-62 | 754b | Howe | 3-10-64 | 231b |
| Harris | 7-7-62 | 770a | Sumner | 3-15-64 | 249a |
| Sherman | 7-8-62 | 771a | Sumner | 3-17-64 | 257a |
| Henderson | 7-10-62 | 795a | Sumner | 3-18-64 | 259a |
| Henderson | 7-10-62 | 795b | Carlile | 3-21-64 | 267a |
| Sherman | 7-10-62 | 796a | Wilkinson | 3-31-64 | 290a |
| Browning | 7-11-62 | 810a | Wilson | 4-7-64 | 307a |
| Sherman | 7-12-62 | 819a | Grimes | 4-12-64 | 319b |
| Sherman | 7-12-62 | 811a | Anthony | 4-14-64 | 325a |
| Sumner | 7-14-62 | 833a | Sherman | 4-19-64 | 348b |
| Sumner | 7-15-62 | 852a | Fessenden | 4-28-64 | 379a |
| Sherman | 7-15-62 | 843a | Chandler | 4-28-64 | 380b |
| Browning | 7-15-62 | 844a | Fessenden | 4-28-64 | 381b |
| Browning | 7-15-62 | 844b | Nesmith | 4-29-64 | 387a |
| Sherman | 7-15-62 | 844c | Howard | 4-30-64 | 388a |
| | | | Conness | 5-2-64 | 394a |
| | | | Henderson | 5-2-64 | 394b |
| | 37 Cong., 3 Sess. | | Sumner | 5-6-64 | 411a |
| | | | Chandler | 5-6-64 | 412a |
| Davis | 1-6-63 | 84a | Collamer | 5-10-64 | 422a |
| Harlan | 1-9-63 | 94b | Collamer | 5-10-64 | 422b |
| Lane, H. S. | 1-12-63 | 99a | Morrill | 5-19-64 | 456a |
| Clark | 1-12-63 | 99b | Howard | 5-20-64 | 462a |
| Wilson | 1-12-63 | 99c | Collamer | 5-24-64 | 469a |
| Fessenden | 1-14-63 | 107b | Sumner | 5-28-64 | 488a |
| Sherman | 1-27-63 | 162a | Harlan | 5-28-64 | 488b |
| Henderson | 1-30-63 | 175a | Sherman | 5-31-64 | 498a |
| Clark | 1-30-63 | 175b | Harris | 6-4-64 | 519b |
| Sherman | 2-10-63 | 229a | Sherman | 6-4-64 | 519c |
| Sumner | 2-12-63 | 241a | Wilkinson | 6-6-64 | 528a |
| Sherman | 2-20-63 | 299a | Sherman | 6-7-64 | 530b |
| Grimes | 2-20-63 | 304a | Harlan | 6-7-64 | 530c |
| Harris | 2-20-63 | 304c | Harlan | 6-7-64 | 531a |
| Sumner | 2-27-63 | 355a | Fessenden | 6-17-64 | 574a |
| Grimes | 2-27-63 | 356a | Anthony | 6-17-64 | 577a |
| Powell | 3-2-63 | 390a | Wilson | 6-17-64 | 578a |
| Lane, J. H. | 3-2-63 | 391a | Sprague | 6-17-64 | 578b |
| | | | Carlile | 6-20-64 | 587a |
| | | | Sumner | 6-21-64 | 600a |
| | 38 Cong., 1 Sess. | | Sumner | 6-21-64 | 601a |
| | | | Sumner | 6-21-64 | 602c |
| Sumner | 1-12-64 | 73a | Sumner | 6-22-64 | 606a |
| Sumner | 2-13-64 | 152a | Brown | 6-22-64 | 608b |
| Grimes | 6-22-64 | 613a | Ten Eyck | 2-3-65 | 129a |
| Lane, H. S. | 6-22-64 | 615b | Lane, J. H. | 2-3-65 | 129b |
| Riddle | 6-22-64 | 615c | Harris | 2-3-65 | 130a |
| Johnson | 6-23-64 | 621b | Trumbull | 2-4-65 | 136b |
| Sumner | 6-25-64 | 645a | Cowan | 2-7-65 | 144a |

APPENDIX D—*continued*

| Moved by | Date | Journal page | Moved by | Date | Journal page |
|---|---|---|---|---|---|
| Sumner | 6-25-64 | 646a | Grimes | 2-21-65 | 211b |
| Wade | 6-30-64 | 685a | Sprague | 2-21-65 | 211c |
| Chandler | 6-30-64 | 692a | Sumner | 2-22-65 | 215b |
| Brown | 7-1-64 | 714a | Trumbull | 2-23-65 | 222a |
| Sumner | 7-1-64 | 714b | Sumner | 2-23-65 | 223a |
| Brown | 7-1-64 | 714c | Chandler | 2-24-65 | 238a |
| Wilson | 7-2-64 | 723a | Wade | 2-25-65 | 244a |
| Sherman | 7-2-64 | 723b | Howard | 2-25-65 | 245a |
| Conness | 7-2-64 | 724a | Sumner | 2-25-65 | 245b |
| Wilson | 7-2-64 | 724b | Howard | 2-25-65 | 245a |
| Wade | 7-2-64 | 726a | Sherman | 2-27-65 | 252a |
| Wilson | 7-2-64 | 738c | Sherman | 3-1-65 | 274a |
| Chandler | 7-2-64 | 738d | Sherman | 3-1-65 | 277a |
| Lane, J. H. | 7-2-64 | 739a | Cowan | 3-2-65 | 292a |
| Sumner | 7-2-64 | 739b | Grimes | 3-2-65 | 292c |
| Lane, J. H. | 7-2-64 | 739c | Sumner | 3-3-65 | 298a |
|  |  |  | Sumner | 3-3-65 | 303a |

38 Cong., 2 Sess.

| Lane, H. S. | 2-2-65 | 125c |

# Index

Abandoned property and purchase of staples, 235-236
*Ableman* v. *Booth,* 309
Abolition of slavery. *See* Blacks, emancipation
Adjournment, 136, 290-295, 302, 304
Alabama Claims Commission, 339
Alexandria and Washington Railroad Company, 201
Allen, Howard W., 100
Anderson, Charles, 275-276
Andrew, John, 169-172
Annapolis. *See* Naval Academy
Anthony, Henry B.: biography, 34, 76, 128, 337; committees, 62-63; confiscation, 226; "double enders," 272; as moderate, 109, 111; Naval Academy, 277-278; taxation, slave owners, 179; vote or other, 69, 135, 162, 164, 178, 201, 322, 325
Appropriations, 172, 194-196, 200, 263, 276, 294, 304, 326
Arbitrary arrests. *See* Habeas corpus
Arkansas: congressional delegation, 248; electoral votes, 256; reconstruction, 257
Army of the Potomac, 239
Arnold, Samuel Greene: biography, 34, 66, 132; as moderate, 141; vote, 266
Arthur, Chester A., 339
Articles of War, 222
Augusta, Dr. Alexander T., 202

Baker, Edward D., 44, 49, 278, 337, 340
Baltimore riots, 276
Banks, 302, 311, 315-325, 330, 333
Banks, Nathaniel P., 248
Bates, Edward, 81-82
Bayard, James A., Jr.: biography, 45, 70,

128, 136; emancipation, D.C., 152-153, 155; oath, 70-71, 286, 289; and Stark, 279-280; vote, 284
Beale, Howard K., 314
Beard, Charles A. and Mary R., 314
Beauregard, Pierre G. T., 284
Benedict, Michael Les, 314
Bill of attainder, 221, 224
Bill-scale correlations, 118-124
Bingham, Kinsley S., 39, 336
Blacks: citizenship, 198; civil rights, 332. Emancipation: confiscation, 223-228, 233; D.C., 95, 99, 118-124, 151-159, 181, 200, 298-300, 334; Missouri, 118-124, 184-188 217, 298, 306; reconstruction, 234, 238, 241, 243-244; West Virginia, 217. Free, 194; segregated railroad cars, 201-205, 298-300. Soldiers: 151, 160-165, 307; emancipation, 120, 167-168, 300-301, 306-307, 334; officers, 166-167; pay, 167-173, 304; recruitment, 173-175, 228, 300. Suffrage: D.C., 209-212, 299-300; Louisiana, 257; Montana, 205-209, 217, 299-300; Wade-Davis bill, 241-242. Witnesses, 197-201, 217, 300-301, 304
Blaine, James G., 44
Blair, Montgomery, 151
Boardinghouses, 26, 126-127
Boston *Commonwealth,* 214
Boston *Journal,* 48, 253
Breckinridge, John C., 36, 43, 47, 136, 278
Bright, Jesse D.: biography, 40, 76, 136, 278; and Stark, 279
Bright, John, 85
Broderick, David C., 45
Brooks, Preston S., 82

Brown, Albert, 271–272, 298
Brown, Benjamin Gratz: biography, 48,
127, 132, 337–338; black soldiers, 167,
173, 300; as radical, 123, 138; reconstruction, 242–245; vote or other, 168, 175,
245, 259
Browning, Orville H.: biography, 41, 127–
128, 262, 337–339; blacks, soldiers,
163–165; confiscation, 221–223, 233–
234; emancipation in D.C., 158; and
Hale, 283; leadership, 133; as moderate,
10, 22, 96, 103, 123; slavery and race,
154–155, 158, 163–164; and Sumner,
218; taxation, slaveholders, 178–179;
vote or other, 162, 166, 225, 287, 289,
291
Bryan, William Jennings, 43
Boutwell, George S., 84
Bowden, Lemuel J., 49
Buckalew, Charles R.: biography, 37; black
witnesses, 200–201; Montana suffrage,
208
Bull Run, 38, 284
Butler, Benjamin F., 166

Calhoun, John C., 264
California: banks, 324; land titles, 313, 325
Camden and Amboy Railroad Company.
See New Jersey railroads
Camden and Atlantic Railroad Company.
See New Jersey railroads
Cameron, Simon, 37, 81
Carlile, John S.: biography, 47. Blacks: soldiers, 168; witnesses, 200. Oath, 286–
287; reconstruction, 239, 243
Caucus. See Republican party
Chandler, Zachariah: abandoned property,
236–237; adjournment, 293–294; biog-
raphy, 38–39, 127–128, 337–338, 340;
and Breckinridge, 136; confiscation, 232,
234; federal Constitution, 309–310; and
Fessenden, 317, 320–321; and Lincoln,
239, 245; New Jersey railroads, 252–255,
259; as radical, 83, 92, 103, 109, 123,
355; Senate rules, secret sessions, 73. Tax-
ation: banks, 316, 320–321; cotton, 179.
Vote or other, 22, 135, 291, 319, 326
Chase, Kate, 34
Chase, Salmon P., 38
Chi square analysis, 53, 354
Chicago Tribune, 41, 48, 162, 226
Cincinnati Commercial, 38
Civil rights. See Blacks
Clark, Daniel: abandoned property, 236;
Alexandria and Washington Railroad,
201; biography, 33, 128, 339; and Albert
Brown, 271; confiscation, 220, 226–234;

economic legislation, 91; emancipation,
Missouri, 187; fugitive slave laws, 188;
Kentucky volunteers, 275; leadership,
133–134; Louisiana recognition, 257–
258; New Jersey railroads, 259; oath, 281–
282; as radical, 111, 323; reconstruction,
243; and Stark, 284; and Sumner, 278,
292; taxation, slaveholders, 178; vote,
291
Clausen, Aage, 352
Clay, Henry, 264
Clubb, Jerome M., 100
Cluster-bloc analysis, 92–93, 345
Coastal slave trade, 194–196, 200, 304
Collamer, Jacob: abandoned property, 236;
biography, 32, 64, 66, 340; black soldiers,
163, 171; coastal slave trade, 195–196;
confiscation, 223–226; economic issues,
91; electoral votes, 242, 247–251; emancipation, Missouri, 186–187; federal
Constitution, 301, 309; fugitive slave
laws, 188; Kentucky volunteers, 275; as
moderate, 92, 111; oath, 288; presidential indemnity, 264–265. Senate rules:
debate limitation, 71, president pro tempore, 71; quorum, 69; secret sessions,
73–74. And Sumner, 218; taxation,
banks, 317, 321, 324–325; vote or other,
76, 188, 194, 196–197, 266
Colonization, 155–157, 181, 223, 228,
299–300, 312
Committee on Confiscation (Select), 99,
133, 225–226, 231–232
Committee on Slavery and Freedmen
(Select), 68, 77–78, 134–135, 168, 200,
212
Committees. See U.S. Senate, committees
Confiscation, 21, 88, 99, 118–124,
133, 219, 260, 292, 298–299, 302, 305,
308, 311, 333–334; explanatory resolution, 234, 333; House bill (H.R. 471),
232–235; Judiciary Committee bill (S.
151), 219–226, 231–232; select committee bill (S. 310), 227–35
Conness, John: adjournment, 293; biography, 45, 132; black soldiers, 168, 170,
174; fugitive slave laws, 192; military
courts, 268; as radical, 113, 123, 138;
vote or other, 259, 294, 319, 321
Conscription, 292, 307
Constitution. See Federal Constitution
Court of Claims, 269–273, 295, 303
Courts. See Federal courts; State courts
Cowan, Edgar: biography, 36–37, 127–128,
132–133, 140, 338–339; black soldiers,
166, 171; confiscation, 221–225, 230–
234; electoral votes, 250–251; federal

Cowan, Edgar (*cont.*)
  Constitution, 307; freedmen's bureau,
  215; military courts, 267–268; as moderate, 10, 92–94, 96, 103, 109–110, 117,
  123; Oregon mint, 328; Pennsylvania
  reimbursement, 240; radicals, 22; reconstruction, 239; taxation, slaveholders,
  178–179; vote or other, 38, 162, 164, 166,
  168, 175, 194, 196, 201, 205, 212, 244,
  287, 289; and Wade, 180
Cue-giving, 304, 314, 326–329, 336
Curry, Leonard P., 102

Dalles City, 326–327
Davis, David, 262
Davis, Garrett: biography, 47–48, 109, 128;
  black witnesses, 198; confiscation, 230;
  D.C., courts, 268; emancipation, D.C.,
  152–158, 181; expulsion motion, 136;
  freedmen's bureau, 213; Kentucky vol-
  unteers, 274–275; leadership, 133; and
  Lincoln, 186–187, 265; oath, 286–287;
  race, 159; reconstruction, 239. Senate
  rules: debate limitation, 71; new commit-
  tees, 71, 135. Taxation, banks, 323; vote
  or other, 193, 205, 236, 276, 288, 291
Davis, Henry Winter, 245
Davis, Jefferson, 43, 47
Declaration of Independence, 199, 256,
  309
Department of Agriculture, 88, 330
Discrimination. *See* Blacks
Disagreement analysis methods, 77, 89,
  313, 353–356
District of Columbia: Code, 269, 298;
  courts, 268–269, 303; emancipation, *see*
  Blacks; Gas Light Company, 298; jail,
  298, water tax, 273
Divisive roll calls, listed, 358–360
Dixon, Elizabeth L., 330
Dixon, James: biography, 35, 128, 339; as
  moderate, 96, 98, 111, 123; and Stark,
  283; southern states, 21–22, 238; and
  Trumbull, 234; vote or other, 266, 283,
  287, 325
Doolittle, James Rood: abandoned property, 236; appropriations bill, 196; biography, 39, 127–128, 132, 262, 337–339.
  Blacks: emancipation, D.C., 156–158;
  Montana suffrage, 206–208. Electoral
  votes, 250–251, 303; federal Constitution, 193, 308; freedmen's bureau, 215;
  fugitive slave laws, 192–193; leadership,
  133; Louisiana recognition, 258; as moderate, 110, 117, 123, 138; Naval
  Academy, 277; oath, 287; race, 157–158;
  reconstruction, 239, 301; and Stark, 283;

and Sumner, 208, 258; taxation,
  slaveholders, 179; Thirteenth Amendment, 217; vote or other, 69, 135, 147,
  168, 175, 194, 203, 205, 225, 244, 266,
  283, 289, 325
"Double enders," 272–273
Douglas, Stephen A., 41, 258
*Dred Scott* v. *Sanford,* 205, 261, 310
Duchess of Argyll, 85

Earnest, as code word, 333–334
East-West disagreement. *See* Republican
  party
Edmunds Act, 339
Electoral College, 74–75, 246–252, 260
Emancipation. *See* Blacks
Emancipation Proclamation, 167, 234, 244,
  303
Emerson, Ralph Waldo, 84, 137, 312
Enlistment, 167–168, 267–269, 293
Expulsions, 75, 136, 279–289

Factor analysis, 123, 352
Farwell, Nathan A., 49, 250
Federal Constitution: Article 1, section 9,
  175; Article 2, section 2, 70; Article 3,
  section 3, 288; black suffrage, Montana,
  206–207; confiscation, 221, 224; Fifth
  Amendment, 70–71, 152, 213, 221–222,
  267, 306; guarantee clause, 243, 250,
  256, 258, 301; interpretation, 21, 190–
  191, 305–312; interstate commerce,
  195–196, 254; "necessary and proper"
  clause, 249–250; oath, 287; Sixth
  Amendment, 267, 306; slaves, 154–155,
  163–164, 175–176, 178, 190–192, 195–
  196, 307; Twelfth Amendment, 252;
  Thirteenth Amendment, 168–169, 188,
  217–218, 252–253, 258, 304; war powers,
  222, 226, 233, 290, 306, 309
Federal courts, 197–199, 303, 306
Federal powers, 301–303, 305, 325, 335
Fessenden, Thomas A. D., 218
Fessenden, William Pitt: absences, 135; adjournment, 290, 292; biography, 29, 32,
  69–70, 77–82, 126–128, 323, 337–338,
  340. Blacks: emancipation, D.C., 151,
  154, Missouri, 186; soldiers, 160, 162;
  Montana suffrage, 206. And Chandler,
  317, 320; committees, 40, 62–63, 66, 68,
  76; confiscation, 231–232; Court of
  Claims, 270–271; diplomatic rank, 302;
  economic issues, 91; federal Constitution,
  306–307, 309; hour of meeting, 289;
  Kentucky volunteers, 275; leadership,
  77–82, 133; military arrests, 265; as moderate, 92, 107–108, 111, 356; Naval

Fessenden, William Pitt (*cont.*)
 Academy, 277; Oregon mint, 326, 328–
 329; radicals, 22, 231–232; reconstruc-
 tion, 245; secret sessions, 73; slavery,
 154; and Stark, 279–280, 282; and
 Sumner, 80, 83, 218, 220, 283. Taxation:
 banks, 318–320, 322; internal revenue
 bill, 1862, 79; slave owners, 175–178.
 Vote or other, 83, 86, 155, 163, 168, 171,
 188, 225, 291; Wade, 231, 234
Field, Richard S., 36, 132, 141, 339
Fifty-Fourth Massachusetts regiment. *See*
 Blacks, soldiers
Fifty-Fifth Massachusetts regiment. *See*
 Blacks, soldiers
Foot, Solomon: biography, 32, 64, 68, 86,
 127–128, 132; economic issues, 91; and
 Waldo Johnson, 136; joint rules, 74;
 leadership, 62; oath, 70; as radical,
 97–98, 110; and Sumner, 218; vote or
 other, 33, 38, 69, 135, 171, 244, 283, 325
Foster, Lafayette S.: biography, 35, 63–64,
 127–128, 132–133, 337–339. Blacks:
 segregated railroad cars, 203; witnesses,
 197–199. And Albert Brown, 271–272;
 conference committees, 288; economic
 issues, 91; federal Constitution, 308–309;
 fugitive slave laws, 192; Louisiana recognition, 258; as moderate, 110, 123; secret
 sessions, 73; vote or other, 69, 135, 168,
 171, 194, 196, 212, 225, 266, 269, 325
Freedmen's bureau: 78, 118–124, 135,
 212–217, 304, 333
Frémont, John Charles, 40
Fugitive slaves, 118–124, 188–194, 196,
 204, 217, 228, 301, 307

Galbraith, John Kenneth, 141
Gambill, Edward, 102
Gamble, Hamilton R., 48
Garfield, James A., 341
Grant, Ulysses S., 209, 211, 320
Grimes, James W.: abandoned property,
 236; adjournment, 291–292; and Charles
 Anderson, 276; biography, 42, 67, 86–87,
 126–128, 339–340. Blacks: segregated
 railroad cars, 204; soldiers, 161, 170–171,
 174–175. D.C.: courts, 268–269; water
 tax, 273. "Double enders," 272–273;
 East-West disagreement, 89–90; ex-
 ecutive nominations, 72; and Fessenden,
 81, 83; freedmen's bureau, 213–215; and
 Ward H. Lamon, 268–269; Naval
 Academy, 276–278, 299; navy grog ration, 195; Northwest, 89–90; as radical,
 108, 111; secret sessions, 73; Supreme
 Court, 262; vote or other, 69, 80, 135,

168, 186, 196, 209, 212, 244, 259;
 Washington Gas Light Company, 100,
 274; Washington and Georgetown Railroad, 203
*Groves* v. *Slaughter,* 196
Grow, Galusha, 37
Guttman scaling methods, 93–97, 102,
 106–107, 118–124, 296, 312–313, 345–
 352, 357

Habeas corpus, 263–266, 295, 306
Haiti, 82, 156
Hale, John P.: adjournment, 289; and
 Charles Anderson, 276; black witnesses,
 198; and Albert Brown, 271; and Browning, 283–284; Court of Claims, 269–270;
 "double enders," 272; electoral votes,
 248–249; freedmen's bureau, 213–214;
 fugitive slave laws, 193; leadership, 78,
 86–87, 134; navy, lash, 195; New Jersey
 railroads, 254, 257; as radical, 109, 326;
 reconstruction, 238, 244; Senate chamber, 29. Senate rules: debate limitation,
 71, 73, 135–136; secret sessions, 73; special orders, 69. State volunteers, 303; Supreme Court, 261; taxation, slaveholders,
 179–180; vote or other, 196, 275, 291
Hamlin, Hannibal, 32, 127, 270, 340
Harding, Benjamin F., 44, 318
Harlan, James: adjournment, 293; biography, 42, 63, 127–128, 338–340; blacks,
 D.C. suffrage, 211; confiscation, 226;
 electoral votes, 250; federal Constitution,
 310; Kentucky volunteers, 275; race,
 159; as radical, 110, 356; reconstruction,
 244; senatorial duties, 28; vote or other,
 171, 291, 294, 319
Harris, Ira: biography, 35–36, 63, 66,
 127–128, 132–133, 339; confiscation,
 223; D.C. courts, 268; electoral votes,
 247–251; emancipation, Missouri, 184;
 federal Constitution, 301, 309; and Fessenden, 79; as moderate, 96–97, 108,
 110, 116, 123; radical influence, 22; reconstruction, 238–240; and Stark, 280–
 283; vote or other, 163–166, 175, 194,
 197, 203, 245, 287, 289, 325
Hayes, Rutherford B., 338
Henderson, John B.: biography, 48. 108,
 336, 355. Blacks: emancipation, Missouri,
 185, 187; soldiers, 162–164, 167. Confiscation, 227, 230; freedmen's bureau,
 214–215; Louisiana recognition, 257;
 oath, 287–288, 306; taxation, banks, 322,
 325; Thirteenth Amendment, 217
Hendricks, Thomas A.: biography, 49, 126,
 205; coastal slave trade, 195; freedmen's

Hendricks, Thomas A. (*cont.*)
  bureau, 213; fugitive slave laws, 189;
  Montana suffrage, 207; taxation, banks,
  324; Thirteenth Amendment, 217
Hicks, Thomas H., 46, 126
Homestead Act, 88, 330
Hook, John, 319
Howard, Jacob M.: biography, 39, 128, 133,
  339; confiscation, 221, 227–229, 233–
  234; electoral votes, 249; Louisiana recognition, 255–258; military courts, 267;
  as radical, 96, 109; reconstruction, 255;
  southern states, 255, 301; and Stark, 282,
  284; taxation, banks, 315, 319; Thirteenth Amendment, 217; mentioned or
  vote, 37, 163, 166, 244–245, 259, 291,
  321
Howe, Timothy O.: biography, 39–40, 128,
  337, 339. Blacks: segregated railroad
  cars, 201; soldiers, 171–172. And Albert
  Brown, 271; electoral votes, 250; Kentucky volunteers, 275; as moderate, 111,
  123; oath, 288; Oregon mint, 327, 329;
  on party, 21; and Stark, 282, 284. Taxation: banks, 317, 323; slaveholders, 177.
  Trumbull, 284; vote or other, 165–166,
  168, 175, 178, 194, 197, 212, 225, 234,
  245, 285, 289, 325

Idaho Territory. *See* Blacks, suffrage,
  Montana
Income tax, 293
Indemnification of the President. *See*
  Habeas corpus
Index of cohesion, 77–78, 101, 343–344
Index of disagreement, 148, 344, 354–355
Index of Likeness. *See* Index of disagree-
  ment
Industrialism, 314, 333
Instruction of senators, 76–77, 154
Insurrection and sedition, 263
Internal revenue, 79, 88, 232, 259, 313,
  322–323. *See also* Taxation
International Monetary Conference, Paris,
  339

James, John, 276
Johnson, Andrew, 49, 108, 340
Johnson, Reverdy: biography, 46, 339.
  Blacks: suffrage, Montana, 205; segregated railroad cars, 202–203; soldiers,
  167, 170. Coastal slave trade, 195–196;
  electoral votes, 252; federal Constitution,
  190–192; fugitive slave laws, 189–194;
  Louisiana recognition, 257; Naval
  Academy, 277; and Sumner, 195–196,
  309; taxation, banks, 323–325

Kansas-Nebraska bill, 258
Kennedy, Anthony, 46
Kennedy, John Pendleton, 46
Kentucky volunteers, 274–275, 298
King, Preston: biography, 35, 128, 132,
  337, 339; black soldiers, 161–162; confiscation, 95, 223–224; executive business,
  198; as radical, 92, 94, 98, 109, 123; taxation, slaveowners, 177; vote or other,
  178, 288, 291

Lamon, Ward H., 268, 298
Land-grant colleges, 88, 90, 330
Lane, Henry S.: biography, 40, 127–128,
  132, 339; confiscation, 234; electoral
  vote, 250–251; freedmen's bureau, 214–
  215; Kentucky volunteers, 275; as moderate, 98, 108, 110, 123; vote or other,
  162, 164, 166, 168, 175, 194, 196, 201,
  203, 205, 212, 283, 291, 319, 321
Lane, James H.: adjournment, 294; biography, 42–43, 66, 128, 205, 340. Blacks:
  emancipation, W. Va., 183; soldiers,
  163–166; suffrage, 242. Electoral votes,
  252; as radical, 111; vote or other, 188,
  244, 266, 285, 291
Lane, Joseph, 44
Latham, Milton S., 44–45, 289, 291
Leadership, 78–87, 133–135, 141–143
Lecompton constitution, 253
Lee, Robert E., 330
Liberal Republicans, 1872, 337
Liberia, 82, 156
Lincoln, Abraham, 22, 35, 38, 40, 81–82,
  85–86, 235, 239, 268, 271, 284, 297,
  302–303, 323, 330; electoral votes, 252.
  Emancipation: D.C., 155–156; Missouri,
  184, 186–187. And Fessenden, 82;
  habeas corpus, 263; judicial appoint-
  ments, 262; 186–187; presidential pow-
  ers, 228, 302–303, 305; reconstruction,
  243, 245, 247–249, 252, 255, 303; trea-
  sury agents, 237
Lincoln, Mary Todd, 330
*Lincoln and the Radicals*, 314
Linden, Glenn M., 314
Loring, Justice Edward G., 270
Louisiana: electoral votes, 118–124, 246–
  252, 298–299, 303, 307–308; recognition,
  120–124, 248, 251, 252, 258–260, 298–299,
  302, 307–308
Loyalty. *See* Expulsions; Oath of office

Mack, 32, 47
Marshall, Justice John, 190, 229
Martial law. *See* Habeas corpus
Maryland volunteers, 274, 298

Mason, James M., 248
Massachusetts regiments. *See* Blacks, soldiers
McLean, Justice John, 196
McClellan, George B., 239, 249, 308
McConachie, Lauros, G., 75–76
*McCulloch* v. *Maryland,* 317, 319, 324–325
McDougall, James A.: biography, 45, 66, 96, 103, 126; and Fessenden, 79; taxation, banks, 224, 322 vote, 294
Merrick, Justice William M., 268
Metropolitan Railroad Company, 202–203
Military arrests. *See* Habeas corpus
Military courts, 267, 303, 311. *See also* Habeas corpus
Militia Act, Amendatory bill, 1862, 95, 118–124, 160–166, 298. *See also* Blacks, soldiers
Miller, Justice Samuel H., 262
Missouri: Compromise, 257; emancipation, 118–124, 184–188; state volunteers, 274, 298
Modernization theory, 311–312, 341
Morgan, Edwin D.: biography, 35, 132; as radical, 123, 141; vote or other, 242, 294
Morrill, Justin S., 32, 81, 84
Morrill, Lot M.: abandoned property, 236; biography, 32, 128, 132, 337–339. Blacks: D.C. emancipation, 152; suffrage, D.C., 211–212, Montana, 208–209; segregated railroad cars, 203. Confiscation, 221; economic legislation, 91; federal Constitution, 308; freedmen's bureau, 215; New Jersey railroads, 259; as radical, 109, 218, 356; slavery and race, 153–154, 158–159; vote or other, 188, 201–202, 210, 212, 291, 319
Morton, Oliver P., 40
Motley, John Lathrop, 84

National banks. *See* banks
Naval Academy, 276–278, 299
Navy Department, 86, 272
Nesmith, James W.: biography, 44, 109; and Albert Brown, 271; New Jersey railroads, 259; Oregon mint, 326–329; and Stark, 279
Nevins, Allan, 88, 117, 240
New Jersey railroads, 252–260, 302, 333
Newport. *See* Naval Academy
New York *Daily News,* 36
New York *Herald,* 69, 215, 234, 253
New York *Tribune,* 86, 161, 263
Nichols, Roy F., 125
Noell, John W., 184
Non-Intercourse Act, 264–265
North Carolina, 238–239

Northwest Ordinance, 183, 238, 217
Nye, James W., 49, 123, 138

Oath of office, 70–71, 136, 286–289, 295, 304, 311. *See also* James A. Bayard Jr., Benjamin Stark
Oregon: branch mint, 284, 313, 326–329; senatorial seat. *See also* Benjamin Stark

Palfrey, John G., 302
Pearce, James A., 46, 68, 128
Peck, Ebenezer, 271
Pennsylvania, militia reimbursement, 241
Philadelphia *Inquirer,* 47
Polk, Trusten, 48, 136
Pollock, James, 327–328
Pomeroy, Samuel C.: biography, 42–43, 75, 127–128, 266, 337; freedmen's bureau, 214; as radical, 111, 123; Senate rules, 72, 294. Taxation: banks, 317–318; slave owners, 178. Vote or other, 242, 244, 291, 319, 321
Powell, Lazarus W.: biography, 47, 133. Blacks: D.C. emancipation, 152–153; naval installations, 159; soldiers, 166. Electoral votes, 251; expulsion motion, 90, 136; and Ward H. Lamon, 269; Louisiana recognition, 258; reconstruction, 239; revenue bill, 294; soldier bounties, 99–100; taxation, banks, 325; vote or other, 41, 265
Power. *See* Leadership
Presidential power, 228, 302–303, 305. *See also* Abraham Lincoln
*Prigg* v. *Pennsylvania,* 189
Providence *Journal,* 34
Provisional governments in the South. *See* Reconstruction

Quartermaster Department, 271
Quorum. *See* U.S. Senate, rules

Racial prejudice, 156–158, 202, 299–300, 332
Railroads: 89–90; transcontinental, 88, 232–233, 330. *See* also New Jersey railroads; Washington, D.C.
Ramsey, Alexander: biography, 43, 132, 339; as radical, 123–124, 141; taxation, banks, 324; vote or other, 319, 321
Randall, James G., 297
Raritan and Delaware Bay Railroad Company. *See* New Jersey railroads
Realignment, 49–50, 335–336
Reconstruction, 118–124, 237–247, 299, 301, 303, 307, 311, 334–335; Harris bill, 238–240; interpretation, 237–238; scales,

Reconstruction (*cont.*)
118-124; Wade-Davis bill, 240-247. *See also* Louisiana
Recruiting agents, 173
Reference groups, 325-329, 336
Regulation of commerce. *See* New Jersey railroads
Republican party: Caucus, 66-67, 75-76, 87, 336; East-West disagreement, 89-91, 100, 117, 138-140, 156-157, 173, 175, 179, 213, 300, 315-316, 321-323, 325, 331. Radicals (and Moderates) defined or evaluated, 9, 13, 21-22, 92-124, 132-133, 137-143, 158, 296-314, 330-336, 345
Revenue. *See* Appropriations; Internal revenue; Taxation
Revisionist historians, 314
Rice, Henry M.: biography, 43, 96, 103, 340; black soldiers, 162; senators, pay, 71; vote, 180
Richardson, William A.: biography, 41-42. Blacks: Missouri emancipation, 186; soldiers, 166. Criticizes Lincoln, 186; oath, 70
Riddle, George R., 49
Riker, William M., 76
Roll-call analysis, 89, 148-149, 343-352
Rothman, David, 51

Salem clique, 44
Santo Domingo Commission, 339
Saulsbury, Willard: biography, 45-46, 109. Blacks: Montana suffrage, 205; segregated railroad cars, 202-203; soldiers, 161. Committee assignments, 62; and Lincoln, 265; New Jersey railroads, 254; oath, 286-287; race, 159; vote, 284
Sawtelle, Charles G., 271-272
Scalograms. *See* Guttman scaling methods
Secret sessions. *See* U.S. Congress, rules
Segregation. *See* Blacks
Senators: ages, 56, 140; departures, 107, 337-340; duties, 27-28; education, 51-54; entry dates, 336-337; ethics, 75; living accommodations, 125-127; party affiliation, 49; place of birth, 54, 56; prior occupations, 53-54; prior public office, 56-58; religious preference, 58-60, 137-138, 140, 312, 331; seating, 127-132; social characteristics, 49-51; social origins, 50-53, 137; successful motions, 133-135
Seward, William H., 40, 64, 76, 82, 128, 279
Shannon, Fred A., 160-161
Sharkey, Robert P., 314
Sharp, Granville, 191

Sherman, John: adjournment, 291-292, 294; and Charles Anderson, 276, appropriation bill riders, 200; biography, 38, 68, 128, 337-338. Blacks: D.C. emancipation, 156; Montana suffrage, 206; segregated railroad cars, 204; soldiers, 161-168, 173-174; witnesses, 200. Coastal slave trade, 194-195; committees, 62-63; confiscation, 223, 226, 234; electoral votes, 249; fugitive slave laws, 189-192; Joint Rules, 291-292, Number 22, 73-74; Kentucky volunteers, 275; legislative strategy, 350; military arrests, 303, 306; military draft, commutation, 307; as moderate, 108-110; presidential indemnity, 265-266; senate rules, quorum, 69, 135; and Stark, 284; and Sumner, 84. Taxation: banks, 315-316, 321-322, 324; cotton, 176, 179; slave owners, 176-178, 306. Thirteenth Amendment, 213; vote or other, 164, 166, 175, 190, 194, 196, 203, 205, 212, 233, 244-245, 250, 259, 276, 287, 319, 325
Significance tests, 53
Simmons, James F.: biography, 34, 75, 128, 132, 336-337; and Fessenden, 79; as moderate, 123; taxation, slave owners, 176-177; vote, 178
Slaves in naval installations, 159. *See also* Blacks, Coastal slave trade, Reconstruction, and Taxation, slaveholders
Slave trade. *See* Coastal slave trade
Soldiers, bounties, 100
Sprague, William: biography, 34, 132, 205, 338, 340; freedmen's bureau, 214; as radical, 123, 138; vote or other, 244, 259, 318, 321
Springfield *Republican* (Mass.), 39, 42, 48, 258
Stanton, Edwin M., 81, 170
Stark, Benjamin: biography, 44; expulsion resolution, 99, 136; seating, 278-285, 295, 304, 311; vote, 239
State banks. *See* Banks
State courts, 197-199
State prisoners, bill discharging. *See* Habeas corpus
State rights, 254, 301-302, 305, 317-318, 324-325, 335
Steamship passengers, bill regulating, 245
Stewart, William M.: biography, 49, 103, 337; as radical, 123, 138; vote, 259
Story, Justice Joseph, 189, 229
Suffrage. *See* Blacks, suffrage
Sumner, Charles: adjournment, 292-294; appropriations bill, riders, 194-195; biography, 33, 128, 340. Blacks: civil

Sumner, Charles (*cont.*)
  rights, 300–304; emancipation, D.C., 95,
  154, Missouri, 187, 306, West Virginia,
  95, 183; segregated railroad cars, 201–
  205; soldiers' pay, 170–172; suffrage,
  D.C., 210–211, Montana, 208–209; witnesses, 197–201, 234, 300. Coastal slave
  trade, 194–196; and Collamer, 32; committees, 64, 132, 134, 290; confiscation,
  222, 229–230, 232–234; and Doolittle, 238;
  Dred Scott decision, 205; Emancipation
  Proclamation, 303; federal Constitution,
  190–191, 307–309; and Fessenden, 81,
  84; and Foster, 258; freedmen's bureau,
  212, 215–217, 304; fugitive slave laws,
  188–194; leadership, 77–78, 80, 82–86,
  99, 133–135, 305, 326; Louisiana recognition, 256–259; Naval Academy, 277;
  New Jersey railroads, 253–255, 302;
  oath, 70, 136, 289; Oregon mint, 328; as
  radical, 83, 92, 103, 106–109, 123, 355;
  reconstruction, 239, 244, 260; Senate
  rules, 69, 72–73; slavery and race, 153–
  155, 158, 211, 217–218; and Stark, 99,
  136, 280–285; state rights, 238, 301–302;
  tariff duties, 326. Taxation: banks, 302,
  317–321, slave owners, 175–180, 305.
  Thirteenth Amendment, 217; treasury
  agents, 237; Trumbull, 238; vote or
  other, 37, 39, 66, 87, 147, 168, 242, 278,
  291, 299, 304, 318, 322
Supreme Court, 197–198, 261–263, 324
Swayne, Noah M., 262

Tariff duties, 88, 99, 249, 313, 326, 330
Taxation: cotton, 176, 179; slave owners,
  151, 175–181, 297. *See also* Banks
Ten Eyck, John C.: biography, 36, 63, 128,
  132–133. Blacks: D.C. emancipation,
  156; soldiers, 174. Confiscation, 220;
  D.C. water tax, 274; East-West disagree-
  ment, 90; electoral votes, 246–247, 250–
  251; as moderate, 103, 110, 117, 123;
  Naval Academy, 277–278; New Jersey
  railroads, 254; reconstruction, 239; taxa-
  tion, slave owners, 178; vote or other,
  164, 166, 168, 171, 175, 179, 194, 202–
  203, 205, 212, 236, 245, 266, 325
Tennessee, 247, 250
Territories, slavery, 195–196
Test oath. *See* Oath of office
Thomson, John R., 36
Thurman, Allen G., 85
Tilghman, Justice William, 229
Treasury agents, 236–237
Treason. *See* Confiscation
Trefousse, Hans L., 74

Trent affair, 82, 87
*Tribune Almanac and Political Register,* 49
Truman, David B., 345
Trumbull, Lyman: adjournment, 290, 293;
  bill to suppress insurrection, 263; biography, 41, 63, 77, 126, 128, 132–133,
  338–339. Blacks: D.C. emancipation,
  156; Montana suffrage, 206–207; segregated railroad cars, 204; witnesses, 199.
  And Browning, 22; and Clark, 232; confiscation, 219–223, 226–228, 231–234,
  333; Court of Claims, 270–271; and
  Cowan, 225; D.C., code, 269; and Dixon,
  21–22; electoral votes, 246, 248, 252;
  federal Constitution, 308; and Fessenden, 82; Kentucky volunteers, 274–275;
  Naval Academy, 277; New Jersey railroads, 254; oath, 70, 286–289; presidential indemnity, 264–265; as radical, 107–
  108, 111, 138, 356; reconstruction, 239.
  Senate rules: 74, 75; debate limitation,
  72; secret sessions, 73. And Stark, 280,
  283–284; and Sumner, 82, 258, 299; taxation, slaveholders, 179; Thirteenth
  Amendment, 217; vote or other, 168,
  175, 178, 194, 196, 203, 205, 212, 244,
  250, 291
Turpie, David, 41, 186
Twain, Mark, 43, 75

Union Pacific Railroad, 339
U.S. Capitol, statuary, 340
U.S. Congress: Joint Committee on the
  Conduct of the War, 41, 68, 72, 85, 133,
  135–136, 340. Joint Rules: 278; bill reading, 291–292; conference committees,
  74; presidential electoral ballots, 75; secret sessions, 72–74, 136. Regulation of
  membership, 303
U.S. Mint, 326–328
U.S. Senate: absenteeism, 70–71, 79, 313;
  adjournment, 291–294; chamber, 28–29;
  committees, 61–69; courtesy, 304. Rules:
  69, 135–136, 278; bill reading, 72, 294;
  meeting time, 289–290; president *pro
  tempore,* 71; quorum, 69–70, 135, 313; secret sessions, 72–74. Working conditions,
  26

Van Horn, Carl, 351–352
Van Winkle, Peter G.: biography, 126, 336,
  355; vote, 205
Voting cohesion, tables, 78, 101, 157

Wade, Benjamin F.: biography, 38, 41, 64,
  85, 128, 133, 339. Blacks: suffrage, D.C.,
  210–212, Montana, 205–206; West

Wade, Benjamin F. (*cont.*)
  Virginia emancipation, 183. Confiscation, 221, 225-226, 228, 231; and Cowan,
  179-180; federal Constitution, 21, 308;
  and Fessenden, 231; electoral votes, 249,
  251; leadership, 133; as radical, 22, 80,
  83, 92, 103, 106-107, 109, 123, 234; reconstruction, 240-245, 249, 303, 307.
  Senate rules: absentees, 135-136; debate
  limitation, 72; secret sessions, 72-74. And
  Sumner, 218; Supreme Court, 262; vote
  or other, 33, 35, 37, 259, 292
Wade-Davis Bill. *See* Reconstruction
Wall, James Walter, 36
War Department, 86, 216
War powers. *See* Federal Constitution, war
  powers; Presidential powers; Abraham
  Lincoln
Washington: voter registration, 210-212;
  war conditions, 26; water tax, 273. *See
  also* District of Columbia
Washington and Georgetown Railroad
  Company, 203-204
Washington Gas Light Company, 100, 274
Webster, Daniel, 264, 281
Welles, Gideon, 67, 86, 272, 276
West Virginia, statehood, 99, 182-183, 292,
  298
Wheaton, Henry, 229
Whigs, 25, 45, 91, 109, 111, 331
Whitman, Walt, 35
Wilkes, Charles, 86
Wilkinson, Morton S.: biography, 43, 63,
  127-128, 337-338. Blacks: Montana suf-
  frage, 205-209, 300; soldiers, 162, 168.
  And Browning and Cowan, 234; and
  Carlile, 243; confiscation, 234; expulsion
  resolutions, 136; as radical, 22, 97, 106,
  109, 123; reconstruction, 239; vote or
  other, 228, 292, 294, 319, 321, 326

Willard, A. H., 126
Willey, Waitman T.: antislavery legislation,
  168; biography, 47, 336, 355; freedmen's
  bureau, 213; and Stark, 284-285; and
  Sumner, 211; West Virginia, 183, 292
Williams, T. Harry, 314
Wilmot, David: biography, 36-37, 127-128,
  132, 271, 339-340; Proviso, 201, 340-
  341; as radical, 92-94, 98, 111, 123; vote
  or other, 178, 228, 291
Wilson, Henry: adjournment, 294; biography, 33-34, 128, 337. Blacks: emancipation, D.C., 152; Missouri, 186; segregated railroad cars, 204; soldiers, 160,
  162, 164, 166-171, 173-174. Confiscation, 226, 230-232; Davis, 136; enlistment laws, 267; freedmen's bureau,
  216-217; habeas corpus, 263, 266; Kentucky volunteers, 275; leadership, 133;
  and Justice Merrick, 268; Naval
  Academy, 277; naval installations, 159-
  160; New Jersey railroads, 259; race,
  158-159; as radical, 109, 123; senatorial
  courtesy, 304; taxation, cotton, 179; treasury agents, 237; vote or other, 167, 178,
  180, 217, 321-322
Wilson, Robert, 48, 181, 239
Wilson, Woodrow, 75
Wisconsin: banks, 232; electoral votes,
  1856, 248; instruction of senators, 76-77
Women's suffrage, 206, 257
Wright, Joseph A.: biography, 40-41, 66,
  90, 96; blacks, D.C., emancipation, 153,
  155; parties, 141; and Stark, 284; vote or
  other, 42, 224, 285, 331
Wright, William, 36

Yates, Richard, 41
Young, James S., 125

*The Earnest Men*

Designed by G. T. Whipple, Jr.
Composed by The Composing Room of Michigan, Inc.
in 10 point VIP Baskerville, 2 points leaded,
with display lines in Baskerville.
Printed offset by Thomson-Shore, Inc.
on Warren's Number 66 text, 50 pound basis.
Bound by John H. Dekker & Sons, Inc.
in Holliston book cloth
and stamped in Kurz-Hastings foil.

*Library of Congress Cataloging in Publication Data*
Bogue, Allan G.
    The earnest men.

    Includes bibliographical references and index.
        1. United States—Politics and government—Civil War,
1861–1865.  2. Republican Party—History—19th century.
I. Title.   II. Title: Republicans of the Civil War
Senate.
E459.B723        973.7′1        81-67176
ISBN 0-8014-1357-5              AACR2